"With both theoretical reflections and examples of new approaches, this volume is a key addition to considering the range of methodologies needed for the writing of liturgical history."

—Lester Ruth
Duke Divinity School

"People throughout the ages have re-created the past in their worship and rituals. This rich and beautifully organized collection by major scholars in the field demonstrates how and why this is so in a multiplicity of ways, across times and cultures, and often with interdisciplinary evidence that points to new methods of working. It will be a classic in the field of liturgical studies and will be gratefully received by scholars in a wide range of disciplines."

—Margot E. Fassler
Keough-Hesburgh Professor of Music History and Liturgy
University of Notre Dame

Liturgy's Imagined Past/s

Methodologies and Materials in the Writing
of Liturgical History Today

Edited by
Teresa Berger and
Bryan D. Spinks

A PUEBLO BOOK

Liturgical Press   Collegeville, Minnesota
www.litpress.org

A Pueblo Book published by Liturgical Press

Cover design by Ann Blattner. Detail of the Dura-Europos Baptistery Wall Painting, 3rd century. Yale University Art Gallery.

Excerpts from the English translation of *The Roman Missal* © 2010, International Commission on English in the Liturgy Corporation (ICEL); excerpt from the English translation of *The Order of Confirmation* © 2013, ICEL. All rights reserved.

Excerpts from documents of the Second Vatican Council are from *Vatican Council II: Constitutions, Decrees, Declarations; The Basic Sixteen Documents*, edited by Austin Flannery, OP, © 1996. Used with permission of Liturgical Press, Collegeville, Minnesota.

Library of Congress Cataloging-in-Publication Data

Names: Berger, Teresa, editor.
Title: Liturgy's imagined pasts : methodologies and materials in the writing of liturgical history today / edited by Teresa Berger and Bryan D. Spinks.
Description: Collegeville, Minnesota : Liturgical Press, 2016. | "A Pueblo book."
Identifiers: LCCN 2015038832 | ISBN 9780814662687 | ISBN 9780814662939 (ebook)
Subjects: LCSH: Liturgics.
Classification: LCC BV176.3 .L585 2016 | DDC 264.009—dc23
LC record available at http://lccn.loc.gov/2015038832

Contents

Part 3: Liturgy's Past/s: Broadening the View

Part 4: The Presence and Future of Liturgy's Past/s

Illustrations

Foreword

A religious act, more often than not, is an act of remembering. A prayer recalls a need in the world or in a human life or offers thanks for a blessing given. The reading of Scripture in an assembly calls to mind the acts of God in human history. Celebration of a ritual such as the Christian Eucharist reenacts the salvific story of Christ. Christian liturgies, especially, are libraries of such historical assertions. But each of these statements is itself a liturgical claim, because each lays hold of a deeply held, though often unspoken, notion that says that as we worship, we recall our histories.

This volume of essays probes and reflects on the acts of history making that liturgies are. To reduce liturgical expression to this notion alone would be an oversimplification, but one of the significant contributions of liturgical studies is that it gives even deeper insights into how individuals and communities construct their identities through the histories they recount. These essays peer back in time like a series of relay lenses, each one allowing us a glimpse around a historical "corner," as it were. Or they function like someone who gazes at a mirror reflecting in a mirror. One reads a liturgy to understand not only how its creators understood their world but also how this understanding was itself shaped by the creators' progenitors. Back and back it goes, each generation adding a layer of knowing.

The essays gathered here share this common goal, but they also focus on contemporary challenges in the writing of liturgy's past. The 2014 Liturgy Conference at the Yale Institute of Sacred Music sought to call attention to the need to reflect on both methodology and contemporary historical research in that process. With regard to the first—methodology—the conference probed the impact of important shifts in historiography (for example, the turns to social history and gender history) on the work of historians of liturgy and on how they imagine and display the past. With regard to the second—historical research itself—the conference presented new scholarship that promises to reconfigure some of the established images of liturgy's past.

The essays in this volume not only bear witness to the historical act that gave birth to them—that international scholarly conference at the Yale Institute of Sacred Music—but they also give evidence to the labors of its conveners, our cherished colleagues Professors Teresa Berger and Bryan Spinks, to whom we owe a great debt of gratitude.

Such a conference and volume are only a small part of a much larger complex of activities at our institute, which employs the sacred arts and ritual as ways to explore the human condition. Such a pursuit is limitless, and our hope is that these essays will not only serve as a small window into our own activity but also inspire others along similar quests. Only by understanding the claims religious actions make can we understand their power to do both good and ill.

Martin D. Jean
Director
Yale Institute of Sacred Music

Acknowledgments

The editors would like to thank a number of people at the Yale Institute of Sacred Music and at Yale Divinity School without whose encouragement, support, and hard work neither the Fourth Yale Liturgy Conference, "Liturgy's Imagined Past/s" 2014, nor this volume would have been possible.

First and foremost, we wish to thank Martin Jean, Director of the Yale Institute of Sacred Music, who generously hosted the 2014 conference and enthusiastically supported the publication of these papers.

We are grateful to Melissa Maier, ISM Manager of External Relations and Publications, for overseeing the organization of the conference, and to Albert Agbayani, who was our "person on the ground."

We owe a debt of gratitude to Rona Johnston for her outstanding editorial work and her commitment to ensure that, at short notice, the manuscript reached the publishers on time.

We express our thanks to Sydney Thomas, ISM MAR '16, for checking bibliographical details.

We continue to be grateful to the wonderful ISM staff, without whose dedication the institute's manifold activities could not flourish, especially Jacqueline Campoli, Kristen Forman, Andrea Hart, Trisha Lendroth, Sachin Ramabhadran, and Elizabeth Santamaria.

As with the past three collections of papers from the liturgy conferences of the Yale Institute of Sacred Music, it has been a pleasure to work with Hans Christoffersen and staff at the Liturgical Press.

Part 1

Foundational Matters

Imagining the Past

Historical Methodologies and Liturgical Study

Bryan D. Spinks

In a book titled *Imagining the Past: East Hampton Histories*, Timothy H. Breen presented his research on the history of the town of East Hampton, Long Island, New York, which had been founded in the 1640s. Breen's original mission was to write about the Mulford Farmstead, which dates from the 1680s, to which end he set out to use artifacts and texts from the town's records. Among the many documents he examined was a sermon delivered in 1806 by the town's Presbyterian minister, the Reverend Lyman Beecher. In his sermon, Beecher reconstructed the history of East Hampton and concluded that the community had prospered not because its inhabitants had been especially clever or diligent, but because they feared God.[1] Writing his history in 1989, Breen decided that in addition to employing archival material, he would listen to contemporary perceptions of the town's history from those who currently lived in East Hampton. He noted, "I soon became aware of a commonly accepted mythic history, a broadly shared sense of how East Hampton got to be the way it is, that bears only problematic relation to what I encountered in the records."[2]

---

[1] The sermon was partly motivated by Beecher's wish to persuade his congregation to raise his salary, which it failed to do. Beecher later moved to the congregational church at Litchfield, Connecticut.

[2] Timothy H. Breen, *Imagining the Past: East Hampton Histories* (Reading, MA: Addison Wesley, 1989), 9–10.

What became obvious to Breen was that "a process, a bundle of values, a set of relations between human beings and the environment have powerfully bound the past and the future in this town."[3] East Hampton's past(s) was/were being imagined to direct the future, and different parties appropriated and interpreted the town's past(s) to validate their particular views on its future identity. A comment by Breen adds another dimension: "I can claim no more than to have presented a personal reading of how various people have thought about East Hampton's past."[4] Thus, in addition to the town's artifacts and records and the imagined histories of many of the then residents of the town, Breen gave a personal reading of the data—*his* imagined past.

The stuff of Breen's history is a reflection of the human mind's tendency and human nature's impulse to explain the way things are, a compulsion that has been called the "cognitive imperative."[5] This process involves interplay between observing, remembering, and imagining. David Hogue has defined the latter:

> Imagination is the distinctively human capacity to envision multiple alternative realities, scenarios, and outcomes. It involves the ability to represent, internally and symbolically, scenarios and configurations of space and time that are not immediately represented to the senses.
>
> Imagination frees us from the tyranny of the present, of the logical, of "real." It also frees us from the constraints of the now, as it pictures what events were like in the historic past or what they might become in the future.[6]

Imagination and imagining thus play important roles in how the past (history) is configured and described. Breen's history of East

[3] Ibid., 11.

[4] Ibid., 15.

[5] Eugene d'Aquili and Andrew B. Newberg, *The Mystical Mind: Probing the Biology of Religious Experience* (Minneapolis, MN: Fortress Press, 1999), 196f. For a more "clinical" account see Kathleen Taylor, *The Brain Supremacy: Notes from the Frontiers of Neuroscience* (Oxford: Oxford University Press, 2012).

[6] David A. Hogue, *Remembering the Future, Imagining the Past: Story, Ritual, and the Human Brain* (Cleveland, OH: Pilgrim Press, 2003), 44–45.

Hampton was different from Lyman Beecher's but no less governed by the imaginings of the human mind.

Historians pride themselves on being objective, and in the nineteenth century, many historians believed they lived up to Leopold von Ranke's aphorism that the task of the historian is simply to show "how it really was."[7] More sober reflections acknowledge that objectivity is always tempered by subjectivity and that recounting and assessing the past involves much more than empirical "facts." At least in the English-speaking world, a change was sounded by E. H. Carr in his 1961 work *What Is History?* His first answer to this question was the assertion that "it is a continuous process of interaction between the historian and his facts, an unending dialogue between the present and the past."[8] Carr questioned historical writing that, as was typical of his time, consisted mainly of political narratives with biography. He defended the growing interest in social and economic history and suggested that understanding the past would help with understandings of the present and possibly change the future. History was a search for causation. Carr is seen as the catalyst for one shift in historical methodology, but other shifts have occurred since. Subsequent historical studies have embraced anthropology, postmodernism, and the "linguistic turn," as well as cultural histories, women's histories, gender studies, and postcolonialism. They have also shifted away from causation and toward meaning and understanding. Historiography has become more interdisciplinary and now makes greater use of artifacts and material culture.

In her recent book *The Look of the Past: Visual and Material Evidence in Historical Practice*, Ludmilla Jordanova notes:

---

[7] Leopold von Ranke, *Histories of the Latin and Teutonic Nations from 1494– 1514* (London: George Bell & Sons, 1909): "History has had assigned to it the office of judging the past and of instructing the present for the benefit of the future ages. To such high offices the present work does not presume: it seeks only to show what actually happened" [*wie es eigentlich gewesen*].

[8] E. H. Carr, *What Is History?* 2nd ed. (New York: Knopf, 1961; repr. Harmondsworth, UK: Penguin Books, 1987), 30.

As in the present, so in the past, the sense of sight shapes experience. The material world is a visual world, which impacts upon human beings through their eyes, and is ultimately bound up with touch. Historians can only benefit from approaching the past with a vivid appreciation of these points, with a willingness to consider what people looked at, how they looked and the roles of objects designed to be looked at. Sight has long been accorded privileged status: that the expression "I see" means "I understand" neatly reveals the point. . . . Artifacts mediate past ideas and experiences, making them ripe for historical analysis.[9]

Reflecting on contemporary historical writing, David Cannadine has noted that in moving from causation to concern for meaning and understanding, we have become much more sophisticated in our comprehension of the past. He adds, however, an important caveat, that "historians . . . are themselves both agents and victims of the historical process. Every generation, scholars have arisen proclaiming that they have found a new key which unlocks the essence of the past in a way that no previous historical approach has ever done. Our own generation is no exception to this rule—and it will probably be no exception to this fate."[10]

An important observation regarding subjectivity, or the historian's own imagination, was made by Keith Jenkins in *Re-thinking History*, when he reflected that "the historian's viewpoint and predilections will shape the choice of historical materials, and our own personal constructs determine what we make of them. The past that we 'know' is always contingent upon our own views, our own 'present.' . . . Epistemology shows we can never really know the past; that the gap between the past and history (historiography) is an ontological one, that is, is in the very nature of things such that no amount of epistemological effort can bridge it."[11] The operative words here are "our own present." How we imagine the past is

[9] Ludmilla Jordanova, *The Look of the Past: Visual Material Evidence in Historical Practice* (Cambridge, UK: Cambridge University Press, 2012), 1.

[10] David Cannadine, ed., *What Is History Now?* (New York: Palgrave Macmillan, 2002), xii.

[11] Keith Jenkins, *Re-thinking History* (London: Routledge, 1991), 12, 19.

mediated to a certain degree by our own present views, needs, and concerns, both conscious and unconscious. As Breen discovered in the contemporary oral histories of East Hampton, to which his own study was an addition, the past is always reconstructed through the lenses of the present. A prime example is the nineteenth-century interest in the medieval world, and that fascination's romantic re-creation of a lost age. The "Romantic" movement was a reaction against a so-called rationalism of the Enlightenment mind and fulfilled a need in rediscovering a mysterious golden past. How far the medieval world imagined by Sir Walter Scott and others bore any resemblance to that era is a study in its own right.[12]

HOW DOES ANY OF THIS RELATE TO LITURGICAL STUDIES?

In *How Societies Remember*, Paul Connerton acknowledges that while texts, other documentary evidence, and works of art are all important sources for the transmission of the past, rituals and commemorative ceremonies as embodied practices are also crucial repositories of the social memory.[13] In other words, liturgy and ritual are extremely revealing resources for history, be it of a denomination, a religion, or a wider society and culture. The older concern with liturgical textual minutiae and close comparison of texts coupled with an apparent obsession with rubrics and correct ceremonial suggested that liturgiology was an arcane discipline pursued by those who had found nothing better to do with their lives. This negative view still persists in many theological and church circles that really should know better. Anton Baumstark (1872–1948) is generally regarded as the father of the older comparative historical

---

[12] Charles L. Eastlake, *A History of the Gothic Revival* (American Life Foundation, Watkins Glen, 1979) was originally published in 1872 and provides what was then a contemporary understanding of the Gothic revival. For more recent reflections, see A. Dwight Culler, *The Victorian Mirror of History* (New Haven, CT: Yale University Press, 1985), and Clare A. Simmons, *Popular Medievalism in Romantic-Era Britain* (New York: Palgrave Macmillan, 2011).

[13] Paul Connerton, *How Societies Remember* (Cambridge, UK: Cambridge University Press, 1989).

liturgical method.[14] The papers presented at a conference held in Rome in 1998 to mark fifty years since his death witnessed to the refinement and expansion of historical liturgical methodologies.[15] They illustrated a vibrant subject, far removed from Dean Inge's (in)famous cryptic comparison of liturgiology with stamp collecting.[16] Those who are committed to serious liturgical scholarship know that their craft has changed dramatically, and it now employs the full range of tools and methodologies of historiography, as well as theological, musicological, and ethnological analyses and approaches, and it frequently embraces the evidence of material culture in the same manner as many other scholarly endeavors.

Liturgical rites are for performance and always have been. When their content is codified for future performance, the result is a liturgical text, or score, in some form. Texts are still important. The older method tended to be concerned with discovering the use of earlier sources—the liturgical antecedents—and/or identifying the author, with exploring the author's theology (always *his* theology), and with interpreting the liturgical texts accordingly. Newer, more complex and sophisticated understandings of "text" have tended to show the limitations of such approaches. The strictures of Robert Morgan and John Barton made in reference to biblical texts are no less applicable to liturgical texts: "Texts, like dead men and women, have no rights, no aims, no interests. They can be used in whatever way readers or interpreters choose."[17]

With reference to studies on the "Euchology of Serapion," Juliette Day has recently written: "The urauthor can be given the

[14] Anton Baumstark, *On the Historical Development of the Liturgy*, introduced, trans., and annotated by Fritz West, with foreword by Robert F. Taft (Collegeville, MN: Liturgical Press, 2011). See also n. 4 in Teresa Berger's essay in this volume.

[15] Robert F. Taft and Gabriele Winkler, eds., *Comparative Liturgy Fifty Years after Anton Baumstark (1872–1948)* (Rome: Pontifical Oriental Institute, 2001).

[16] A comment made by Inge to Edward Ratcliff, recorded by A. H. Couratin, in "Liturgy," in *The Pelican Guide to Modern Theology*, vol. 2, ed. J. Daniélou, A. H. Couratin, and John Kent (Harmondsworth, UK: Penguin Books, 1969), 131.

[17] Robert Morgan and John Barton, *Biblical Interpretation* (New York: Oxford University Press, 1988), 7.

name Serapion, but our construction of him may well not be the same as the historical Serapion whom, in any case, we cannot recover. The historical Serapion cannot control the interpretations we place upon the prayers which bear his name, but starting with whatever (historical) information we can gather from within and without the text, we are then free to interpret."[18] Day's book usefully explores the dimensions of text, authorship, genre, narrative, and intertextuality and their implications for liturgical studies. The application of a broader textual methodology to liturgical study is also illustrated by the methodology developed at the Pontifical Institute of Liturgy at Saint Anselmo, Rome, by Renato De Zan and now adapted for the Institute of Liturgy at Ealing Abbey, England. According to De Zan, study begins with textuality (historical-semantic dimension) and leads to liturgicity (pragmatic dimension), which is situated within liturgical celebrations and linguistic-pragmatic contexts. That process requires understanding of how a text relates to other texts of a rite, the gestures, the mystery being celebrated, and the liturgical season and leads eventually to a liturgical theology.[19] De Zan has recently demonstrated this form of engagement with particular reference to collects.[20]

Morgan and Barton's comment that texts have no aims and interests is not entirely accurate for liturgical texts, which quite often have particular interests—theological, ideological, or even functional. Matthew Cheung Salisbury has remarked of medieval liturgical manuscripts of the Sarum use, "The extant sources vary in a surprising range of aspects, but within individual Uses some contents are absolutely consistent. It would seem that some changes to

---

[18] Juliette J. Day, *Reading the Liturgy: An Exploration of Texts in Christian Worship* (London: Bloomsbury, 2014), 36.

[19] Renato De Zan, "Criticism and Interpretation of Liturgical Texts," in *Handbook for Liturgical Studies*, vol. 1: *Introduction to the Liturgy*, ed. Anscar J. Chupungco (Collegeville, MN: Liturgical Press, 1997), 331–65.

[20] Renato De Zan, "How to Interpret a Collect," in *Appreciating the Collect: An Irenic Methodology*, ed. James G. Leachman and Daniel P. McCarthy (Farnborough: Saint Michael's Abbey Press, 2008), 57–77. Leachman and McCarthy have adapted this methodology for the institute at Ealing Abbey in which they teach.

liturgical texts were deliberately applied or enforced, in attempts to create or preserve specific traditions, and that others simply reflected contemporary trends in the transmission of text and music, and varying adherence to authority."[21]

An obvious example from the early centuries that is discussed further in this collection is the so-called *Apostolic Tradition* attributed to Hippolytus. Liturgical revisers of the 1960s approached this text as though it not only represented the practice of all the churches of Rome in circa 215 but also was normative for the whole West and normative for liturgical revision in the late twentieth century. Dom Gregory Dix had written confidently in 1937: "Here from the pen of a disciple of St. Irenaeus is what claims to be an accurate and authoritative account of the rites and organization of the Church as the men of the later second century had received them from the sub-apostolic age. . . . It represents the mind and practice not of St. Hippolytus only but of the whole Catholic Church of the second century. As such it is of outstanding importance."[22] In 1970 Dom Bernard Botte wrote of the anaphora in this text, "It is certainly one of the oldest examples of Christian prayer literature so it is hardly surprising that when the liturgical reform was initiated consideration was given to restoring to use this admirably simple prayer."[23] The influence of "Hippolytus" on liturgical revision in many Western churches in the post–Vatican II decade was widespread and notable, for example, in the new Roman Catholic ordination rites of Vatican II and of the Episcopal Church of the United States.

More recent scholarship suggests that this particular text is a composite document, redacted in the late third or, more probably, early fourth century. The text now seems to be itself the imagined past of a particular group in Rome and was an attempt to estab-

---

[21] Matthew Cheung Salisbury, *The Secular Liturgical Office in Late Medieval England* (Turnhout: Brepols, 2015), 7.

[22] Gregory Dix, *The Treatise on The Apostolic Tradition of St. Hippolytus of Rome*, 2nd ed. (London: SPCK, 1968), xi, xliv.

[23] Bernard Botte, "The Short Anaphora," in *The New Liturgy: A Comprehensive Introduction*, ed. Lancelot Sheppard (London: Darton, Longman & Todd, 1970), 194–99.

lish some sort of authority through an imagined tradition. Church orders are not innocent, neutral documents. The text *Apostolic Tradition* used by revisers in the 1960s was itself a scholarly reconstruction from other church orders. A manuscript called *Apostolic Tradition* is no greater reality than New Testament scholars' supposed manuscript of "Q." What was/is presented has been/is a scholarly imagining. As Morgan and Barton note, "The balance of power and moral rights then shifts to the interpreters. They are the masters or judges of meaning now, for better or worse. The interpreters are never mindless servants of the text, or midwives at the birth or communication of meaning. They are human agents with their own aims, interests, and rights."[24]

Liturgical scholars and revisers of the mid-twentieth century gave the *Apostolic Tradition* an assumed authority to help direct their ideas and ideals of liturgical revision. They reimagined what appears to have been an already imagined past. Although this scenario seems obvious to twenty-first-century liturgical scholars in hindsight, it was not obvious to those revisers of the twentieth century.

Current agendas often color how a liturgical past is imagined, and some biases are less opaque than others. The preface to the first *Book of Common Prayer*, presumably penned by Archbishop Thomas Cranmer, stated, "And where heretofore, there hath been great diversitie in saying and synging in churches within this realme: some folowyng Salsbury use, some Herford use, some the use of Bangor, some of Yorke, and some of Lincolne: Now from hencefurth, all the whole realme shall have but one use." Nigel Morgan has rightly said that not only has no evidence ever been found of a use of Bangor and it is unlikely to have existed (the Bangor Pontifical sheds no light on the subject) but also no evidence exists for a distinct use of Lincoln, only minor differences from a basically Sarum use.[25] Richard Pfaff came to a similar

---

[24] Morgan and Barton, *Biblical Interpretation*, 6–7.

[25] Nigel Morgan, "The Introduction of the Sarum Calendar into the Dioceses of England in the Thirteenth Century," in *Thirteenth Century England VIII: Proceedings of the Durham Conference 1999*, ed. Michael Prestwich, Richard

conclusion.[26] By the sixteenth century, Sarum use seems to have been almost universal in the English church other than in Hereford and York. Why, then, did Cranmer multiply the uses? Did he believe there were Bangor and Lincoln uses? Did he hear that each of these cathedrals had its own use and imagined those accounts to be true? Or with Sarum use the sole use in the province of Canterbury since 1542, did Cranmer deliberately exaggerate the diversity in order to justify the enacted uniformity of the new 1549 liturgy?[27]

A recent example of undisguised bias is found in *Resurgent in the Midst of Crisis: Sacred Liturgy, the Traditional Latin Mass, and Renewal in the Church*, by Peter Kwasniewski. Kwasniewski is a theologian whose sympathies lie with the "Reform of the Reform" movement in the Roman Catholic Church, which regards the *Novus Ordo Missae* of Pope Paul VI as a departure from Catholic tradition and a product of modernity. The *Novus Ordo Missae* is described as possessing symbolic value as "a kind of rough-and-ready repudiation of the Council of Trent, of Boniface VIII's Unam Sanctam, of patristic mystagogy and the antithesis of the ancient and medieval heritage."[28] Whether the revised Mass actually is any of these things is highly questionable. Kwasniewski clearly prefers the older Latin Rite as found in the Missal of Pope John XXIII of 1962, which he refers to as "The Classical Roman Rite." Although a footnote acknowledges historical development and regional accretions, the author asserts the existence of a core that constitutes the traditional Latin Mass "going back substantially to the first millennium and even the first half of the first millennium."[29] This definition is con-

---

Britnell, and Robin Frame (Woodbridge: Boydell, 2001), 179–206, see in particular 182–83.

[26] Richard Pfaff, *The Liturgy in Medieval England: A History* (Cambridge, UK: Cambridge University Press, 2009), 458, 502–5.

[27] *Concilia Magnae Britanniae et Hiberniae, a synodo Verolamiensi AD 496 ad Londinensem AD 1717*, ed. David Wilkens, 4 vols. (London: R. Gosling, 1737), 3:861f.

[28] Peter Kwasniewski, *Resurgent in the Midst of Crisis: Sacred Liturgy, the Traditional Mass, and Renewal in the Church* (Kettering, OH: Angelico Press, 2014), 151.

[29] Ibid., 151n1.

flated and misleading history, yet this imagined past is used to legitimate the author's view of the 1970 missal as the source of most of what is wrong in the contemporary Catholic Church.

A more measured approach is found in an essay by Paul Gunter.[30] Although we might take issue with some of his statements (his attribution of the Supplement to the Hadrianum to Alcuin of York, for example), Gunter is on solid ground when he proposes, "In order to avoid the misconception that the Ordinary Form of the Mass in its 2002 edition and the Extraordinary Form of 1962 are two distinct entities irreconcilably at odds with each other (since each, in its distinctive form, represents the Roman Rite), we need to trace the historical developments out of which the missal of 1570 arose."[31] The 1962 missal carries a more cultic view of priesthood, understood through its links to the 1570 Mass and that Mass's theology and beauty of form and artifact, while the missal of 1970, with its emphasis on the assembly, requires that the content of the celebration and the rites should be self-explanatory.[32] Gunter may have a personal preference, but that inclination cannot be easily gleaned from his historical narrative. As Richard Muller has said, "Historiography ought not to be grounded in theological assumptions."[33]

Having a preference or a personal (even group-shared) liturgical agenda is entirely legitimate. When, however, a particular agenda drives and distorts the interpretation of the historical data, the resulting assumed narrative is problematic. The "organic" development of the 1962 rite to which Kwasniewski appeals over against the "genetic engineering" of the new rite actually came to an abrupt end with the Council of Trent, when reform was put in the hands of the pope and all local "organic" changes were ended. The

---

[30] Paul Gunter, "'Sacerdos paratus' and 'Populo congregato': The Historical Development of the Roman Missal," in *Benedict XVI and the Roman Missal*, ed. Janet E. Rutherford and James O'Brien (Dublin: Four Courts Press, 2013), 40–69.

[31] Ibid., 41.

[32] Ibid., 66.

[33] Richard A. Muller, "Historiography in the Service of Theology and Worship: Toward Dialogue with John Frame," *Westminster Theological Journal* 59 (1997): 301–10.

revisers who compiled the *Novus Ordo Missae* believed they were restoring an older, more classical shape using the best scholarship of the 1960s. From today's perspective, it seems that they simply created an imagined retrieval and that the result is a product of modernity. Equally though, whatever the age of certain elements of the 1962 Latin Mass, its codification and control at Trent make it an early-modern liturgy, and the 1962 version is simply a recycling of material that generates, in turn, a product of twentieth-century modernity.

Contemporary liturgical scholars often try to be mindful of their prejudices and agendas, though the suggestion that those studies whose ultimate ancestry is the liturgical movement are more agenda driven than are the critical editions of important liturgical texts, as Richard Pfaff has claimed, is something of a self-deception.[34] On the whole, liturgists do their best (though not always successfully) to avoid searching for a "golden age" of liturgy. They are also well aware of and employ more recent methodologies. In addition, they make no apology for discussing implicit and explicit theology, since their training allows them to do just that. Robert Taft exemplifies the older textual comparative method in his monumental volumes on the liturgy of St. John Chrysostom. His copious footnotes witness to tireless comparison of manuscripts and readings in order to establish the best text. As a theologian, Taft also discusses theological issues raised by the texts. Yet he has pioneered structural analysis of liturgical units.[35] He has also written *Through Their Own Eyes: Liturgy as the Byzantines Saw It*, which attempts a social history of the Byzantine Rite, using then-contemporary lay sources.[36] Taft says, "One can no longer re-

[34] Richard W. Pfaff, "Liturgical Studies Today: One Subject or Two?," *Journal of Ecclesiastical History* 45 (1994): 325–32. The production of a critical text is not an entirely neutral undertaking, as Pfaff seems to think. The process may not be driven by theological or pastoral concerns, but it is not necessarily without an agenda.

[35] R. F. Taft, "The Structural Analysis of Liturgical Units: An Essay in Methodology," *Worship* 52 (1978): 314–29.

[36] R. F. Taft, *Through Their Own Eyes: Liturgy as the Byzantines Saw It* (Berkeley, CA: InterOrthodox Press, 2006).

construct the past only from the top down. What we find in liturgical manuscripts was embedded in a socio-cultural ambiance outside of which it cannot be understood as liturgy, something that real people did. Furthermore, such literary monuments are a product of high culture, and hence only half of the story."[37]

Historians and musicologists have also rediscovered the importance of liturgy, and the late classical and medieval eras have proved particularly fruitful for interdisciplinary studies. Éamonn Ó Carragáin has woven together explorations of the Ruthwell Cross, the poetry of the Dream of the Rood, and the liturgical themes central to Lent and Easter as celebrated in the seventh and early eighth centuries, which were adapted by the Ruthwell community for their own local needs.[38] His work is an outstanding example of interdisciplinary methods. Carolyn Marino Malone decoded the façade of Wells Cathedral in relation to the reforms of the Fourth Lateran Council, the homilies of the period, and the liturgical processions described in the Sarum Customary, which Wells had adopted under Bishop Jocelyn. She brought together architecture, decoration, homiletic material, and liturgy.[39] Susan Boynton explored the monastic community at Farfa in the eleventh and twelfth centuries, arguing that it can be adequately perceived only by taking into account the centrality of liturgical performance in shaping and reflecting its identities. Changes in liturgical chant are a central facet of her study.[40] Helen Gittos has interlaced Anglo-Saxon architecture, archeology, and the Anglo-Saxon liturgical text, explaining processions between buildings in the same compound and giving context to the rites for dedicating churches.[41] Owen

---

[37] Ibid., 7.

[38] Éamonn Ó Carragáin, *Ritual and the Rood: Liturgical Images and the Old English Poems of the Dream of the Rood Tradition* (London: The British Library; Toronto: University of Toronto Press, 2005).

[39] Carolyn Marino Malone, *Façade as Spectacle: Ritual and Ideology at Wells Cathedral* (Leiden: Brill, 2004).

[40] Susan Boynton, *Shaping a Monastic Identity: Liturgy and History at the Imperial Abbey of Farfa, 1000–1125* (Ithaca, NY: Cornell University Press, 2006).

[41] Helen Gittos, *Liturgy, Architecture, and Sacred Places in Anglo-Saxon England* (Oxford: Oxford University Press, 2013).

Phelan has explored Alcuin's teaching on *sacramentum* and baptism and the implications of a binding oath of political allegiance in the Carolingian Kingdom.[42] In all these studies, liturgical scholars can recognize a grasp of the liturgical materials that has been given deeper and richer meaning through engagement with cognate disciplines.

In a variety of ways, the faculty of Yale Institute of Sacred Music (ISM), past and present, have attempted in their own works to exemplify the fruits of modern historiography and interdisciplinary approaches in their study of liturgy. Former faculty member Lester Ruth wrote in his introduction to worship at early Methodist quarterly meetings:

> A new portrayal of early American Methodists at worship, listening to their voices and accepting them on their own terms, is the goal of this book. To pursue this end, I will use a wealth of materials dating from before 1825: journals, diaries, letters, liturgical fragments, hymns, circuit records, histories, and autobiographies. Much of this material is unpublished and has been little considered by liturgical historians. I also give careful attention to distinctive elements of Methodist polity since it provides the flavor and context for other aspects of Methodist life, including worship. In the end, the reader must judge whether I succeed in giving voice to these early Methodists, for I believe people truly are the primary liturgical documents.[43]

In assessing worship and sacramental theology in England and Scotland in the seventeenth and eighteenth centuries, in addition to published and unpublished liturgical documents, I drew on contemporary accounts of worship as well as catechisms, sermons, theological works, and hymns to give a thicker description of worship and sacramental understanding in that period, adding views from the pew.[44] Former ISM director Margot Fassler has combined

---

[42] Owen M. Phelan, *The Formation of Christian Europe: The Carolingians, Baptism, and the Imperium Christianum* (Oxford: Oxford University Press, 2014).

[43] Lester Ruth, *A Little Heaven Below: Worship at Early Methodist Quarterly Meetings* (Nashville, TN: Abingdon/Kingswood Books, 2000), 14.

[44] Bryan D. Spinks, *Liturgy in the Age of Reason: Worship and Sacraments in England and Scotland 1662–c. 1800* (Farnham: Ashgate, 2008).

musicology, liturgy, sermons, and architecture to reconstruct processional liturgies in Chartres through the central *Portail Royal*. The meanings of the liturgy—its tropes, hymns, and prayers—can be correlated with the imagery that marks out liturgical pathways, both outside and inside the church. The introit tropes find their visual echo in sculpture.[45] Vasileios Marinis has examined the interchange between ritual and architecture in the late Byzantine churches of Constantinople, employing archeological data, liturgical texts and commentaries, and monastic *typika*.[46] Teresa Berger has begun to fill a huge vacuum in liturgy and gender studies. Drawing on historical case studies and focusing particularly on the early centuries of Christian worship, she has lifted a veil on liturgy's past to allow for a rich and diverse notion of gender difference and has asked whether we can assume that the struggle for holiness was so unevenly and gender-specifically successful.[47] Melanie Ross has utilized ethnographical studies to illuminate worship in evangelical congregations and drew on historical analysis, systematic theology, and the worship life of two congregations to show the common ground occupied by evangelical and so-called liturgical churches.[48] Markus Rathey's two forthcoming books on J. S. Bach combine the study of oratorios, passions, and the B-minor Mass with eighteenth-century Lutheran liturgy and theology to give a richer contextualization of Bach's music.[49] Henry Parkes has examined the writing and design of four important manuscripts from the city of Mainz—a musician's troper, a priest's

---

[45] Margot E. Fassler, *The Virgin of Chartres: Making History through Liturgy and the Arts* (New Haven, CT: Yale University Press, 2010).

[46] Vasileios Marinis, *Architecture and Ritual in the Churches of Constantinople: Ninth to Fifteenth Centuries* (Cambridge, UK: Cambridge University Press, 2014).

[47] Teresa Berger, *Lifting a Veil on Liturgy's Past: Gender Differences and the Making of Liturgical History* (Farnham: Ashgate, 2011).

[48] Melanie Ross, *Evangelical versus Liturgical? Defying a Dichotomy* (Grand Rapids, MI: Eerdmans, 2014).

[49] Markus Rathey, *Johann Sebastian Bach's Christmas Oratorio: Music, Theology, Culture* (Oxford: Oxford University Press, forthcoming 2016); *Bach's Major Vocal Works: Music, Drama, Liturgy* (New Haven, CT: Yale University Press, forthcoming 2016).

ritual handbook, a bishop's pontifical, and a copy of the enigmatic compilation now known as the Romano-German Pontifical—to open up new ways of understanding how religious ritual was organized, transmitted, and perceived in early medieval Germany and, by implication, elsewhere.[50]

All this is to say that we believe that the ISM already exemplifies many of the current major trends in liturgical studies. Having made such a claim, I also acknowledge that the present faculty all seek to learn more from others in affiliated fields. Such exploration was one purpose of the ISM's 2014 conference titled "Imagining Liturgies Past/s." We invited leading liturgical scholars together with historians who have pioneered interdisciplinary studies and who themselves have made significant contributions to liturgical subjects to present papers bringing new light to old subject matter and showcasing new material. Many of those papers are included in this collection. We hope that we can all learn from one another's insights, methods, and methodologies, discovering new keys we can use to unlock the liturgical past. And we remain aware that both our own shortcomings and our present concerns will sooner or later be exposed by those who will come after us. As Cannadine so rightly observed, "We are ourselves both agents and victims of the historical process."[51] That process encompasses *our* imagined past/s of liturgy. Since liturgical scholars are only human, we will continue to imagine.

---

[50] Henry Parkes, *The Making of Liturgy in the Ottonian Church: Books, Music and Ritual in Mainz, 950–1050* (Cambridge, UK: Cambridge University Press, 2015).

[51] Cannadine, *What Is History Now?*, xii.

Liturgy's Present

How Historians Are Animating a
"New" History of Liturgy

Miri Rubin

In winter 2010, a doctoral student at the School of History, Queen Mary University of London, sent out a call for papers for a workshop titled "Rethinking Medieval Liturgy: New Approaches across the Disciplines." She had in mind a small gathering of early career researchers for the exchange of research, training, and community building. The response was overwhelming, and it came from Warsaw and Dublin, Padua and York; one person even crossed the Atlantic from the University of Pennsylvania. There were sessions on particular offices and prayers—the *Officium stellae* and the *Ave Maria*—the traditional terrain of liturgy, and there was a great deal that was new, with papers on sculptures and articulated figures used in liturgical processions, liturgical drama, and treatises about the liturgy. The source material was both Latin and vernacular, and a great deal of attention was paid to music and performance. The vibrant meeting ended with hopes and promises to meet again.

The next gathering took place in November 2013, as "Liturgy in History." It too attracted a great deal of interest, with a heavier emphasis on chant and music. It drew young researchers from Berlin to Dublin, from Winchester to Trondheim, and was led by a team of seasoned scholars: Emma Dillon, Sara Lipton, Nils Holger Petersen, and Beth Williamson. The day ended at the twelfth-century church of St. Bartholomew's, Farringdon, London, with performances led by one of the day's organizers, Matthew Champion, medieval historian, singer, and choirmaster.

I open this discussion of the present state of the study of liturgy with these examples since they convey something of the enthusiasm, innovation, diversity, and collaboration that animate that study. Over the last decade or so, many more medievalists have begun to use liturgical sources and have sought to be trained in the traditions of liturgical scholarship. As we shall see, developments in the study of history in the later decades of the twentieth century raised challenges for historians that have more recently matured into a new engagement with liturgical sources. Historians of religion, art, politics, women, communities, and courts are asking questions to which liturgical sources offer answers. Historically minded inquiry now guides the study of liturgy, a domain that was traditionally led by priests, pastors, and monks.

The historical interests that animate Liturgy's Present are the product of formative changes in the interests and priorities of many historians. The second half of the twentieth century saw a broadening of the field of historical inquiry to include groups and practices that previous generations of historians had not included in the historical enterprise. Great institutions of state and church had underpinned history making over the centuries—and affected what history was—when it emerged in the nineteenth century as an academic discipline to be taught and researched. Law, politics, diplomacy, war, and, later, economics and demography were the stuff of history, often organized along national lines. History was taught—just as the Classics were—as an endeavor that communicated insight, taught reasoning, and imparted lessons and examples to those destined to rule. Historians argued at length about roots and causes of great moments in history: the Reformation, the French and American Revolutions, the rise and fall of empires.

Some of these assumptions about history were questioned in the early twentieth century, after the First World War, as intellectuals like Marc Bloch sought to find a way of making history that touched people's lives as embedded within local landscapes, agrarian regimes, families, and communities. Theirs was a challenge to the Europe of nation-states that had just "sleepwalked" into catastrophe. What developed over the next decades, and is often associated with the French journal *Annales*, was an approach that imputed to "ordinary" people ideas and interests. The next generation, after the Second World War, continued the project with gusto. Its aims soon intersected with political and cultural movements of the 1960s and 1970s: the democratization of higher education in Europe, feminism, civil rights, and workers' movements, and with people in emergent postcolonial situations. New terms and concepts emerged from these aspirations: interest in ideologies and in resistance to those ideologies, in deviations from expected social norms, in popular culture, in the workings of communities, in the rhythms—and rituals—of daily life. The influence of Michel Foucault enhanced attention to those excluded or marginalized, such as witches, heretics, and the sick and poor. Already in 1986, Robert Darnton described the resulting historical activity as something of an "odd turn":

> But the most recent run of publication suggests a new range of subjects, some stranger than the other. We have had books on the lesbian nun, the anorexic saint, the wild boy, and the pregnant man. We have had dog saints and cat massacres. We possess a whole library of works on madmen, criminals, witches, and beggars. Why this penchant for the offbeat and the marginal?[1]

Such disdain did not dampen the desire of historically minded scholars in the humanities to give voice. Indeed, to the "strange" subjects of history, we can even add strange new shapes, with histories that are now recognized as global or that expect beliefs and practices to transcend the borders laid down by laws and rules in any sphere. In the study of religion, historians expect official knowledge and practice to be realized in forms that display the agency and cultural resources of lay users. Histories are also perceived as being "braided"—as Natalie Davis calls it—or entangled in intricate ways across borders, *histoire croisée*, in the helpful term

---

[1] Robert Darnton, "Pop Foucaultism," *New York Review of Books*, October 9, 1986.

coined by Michael Werner and Bénédicte Zimmermann.[2] They are made of interlocking strands of different hues and textures but necessarily meeting, intersecting, and always in flux.

In seeking to treat history in its complexity and to recognize its many voices, historians turned avidly to other disciplines in search of insights and concepts. Now there was psychohistory, cliometric history, and history informed by sociology or demography. The burgeoning interest in "religious cultures" found two disciplines to be particularly useful, literary criticism and anthropology, for our sources are so often texts, and religious life is so often patterned around ritual performance. More recently, psychology and neuroscience have been exciting research.

All these strands have produced a great deal of change in the study of religious ideas, practices, and experiences, the field of interest to us here. From the centrality of the study of theology and religious institutions have developed interests best captured by that term "religious culture."[3]

In a lecture delivered in London in 2007, Giles Constable reflected on the changes he had seen over his long and still fruitful life in scholarship, which he termed a shift "from church history to religious culture." He described how as a young scholar interested in twelfth-century spirituality, he was advised to develop a career in departments not of history but of religious studies. Tracing the trajectory in the United States above all, he noted that "Academic historians of the nineteenth and the early-twentieth century . . . inherited much of the secularism and the anti-clericalism of the eighteenth century, often without the learning, and tended to neglect the study of religion."[4]

---

[2] Michael Werner and Bénédicte Zimmermann, "Beyond Comparison: *Histoire croisée* and the Challenge of Reflexivity," *History and Theory* 45 (2006): 30–50.

[3] On some of the uses of liturgical sources by literary scholars and historians, see Clifford Flanigan, Kathleen Ashley, and Pamela Sheingorn, "Liturgy as Social Performance: Expanding the Definitions," in *The Liturgy of the Medieval Church*, ed. Thomas J. Heffernan and E. Ann Matter (Kalamazoo, MI: Medieval Institute Publications, 2005), 635–52.

[4] Giles Constable, "From Church History to Religious Culture: The Study of Medieval Life and Spirituality," in *European Religious Cultures: Essays Offered to*

The study of religion in the United States was often conducted by scholars in colleges with explicit denominational affiliations. In Europe, it was traditionally the business of priests, pastors, and monks. That characterization is particularly true for the study of liturgy. We still rely heavily on scholarly traditions laid down by the Maurists and the Bollandists for critical editions and reference books. The study of liturgy has been enriched by monks from Downside, Solesmes or Ligugé abbeys, with their scholarly preparation and study of textual texts, as well as their traditions of practice.

Some historians approach liturgical sources for answers to wide-ranging questions about the nature of social relations in societies where religion was a pervasive cultural resource for making sense of the world and understanding human relations, as well as the route to salvation. Liturgy has increasingly been used in recent decades as a key to understanding social relations as rituals that contained and transmitted—and also enacted—core values. John Bossy's highly influential article "The Mass as a Social Institution" (1983) was inspired by an insight offered by Émile Durkheim in *Les formes elementaires de la vie religieuse* (1912): that in ritual was encoded the whole set of a society's values, and that through ritual these values were imprinted and regularly conveyed to members anew.[5] Bossy offered an analysis of the Mass as an occasion for social integration culminating in the moment of charity par excellence, the *pax*. Scholars of liturgy like Paul Post deemed the approach too schematic, as it emphasized one moment over others and assumed liturgy's effect to be accomplished.[6] Liturgy scholars were, on the whole, much more satisfied with Eamon Duffy's 1992

Christopher Brooke on the Occasion of His Eightieth Birthday, ed. Miri Rubin (London: Institute of Historical Research, 2008), 3–4.

[5] John Bossy, "The Mass as a Social Institution, 1200–1700," *Past and Present* 100, no. 1 (1983): 29–61.

[6] Paul Post, "John Bossy and the Study of Liturgy," in *Omnes circumadstantes: Contributions towards a History of the Role of the People in the Liturgy, Presented to Herman Wegman on the Occasion of His Retirement*, ed. Charles Caspers and Marc Schneiders (Kampen: Kok, 1990), 31–50.

publication *The Stripping of the Altars*.[7] Duffy's capacious exercise embraced a vast array of images and prayers, devotional texts and objects. Duffy went on to write about prayer, thus suggesting that liturgy could be taken outside the church, into private chapels and homes, and even practiced alone.[8]

Historians have found liturgical sources to be useful witnesses to processes of change. The study of Merovingian society, for example, had often been obscured by the use of material colored by the dismissive attitude of Carolingian writers. Yitzhak Hen was impressed by a report from the 560s or 570s by the Byzantine historian Agathias, who recorded, "The Franks are not nomads, as some of the Barbarians certainly are. . . . They are all in fact Christian, and completely orthodox. They have magistrates and priests in their towns and celebrate the festivals just as we do."[9] Hen turned to liturgy and to the religious rituals that acted as bridges between the values superseded and the new Christian hegemony.

A good example is Hen's treatment of the *barbatoria*, the rite of passage by which male adolescents became men. While in pre-Christian times this event was a ceremony of the first arms bearing, it became a ceremony of the first shave and haircut, administered by the subject's father or closest male blood kin. Merovingian liturgical sources, such as the Old Gelasian Sacramentary (seventh century and probably from Gaul), offered a prayer for the first cutting of hair, and that prayer persisted into the Gregorianum (or the Hadrianum) that Charlemagne received from Pope Hadrian in 784.[10]

[7] Eamon Duffy, *The Stripping of the Altars: Traditional Religion in England, 1400–1580* (New Haven, CT: Yale University Press, 1992).

[8] Eamon Duffy, *Marking the Hours: English People and Their Prayers, 1240–1570* (New Haven, CT: Yale University Press, 2007); see also Virginia Reinburg, *French Books of Hours: Making an Archive of Prayer, c. 1400–1600* (Cambridge, UK: Cambridge University Press, 2012).

[9] Yitzhak Hen, *Culture and Religion in Merovingian Gaul A.D. 481–751* (Leiden: Brill, 1995), 1.

[10] Rosamund McKitterick, *The Frankish Church and the Carolingian Reforms, 789–895* (London: Royal Historical Society, 1977), 123–38.

As interesting for our purpose here is that Hen, a historian of Merovingian Gaul, is now also a scholar of liturgy, with distinguished contributions to the field such as his edition of the Sacramentary of Echternach[11] and his interdisciplinary collection of essays on the Bobbio Missal, edited with Rob Meens.[12] Here is an important development, for historians of liturgy are not born but made, and, moreover, nowadays they rarely treat liturgical sources alone but rather insert them alongside other textual, visual, and musical sources.

Historians of liturgy have traditionally concentrated their efforts on the history of texts, whereby they sought to establish authoritative versions of liturgies, trace variation and dissemination, and often link these studies to the histories of religious orders, not infrequently orders of which they were members. Liturgy, in both past and present, is associated with the identities of its practitioners and of its historians too.[13] When present, new trends in the study depend on these achievements and traditions of erudition, but they tend to pose questions arising from without the liturgical domain.

As we have seen, historians now approach liturgy with the diversity, changeability, and fragility of practice in mind. They are mindful of the varying levels of training and ability among the liturgical performers in parishes, who were the parish priests, and of the vastly differing spaces of performance: cathedral, parish, private chapel, confraternity altar, wayside cross, or parish boundary.

Liturgy is the *opus dei*—be it in a monastery or a parish church— and its effects are many. It was designed to shape belief and

[11] *The Sacramentary of Echternach (Paris Bibliothèque Nationale, lat. 9433)*, ed. Yitzhak Hen, Henry Bradshaw Society 110 (Cambridge, UK: Cambridge University Press, 1997).

[12] *The Bobbio Missal: Liturgy and Religious Culture in Merovingian Gaul*, ed. Yitzhak Hen and Rob Meens (Cambridge, UK: Cambridge University Press, 2004).

[13] Susan Boynton, *Shaping a Monastic Identity: Liturgy and History at the Imperial Abbey of Farfa, 1000–1125* (Ithaca, NY: Cornell University Press, 2006); Susan Boynton, *Silent Music—Medieval Song and the Construction of History in Eighteenth-Century Spain* (New York: Oxford University Press, 2011).

perform sacramental action, to structure time and facilitate the route to salvation. Its rhythms included the daily, weekly, seasonal, and yearly rhythms with the added punctuations of feasts, alongside urgent calls to celebrate victory or coronation, or to petition desperately for the cessation of war and disease. It was always the product of local practices and interests, based in the traditions of local cathedrals, minsters, and monasteries and affected by initiatives from regional and ecumenical ecclesiastical councils as well as by directives from the chapters of religious orders.

Like all programmatic sources—law or conduct books, for example—liturgical texts are but a starting point in the unfolding of practice, a script for a play that depended a great deal on the contributions of its actors, the setting in which it was staged, and the attitudes and responses of its audiences. In short, that play was bound to be messy and to vary vastly from performance to performance. Historians of liturgy are working in archives in order to supplement the knowledge of liturgical design contained in liturgical books and their rubrics with knowledge of practice. My own work on provision for the celebration of the Mass encompassed the directives of councils and synods in England and France—but with indications of the provision of lights, cloths, chalices, pyxes, and missals arising from a whole variety of sources.[14] There is a long historical tradition—often polemical in tone—of using visitation records to expose lapses in liturgical practice, a tradition informed by polemical interests. This practice does not describe the orientation of the "new" history of liturgy, for, above all, recent attempts have been interested in experience: in how rules of conduct, traditions designed for practice, were in fact enacted by individuals in vastly variable spaces. Think, for example of the rich cathedral establishment of Cambrai, whose capitulary—a book of expenses paid and actions taken by the cathedral's officials—has been studied by Craig Wright. This work shows that monophonic service books contained added sections and pages of polyphonic chant, that comments and notes in margins directed attention to the dif-

---

[14] Miri Rubin, *Corpus Christi: The Eucharist in Late Medieval Culture* (Cambridge, UK: Cambridge University Press, 1991), 35–48.

ficulty of achieving harmony and balance between the two sides of the choir, and that members of the choir were troublesome too. An entry from 1493, which Wright rightly calls "bizarre," records the chastisement of vicars who threw meat and bones at each other during the divine service.[15]

Historians of liturgy are interested more than before in the challenges posed by practice, and that concern has extended the frame within which liturgy is studied. Alongside the Latin liturgy, a wide range of vernacular liturgy is now taken very seriously.[16] Religious women used such vernacular liturgy, as did priests and friars providing pastoral care to communities. Historians have thus turned away from the normative texts and toward the dissemination of these texts' ideas. Once passed on, such ideas are possessed in people's lives, a process that linguists would describe as a movement from structure to enunciation. The historians do not call these enunciations "folk," "superstitious," or "deviant," but seek to understand them in terms of the vast opportunities for self-expression and exploration of the world offered by the language of Christian religion. Caroline Bynum has led by exploring the language of medieval religious women, inspired by the Eucharist and appropriated into cells and city streets.[17] Jean-Claude Schmitt traced the cult of a healing greyhound, unlikely as it sounds, within the traditions of pilgrimage and the cult of saints.[18] Voices of participants in liturgical events, clerical practitioners and lay audiences alike, are being made to speak from the registers of inquisitors, from ego-documents, and in moments of correction and chastisement. Particularly novel is our emergent view of the

[15] Craig Wright, "Performance Practices at the Cathedral of Cambrai 1475–1550," *Musical Quarterly* 64 (1978): 295–328, see especially pp. 297, 303.

[16] See, for example, Eyal Poleg, *Approaching the Bible in Medieval England* (Manchester: Manchester University Press, 2013); see also Helen Gittos and M. Bradford Bedingfield, eds., *The Liturgy of the Late Anglo-Saxon Church* (Woodbridge, Suffolk: Boydell, 2005).

[17] Caroline Walker Bynum, *Holy Feast and Holy Fast: The Religious Significance of Food to Medieval Women* (Berkeley, CA: University of California Press, 1987).

[18] Jean-Claude Schmitt, *The Holy Greyhound: Guinefort, Healer of Children since the Thirteenth Century* (Cambridge, UK: Cambridge University Press, 1983).

liturgical understanding and skills of lay people, and of liturgy as amenable to absorption into intimate personal identity and experience.[19]

The elevation of the Host in the Mass is much described and interpreted in theological, liturgical, and pastoral texts, but it has also emerged as a highly personal experience inspired by the proximity to God made flesh in the form of bread. Such was the case for Aude Fauré, a woman we know from the records of her interrogation on suspicion of heresy by the bishop of Pamiers in 1318, the sources of Montaillou fame. On her first visit to church in the village of Merviel after giving birth, Fauré was troubled on viewing the elevated Host by thoughts about the pollution of childbirth, above all the bloody placenta, as associated with Christ's birth. For Fauré the consoling, salvific presence of Corpus Christi prompted doubt and anxiety at a moment of high awareness of her body, of her motherhood. The liturgy prompted a string of thoughts and feelings that Fauré shared with her kin, and thus ultimately these private cogitations became the stuff of public scrutiny.[20]

Fauré's testimony to her investigators was given in Occitan but recorded in Latin, with some of the original words retained in the official record. It is in the vernacular that historians are finding women's utterances related to liturgy and devotional practices. And so the new history of liturgy meets one of the most fruitful trends to have animated history writing since the last century: the desire to include women. Although the extraordinary Hildegard of Bingen (d. 1179), a sophisticated writer, composer, and musician, worked within the Latin liturgical traditions, most women's writings on religion and its practice, such as those of Angela da Foligno, Marguerite Porete, and Margery Kempe, were in the vernacular. Provision for women's devotions and liturgy was made in the vernacular and often composed by women, as Nancy Bradley Warren has shown in the case of veiling liturgies in English for

---

[19] See, for example, Derek Krueger, *Liturgical Subjects: Christian Ritual, Biblical Narrative, and the Formation of the Self in Byzantium* (Philadelphia, PA: Pennsylvania University Press, 2014).

[20] Rubin, *Corpus Christi*, 343–44.

both Benedictine and Brigittine nuns.[21] There was guidance for religious women provided in Latin and the vernacular, while prayers and devotional texts linked to the liturgy were often composed by women, like those explored by June Mecham for the nuns of Wienhausen.[22] The concept of vernacular theology, coined just a few years ago, has marked fields of creativity beyond Latin and clerical formations. It includes sermons, prayers, and hymns and is associated with imagery to be used in church or home.

Liturgy's Present explores how the liturgy became part of the existence of those who absorbed it and was thus transported to other areas of life. Pamela King has found in the York cycle of vernacular biblical plays many Latin liturgical cues, which people could repeat and intone.[23] Similarly, Penny Granger has analyzed the English N-Town Play, another fifteenth-century English biblical drama, with a strong Marian emphasis.[24] The play of the Visitation has Mary and Elizabeth reciting the *Magnificat*, Mary in Latin and Elizabeth in English, a performance of liturgy on stage that may have invited audience participation.

Historians of medieval literature in all the European vernaculars are unearthing a shadow world of translations of parts of the liturgy and especially those sections that carry important theological messages or form part of a sacramental action. Marian hymns and prayers in all European vernaculars developed alongside special Marian devotions, with explications of the *Ave Maria* and the *Pater Noster* provided in all vernaculars and sometimes directed at children or the literate laity. The work on vernacular liturgy thus

[21] Nancy Bradley Warren, *Spiritual Economies: Female Monasticism in Later Medieval England* (Philadelphia, PA: University of Pennsylvania Press, 2001); see also Judith H. Oliver, *Singing with Angels: Liturgy, Music, and Art in the Gradual of Gisela von Kerssenbrock* (Turnhout: Brepols, 2007).

[22] June L. Mecham, "Reading between the Lines: Compilation, Variation, and the Recovery of an Authentic Female Voice in the Dornenkron Prayer Books from Wienhausen," *Journal of Medieval History* 29 (2003): 109–28.

[23] Pamela M. King, *The York Mystery Cycle and the Worship of the City*, Westfield Medieval Studies 1 (Woodbridge, Suffolk: D. S. Brewer, 2006).

[24] Penny Granger, *The N-Town Play: Drama and Liturgy in Medieval East Anglia* (Woodbridge, Suffolk: Boydell, 2009).

amplifies the picture that arose some thirty years ago from R. W. Scribner's excellent work on popular religion on the eve of the Reformation:[25] sacramentalia, the creative and practical use of sacred materials in the search for fertility and health, now seems to be in keeping with the capacities of the informed medieval laity after, say, 1250.

The extensive attention to performance and audience, and perhaps also the anthropological bent of many of those who study religious cultures, has meant that the material environment of liturgy is now of great interest. What could be heard or seen? Did people stand or sit? Could anyone see the elevation through thick screens and in ill-lit spaces? We know these issues mattered to people in the past, since they occasionally voiced complaints, made provision, or sought solutions, tackling, for example, drafts that might extinguish the light on the altar.

The liturgy marked a place, a space, and a time, and its effects could be spectacular: it taught; it induced emotions; it created communities with shared lore.[26] The challenge of combining sources and approaches into a capacious view of liturgical life has been realized by Margot Fassler in exemplary fashion in her *The Virgin of Chartres: Making History through Liturgy and the Arts.*[27] Here art history, the history of music in architectural spaces, and the history of an urban community all come together through the tracing of a sole strand: the local cult of a miraculous Virgin. Moving across time and equally ambitious is the collaborative enterprise that resulted in the volume *The Medieval Art, Architecture and*

[25] R. W. Scribner, *Popular Culture and Popular Movements in Reformation Germany* (London: Hambledon Press, 1987), 10.

[26] For particular attention to space, see Eric Palazzo, *L'espace rituel et le sacré dans le christianisme: la liturgie de l'autel portatif dans l'Antiquité et au Moyen Âge* (Turnhout: Brepols, 2008). See for the treatment of space also Teresa Webber, "Monastic Space and the Use of Books in the Anglo-Norman Period," *Anglo-Norman Studies*, ed. David Bates (Woodbridge, Suffolk: Boydell, 2013), 221–40.

[27] Margot Fassler, *The Virgin of Chartres: Making History through Liturgy and the Arts* (New Haven, CT: Yale University Press, 2009).

History of Bristol Cathedral: An Enigma Explored,[28] which brought together scholars of different periods and orientations to study this complex space where a community of St. Augustine became a cathedral after the Reformation. The community of canons monks had elaborately decorated liturgical spaces that formed a *Gesamtkunstwerk* and a factory for prayer and for the commemoration of the Berkeley benefactors, which are to be studied in their many parts. Deborah Howard and Laura Moretti's *Sound and Space in Renaissance Venice: Architecture, Music, Acoustics* combined studies of sacred music and architecture in order to understand how the two interacted, asking whether new architectural styles put liturgical considerations to the fore and, if so, to what effect?[29] Their investigation involved performing in the spaces and using modern technology to measure the level and quality of the sound. Their undertaking was a joint project, funded by a large grant, and collaboration characterizes a great number of the current interdisciplinary endeavors in the field of Liturgy's Present.

The spaces of liturgy were neither uniform nor unified. Through the course of the medieval centuries, an increased differentiation is evident as families and confraternities were allocated spaces in parish churches and cathedrals and as new devotional emphases led to new designations of spaces, like the Lady Chapels of Marian devotions or the *Sakramentshäuser* that towered over chancel spaces in German churches by the later Middle Ages. Thirty years ago, Clive Burgess argued that such chapels and chantries also enriched the liturgy with their introduction of professional performers and innovative chant.[30]

Confraternities were particularly lively consumers and inspirers of liturgical compositions that are sometimes called "paraliturgy," a term that is far from illuminating. In towns, above all

---

[28] Jon Cannon and Beth Williamson, eds., *The Medieval Art, Architecture and History of Bristol Cathedral: An Enigma Explored* (Woodbridge, Suffolk: Boydell, 2011).

[29] Deborah Howard and Laura Moretti, *Sound and Space in Renaissance Venice: Architecture, Music, Acoustics* (New Haven, CT: Yale University Press, 2010).

[30] Clive Burgess, "'For the Increase of Divine Service': Chantries in the Parish in Late Medieval Bristol," *Journal of Ecclesiastical History* 36 (1985): 46–65.

in their heyday from the thirteenth century, laypeople were guided by friars in the development of devotional activities to be performed alongside parochial liturgical practices. These activities were not habitual offices on the model of those contained from the thirteenth century on in books of hours and thus used by the privileged literate laity. Rather, in Tuscan cities, compositions in the local dialect dramatized the Christian story, most commonly the crucifixion. A particular form of performance animated the emotional drama of mother and son, with the laude performed as collective chant, often in front of images.

Art and chant came together in Orsanmichele in Florence around 1360, when the artist Orcagna painted a crucifix with a powerful depiction of Christ's tortured body. By 1388 the image was accompanied by an inscription with the first lines of the *Stabat Mater*.[31] The Marian theme prevailed in the laude chanted in confraternities, like that of Urbino:

> Oh son, son, son
> Oh beloved jewel
> Son, who gives comfort
> To my anguished heart?
> My gracious son
> my delectable son
> my fragrant son
> Why is he imprisoned?[32]

The rhythmic chants described in detail every aspect of Christ's unmaking and often emphasized a causal link between Mary's sorrows and the Jews. The drama of the Passion unfolded in image and sound:

[31] Diane F. Zervas, "Niccolò Gerini's 'Entombment and Resurrection of Christ,' S. Anna/S. Michele/S. Carlo and Orsanmichele in Florence: Clarifications and New Documentation," *Zeitschrift für Kunstgeschichte* 66 (2003): 33–64, see esp. pp. 54–55.

[32] "O fillo, fillo, fillo/ oi amoroso gillo/ fillo ki da consillo/ al cor mio angustiato?," G. Grimaldi, "Il Laudario dei disciplinati di S. Croce di Urbino," *Studj Romanzi* 12 (1915): no. 16, p. 22.

Down the white flesh
the red blood trickled
Behold the bitter life
that Mary's son has had.
The crazed crowd
ordained in counsel:
death and destruction
of the good pastor.[33]

There is strong polemical content to these chants, and liturgy is emerging as a site for the expression of polemical sentiment. In one of the most powerful projects using liturgical materials, Israel Yuval has analyzed both the Passover Haggadah and the medieval synagogue chants as vehicles for potent polemical and emotional expression.[34] And so, following the appalling violence inflicted on the Jewish communities of the Rhineland in 1096, liturgical laments—*piyyutim*—formed an act of commemoration and defiance:[35]

The gentiles call their holiness which is a sin of lechery
Your chosen ones reject the lineage of the woman of lechery
The gentiles raise an image higher than God
Your people bear witness to your lordship, God of Gods,
The gentiles have a defeated corpse as their nonsensical folly
Your cohort has you as holy seated in praise.[36]

[33] "Per la carne pollita . currea sangue vermillo/ orecco amara vita . kavera maria del/ fillo/ Lagente desmentita . ordenaro consillo. / la morte elo dessillo delo bono pastore," ibid., no. 7, p. 9.

[34] Israel Yuval, *Two Nations in Your Womb: Perceptions of Jews and Christians in Late Antiquity and the Middle Ages* (Berkeley, CA: University of California Press, 2008).

[35] For a pioneering engagement with this material, see Anna Sapir Abulafia, "Invectives against Christianity in the Hebrew Chronicles of the First Crusade," in *Crusade and Settlement: Papers Read at the First Conference of the Society for the Study of the Crusades and the Latin East, and presented to R. C. Smail*, ed. Peter W. Edbury (Cardiff: University of Cardiff Press, 1985), 66–72.

[36] *Sefer Gezerot Ashkenaz ve-Zarefat*, ed. Abraham Habermann (Jerusalem: Tarshish, 1945); see also Evyatar Marienberg, *Niddah. Lorsque les juifs conceptualisent la menstruation* (Paris: Les Belles Lettres, 2003), 177.

Polemic suggests otherness and difference, and the new types of otherness found by the late Middle Ages make the study of liturgy all the more necessary and obviously global. In his *Colonial Counterpoint: Music in Early Modern Manila*, David R. M. Irving explores the uses that Christian literary and religious drama made of native traditions of song and drama.[37] A rich public processional life—for the feast of the Assumption above all—was a celebration of the local and the Christian, a product of concerted effort by friars and Jesuits. And the global could be apprehended far closer to home, in Europe itself. The offerings of those who had been pilgrims or travelers to Jerusalem, and beyond, resided in churches, as did, more mundanely, wine and chrism from afar. The collegiate church at Goslar possessed a letter of *intitulatio* of Emperor Henry III from 1049, parchment dipped in porphyry as befits an imperial letter, which was first used to cover the altar and later arranged as an antependium.[38]

The range of underlying interests brought by scholars to the study of liturgical texts is now broader than ever, just as are the diverse skills and intellectual orientations applied to the study of liturgy. Liturgy now habitually meets the study of politics and of urban life, as seen in Meredith Cohen's work on Sainte-Chapelle, in Paris, and Andrew Brown's work on civic life in medieval Bruges.[39] Liturgical study also sees new types of engagement with liturgical manuscripts, often in a collaborative setting, of which a collection edited by Jonathan Wilcox, *Scraped, Stroked, and Bound: Materially Engaged Readings of Medieval Manuscripts*, is an excellent

[37] David R. M. Irving, *Colonial Counterpoint: Music in Early Modern Manila* (Oxford: Oxford University Press, 2010).

[38] Such findings arise from Tillman Lohse's research on the *Libri ordinarii*, see Tilmann Lohse, "Stand und Perspektiven der Liber ordinarius-Forschung," in *Liturgie in mittelalterlichen Frauenstiften. Forschungen zum Liber ordinarius*, ed. Klaus Gereon Beuckers, Essener Forschungen zum Frauenstift 10 (Essen: Klartext, 2012), 215–55.

[39] Meredith Cohen, *The Sainte-Chapelle and the Construction of Sacral Monarchy: Royal Architecture in Thirteenth-Century Paris* (Cambridge, UK: Cambridge University Press, 2014); Andrew Brown, *Civic Ceremony and Religion in Medieval Bruges c. 1300–1520* (Cambridge, UK: Cambridge University Press, 2011).

example.[40] Several contributors to this volume have pondered the traces of collective effort—in copying manuscripts and in performing liturgy—that the study of devotional and liturgical texts offer. Projects animated by Digital Humanities will facilitate and inspire further access to these rich materials.

From the erudite tradition of liturgy scholarship to the imaginative engagement with music and art, Liturgy's Present is vibrant, a leading force in medieval studies and in historical reflection. The "new" history of liturgy builds on traditions of scholarship but now is animated by questions of agency and gender, takes seriously lay contributions and experiences, and always remembers that liturgy's makers were embodied, feeling individuals.[41] That new history of liturgy is set to enrich many areas of historical reflection, beyond Europe, beyond Christianity.

[40] Jonathan Wilcox, ed., *Scraped, Stroked, and Bound: Materially Engaged Readings of Medieval Manuscripts* (Turnhout: Brepols, 2013). See also Henry Parkes, *The Making of Liturgy in the Ottonian Church: Books, Music and Ritual in Mainz, 950–1050* (Cambridge, UK: Cambridge University Press, 2015).

[41] Éric Palazzo, *L'invention chrétienne des cinq sens dans la liturgie et l'art au Moyen Âge* (Paris: Cerf, 2010).

Part 2

New Perspectives on Liturgy's Past/s

New Reflections on the Image of Late Antique and Medieval Ethiopian Liturgy

Emmanuel Fritsch

There was a time when the outsider's image of the Ethiopian liturgy was negative, to say the least.[1] For example, in *Églises orientales et rites orientaux*, published in 1922, Raymond Janin recorded, "In general the mass and the offices present the aspect of barbarous ceremonies because of the carelessness in the way they dress and of the contortions whereby the ceremonies are embellished" and "The secular clergy enjoys the most horrible notoriety, which they seem to deserve fully. . . . They actually demonstrate very little care for the Divine service, most of the time wear only dirty and worn out vestments and sometimes officiate half naked." He concluded his informatory piece: "It is barbarism in the sanctuary."[2] His description of the liturgy was very vivid indeed. And we can find still much worse from the pen of the famous missionary

---

[1] I am deeply indebted to Marie-Laure Derat, who allowed me access to her important work *Enquête sur les rois Zāgwē: Royaume chrétien d'Éthiopie, XIᵉ–XIIIᵉ siècle* (Habilitation thesis HDR, Université Paris 1 Panthéon-Sorbonne, 2013) long before its publication and commented on a draft of this paper. I also thank Anaïs Wion, with whom I discussed elements of this paper, Claire Bosc-Tiessé, and Ugo Zanetti, who commented on a draft and offered constructive remarks, as well as Heinzgerd Brakmann, who communicated to me yet unpublished material in addition to engaging in enlightening conversations.

[2] Translation mine. Original French texts in Raymond Janin, *Les églises orientales et rites orientaux* (Paris: Letouzey & Ané, 1922), 678 and 682.

and specialist Guglielmo Cardinal Massaja, in an account written just a few years before Pope Leo XIII issued *Orientalium Dignitas* on November 30, 1894. Massaja described the Ethiopian Rite as "a worm of a rite" (*questa larva di rito*) insofar as it was a rite at all.[3] Although the vocabulary was changed in Janin's amended second edition of 1954,[4] things Ethiopian or Eritrean were not valued until the work of Bernard Velat on the Divine Office, in particular, contributed to giving credence to the Ethiopian patrimony. Much done since in different disciplines has contributed to the history of liturgy, changing the tone from paternalistic and judgmental on theological and ethnocentric grounds to one of (moderate and by no means general) respect.

Taking as its starting point the Ethiopian liturgical tradition itself, the following discussion will highlight various approaches as well as indicate research that is still to be done. Liturgy is not worked out in a vacuum, as certain facts will make evident even to those who are unprepared for such a realization. From a scholarly standpoint, the work accomplished so far has begun to do justice to the Ethiopian church and its liturgical patrimony. Research in this field makes use of all available means, and interdisciplinary study leads to progress. As illustrated by what follows, leaps may be made or (educated) guesses confirmed by particular individual discoveries. From amongst examples of recent finds, this chapter will consider very unexpected elements contained in a manuscript discovered some twenty years ago. Moreover, a supposedly well-known structure has recently been identified as something previously unheard of on Ethiopian soil. Taken together with a freshly interpreted Ge'ez document, that discovery helps account for the initial appearance of a definitely new type of church. Finally, investigation of the origins of the type of church that is now most common will take us through various witnesses, trends of thought, and sites.

[3] See Giuseppe Mojoli, *Attività liturgica della S. Congregazione "De Propaganda Fide" per gli affari di Rito Orientale nel periodo 1893–1917* (Vicenza: Esca, 1979), 65–71.

[4] Raymond Janin, *Les églises orientales et rites orientaux*, 2nd ed. (Paris: Letouzey & Ané, 1954), 497 and 500.

The following pages shed new light on our understanding of liturgical development in the Ethiopian tradition, though certain questions remain unanswered.

PART 1: THE EUCHOLOGY IN THE AKSUMITE COLLECTION

Our ignorance of the Ethiopian past is fed by a lack of manuscripts. In addition to the present campaign to prevent not only tourists but also researchers, both Ethiopian and foreign, from accessing surviving manuscripts, many manuscripts were also destroyed, especially during the *ğihad* of Muḥammad ibn Ibrāhīm al Ġāzī in the sixteenth century but also by other hazards. We can list, however, a number of examples of promising material. Very significant information has come to light through the discovery of a catechesis of initiation to the eucharistic celebration contained in the fifteenth-century manuscript BnF ms. 66-66bis d'Abbadie, first published by Robert Beylot in 1984, then by Gérard Colin.[5] The seventh-century monastic story from Lower Egypt attributed to Bishop James of Wasim that stages the noblewoman Hilaria is also well known.[6] Several other texts are not so old but still have interesting liturgical potential. We might cite here, for example, the sixteenth-century Rās Sem'on, who wrote his own unusual story, which included a piece he had composed that was to be inserted in the book of the *Miracles of Mary* and a homily for the *Gebra Ḥemāmāt*, the Ritual and Lectionary for Holy Week,[7] or a

[5] "Sermon éthiopien anonyme sur l'Eucharistie," ed. Robert Beylot, *Abbay* 12 (1983–1984): 113–16; Gérard Colin, trans., *Le synaxaire éthiopien: mois de ṭerr*, Patrologia orientalis 45, no. 201 (Turnhout: Brepols, 1990), 214–31.

[6] *Quadraginta historiae monachorum*, ed. Victor Arras, Text: Corpus Scriptorum Christianorum Orientalium 505, Scriptores Aethiopici 85 (Louvain: Peeters, 1988), 235; Versio: Corpus Scriptorum Christianorum Orientalium 506, 154, in chap. 35 §3. On those documents, see Heinzgerd Brakmann, "Le déroulement de la messe copte: structure et histoire," in *L'eucharistie: célébrations, rites, piétés. Conférences Saint-Serge, 41ᵉ Semaine d'Études Liturgiques, Paris 1994*, ed. A. M. Triacca and A. Pistoia (Rome: Edizioni liturgiche, 1995), 109, 118–19.

[7] Getatchew Haile, "The Works of Ras Səm'on of Hagärä Maryam," *Journal of Ethiopian Studies* 38, nos. 1–2 (June–December 2005): 5–95.

seventeenth-century text concerning Zēnā Gabre'ēl, which was presented by Getatchew Haile in Moscow in 1988.[8]

The more ancient texts mentioned, which are in Ge'ez, are not direct descriptions of the Ethiopian liturgy but by chance—or providentially—describe Egyptian liturgy. A small number of other little-known stories from Egyptian sources should be added to our list because they help build a picture of early liturgical development in Egypt, which serves as backdrop for Ethiopia.[9] This Egyptian material will reflect Ethiopian liturgy insofar as the latter followed the former. But how can we know that such parallels did exist, beyond the educated guesses of scholars such as Heinzgerd Brakmann, who has been proposing for years that the Aksumites most likely used an Alexandrian liturgy?

The stunning recent discovery of a possibly twelfth-century parchment codex, found in Tegrāy, revealed what Alessandro Bausi, its editor, has named the "Aksumite Collection."[10] It contains what Bausi describes as "approximately thirty-six main pieces of patristic, liturgical, and canonical literature, as well as a historical text that is a *unicum*."[11] Composed in an Egyptian milieu,

[8] Getatchew Haile, "On the House of Lasta from the History of Zena Gäbrə'el," *Proceedings of the 9th International Conference of Ethiopian Studies* (Moscow: Nauka Publishers, Central Department of Oriental Literature, 1988), 6:7–21.

[9] For example, Enzo Lucchesi, "Trois nouveaux fragments coptes de la vie de Paul de Tamma par Ezéchiel," in *Ægyptus Christiana: Mélanges d'hagiographie égyptienne et orientale dédiés à la mémoire du P. Paul Devos, Bollandiste,* Cahiers d'orientalisme, ed. Ugo Zanetti and Enzo Lucchesi (Geneva: Patrick Cramer, 2004), 220n2, 5; "A Eucharistic Miracle," in *The Monasteries of the Wadi'n Natrun,* part 1, *New Coptic Texts from the Monastery of Saint Macarius,* ed. Hugh C. Evelyn White (New York: Metropolitan Museum of Art Egyptian Expedition, 1926), 176–77; Ugo Zanetti, "La Vie de Saint Jean, higoumène de Scété au VIIe siècle," *Analecta Bollandiana* 114, no. 3–4 (1996): 273–405.

[10] The first published reference to this document is the work of its discoverer, Jacques Mercier, "La peinture éthiopienne à l'époque axoumite et au XVIIIe siècle," *Comptes-rendus de l'Académie des Inscriptions et Belles-Lettres* (January–March 2000): 36n6.

[11] Alessandro Bausi, "The *Aksumite Collection,*" in *Comparative Oriental Manuscript Studies: An Introduction,* ed. Alessandro Bausi et al. (Hamburg: COMSt,

it was translated from Greek into Ge'ez between 477 and 686/687, possibly under the name *Sanidos za-ḥegg*, "Synodicon of the Law," a title that emphasizes an important part of its content as liturgical-canonical.[12] Bausi has provided introductions to this text in several papers and has published a number of its sections. Although a full edition is still in progress and the present translation is provisional, it is opportune to present some of the more interesting segments from the liturgical section of the Aksumite Collection.[13]

2015), 367; Alessandro Bausi, "La *Collezione aksumita* canonico-liturgica," *Adamantius* 12 (2006) (= *Il Patriarcato di Alessandria nella tarda antichità e nel Medioevo*, ed. Alberto Camplani): 43–70.

[12] According to references to that name in the *Acts of Peter of Alexandria*, itself part of the "Aksumite Collection." See Bausi, "La *Collezione aksumita* canonico-liturgica," 50 (p. 45 for the dating); Bausi, "The *Aksumite Collection*," 368–69.

[13] On this now abundant literature and in addition to the works in note 11, see Alessandro Bausi, "The 'So-called Traditio apostolica': Preliminary Observations on the New Ethiopic Evidence," in *Volksglaube im antiken Christentum*, ed. Heike Grieser and Andreas Merkt (Darmstadt: Wissenschaftliche Buchgesellschaft, 2009), 291–321; Alessandro Bausi, "La 'nuova' versione etiopica della Traditio apostolica: edizione e traduzione preliminare," in *Christianity in Egypt: Literary Production and Intellectual Trends*, ed. Paola Buzi and Alberto Camplani, Studia Ephemeridis Augustinianum 125 (Rome: Institutum Patristicum Augustinianum, 2011), 19–69; Alessandro Bausi, "The Aksumite Background of the Ethiopic 'Corpus Canonum,'" in *Proceedings of the XVth International Conference of Ethiopian Studies, Hamburg 2003*, ed. Siegbert Uhlig et al., Aethiopistische Forschungen 65 (Wiesbaden: Harrassowitz Verlag, 2005), 532–41; Alessandro Bausi, "Liste etiopiche di vescovi niceni," in *Orientalia Christiana. Festschrift für Hubert Kaufhold zum 70. Geburtstag*, ed. Peter Bruns and Heinz Otto Luthe, Eichstätter Beiträge zum Christlichen Orient 3 (Wiesbaden: Harrassowitz Verlag, 2013), 33–62 (author's approved text on http://www.academia.edu/3177140/Liste_etiopiche_di_vescovi_niceni); Alessandro Bausi and Alberto Camplani, "New Ethiopic Documents for the History of Christian Egypt," *Zeitschrift für Antikes Christentum* 17, no. 2 (2013): 215–47. I am very indebted to Alessandro Bausi, who generously shared with me the euchological section of the Aksumite Collection (which he had already largely edited, albeit it remained in a somewhat provisional condition) long before its publication and permitted me to prepare an English translation and a liturgical commentary on the text. Thus, I have previously made use of part of this material in E. Fritsch, "The Anaphoras of the Ge'ez Churches: A Challenging Orthodoxy," in *The Anaphoral Genesis of the Institution Narrative in Light of the Anaphora of Addai and Mari. Acts of the International Liturgy Congress, Rome*

This liturgical section includes forty items spread across nineteen folios, among which are prayers for the day and the night, for monastic life and matrimony, for the house, and for children, a set of prayers belonging to a baptismal ritual,[14] and an almost full collection of the *Mastabqʷeʾat* ("Supplications") still in use.[15] Let us begin with the Supplication for the Kings, addressed to God the Father, in a provisional translation.

> And again we beseech the Almighty Lord, the Father of the Lord our Savior Jesus Christ, for the beloved (pl.) of the Lord, Kings N. and N., so that the Almighty Lord may keep their reigns without suffering, in peace and in righteousness.
>   And the deacon says: Pray for the kings!
>   Almighty Lord, we pray and beseech for the kings of this land, the beloved of the Lord, and endow them with profitable things. And submit the enemy, the nations, for our tranquility. Speak in their hearts about your Church. Grant them what is without fault. May they keep [their] understanding about the faith in your good worship. Through your only Son, through whom, to you, together with him and with the Holy Spirit, be glory and dominion, now and ever, forever and ever. Amen.

25–26 October 2011, ed. Cesare Giraudo (Rome: Pontificio Istituto Orientale, 2013), 275–316; E. Fritsch, "Alcune caratteristiche del cristianesimo etiopico," (lecture, XXXV Settimana europea, Storia Religiosa Euro-Mediterranea, September 3–7, 2013), in *Popoli, Religioni e Chiese lungo il corso del Nilo Dal Faraone cristiano al Leone di Giuda*, ed. Cesare Alzati (Rome: Libreria Editrice Vaticana, 2015); E. Fritsch, "The 'Order of the Mystery': An Ancient Catechesis preserved in BnF Ethiopic Ms. d'Abbadie 66-66bis (fifteenth century) with a Liturgical Commentary," in *Studies on the Liturgies of the Christian East: Selected Papers of the Fifth International Congress of the Society of Oriental Liturgy, St. Vladimir's Orthodox Theological Seminary, New York, June 10–14, 2014*, ed. Bert Groen, Daniel Galadza, Nina Glibetić, and Gabriel Radle, Eastern Christian Studies (Louvain: Peeters, 2016).

[14] This set of prayers follows the actual baptismal ritual and is made up of texts published long ago. See Bausi, "La *Collezione aksumita* canonico-liturgica," 60n9; A. Salles, *Trois antiques rituels du Baptême*, Sources Chrétiennes 59 (Paris: Éditions du Cerf, 1959).

[15] Bausi, "La *Collezione aksumita* canonico-liturgica," 43–70.

Much in this text is well known, but one detail stands out: the use of the plural. It is a prayer not for kings in general or for a king and his consort but for two specific reigning kings, who will be named in this supplication. The plural also appears at other points of the euchology where the authorities are mentioned. Is the reference to Constantinople, or Egypt, or the kingdom of the Aksumites?[16]

The Anaphoras

The euchology contains very remarkable elements under §26 and §40, namely, the two anaphoras that are presented in their entirety side by side below, in a provisional English translation, as the anaphora of St. Mark and the anaphora of the *Apostolic Tradition*. Although the *Apostolic Tradition* is itself a very significant part of the codex, this latter anaphora does not appear within the *Apostolic Tradition* according to its usual presentation and location. Rather, it is placed in the euchological section and is found already edited for the liturgy, in the form that we will call the "Anaphora of the Apostles."[17] This second anaphora of the Aksumite Collection is an exceptional witness that vindicates earlier scholarly positions. Heinzgerd Brakmann assumed the early Ge'ez anaphoral tradition was Alexandrian and expected the normal anaphora to be that of St. Mark, while José L. Bandrès argued that the *Anaphora of the Apostles* had always been in use in the Aksumite kingdom.[18]

---

[16] Alexander Lingas pointed me to H. J. W. Tillyard, "The Acclamation of Emperors in Byzantine Ritual," *Annual of the British School at Athens* 18 (1911–12): 239–60, in which a couple of pages from a text from late fourteenth-century Athens, National Library of Greece MS 2062, include acclamations from the "Rite of the Trullo" sung at the vigil of September 14. The kings are commemorated in the plural, with acclamations that mention John V, his queen Helena, and Andronikos IV. I am grateful to Alexander Lingas for pointing this out to me following the 2014 Yale ISM liturgy conference.

[17] The convenient title "Anaphora of the Apostles" is used here, identifying this text with the well-known anaphora of the same name, without prejudging ways of explaining that identity.

[18] Heinzgerd Brakmann, Τὸ παρὰ τοῖς βαρβάροις ἔργον θεῖον; *Die Einwurzelung der Kirche im spätantiken Reich von Aksum* (Bonn: Borengässer, 1994), 160; José L. Bandrès, "The Ethiopian Anaphora of the Apostles: Historical Considerations," *Proche-Orient Chrétien* 36 (1986): 6–13; Habtemichael Kidane, "Origine

In 2010 Bausi wrote, "The *Anaphora of the Apostles* as well as some of the *mästäbqʷaʾat* certainly belong to the earliest layer of the Ethiopian liturgy (. . . e.g., the *Euchologion* in the so-called 'Aksumite Collection')."[19] Mapping the precise historical development is complex. A sentence by the fifteenth-century Ethiopian king Zarʾa Yãʿeqob might be read as implying that the Anaphoras of the Apostles and of the Lord go back only to his time.[20] Bausi has

---

ed evoluzione della 'Liturgia Gǝʾǝz,'" in *Acts of the First SOL Congress, Eichstätt 2006*, Bollettino della Badia Greca di Grottaferrata 5 (Rome: Poligraphica Laziale, 2008), 130; Irénée-Henri Dalmais, "La Tradition apostolique et ses dérivés dans les prières eucharistiques éthiopiennes," *Augustinianum* 20, fasc. 1–2 (August 1980): 109–17; Paulos Tzadua, "The Divine Liturgy according to the Rite of the Ethiopian Church," in *The Eucharistic Liturgy of the Christian East*, ed. J. Madey (Kottayam/Paderborn, West Germany: Prakasan Publications, 1982), 47; Takla-Maryam Semharay Salim, "Textus aethiopicus anaphorae sancti Marci," *Ephemerides Liturgici* 42 (1928): 507. See, for comparison, Ernst Hammerschmidt, *Studies in the Ethiopic Anaphoras*, 2nd ed., Äthiopische Forschungen 25 (Stuttgart: F. Steiner Verlag, 1987), 43–44.

[19] Alessandro Bausi, "Qǝddase: Mäṣḥäfä qǝddase," *Encyclopedia Aethiopica*, ed. S. Uhlig in cooperation with A. Bausi (Wiesbaden: Harrassowitz Verlag, 2010) (henceforward *EAE*), 4:281, referring to Bausi, "La *Collezione aksumita canonico-liturgica*," 60f. Bausi had already listed the following relevant anaphoral sections: on the one hand, *Initium gratiae actionis, Oratio supra fractionem, Oratio postquam acceperunt Dominum omnipotentem, i.e. postquam Dominus eis communicatus est, Oratio cum se demittunt postquam acceperunt*, which refer to the *Anaphora of St. Mark*, and on the other hand, the *Oratio oblationis (eucharisticae)* and *Oratio supra fractionem*, which refer to the *Anaphora of the Apostles*. I stated my identification of the Anaphoras of St. Mark and of the Apostles at the 2011 Addai Congress: see Fritsch, "The Anaphoras of the Geʾez Churches: A Challenging Orthodoxy," 275.

[20] Reinhard Meßner and Martin Lang, "Ethiopian Anaphoras: Status and Tasks in Current Research via an Edition of the Ethiopian Anaphora of the Apostles," in *Jewish and Christian Liturgy and Worship: New Insights into its History and Interaction*, ed. A. Gerhards and C. Leonhard, Jewish and Christian Perspectives Series 15 (Leiden: Brill, 2007), 203; Paul F. Bradshaw and Maxwell E. Johnson's presentation *The Eucharistic Liturgies: Their Evolution and Interpretation* (Collegeville, MN: Liturgical Press/A Pueblo Book, 2012) suffers from adhering to the provisional results of research, as is partly indicated in the footnotes (pp. 159, 161), especially the reference to Henoch to explain the "Benedictus." On this, see Gabriele Winkler, *Das Sanctus. Über den Ursprung und die Anfänge des Sanctus und sein Fortwirken*, Orientalia Christiana Analecta 267 (Rome: Pontificio Istituto Orientale, 2002); Heinzgerd Brakmann,

shown that the contents of the Aksumite Collection eventually merged with the liturgico-canonical documentation that came from Egypt through Arabic from the fourteenth century onward.[21]

Below, the Anaphoras of Mark and of the Apostles are placed in parallel to facilitate comparison.

Anaphora of St. Mark	Anaphora of the Apostles
1. Beginning of the Thanksgiving	Prayer of the Offering
The deacon says: Stand well in order to offer! Look to the east! We watch!	The deacon says: Stand well in order to offer! Look to the east! We watch!
The bishop (*epis qopos*) says: The Lord [be] with you all.	The pope (*pippas* [sic!]) says: The Lord [be] with you all.
People: And with your spirit.	People: With your spirit.
Lift up your hearts!	Lift up your hearts!
People: We have them with the Lord.	People: We pray to the Lord.
Let us give thanks to the Lord!	Let us give thanks to the Lord!
People: It is right and just.	People: It is right and just, he is worthy.
2. *epis qopos:* It is right and just that we praise you, glorify you, bless you. We confess you by night and by day. To you who made heaven and all that is in it, the earth and all that is on the earth, the sea and all that is in it; to you who created man in your own image and likeness, you created all by this your wisdom, the true light, the Lord our Saviour Jesus Christ, through whom to you, with him and through the Holy Spirit, as we give thanks we offer the reason-	We give you thanks, O Lord, through your beloved Son our Saviour Jesus Christ whom in the last days you sent to us as saviour and redeemer and the angel of your council. He is the Word while he is faithful, him through whom you made all things, you having decided, and you sent him from heaven into the womb of a virgin.

"Schwarze Perlen aus Henochs Erbe? Zu 'Sanctus' und 'Benedictus' der äthiopischen Apostel-Anaphora," *Oriens Christianus* 91 (2007): 56–86; Gabriele Winkler, "Über das christliche Erbe Henochs und einige Probleme des *Testamentum Domini*," *Oriens Christianus* 93 (2009): 201–47.

[21] This is how it was quoted by, for example, Abbā Giyorgis of Saglā. See Bausi, "La *Collezione aksumita* canonico-liturgica," 44–45, and Bausi, "The Aksumite Background of the Ethiopic 'Corpus Canonum,'" 532–41.

able sacrifice, this bloodless worship of yours, which all the peoples offer to you from the rising of the sun to the west, from south to north, for your name is great among all nations and in every place incense is offered to your holy name and a pure sacrifice.

3. In this sacrifice and offering we pray and beseech you: remember the one, your holy Church which is spread everywhere; surround all the people and all the flock with the peace from the heavens; grant to the heart of all of us the peace of this life; adorn with all peace the kings, the armies, the governors, the peoples, our neighbourhood, our coming in and our going out.
O King of peace, give us peace, because you have rewarded us in all. Take possession of us, Lord. Except you only, there is nobody we know: we call your Name.

4. Having visited the sick of your people, heal them, having generously given comfort, strength and firmness to those who travel or will be travelling and are in difficulty; send your rains in the areas where it is needed; rejoice the face of the earth; bring about the seed and the harvest for the poor of your people and for all who hope in you. For you are the nourisher of all flesh. Rest the souls of those who are asleep.

5. Remember therefore the blessed fathers our popes. Give us to receive a share and an inheritance with your saints as you remember them, and to commemorate them on this day.

Here let be read the names of the commemoration and let the deacons tell a second and a third time.	Let the names be read here.
And [remember] your servant N., or that woman, if it is the case. Rest his soul in your eternal dwelling-place, by the luminous angels, together with your saints. And if there is someone who transgressed human law, remit.	
Accept in your heavens those who bring sacrifices, and a sacrifice of the word. Reward them with what is incorruptible instead of what is corruptible and with what is in the heavens instead of what is on earth. And remember the blessed Pope N., keep him for many years for days of peace, as well as all the orthodox bishops, priests, deacons.	
6. My Lord, also remember us with compassion and with mercy and destroy our sins for you are good and a friend of man. You, Lord, be with us who serve your Name which is holy on all accounts; bless our community.	He became flesh and was carried in the womb and your Son was known from the Holy Spirit.
And the deacon says: You who are seated stand up!	And the deacon says: You who are seated, stand up!
Uproot idolatry from the world for ever. Tread down Satan and trample under our feet every power which opposes you. Cut short now the enemies of your Church, and strip them of their pride, show them quickly their weakness; destroy their jealousy and their slander; let their evil accusation be one which is useless; their plots and devices and schemings which they contrive against us.	

7. Arise, my Lord, and let your enemies be scattered and let all who hate your holy Name flee away. But your people, make them thousands and thousands and myriads of myriads. Ransom the prisoners, save those in distress, feed the hungry, console the afflicted, raise those who have fallen, send back those who got lost, lead all to the path of salvation and unite them to your people. As for us, save us from our sins as you are our guardian.
The deacon says: Look to the east!
It is you who are above every rank and authority and power and dominations and every name which is named; before you stand millions of millions and myriads of holy angels and archangels; before you stand your glorious living creatures, the seraphs with six wings and the cherubs.

To you, whom sanctify the thousands and countless thousands of holy angels and archangels and your glorious animals, the seraphim and cherubim who have six wings,

8. With two wings they cover their face, with two their feet, with two they fly and all of them always sanctify you. Accept our own sanctification as, together with all those who sanctify you, we say to you:

The people says together with the one who offers:
Holy holy holy Lord Sabaoth!
<u>Perfect</u> [is] the holiness of your glory in heaven and on earth!
The one who offers says: <u>Perfect</u> therefore is all the heaven and the earth by the holiness of your glory through the Lord our Saviour Jesus Christ. <u>Perfect</u>, O Lord, this sacrifice which is a blessing from you by the Holy Spirit because it is your only Son, the Lord (*Egzi'a beḥēr*) and God and our King over all, Jesus Christ.

with two wings they cover the face, and with two they cover their feet, and with two of their wings they fly and all of them continuously sanctify you together with all those who sanctify you, accept our own sanctification (*qeddest*) as we say to you: Holy!
And the people says together with the one who offers:
Holy holy holy Lord Sabaoth!
Heaven and earth are <u>filled</u> with the holiness of your glory!
Truly the holiness of your glory <u>fills</u> heaven and earth through our Lord and our Saviour Jesus Christ. Your holy Son having been born of a virgin in order to fulfill your will and to make a people for you, stretched his hand(s), suffering in order to set the sufferers free, those who rely on you, he was given to suffering by his

50

	will in order to overcome death and break the bounds of [the devil (Latin) / Satan] and tram[ple she]ol and lead the holy ones and establish a covenant, and make known the resurrection.
9. In the night when they <u>handed</u> him over he took bread <u>with</u> his holy and blessed hands and, having blessed and broken it, he gave (it) to his very disciples and to his apostles as he said: "Take, eat from it all of you: This is my body which is given for you unto the remission of sin." Again, likewise for the chalice after they had supper, having taken (it), he gave thanks and gave as he said: "Take, drink from it all of you: this is my blood of the new covenant which is poured for you unto the forgiveness of sins." <u>As often</u> as you eat this bread and drink this cup then you <u>announce</u> this my death and you believe in my resurrection.	In the night in which they <u>betrayed</u> him he took bread <u>on</u> his holy [hand] and looked up towards you, towards his Father, and blessed and broke and gave to them his own disciples and said to them: "Take, eat, all of you: This is my body. It is given to you, this by which sin is remitted." And likewise the chalice, having given thanks he said: "Take, drink all of you, this is my blood which will be poured for you, by which sin is remitted." <u>When</u> you do this, you will do it for the <u>commemoration</u> of me.
10. As we <u>announce</u> the death of my Lord almighty, your Only Son, the Lord (*Egzi'*) and God (*Egzi'a beḥēr*), the king over all and our Saviour Jesus Christ, as we believe in his resurrection, his ascension in the heavens, we have offered to you this your own gift from your own gift. We pray and beseech you to send the *Holy Spirit and power* in this offering upon the bread and the cup and to make the bread the body and the cup the blood of the new covenant of the Lord God (*Egzi'a beḥēr*), our king everywhere, Jesus Christ. The deacon only whistles.	As we <u>commemorate</u> his death and resurrection, we offer to you this bread and cup as we thank you. Thereby you made . . . for us so that we may stand (before) you and serve you sacerdotally. We pray and beseech you so that you may send the *Holy Spirit and power* to this bread and cup and (that) you may make it the body and the blood of the Lord our Saviour Jesus Christ. Amen.

So that it may be for all who take from it for faith, for understanding, for healing, for a renewal of soul, body and spirit, so that to you, in this as in all things, be glorified your holy and blessed name in everything, with Jesus Christ and the Holy Spirit.
The people says: As it was, is and shall be, and become for generations of generations for ever and ever. Amen.

Having united, may you give to all those who take (of it) that they will be for holiness and the fullness of the Holy Spirit, [the strengthening] of the (true) faith so that they may glorify and praise you and your Son our Saviour Jesus Christ with the Holy Spirit.
And the people says: As it was, is, and shall be for ever and ever. Amen.

11. Prayer upon the Fraction
And again we beseech the Almighty Lord, the Father of the Lord our Saviour Jesus Christ, that he may give us to receive with blessing this holy mystery and, if it happens that there is someone unworthy among us, that he may not condemn any of us but cause worthiness in all of those who take the reception of the holy mystery, the body and the blood of Christ, almighty Lord our God.
Let the deacon say: Pray!
Almighty Lord, grant to us the reception of your holy mystery as our strengthening; do not condemn any one of us but bless all through Christ, through whom, to you, with him and with the Holy Spirit, be glory and power forever, for ever and ever. Amen.

Prayer upon the Fraction
I humbly praise you, O Lord Almighty, who sit on the chariot of the cherubim, who rest in the height and know the humble, who are in the light, who make the universe rest: it is you who showed the hidden mystery of the cross. And who is a god like you? Do not remove far away from us your authority, like the authority that you gave to your apostles, for those who serve you with gentleness of heart and who offer to you a fragrant perfume which is about our Lord Jesus Christ. To you and to him glory and honour, to the Father and the Son and the Holy Spirit and the holy Church.

12. Let the deacon say: As you stand, lower your heads!
Eternal Lord, who knows the hidden things, it is towards you that your people have bowed their heads and towards you that they have bent the hardness of heart and flesh. Look from your worthy dwelling-place and bless them, men and women;

incline your ear towards them and listen to their prayer; strengthen them by the might of your right hand, protect them from evil sickness, be for them a guardian of the body and of the soul, increase in both them and ourselves the faith and the fear of you through your only Son, through him, to you, with him and with the Holy Spirit, be glory and power forever, for ever and ever. Amen.

The deacon says: Let us watch!
Let the one who offers say: The holy things for the holy.
Let the people say: One is the holy Father, One is the holy Son, One is the holy Spirit.
Let the one who offers say: The Lord is with you all.
The people: With your spirit.

13. Prayer after they have received
O Lord, Lord, Almighty, Father of the Lord our Saviour Jesus Christ, we give you thanks because you have shared with us that we take from your holy mystery. Let it not be for guilt or condemnation, but for the renewal of soul and body and spirit. Through your only Son, through whom, to you, with him and with the Holy Spirit, be glory and power forever, and for ever and ever. Amen.

Prayer when they bow their heads after they have received
O Lord, Eternal, Almighty, Father of the Lord our Saviour Jesus Christ, bless your servants and handmaids; cover and help and send (them) away with the strength of the angels;

protect and strengthen (them) by the fear of you; keep (them) in the fear of you, adorn what belongs to you by your greatness; grant that they may think about what is yours and may believe what is yours; and grant that they may want what is yours; grant concord without fault or wrath. Through your only Son, through whom, to you, with him and with the Holy Spirit, be glory and power forever, and for ever and ever. Amen.	

The utilization of material from the Anaphora of St. Mark to create the new Anaphora of the Apostles from that of the *Apostolic Tradition* is obvious[22] and emphasized by the fact that the structure of the rite is largely carried by Mark. The presentation, the contents, the translation system (sometimes surprisingly poor as for example with "prospherein / *(za-)yeqērreb*" in the initial dialogue and "orthodox / *retu'āna sebḥat*," that is, those who adhere to the right "glory" rather than "faith"[23]), and the relationship between Alexandrine and Antiochene anaphoras, as well as the sometimes independent way in which similar texts such as the *Sanctus* are rendered, are all paths for future investigation and will likely be as informative for Egypt as for Ethiopia.[24]

The only serious difference from today's text is that the conclusion of the thanksgiving of the *Testamentum Domini* is missing.[25] Composed in Greek in a fifth-century Palestinian, rather than

[22] As has been demonstrated by Meßner and Lang, "Ethiopian Anaphoras," 185–205.

[23] Ugo Zanetti points out that this mistake, which also occurs in the Slavic case of *pravo-slavie*, is understandable in light of the double meaning of δόξα.

[24] It is worth noting here that the Anaphora of St. Mark was documented in a very fragmentary manner that reflected similar translation difficulties in the fifth-century Alexandrian Catechesis. See my "The 'Order of the Mystery.'"

[25] The *Habanna neḥebar*, during which the rite of the fraction is performed. See Winkler, "Über das christliche *Erbe Henochs* und einige Probleme des Testamentum Domini," and Brakmann, "Schwarze Perlen aus Henochs Erbe?"

Antiochene, milieu,[26] the *Testamentum Domini* was present in Egypt in the sixth century, and according to Bausi, its "Ge'ez version is probably an independent translation upon a Greek *Vorlage*."[27] Nevertheless, it remains unclear when the edition of its anaphora as the Anaphora of the Lord was redacted or when material from it was used to enrich the Ge'ez eucharistic *Ordo*.

Another interesting feature is that the *cauda* of the Prayer of the Fraction reads: "To you and to him glory and honor, to the Father and the Son and the Holy Spirit and the holy Church." This wording uses the conclusion of the anaphora of the *Apostolic Tradition*: "May we be able thus to praise and glorify you through your Child, Jesus Christ. Through him glory to you and honor, to the Father and the Son, with the Holy Spirit, in your holy Church, now and forever." This adaptation could suggest that this prayer was considered part of the anaphora, a kind of doubling of the *Dammira-ka*. It has disappeared from the text of the Prayers of the Fraction and Embolism of the Anaphora of the Lord, to which, divided into two parts, it had once migrated.[28]

The use of the term "euchology" in connection with the Aksumite Collection is inappropriate insofar as the texts are incomplete and in apparent disorder and because this book could not be used for an actual liturgical service. Its inadequate character, however, and

[26] As can be deduced from church arrangement in Georges Descoeudres, *Die Pastophorien im syro-byzantinischen Osten*, Schriften zur Geistesgeschichte des östlichen Europa 16 (Wiesbaden: Harrassowitz Verlag, 1983), 45–49; Robert F. Taft, *The Diptychs*, vol. 4 of *A History of the Liturgy of St. John Chrysostom*, Orientalia Christiana Analecta 238 (Rome: Pontificium Institutum Studiorum Orientalium, 1991), 39–40.

[27] Alessandro Bausi, "Testamentum Domini," *EAE* 4:928. See also René-Georges Coquin, "Le Testamentum Domini: problèmes de tradition textuelle," *Parole de l'Orient* 5 (1974): 186; Robert Beylot, ed., *Testamentum Domini éthiopien* (Louvain: Peeters, 1984), viii.

[28] E.g. in Vatican ms aeth. 22 (15th cent.), f. 93va. See G. Horner, *Canones Ecclesiastici* (London: Williams & Norgate, 1904), 139–43; Hugo Duensing, ed., *Der aethiopische Text der Kirchenordnung des Hippolyt* (Göttingen: Vandenhoeck & Ruprecht, 1946), 20–31; Paul F. Bradshaw, Maxwell E. Johnson, and L. Edward Phillips, *The Apostolic Tradition: A Commentary*, Hermeneia Commentary Series (Minneapolis, MN: Augsburg Fortress Press, 2002), 37–54.

the contrast it presents with the Synodicon translated from Arabic in the fourteenth century, strongly suggest that we have here authentic liturgical material meant to be used, although, admittedly, not with this codex in hand. The Aksumite Collection may contain an "actualized" *Apostolic Tradition* and anaphora, suggesting that these texts were intended not simply as a repository of information but for the presentation of material that was to be put to use. Thus, this collection raises intriguing questions about the evanescent nature of liturgico-canonical documentation.

PART 2: TWO MOMENTS IN THE DEVELOPMENT OF ETHIOPIAN CHURCHES

Another field of research that documents the development of liturgy is the study of church architecture. For the relationship between liturgy and architecture as evinced by the churches of Eritrea and Ethiopia, two episodes are particularly compelling: the appearance of churches with several sanctuaries instead of pastophoria (sacristies) and the appearance of circular churches.

The Appearance of Churches with Several Sanctuaries

Egyptian influence caused the first major revolution in Ethiopian liturgy. The pastophoria were replaced by additional sanctuaries, which in turn caused the rearrangement of the beginning of the eucharistic rites as well as of the pre-anaphora.[29] The first extant monument that is both identifiable and datable, and that is likely to have been the first monument of its kind, is the church of Mikā'ēl

---

[29] See Emmanuel Fritsch and Michael Gervers, "*Pastophoria* and Altars: Interaction in Ethiopian Liturgy and Church Architecture," *Aethiopica* 10 (2007): 7–50; Emmanuel Fritsch, "The Preparation of the Gifts and the Pre-anaphora in the Ethiopian Eucharistic Liturgy in around 1100 AD," in *Rites and Rituals of the Christian East: Proceedings of the Fourth International Congress of the Society of Oriental Liturgy, Lebanon, 10–15 July, 2012*, ed. Bert Groen, Daniel Galadza, Nina Glibetić and Gabriel Radle, Eastern Christian Studies 22 (Louvain: Peeters, 2014), 99–100. It should be underscored that the exact circumstances and the timing of the changes mentioned remain elusive because of the unavailability of written documents. The rite may already have largely evolved, due to the earlier progress and influence of the Copts.

Ambā (East Tegrāy). It was arranged with three sanctuaries side-by-side—no longer following the model of a sanctuary and two pastophoria—as is demonstrated by the walls constructed later in that rock-hewn church in order to close off the lateral sanctuaries that would originally have been open and the triple chancel.[30] How did this come to happen? Fortunately, the monastery of Mikā'ēl Ambā still holds a six-teenth- or seventeenth-century book of the four gospels in which a note transcribed later by another hand preserved a text composed in the twelfth century by a certain Metropolitan Mikā'ēl. That note reads:

> In the name of the Father and of the Son and of the Holy Spirit, One God. I Mikā'ēl the sinner, a son of saint Abbā Entonyos in the monastery of the Arabeh which is on the shore of the Red Sea, and Abbā Maqāryos the arch-bishop of Alexandria appointed me pope of Ethiopia at the time of King Anbasā Wedem. And by the good

Fig. 1. *View of the church of Mikā'ēl Ambā*

Fig. 2. *Later-built partition closing off the once-open north sanctuary of Mikā'ēl Ambā*

Fig. 3. *The three chancels of Mikā'ēl Ambā*

---

[30] On this church see Ewa Balicka-Witakowska, "Mika'el Amba," *EAE* 3:959–61.

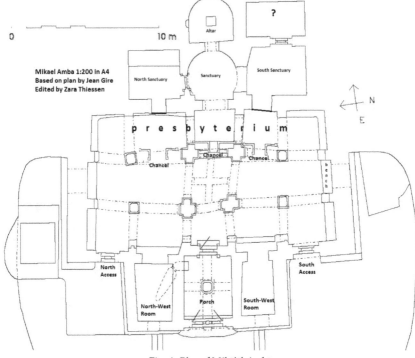

Fig. 4. *Plan of Mikā'ēl Ambā*

pleasure of God I have anointed 7 kings and consecrated 1,009 churches, and I have consecrated this monastery by the name of Saint Michael the archangel so that he may listen to my sorrow. And this matter took place in the Era of the Martyrs 866. . . . And I have built 70 churches [as a whole, including] at Nāzrēt, 4 at Ḍolā'et and 1 at Norā. Out of them, 1 by the name of Mary and another next to her by the name of Michael and Gabriel, . . . and all of you my male-slaves and my female-slaves, I have freed you from servitude for the sake of our Lord Jesus Christ and our Lady Mary the Mother of God, I Abbā Mikā'ēl, who consecrated her [i.e., the church of Mikā'ēl Ambā]. Remember me in your [pl.] prayer."[31]

[31] Inventory no. C3-IV-415, f. 102rv. See Derat, *Enquête sur les rois Zāgwē*, 30–36 for the text and a French translation. A partial translation of the note was published by Sergew Hable Sellassie, *Ancient and Medieval Ethiopian History to 1270* (Addis Ababa: United Printers, 1970), 203n117.

Historian Marie-Laure Derat, who has examined this note closely, identifies the years 1149/1150 as equivalent for the dating given above and has deemed the text authentic: the ascription of a church to an Egyptian metropolitan is exceptional in Ethiopia and the name Anbasā Wedem most unexpected; the authors of a later forgery would surely have picked a more illustrious name. Derat also suggests that the anointment of seven kings would not have been impossible for a bishop who served so long.[32] The exaggerations noted by some authors appear as such only because of insufficient knowledge of the ecclesiastical culture shared by Copts and Ethiopians regarding the consecration of churches.[33]

Furthermore, as Mary K. Farag has pointed out, the end of this statement by the long-reigning Metropolitan Mikā'ēl contains words that are crucial for a proper understanding of the very nature of the document: "and all of you my male-slaves and my female-slaves, I have freed you from servitude." The manumission of slaves is characteristic of wills according to a tradition that originated in a constitution issued by Constantine to Bishop Hosius in AD 321 and is contained in the Theodosian Code published in AD 438.[34] Mikā'ēl's twelfth-century note shows that Constantine's

[32] Derat, *Enquête sur les rois Zāgwē*, 31–32, 34. See also Denis Nosnitsin, "Mika'el I," *EAE* 3:953.

[33] Metropolitan Mikā'ēl did not visit these 1,009 churches but did consecrate for them the mobile altars or altar-tablets sent to him, the *tābotāt*. Having been consecrated by the bishop, the *tābot* was brought back to the church for which it was meant. Its solemn introduction was, and still is, tantamount to its consecration. The Copts used to, and continue to, employ mobile altars, the model for the Ethiopian *tābotāt*. See Emmanuel Fritsch, "The Altar in the Ethiopian Church: History, Forms and Meanings," in *Inquiries into Eastern Christian Worship: Selected Papers of the Second International Congress of the Society of Oriental Liturgy, Rome, 17–21 September 2008*, ed. Bert Groen, Steven Hawkes-Teeples, and Stefanos Alexopoulos, Eastern Christian Studies 12 (Louvain: Peeters, 2012), 443–510.

[34] For the text of the Theodosian Code, Clyde Pharr, *The Theodosian Code and Novels and the Sirmondian Constitutions: A Translation with Commentary, Glossary and Bibliography*, in collaboration with Theresa Sherrer Davidson and Mary Brown Pharr, Corpus of Roman Law 1 (Princeton, NJ: Princeton University Press, 1952). I thank Mary K. Farag, a doctoral candidate in the department of Religious Studies at Yale University for this information.

Fig. 5. *Māryām Nāzrēt, eastward*

constitution was known and observed before it was eventually
included in chapter 32 of the nomocanon compiled around 1240
by Al-Ṣafī abū l-Faḍā'il ibn al 'Assāl.[35] When we recognize that
Mikā'ēl's note is the prelate's last will, written in the context of
ancient Coptic jurisprudence, and not merely a record of a foundation of a church, we are no longer surprised to see him list his
achievements and ask as he signs the document for the support of
the faithful's prayers even after his death.

Of immediate interest to us is that Mikā'ēl states that he consecrated Mikā'ēl Ambā in the mid-twelfth century and that he "built
70 churches [as a whole, including] at Nāzrēt, 4 at Ḍolā 'et and 1 at
Norā. Out of them, 1 after the name of Mary."[36] Accordingly, while

[35] See William A. Hanna, trans., *Magmou Al-Safawy Ibn Al-Assal* (St. Louis,
MO: St. Mary & St. Abraam Coptic Orthodox Church, 1996), chap. 32, sec. 9,
120.

[36] Derat (*Enquête sur les rois Zāgwē*, 101) identified the site of Nāzrēt with the
place mentioned in Metropolitan Mikā'ēl's note as figuring also in the *Kebra
Nagaśt*. The number of "70 churches made at Nāzrēt" contrasts with the rest

Māryām Nāzrēt is listed in the same source as Mikā'ēl Ambā, they are differentiated. While Metropolitan Mikā'ēl mentioned on two occasions that he had *consecrated* Mikā'ēl Ambā, he *built* Māryām Nāzrēt and called it by Mary's name, in the same stroke identifying its main, central, altar. Indeed, an authentic grand Coptic church is found to this day at Māryām Nāzrēt, a location also known as 'Adi Abun, "the Place of the Metropolitan," reputed to have been a traditional seat of Coptic metropolitans in Ethiopia. It is a much-visited monument but hitherto has not been understood for what it

Fig. 6. *Māryām Nāzrēt, string of sanctuaries northward*

once was.[37] A large Aksumite base supports a building that includes no fewer than five sanctuaries (the northernmost is largely ruined) which communicate with one another via narrow doorways. They all open onto a common nave through a long west wall, which in light of the way it is built seems to be largely original. A tall niche adorns the east wall of each sanctuary, and a cupola serves as the ceiling,[38] while the wider central sanctuary has a variation, as its whole ceiling comes down in the east to form a wide apse.

---

of the list: "4 churches at Ḍola'ət and 1 at Norā." Mikā'ēl did mention earlier in the text that he consecrated 1,009 churches, ending this statement with the consecration of "this monastery," Mikā'ēl Ambā.

[37] Māryām Nāzrēt, or Nāzrē (Endertā, Ambā Alāgi, Tegrāy), 9.5 km east of May Nebri. I first visited Māryām Nāzrē in June 2013 with Anaïs Wion and Philippe Sidot, thanks to the support of the Centre français des études éthiopiennes (CFEE, Addis Ababa). A longer visit was arranged in October 2014 in the framework of the Lālibalā Mission directed by historians Claire Bosc-Tiessé and Marie-Laure Derat, with archaeologist Romain Mensan, Antoine Garric, head of the reconstruction works of the temples of Karnak, and myself participating.

[38] Measurements: ca. 3.50 m east-west; cupola height: 6.70 m to 7.50 m (field notes, June 13, 2013).

Fig. 7. *Māryām Nāzrēt, second sanctuary from the north, eastward*

Murals, now lost, used to cover the walls, as is suggested by the extensive plaster on the walls and by a few remainders of red bands that would have framed the images. The orientation, the existence and type of niches, the symmetry in the distribution of the cupolas, the connections between the rooms, the west doors of the side sanctuaries that contrast with the original large western opening of the main

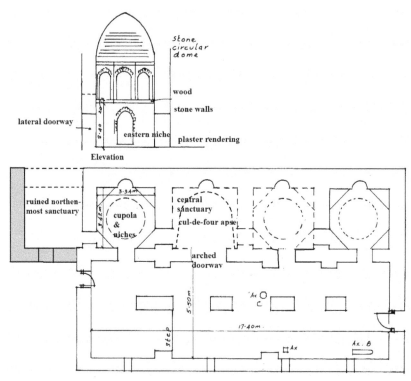

Fig. 8. *Māryām Nāzrēt*

sanctuary,[39] and the murals concur in demonstrating that this construction was created as the sanctuary of an exceptionally important Coptic church.

Architecturally, the edifice is constructed in a way developed at the time of the Fatimid

Fig. 9. *Angle niche in Saint Mark's Sanctuary, Deir Abu Maqar (Egypt)*

Dynasty (909–1171). It is strikingly similar to the sanctuary of St. Mark in the main church of the monastery of St. Macarius the Great (Wadi n'Natroun, Egypt) as to both construction time frame and construction style.[40] One detail is particularly striking: the design with the niches in the two edifices—bricks were employed in Egypt, while stones imitating bricks were used at Nāzrēt. Characteristically, at the latter location, twin rows of voussoirs made of cut stones imitating bricks are placed radiating out, to shape the eight niches at mid-height in each of the four side-sanctuaries they adorn, resting on horizontal timber boards.

---

[39] As observed by Claire Bosc-Tiessé, Antoine Garric and Romain Mensan. It was filled later.

[40] See Jules Leroy, *La Peinture murale chez les Coptes II: Les Peintures des couvents du Ouadi Natroun* (Cairo: Institut Français d'Archéologie Orientale, 1982), 11–12; 28ff; plates 28–70. The first mention ever of the sanctuary of St. Mark goes back to 1133 (E.M. 849) in the story of the Consecration of the Chrism by Gabriel III, Cod. Copt. Vat. XLVIII, f° 70 (cf. White, *Monasteries of the Wadi'n Natrun*, 2:37n1). Its erection took place between the years 1010 and 1050 (White, *Monasteries of the Wadi'n Natrun*, 3:57). Thanks to the understanding of the monastic community and under the guidance of *Abuna* Wadid, the churches of the monastery of St. Macarius and their murals were examined by Ewa Balicka-Witakowska, Michael Gervers, and myself in September 2007. This is the occasion to express our warm gratefulness to *Abuna* Wadid and the community of Deir Abu Maqar.

That Ethiopia has preserved, although in rather derelict condition, an authentic Coptic church built in a style that had been developing in Egypt since about the tenth century is little known. That it is a constructed building, not a rock-hewn church, should be underscored, as it must be added to the rather short list of extant monuments that still stand in the open.[41]

Interestingly, in his note Mikā'ēl identified himself as having been sent as *p̄āp̄p̄ās* of Ethiopia by Pope Macarius II of Alexandria (1102–1128), little remembered by his chroniclers.[42] In contrast, Macarius's successor on the throne of St. Mark, Pope Gabriel II ibn Turayk (1131–1145), is described with great interest, for he was a reformer at a time when the Fatimid authorities were by and large favorable to Christians.[43] Among the regulations pronounced by Patriarch Gabriel II is this canon:

> It has reached my feebleness that certain people in the provinces of the Sa'id celebrate the Liturgies not in conformity with, and otherwise than the three known ones which are the Liturgy of Saint Basil, and that of Saint Gregory, and the Liturgy of Saint Cyril. I have forbidden anyone to act deliberately thus, until he has come to the Cell, and his Liturgies have been verified.[44]

[41] They are only Endā Abuna Aragāwi (Dabra Dāmmo, although it has been reconstructed), Giyorgis Zāramā (Wambertā, between the seventh and ninth centuries at the latest) and Bēta Leḥēm (Gāyent, ca. 1400), to which we could have added the Eritrean "Old Church of Asmara" (before tenth century), destroyed in 1920, and also Dabra Libānos of Hām, had not the monks replaced it themselves with a new building in 1959/1960. The churches of Qirqos Agobo (Wambertā, ca. eleventh century), the mixed churches of Ṣabā' 'Aynā and Dabra Salām Mikā'ēl (Wambertā, ca. eleventh and twelfth centuries respectively?) as well as the churches in cave of Yemreḥanna Krestos, Emmakinā Madḥanē 'ālam, Wālyē Iyasus, Emmakinā Ledatā (Lasta and wider region of Lālibalā, thirteenth century) are still extant because they were sheltered from the elements.

[42] This appointment is confirmed by Antoine Khater and O. H. E. Burmester, ed., *Macarius II–John V (A.D. 1102–1167)*, vol. 3, pt. 1 of *History of the Patriarchs of the Egyptian Church* (Cairo: Société d'Archéologie Copte, 1968), 90–91.

[43] Although with exceptions, to the point that the patriarch was thrown into prison, his pontificate ending with troubles brought about by years of famine.

[44] O. H. E. Burmester, "The Canons of Gabriel Ibn Turaik, LXX Patriarch of Alexandria, (First Series)," *Orientalia Christiana Periodica* 1 (1935): 41. The Cell is the patriarchal residence.

Although Pope Gabriel II required uniformity of the eucharistic prayers, it is certainly possible that Ethiopia continued to enjoy her customs as before, thanks to the geographical distance between the mother and daughter churches, or simply because the decree only concerned people living "in the provinces of the Sa'id," as the canon states. Perhaps ill feelings also added to that distance: when an unnamed Ethiopian king of Mikā'ēl's time asked to have the number of bishops increased, Pope Gabriel II turned down his request, thereby reversing the favorable attitude of the Muslim ruler of Egypt, lest the Ethiopians form a holy synod able to elect their own primate. Although Pope Gabriel's immediate concern may have been with doctrine, the waves his decree generated would engulf all the liturgy of his patriarchate, in the process creating a uniformity that was eventually complete for all Egypt according to the customs of the north. This same tendency appears also to have been at work in Ethiopia at precisely the time of the first church building, when several sanctuaries took the place of the hitherto regular pastophoria. Even more effective than the edict was the physical model that had been erected on Ethiopian soil for all to see and study.

How Egypt's evolution was transmitted and how this trend was materialized in Ethiopia can be better explained thanks to the discovery of Saint-Mary Fatimid church of Nāzrēt. It is hardly surprising now that *Ṗāṗṗās* Mikā'ēl consecrated the church of Mikā'ēl Ambā in AD 1149/1150 as a church where an important new liturgical shift was taking place, as at Māryām Nāzrēt, thereby joining in current Coptic developments. To see something more definitely Coptic in Mikā'ēl Ambā, one need only look to the poor but certain relics of the *Maiestas Domini* and the saintly faces hanging in the northwestern part of the church.

Fig. 10. *Jesus Christ*, Maiestas Domini, *Mikā'ēl Ambā mural*

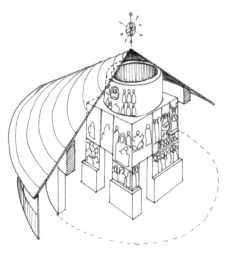

Fig. 11. *Sketch of a circular church*

The Circular Churches

The circular church has become the omnipresent Ethiopian church and, as far as the architectural development of Ethiopian churches in connection with liturgical evolution is concerned, such churches constitute a revolution that was as important as the earlier appearance of churches with multiple sanctuaries and altars.

There is no direct evidence as to the place, precise time, or manner in which such circular churches began. We therefore know neither the occasion that triggered their appearance nor the reason why they were circular. The discussion that follows seeks to examine clues gathered wherever possible in hope of increasing our understanding of this phenomenon. We begin with a description of a circular church, enabling identification of the essence of this type of building, and then investigate the data available to date their appearance, drawing first on contemporaneous witnesses from Europe and then on more recent writings. Finally, we consider how scholars have interpreted such buildings, looking in particular at possible Hierosolymitan archetypes in the temple or the Holy Sepulcher, and we see a Nubian connection emerge from the sands. The *status quaestionis* sums up the essay.

A round church is in essence a structure with a circular wall—or concentric walls—surrounded by a verandah, with a square sanctuary (the *Maqdas*) surmounted by its dome, occupying the center. It follows that the roof generally forms a cone, with its peak atop the drum sitting on the sanctuary and its lower end resting on supporting beams running all around the circular wall(s). Resting on its own foundations, the sanctuary is raised several steps above the floor of the rest of the church. Although there is no sign of the more

Fig. 12. *Round church of Dabra Sinā, Gorgorā*

ancient *Qeddest* step(s) that used to extend the sanctuary westward but had already disappeared by the first part of the thirteenth century, the area down the steps retains the same functions as previously, with the addition of the distribution of Holy Communion. To the east is the traditional window, while the sanctuary is entered on the west, through, generally, a double set of large doors, with a simple door guarding the north and south sides. In contrast to Coptic usage, which was introduced to Ethiopia during the mid-twelfth century, and perhaps paradoxically following on from it, a single altar fills the center, kept hidden by a fixed red screen, while curtains cover the outside of the doors. Also contrary to a trend developed in Ethiopian hall churches from the thirteenth to the fifteenth centuries, where everything was wide open,[45] in the circular churches all was divided up, with doors and curtains blocking the view and preventing free circulation. The wall that encloses the

[45] Fritsch and Gervers, "*Pastophoria* and Altars," 16 and 33.

67

sanctuary, the doors and the curtains that maintain secrecy, and the partitioning of the whole place by additional walls and curtains are common Egyptian features.

Curtains and Doors

Partitioning with curtains must have entered Ethiopia shortly before the spread of the round churches. Curtains therefore should be seen as nonstructural details rather than as part of the essence of a round church, although they always are part of their makeup. One of our witnesses is Father Francisco Alvares, the first outsider to have bequeathed an extensive report of what he saw in the lands of Prester John, which he traversed extensively from 1520 to 1526.[46] He described the church of St. Michael near Dabra Bizan in Eritrea as having "a sanctuary and a crossing; in the crossing are curtains from end to end; and there are other curtains before the side doors, from wall to wall. They are curtains of silk: the entrance through these curtains is in three places, they are open in the middle, and they reach one to another, they can also be entered close to the walls."[47] This text describes how curtains were used to divide up the space of the church, but the church itself is not described as round. Curtains were used in Ethiopia as were lattice barriers in Egypt, where, as we run east to west, they separated off the choir, then the men, then the women.

Although this partitioning with curtains is of Egyptian origin and likely to have preexisted the round churches, one particularity of the Coptic *hiğab*, namely, the solid and lockable sanctuary doors, does not seem to be documented independently of this new type of construction, where such doors are universally present. As long as separate lockable pastophoria (sacristies) existed on either side

---

[46] Alvares († before 1542) was a member of the embassy sent by Manoel I of Lisbon in 1515. His book was published in 1540.

[47] *The Prester John of the Indies: A true relation of the lands of Prester John, being the narrative of the Portuguese embassy to Ethiopia in 1520 written by Father Francisco Alvares*, trans. Lord Stanley of Alderley, rev. and ed. C. F. Beckingham and G. W. B. Huntingford, The Hakluyt Society, 2 vols. (Cambridge, UK: Cambridge University Press, 1961), 1:75; Francisco Alvares, *Historiale Description de l'Ethiopie* (Anvers: Iehan Bellere, 1558), after 57.

of the central sanctuary, that sanctuary could readily be identified with the open area where the altar stood. But with the abolition of such secure areas, there was no longer a place inside the church itself where precious items could be safely stored; the only option was to lock the whole building. Additional rooms or outdoor sacristies and treasuries had previously also been used, but they too were now replaced through a new approach that saw the sanctuary serve as pastophorion and be locked between services.

While the iconostasis developed in Byzantine areas in the fourteenth century, during the Mamluk period (thirteenth to sixteenth century), the *khurus* wall, which separated the choir of clerics from the faithful, gradually disappeared in Egypt in the wake of the multiplication of altars. It was replaced by the *hiğab*, literally, "curtains," which then took over the function of concealing the sanctuary, closing it off on the west from both choir and nave.[48] This closing system greatly affected the evolution of Ethiopian liturgy. Claire Bosc-Tiessé has documented how, making a positive out of a negative, painters developed entire iconographic programs significant in terms of both liturgy and, often, artistic quality, on the large surfaces the outer walls of the sanctuary now provided.[49] Our prime concern here, however, is with the circular (or polygonal or even square) shape of the church itself and with the characteristic location of the sanctuary in the center of the building.

Time Frame

No Ge'ez text concerning the beginnings of the round churches has so far been found. Reviewing the available material, we can turn first to Abbā Giyorgis of Saglā. In a passage of his *Maṣḥafa Meṣṭir*, written circa 1424, while underscoring the contrast between the poor appearance of an ordinary church and the glorious reality that inhabits it, the writer incidentally confirms that the building is

[48] Peter Grossmann, "Architectural Elements of Churches," *The Coptic Encyclopedia*, ed. Aziz S. Atiya (New York: Macmillan, 1991), 1:211–214, 221.

[49] Claire Bosc-Tiessé, *Les îles de la mémoire: Fabrique des images et écriture de l'histoire dans les églises du lac Tana, Éthiopie, XVIIᵉ–XVIIIᵉ siècle* (Paris: Publications de la Sorbonne, 2008).

not round. The text reads, "The fourfold structure of its sides [are] in the image of the four living creatures."[50] The terms indicate a parallelepiped of a sort, not surprising for the fifteenth century.[51]

Another document is the *Acts of Marḥa Krestos*. Marḥa Krestos was abbot of Dabra Libānos († 1497); this work was written during the lifetime of his successor P̣ēṭros, who died circa 1524, while Alvares was in Ethiopia. All the details gleaned from the account point to the church of Dabra Libānos' having been rectangular at the time.[52] This negative literary witness is congruent with the little we know or might surmise about the churches of King Nā'od and Lebna Dengel as well as the ruins of all the known churches of the Amhara.[53]

---

[50] ወተርብዕተ፡ ገበዋቲሃስ፡ ፬ እንስሳ፡ (*wa-terbe'eta gabawātihā-sa ba-śe'ela 4 ensesā*), Yaqob Beyene, ed. *Giyorgis Sagla:Il Libro del Mistero (Mashafa Mestir)*, vol. 2, CSCO 532 (Louvain: Corpus Scriptorum Christianorum Orientalium, 1993), text 87,55.3–16); Italian translation reads: "la quadratura dei suoi lati è fatta a immagine dei quattro animali . . . ," trans. 98, 33.33–34.9. *Terbe'et* is used for the four sides of a square.

[51] Beyene, *Giyorgis Sagla: Il Libro del Mistero*, 2:125–29 [text] = 76f. [tr.]. This reference is found in Robert Beylot, "Les règles de l'Église (d'après le ms éthiopien D'Abbadie 156) relues d'après de nouveaux documents, avec un texte inédit sur les anges et les ordres du clergé," *Pount* 5 (2011): 130–31.

[52] See Stanislas Kur, ed., *Actes de Marha Krestos*, Corpus Scriptorum Christianorum Orientalium 330–31, Scriptores Aethiopici 62–63 (Louvain: Corpus Scriptorum Christianorum Orientalium, 1972), xvi. Again, the four angles of the church are mentioned in text 67; trans. 62.

[53] See, for example, Lanfranco Ricci, "Resti di antico edificio in Gimbi (Scioa)," *Annales d'Éthiopie* 10 (1976): 177–211; Stanislaw Chojnacki, "Day Giyorgis," *Journal of Ethiopian Studies* 7, no. 2 (1969): 43–52; Stanislaw Chojnacki, "New Discoveries in Ethiopian Archaeology Dabr Takla Haymanot in Dawnt and Enso Gabre'el in Lasta," (paper presented at the First International Littmann Conference, Munich, 2002), in *Afrikas Horn: Akten der Ersten Internation-alen Littmann-Konferenz*, ed. Walter Raunig and Steffen Wenig (Wiesbaden: Harrassowitz Verlag, 2005), 44–50; Paul B. Henze, "The Monastery of Mertule Maryam in Gojjam: A Major Medieval Ethiopian Architectural Monument," in *Äthiopien gestern und heute*, ed. Piotr Scholz, Nubica et Aethiopica, vol. 4–5 (Warsaw: ZA'S PAN, 1999), 520–50; Marie-Laure Derat, *Le domaine des rois éthiopiens 1270–1527* (Paris: Publications de la Sorbonne, 2003); Deresse Ayenachew, "Le kätäma: la cour et le camp royal en Éthiopie (XIVᵉ–XVIᵉ siècle): Espace et pouvoir" (PhD diss., Université Paris 1 Panthéon-Sorbonne,

Alvares, already quoted above, did not provide us with a single example of a church that we might understand to have been round. But only some fifteen years after Alvares's departure in 1526, Miguel de Castanhoso († 1565?) was in Ethiopia, from 1541 to 1543, as a member of the Portuguese force sent to rescue the Christian kingdom facing the *ǧihad* led by *Imām* Aḥmad b. Ibrāhīm al-Ġāzī, nicknamed *Grāñ*, "the Left-handed" (ca. 1506–22 February 1543). He tells us of the general existence of round churches right in the midst of the *imām*'s devastating campaigns, which lasted from September 1528 to February 1543, describing them in a simple statement: "These churches are round, with a holy place in the centre, and all around outside are verandahs."[54]

The account of Jesuit Manoel de Almeida († 1646)[55] makes the first identification of a circular church, that of St. Mary on Ambā Gešan (South Wallo), founded by King Nāʾod (1495–1508) and completed by his son King Lebna Dengel (1508–1540). Although Almeida adds that miraculously the church had escaped destruction by ǧihadist Aḥmad Grāñ's troops, the Short Chronicle states bluntly that in 1540 "Gešše was destroyed and burnt down."[56]

2009); Emmanuel Fritsch and Marie-Laure Derat, "Une lecture architecturale et liturgique des ruines de Gabriel," in *Gabriel, une église médiévale d'Éthiopie. Interprétations historiques et archéologiques de sites chrétiens autour de Mashala Māryām (Manz, Éthiopie), XVᵉ–XVIIᵉ siècles*, dir. Marie-Laure Derat and Anne-Marie Jouquand (Paris: De Boccard, 2012), 195–204.

[54] Miguel Castanhoso, *The Portuguese Expedition to Abyssinia in 1541–1543 with some contemporary letters, the short account of Bermudez, and certain extracts from Correa*, trans. and ed. Richard Stephen Whiteway, Hakluyt Society Papers, 2nd ser., 10 (London: Hakluyt Society, 1902), 90.

[55] See *Notizia e Saggi di opere e documenti inediti riguardanti la Storia di Etiopia durante i secoli XVI, XVII e XVIII, con otto facsimili e due carte geographiche*, ed. Camillo Beccari (1903; repr. Brussels: Culture et civilization, 1969), 5:217; "Almeida on Ethiopia," in *Some Records of Ethiopia, 1593–1646: Being Extracts from the History of High Ethiopia or Abassia by Manoel de Almeida, together with Bahrey's History of the Galla*, ed. and trans. Charles Fraser Beckingham and George Wynn Brereton Huntingford, Hakluyt Society Works 2nd ser., 107, 2nd ed. (Nendeln, Liechtenstein: Kraus Reprint Limited, 1967), 99. See also Marilyn E. Heldman, "Church Buildings," *EAE* 1:739.

[56] Šihabaddīn Aḥmad ibn ʿAbdalqādir, *Futūḥ al-Ḥabaša. Histoire de la conquête de l'Abyssinie (XVIᵉ siècle) par Chihab Eddin Aḥmed ben ʿAbd el-Qāder, surnommé*

King Nā'od is known to have been responsible for the construction of two other churches: Berārah, for which no detail is available and which is mentioned only in the *Futūḥ al-Ḥabaša* as "a church that belonged to the former king"[57] and Makāna Śellāsē, which was a grand edifice, rectangular in shape, the base of which still exists.[58] The third church ascribed to Nā'od on Ambā Gešan could have been of the same basic form as Makāna Śellāsē, a possibility that seems all the more likely in light of the absence of any comment on its originality, but as no evidence is documented, a change cannot be ruled out.[59]

With Castanhoso present in Ethiopia from 1541 to 1543 and in light of the character of his statement, these dates can safely be regarded as a *terminus ante quem* for the circular church, but little can be said regarding the beginnings of this phenomenon, other than that the first circular churches likely appeared under King Lebna Dengel (1508–1540).[60]

How Did the Circular Churches Come into Existence?

As noted, to date no helpful text in Ge'ez mentioning circular churches has been found. Material from Egypt, too, is silent. Pope John XIII of Alexandria (1484–1524) stresses that his was a time of "great destruction, ruin, and want in every place."[61] The prevailing

---

Arab-Faqih, ed. and trans. René Basset, Publications de l'École des lettres d'Alger 19, vol. 20 (Paris: Ernest Leroux, 1897), f. 7, 17 (text) / 109 (trad.).

[57] Šihāb ad-Dīn Aḥmad bin 'Abd al-Qāder bin Sālem bin 'Utmān, also known as 'Arab Faqīh, *Futūḥ al-Ḥabaša, The Conquest of Abyssinia*, trans. Paul Lester Stenhouse (Hollywood, CA: Tsehai, 2003), 165; "une église construite par le roi précédent Nâod," Šihabaddīn . . . , Basset, *Histoire de la conquête de l'Abyssinie*, 217. See Marie-Laure Derat, "Na'od," *EAE* 3:1134–1135 on 1135a; Derat, *Le domaine des rois éthiopiens*, 209, 214, 328.

[58] Marie-Laure Derat, "Mäkanä Śəllase," *EAE* 3:672.

[59] The site was visited with Claire Bosc-Tiessé on the occasion of a mission in South-Wallo set up under the aegis of the Centre français des études éthiopiennes (CFEE, Addis Ababa) in February 2010.

[60] *The Prester John of the Indies*, Beckingham and Huntingford, 1:80.

[61] Quoted from Mark N. Swanson, *The Coptic Papacy in Islamic Egypt (641–1517)*, The Popes of Egypt 2 (Cairo: American University of Cairo Press, 2010), 127. There does not seem to be anything particularly relevant to the wide

situation would not have been conducive to a redirection under Coptic influence of the course already being followed by Ethiopians, although around this date sanctuaries were equipped with doors and divided off with curtains, creating or reinforcing a lasting trend of secrecy in the ethos of the whole community.

A good number of researchers have proposed that circular churches could have been purely locally inspired, as an expression of a deeply inculturated Ethiopian Christianity that drew from the traditional model of a home and that in repeating the concentric areas surrounding the fire-place matched everyday experience.[62] The sanctuary itself would have remained square in order to satisfy the strict ecclesiastical regulations concerning the performance of the liturgical rites.

Ethiopian tradition on such matters is accessible today only through the words of learned scholars, sometimes documented in recent publications, or as found in texts called *Ser'āta Bēta krestiyān*, literally, "church orders," which influenced each other. This "living literature," living even today, has been documented by Marcel Griaule[63] and Roger Schneider[64] and was printed by *Qasis* Kenfa Gabre'ēl Altāya by a longtime teacher at the Holy Trinity Theological College of Addis Ababa.[65] Denis Nosnitsin describes

---

period in Antoine Khater and O. H. E. Burmester, ed., *Cyril II–Cyril V (AD 1235–1894)*, vol. 3, pt. 3 of *History of the Patriarchs of the Coptic Church of Alexandria* (Cairo: Société d'Archéologie Copte, 1968), 274–75. Egypt became a province of the Ottoman Empire in 1517.

[62] Ernst Hammerschmidt, among others, observes this possibility while considering the influence of the *mausolea* of Rome and the East, to which we shall return, in *Äthiopien. Christliches Reich zwischen Gestern und Morgen* (Wiesbaden: Harrassowitz Verlag, 1967), 92. I am not considering here the hypothesis according to which "hall-churches" would have originally been covered with a conical thatched roof so as to hide them from the Muslims of Grañ.

[63] Marcel Griaule, "Règles de l'Église (Documents Éthiopiens)," *Journal Asiatique* 221 (July–September 1932): 1–42.

[64] Roger Schneider, "Nouveaux témoins du texte éthiopien des *Règles de l'Église* (Documents Éthiopiens)," *Journal Asiatique* 276 (July–September 1988): 71–96.

[65] Last of several editions: *Liqa kāhenāt* Kenfa Gabre'ēl Altāya, *Ser'āta Bēta krestiyān* ("The Order of the Church,"), vol. 1 (Addis Ababa: Tensae Publishing

this form of writing as "akin to the tradition of Bible interpretation, i.e., the *Andemtā* and *Terg*^{w}*āmē*, using partly similar methods and expressive means . . . The eighteenth century may be considered as the time when this kind of treatise started to appear, along with intensified church construction and the emergence of the traditional exegetical schools during the Gondärine kingdom."[66] Robert Beylot pushed the roots of the *Ser'āta Bēta krestiyān* further back in time, pointing in particular to a passage of the fifteenth-century Abbā Giyorgis Saglāwi's *Book of the Mystery* as using the genre.[67] This literary genre may also be found formally in chapter ten of the Ge'ez *Testamentum Domini*, from the title down to several details.[68] This general and quite popular form of teaching produces similar symbolical interpretations, simply presented, based on what certain figures evoke. Griaule's and other documents all describe the church as a round structure.[69] The circular shape may tie in with the idea of the church as the "symbol of this world," and the priests "turning three times around" as they spread the incense can be seen as "the symbol of Jesus Christ who taught the Gospel by circulating in this world three years and three months."[70] But these interpretations exist alongside others and therefore are not decisive.[71]

House, 1983 EC/AD 1991) and vol. 2 (Addis Ababa: Tensae Publishing House, 1993 EC/AD 2000).

[66] Denis Nosnitsin, "Śər'atä Betä krəstiyan," *EAE* 4:631–34. See also Bosc-Tiessé, *Les îles de la mémoire*, 336–37.

[67] See Beylot, "Les règles de l'Église relues," 130.

[68] See Beylot, *Testamentum Domini éthiopien*, 19–21 (text, which reads *qannonā bēta krestiyān*, "Rule of the Church") and 157–58 (translation).

[69] Which is no proof that there cannot be an Arabic or another foreign *Vorlage* as that would be an easy adaptation to the local situation (cp. "The Ge'ez may indeed be a treatise regarding the structure of an individual church and the organization of the clergy, based on the translated writings of the Church Fathers [cp. *Project Vol. V: Numbers 1501–2000* of Ethiopian Manuscript Microfilm Library, ed. Getatchew Haile and William F. Macomber (Collegeville, MN: HMML, 1981), 437, 467]. The text, however, may also be an Ethiopian one; the existence of a foreign [Arabic?] *Vorlage* has been doubted since the work—an allegorical description of the church—seems to refer to an Ethiopian round church," Denis Nosnitsin, *EAE* 4:631–34.

[70] Griaule, "Règles de l'Église," 30.

[71] Ibid., 33. The *Fetḥa Nagaśt* says nothing about this matter.

As if echoing what travelers had been thinking, a church publication by Sergew Hable Selassie states: "In the late medieval period, ecclesiastical architecture underwent radical change. Churches of octagonal or circular shape were constructed. It seems probable that these forms were increasingly adopted as Ethiopian power moved southward and the churches acquired the form of the round dwellings common in the south. This type of circular or octagonal church is abundant in the southern and western areas where Christianity was introduced later."[72] Recently, *Qasis* Alemnew Azene similarly reported that today's *liqāwent* say that the churches are constructed in accord with the area's traditional dwellings. It follows that if people were used to building their homes as round structures with thatched roofing, churches would also have been built thus, with a difference in size only. We see this association in the Lake Ṭāna area in the north, for example, where because people are used to building four walls with hewn stone, the churches too are made of stone and also have four walls that meet at right angles. Fr. Alemnew further reports the claim that "the circle is perfect, our religion (*hāymānot*) is perfect, and we make a church as the ark of Noah was, that is circular and compartmented according to species."[73] We note the biblical reference to 1 Peter 3:20, with modern homiletics often making reference to the church as the "ark of salvation," based on the understanding that the flood is a type of baptism.

Discussion of this literary genre should also make reference to the *Ya-Qeddāsē Tārik*, "History of the Sanctification (the Mass)" presented by *Mamher* Garimā, later Archbishop Mikā'ēl, in his *Maṣḥafa Qeddāsē andemtā*, "Commentary of the Missal."[74] There,

[72] Sergew Hable Selassie and Belaynesh Mikael, "Worship in the Ethiopian Orthodox Church," in *The Church of Ethiopia: A Panorama of History and Spiritual Life*, ed. Sergew Hable Selassie (1970; repr. Addis Ababa: Ethiopian Orthodox Church, 1997), 64.

[73] I am grateful to *Qasis* Alemenew who kindly discussed this matter with me on February 19, 2015.

[74] *Mamher* Garimā Walda Kidān (later Archbishop Mikā'ēl), ed., *Maṣḥafa Qeddāsē. Ka-qaddemo abbātoč siward siwārad ya-maṭāw nebābu-nnā tergʷāmēw* [The Book of the Sanctification: Text and interpretation come from the Fathers'

after a review of the places of worship found at different stages in the Old Testament, in which the ark of Noah holds a prominent place, the institution of the Eucharist is placed in the home of Lazarus,[75] while the first church, at Philippi in Macedonia, where Paul and Barnabas preached (Acts 16), is ascribed to Jesus Christ himself and signals the beginning of church construction.[76] Again, three areas are indicated but named as Adam's *tābot*, Moses' *tābot*, and Jesus' *tābot*. Remarkably, Jerusalem is mentioned only to say that Peter and John were joined there in their apostolic work and did not leave the city until Jesus Christ gathered them in Philippi. As for the shape of the building, the three stones assembled as its base suggest a circular church—four would be expected for a parallelepiped—besides naturally referring to the Holy Trinity.[77]

It should be noted, however, that an inexactitude such as Schneider's translation of *Maqdas* by "Holy of Holies"[78] can be misleading in suggesting a reference to the Jerusalem temple, for the reference

---

tradition] (Addis Ababa: 1918 EC/AD 1926; last printed 1988 EC/1996 GC), 5–9, on 6b (henceforward: "Missal Commentary").

[75] Also referred to in the Institution of the Anaphora of Epiphanius.

[76] Coptic 21st Ba'ûnah and Ethiopian Sanē 20th and 21st (Julian 10 and 11 July / Gregorian 27 and 28 June, respectively) commemorate the building by Jesus Christ of the first church for the Virgin Mary, as a model, and the consecration of the same through the first Eucharist that took place there. It was celebrated by Jesus Christ himself in order to show that "it is his will that the apostles built churches named after his Mother from one end of the world to the other" ("Missal Commentary," 6b). The story in the "Missal Commentary" derives from the reading found in the Synaxary (see Sir Ernest Alfred Thompson Wallis Budge, trans., *The Book of the Saints of the Ethiopian Church*, 4 vols. [1928; repr. Hildesheim: G. Olms, 1976]), 1051 (the PDF version available online does not have this commemoration); *Le Synaxaire éthiopien: Le mois de sanê*, ed. and trans. Ignazio Guidi, Patrologia Orientalis 1, fasc. 5, no. 5 (1905, repr., Turnhout: Brepols, 2003), 645–47. There is no entry on Sanē 20th but the reading for Sanē 21st visibly is the same story as that recorded by the "Missal Commentary," despite significant differences. See also Emmanuel Fritsch, *The Liturgical Year of the Ethiopian Church*, Ethiopian Review of Cultures 9–10 (Special Issue) (Addis Ababa: Master Printing Press, 2001), 63–64, 71.20, 300–301.

[77] "Missal Commentary," 6b.

[78] "Saint des saints." See Schneider, "Nouveaux témoins du texte éthiopien des *Règles de l'Église*," 81.17 and 84.9.

is in fact only to a "sanctuary" in the sense of the area in the church where the altar is placed.[79] While it is true that the word *Maqdas* can sometimes be used for "Holy of Holies," that usage is found not in primary source documents but in modern presentations. The actual connection to the temple is rather thin. The Amharic-English bilingual official self-presentation *The Ethiopian Orthodox Tewahedo Church Faith, Order of Worship and Ecumenical Relations* mentions the ark of Noah, the tent of Abraham, the tabernacle, and the temple of Solomon as Old Testament "examples of churches where offerings and worship to God were made" but does not apply them to New Testament times at all or to any sort of Ethiopian church type, while declaring the church's attachment to the Old Testament *tābot*, the ark of the covenant.[80]

On the prevalence of round churches, Archbishop *Abuna* Malka Ṣēdēq states, "It is not known when or how it started but all the country churches are round [*bēta neguś*, i.e., "the house of the king"] in style. Even today, when a new church is built in the countryside, people like to build it in this form." No other reference is given. Only when he discusses the divisions found within the church does the archbishop refer to Solomon: "The division of a church. Any church, whatever its style [i.e., basilican or round], has three divisions in the likeness of the temple of Solomon because the Jewish order (*śer'āt*) is the foundation and example of all the faith, teaching, service of Christianity." His statement is universal, not in any way specific to the round churches.[81]

Qasis Kenfa Gabre'ēl Altāya says that the way the Tent of the Law (*Dabtarā 'Orit*) and the Sanctuary of the Law (*Maqdasa 'Orit*)

---

[79] Stuart Munro-Hay, *Ethiopia, the Unknown Land* (London: I. B. Tauris, 2002), 50, also mentions the *qeddesta qeddusan*, Holy of Holies, as an alternative name of the *maqdas* without further explanation.

[80] *The Ethiopian Orthodox Tewahedo Church Faith, Order of Worship and Ecumenical Relations* (Addis Ababa: Tensae Publishing House, 1996), 62–67, on pp. 63 and 65. The Amharic texts do not differ (pp. 59–61).

[81] Archbishop Malka Ṣēdēq, *Temherta Krestenna* ("Catechism"), Part 2 (Addis Ababa: Tensae Publishing House, 1984 EC/AD 1992), 128–30. *Abuna* Malka Ṣēdēq was once the renowned *Liqa śelṭānāt* Habtamāryām Warqneh, dean of the Holy Trinity Cathedral in Addis Ababa.

were made has a *messālennat*, in this context an exemplary—or symbolical—character, which refers us to the typological language for the manner in which the church building is constructed.[82] He explains further: "As the Tent of the Law and the Sanctuary of the Law used to be made in three parts, every church is made in the three parts of the *qenē māḥelēt, qeddest, maqdas*."[83]

Kenfa Gabre'ēl counts three sorts of church plan. The first is like a rectangular hall (*saqalā*) and oblong (*molālā*); the second circular (*kebb*), a shape known as *bēta neguś*, literally "the house of the king," in which the three compartments are defined according to their purpose (*gebru*); the third is the church-in-cave (*wāšā*), which has only one entrance door and one sanctuary door, with its different areas defined by curtains only.[84] Kenfa Gabre'ēl grants a particular rationale to the first type only, which he says imitates both the temple of Solomon and, in the New Covenant, the churches built by St. Helen at Jerusalem and Bethlehem. The temple and the basilica are now united in the rectangular plan, while no particular meaning is ascribed to the circular church or the central sanctuary. It follows that a round church is made in the image of Old Testament sacred places in that it is divided into three areas, like any other church type, which is not really helpful.

Aymro Wondmagegnehu and Joachim Motovu identified a definite association between the Jerusalem temple and the circular church only in relation to the prevalence of round churches: "The form of the Hebrew sanctuary was preferred by Ethiopians to the basilica type."[85] No other detail is cited to explain how the parallelepiped Jerusalem temple would have been closer in form to the round church than to the basilica. Curiously, even though neither the present stage of tradition development nor objective observation, let alone any sources, supports a specific tie between

[82] Kenfa Gabre'ēl, *Ser'āta Bēta krestiyān*, 5.

[83] Ibid., 5–6.

[84] Ibid., 13.

[85] Aymro Wondmagegnehu and Joachim Motovu, *The Ethiopian Orthodox Church* (Addis Ababa: Ethiopian Orthodox Mission, 1970), 46. The sentence, hardly touched up, is taken from Ullendorff's quote below.

the round church and the Jerusalem temple, that notion continues to attract interest. Here, then, is evidence of Edward Ullendorff's lasting authority. Ullendorff stated:

> The way in which Abyssinian churches are built is clearly derived from the threefold division of the Hebrew temple. . . . The outside ambulatory of the three concentric parts of the Abyssinian church (which is either round, octagonal or rectangular) is called *k'əne maḥlet*, i.e. the place where hymns are sung and where the *däbtära* or cantors stand. This outer part corresponds to the *ḥäṣēr* of the Tabernacle or the *'ulām* of Solomon's Temple. The next chamber is the *k'əddəst* where communion is administered to the people; and the innermost part is the *mäk'däs* where the *tabot* rests and to which only priests and the King have access. . . . This division into three chambers applies to all Abyssinian churches, even to the smallest of them. It is thus clear that the form of the Hebrew sanctuary was preferred by Abyssinians to the basilica type which was accepted by early Christians elsewhere. [The idea is reproduced by Wondmagegnehu and Motovu.] Similarly, churches throughout Ethiopia are usually built upon a small hill overlooking the village or, at any rate, at the most elevated place available.[86]

The following remarks seem to be called for. (1) The model of the Hebrew sanctuary is universally applied to all Ethiopian churches, whether basilican or circular, giving them a commonality despite the new characteristics of the latter, with its central sanctuary and circular form. Therefore, its being round would not relate a church to the temple, only its three divisions would do so. (2) Although Uttendorff writes of the Abyssinians' preference for the "Hebrew sanctuary" over "the basilica type, which was accepted by early Christians elsewhere," from the earliest churches of the kingdom of the Aksumites up until the end of the fifteenth-century King Nā'od's Makāna Śellāsē, all churches without exception were basilicas, at least in their ground plans, sharing that structure with

---

[86] Edward Ullendorff, "Hebraic-Jewish Elements in Abyssinian Christianity," *Journal of Semitic Studies* 114 (1956): 235–36; Edward Ullendorff, *Ethiopia and the Bible* (Oxford: The British Academy, 1968), 87–89.

the other basilicas of the Christian world. The latter should there-fore also be referred to the Hebrew temple, but basilicas are not in essence modeled on any cultic place, be it the temple at Jerusalem or pre-Christian temples elsewhere. (3) In addition, the triple space division follows an order that is quite natural, and it is therefore not surprising that they could be found everywhere, not just in Ethiopia. Or, to put it another way, such divisions are frequent and are found both in the Hebrew temple and in Christian churches, including the Ethiopian churches. And a number of Ethiopian churches contain two, not three, divisions, with Yemrehanna Kres-tos, near Lālibalā, a famous example. (4) The terminology used to name the three areas of the church is of no importance. The *Maqdas,* "sanctuary," and *Qenē māḥlēt,* "service of praise," are de-scriptive, while *Qeddest,* "holy place," refers to the presbyterium that, until at least the twelfth century, was protected by a chancel. Lay people received Holy Communion outside the presbyterium, in the nave. That simple fact removes the universality from the statement, "the next chamber is the *k'addast* where communion is administered to the people." Another example: the porch is not the *Qenē māḥlēt,* which is not an outer ambulatory either. The term *Qeddesta qeddusān* is traditionally employed by Ethiopians not for the *Maqdas* but in speaking of the Jerusalem temple. The vocabu-lary and the ascription are approximate.[87] Moreover, the appear-ance of these names cannot be dated and, in any case, they do not exist in the circa sixth-century *Testamentum Domini.*[88] It follows that the universality of these names and of what they might evoke is questionable.

If there ever was a connection, it was probably literary, a product of the common reading of Scripture and, on the Christian side, the application of the typology of the temple to the ἱερωσύνη of Jesus Christ as in the Letter to the Hebrews 9, which was not particu-lar to Ethiopia but affected all Christian churches. We have, then, no tangible link between the temple and the circular Ethiopian church, only a general feeling that such a link is in accord with

[87] See, for example, Ullendorff, *Ethiopia and the Bible,* 88.
[88] Cf. Bausi, "Testamentum Domini," *EAE* 4:927–28.

the so-called special Judeo-Christian emphasis of the Ethiopian Church or, rather, the leanings for the Old Testament found in the Ethiopian Church, an altogether different story.

The Holy Sepulcher, Then?

A more convincing explanation for the development of the circular church in relation to Jerusalem might look instead to the Holy Sepulcher, a persistent focus of great spiritual interest for the Ethiopians as for the members of all other Christian churches. Even after the fall of Jerusalem in AD 1187, Ethiopians do not seem to have been prevented from reaching the holy places, whatever other views have suggested.[89] Pilgrimages and monastic settlements bear witness to that travel. But not everyone could undertake such a journey, and some sort of relay could therefore have been desirable, for example, in the form of a symbolic relationship with Jerusalem. Might the circular shape of Ethiopian churches have been inspired by the shape of the rotunda surrounding the empty tomb of Jesus Christ in Jerusalem?

Marie-Laure Derat has recently studied the history of the *Life of Lālibālā*, known for the eponymous place where the famous churches were hewn. In Lālibālā, the church of Golegotā even holds a lasting *translatio Hierosolymae*.[90] The *Life of Lālibālā*, the oldest text to refer to the *translatio Hierosolymae*, must have been written before the middle of the fifteenth century since a copy of the work (BL ms Or. 719) was offered by King Zar'a Yā'eqob (1434–1468) to the church of Golegotā, revealing that a relationship had in fact been established between King Lālibālā and that particular church.[91] The text states that the saintly king established marvelous things in that place, referring to "the dead body, glorious, which belongs to the Lamb whose body does not become corrupted, and several other representations (*se'elt*) which he [Lālibālā] was

---

[89] Emery Van Donzel, "Ethiopia's Lalibäla and the fall of Jerusalem 1187," *Aethiopica* 1 (1998): 43–44, 47.

[90] As emphasized by Derat, *Enquête sur les rois Zāgwē*, 161.

[91] Ibid., 169.

thinking of night and day."[92] This reference is to the recumbent statue of Jesus Christ and the sculptures of saints standing around the church of Golegotā. It confirms that the funerary recess of the recumbent figure was an actual representation of Christ's Holy Sepulcher, as is stated in the *Life*, where we find this comment: "Any Ethiopian who, having heard about those so remarkable churches, does not go to the holy city of Roha [i.e., Lālibalā] is like a man who would not have any desire to behold the face of our Lord and Saviour Jesus Christ."[93]

Fig. 13. *Recumbent Christ in the Bēta Golegotā chapel, Lālibalā*

That notion has momentum. For example, according to the *Acts of Marḥa Krestos*, it was from Jerusalem that Marḥa Krestos, abbot of Dabra Libānos († 1497), received new sacred vessels for his church during the reign of Nā'od.[94] Later still, around 1520 and therefore right in the middle of the period that concerns us most, when Francisco Alvares visited the church of Golegotā, he was shown the tomb of the holy King Lālibālā. He recalled, "On the left-hand side, going from the principal door in front of the chancel, there is a tomb cut in the same rock as the church, which they say is made like the sepulchre of Jesus Christ in Jerusalem. So they hold it in honour and veneration and reverence."[95] Alvares also recorded the contemporary importance of the link of Ethiopia with the Holy Sepulcher in Jerusalem itself:

[92] The French by Marie-Laure Derat reads: "le corps (mort) glorieux qui appartient à l'agneau au corps indestructible et plusieurs autres représentations (*se'elt*) auxquelles il [Lālibalā] pensait nuit et jour" (Derat, *Enquête sur les rois Zāgwē*, 166n83).

[93] *Gadla Lālibalā*, 127, quoted in Derat, *Enquête sur les rois Zāgwē*, 166.

[94] *Actes of Marḥa Krestos*, ed. Stanislas Kur, 101 and 92.

[95] *The Prester John of the Indies*, Beckingham and Huntingford, 1:207–21, on 221.

As to the silks and brocades, Pero de Covilham said that they often took them out to give them to churches and monasteries, as was done three years before our arrival, when the Prester sent large offerings to Jerusalem of the silks and brocades from the caves, because of the multitude he possessed; they were so many that they covered the walls of the church of the Holy Sepulchre. He also sent some of the other gold.[96]

And a little later, Alvares mentioned a caravan of monks going on pilgrimage to Jerusalem.

Yet although Ethiopians knew the Holy Sepulcher was circular, the church of Golegotā in Lālibalā, which contains the recumbent Christ, is *not* circular. The recumbent Christ found in Golegotā was meant to refer to the tomb *inside* the aediculum in the center of the circular church of Jerusalem rather than to that church as such, and the wall-niche tomb represents the aediculum of Jerusalem. The space around—the circular ambulatory—is evidently of no particular importance in Lālibalā.

What then suggested that Ethiopian churches had to be circular on account of the shape of the Holy Sepulcher? Perhaps we have a clue as to the event that generated that idea and led to its realization in a circular architectural style in one location that was subsequently repeated all over the country. Cerulli noted, "In 1522 the French pilgrim Bartholomé de Salignac informs us that the Ethiopian community of Jerusalem had disappeared altogether."[97] Kirsten Stoffregen Pedersen further records, "The rise of Ottoman Turkey and the wars of Aḥmad b. Ibrāhīm al-Ġāzī caused a swift impoverishment and decline of the Ethiopian community in Jerusalem. . . . From descriptions of the Ethiopian community in Jerusalem in foreign sources from the sixteenth till the end of the nineteenth century it is clear that it lost its privileges in the holy places and was finally confined to the dilapidated Dayr al-Sulṭān."[98] In this connection, we might explore a possible analogy

[96] Ibid., 2:448.
[97] Enrico Cerulli, *Etiopi in Palestina*, vol. 1 (Rome: Libreria dello Stato, 1943), 395.
[98] Kirsten Stoffregen Pedersen, "Jerusalem," *EAE* 3:275.

Fig. 14. *Bēta Giyorgis, Lālibalā*

with the building by King Zar'a Yā'eqob of a new Dabra Meṭmāq after he received a message from Pope John of Alexandria in 1441 informing him that the Egyptian original place of the Bath (Arabic: *maǧṭis/miǧṭas*), which had served as a station for Ethiopian pilgrims on their way to the Holy Land, had been destroyed.[99] Similarly, the adverse circumstances affecting the Ethiopians in Jerusalem may have triggered a demonstration in their homeland of attachment to Jerusalem and of a decision to host the Holy Sepulcher—or to be hosted by it. That suggestion lacks, however, textual support.

Who or What Authorized the Novelty of a Central Sanctuary and Altar?

The sanctuary placed right in the middle of the church is one central element of the puzzle, and a complex element at that. If that design was not an imitation of the circular Holy Sepulcher, what might have been behind the displacement of the sanctuary from the east to the center of the building? Among earlier monuments that moved furthest in this direction was the thirteenth-century cruciform church of Bēta Giyorgis at Lālibalā.[100] In an earlier study,

---

[99] Marie-Laure Derat, "Däbrä Mäṭmaq," *EAE* 2:34–35.

[100] Claude Lepage adds to Bēta Giyorgis the much earlier church of Zāramā in "L'Église de Zaréma (Ethiopie) découverte en Mai 1973 et son apport à l'histoire de l'architecture éthiopienne," Académie des Inscriptions et Belles-Lettres (Paris: CRAIBL, 1973), 446 ff.; this notion, however, has not been proposed again in the more recent work by Claude Lepage and Jacques Mercier, *Art éthiopien: Les églises historiques du Tigray* [Ethiopian Art: The Ancient Churches of Tigray] (Paris: Editions Recherche sur les Civilisations, 2005), 64. Even when we discount Zāramā from the number of cruciform churches in general, several considerations in the former study remain of interest.

Fig. 15. *(Old) Dongola Cruciform Church*

I followed Jean Doresse's views on the relationship of this renowned rock-hewn church to the now-submerged Nubian Church
of the Archangels at Tāmit.[101] Several features of the monolithic
churches of Lalibālā point to Nubia as a likely source of inspiration.[102] In the specific case of cruciform Bēta Giyorgis, the sanctuary
is found in the eastern arm of the cross, not in its center. A central
plan had not been appropriated although it could well have been
by reference not to the church of the Archangels of Tāmit but to the
"Cruciform Church" of (Old) Dongola, the capital of the Nubian
kingdom of Makuria.

[101] Emmanuel Fritsch, "The Churches of Lalibäla (Ethiopia) Witnesses of Liturgical Changes," Proceedings of the First SOL Congress, Eichstätt 2006, *Bollettino della Badia Greca di Grottaferrata*, vol. 5 (Rome: Grottaferrata, June 2008),
69–112, on p. 105.

[102] I initiated a discussion of this matter in "Liturgy and Architectonics in Lālibalā Monolithic Churches: Accounting for a Mismatch," a paper delivered at
the Eighteenth Conference of Ethiopian Studies, Dire Dawa (Ethiopia), 2012 (no
Proceedings). The topic is under further study. A remote possibility exists that
some features I call Nubian might pastiche ancient Aksumite precedents rather
than contemporaneous Nubian monuments, but this has not been documented
so far archaeologically. See Lepage, "L'église de Zarema," 450; David Buxton,
"The Christian Antiquities of Northern Ethiopia," *Archaeologia or Miscellaneous
Tracts relating to Antiquity* 92 (London: Society of Antiquaries, 1947), 29–30.

The "Cruciform Church" in Old Dongola

Even covered by sands, the ruins of this church reveal an impos-
ing building with its origins as early as the ninth century. These
ruins have been identified with the church of Sus or Usus (= Jesus)
that Mamlouk Baibars's troops destroyed in 1275, shortly after the
demise of the Zāg^{w}ē Dynasty at the hands of Yekunno Amlāk in
1270. The troops looted in particular a golden cross estimated to
be worth 4,640.50 dinars.[103] A basic description of the Cruciform
Church would include the following: the center is formed by a 14
meter by 14 meter domed square, which contains an inner square
space that is marked by four columns 6.6 meters tall and surrounds
a structure covered with a stone ciborium. A two-column portico
forming a trifolium opens in the middle of each side, from which
the arms of the cross radiate toward the four corners, ending in
porches on the north, south, and west. On the east, the arm was
longer and its easternmost segment was separated from the rest by
a wall with a doorway. A synthronon lay at the foot of its trifolium,
with side chancels that prevented the laity from going farther east,
where, beyond a door, a red brick table leaned against the far east
wall, and opposite it a low elongated structure in the shape of a
Latin cross was found on the pavement.[104]

---

[103] Al-Malik az-Zâhir Rukn ad-Dîn Baybars al-Bunduqdari, better known
under the name of Baybars, a Bahrite Mamluk sultan of Egypt (r. 1260–1277).
See Joseph Cuoq, *Islamisation de la Nubie chrétienne. VIIe–XVIe siècles*, Bibliothèque d'études islamiques 9 (Paris: Librairie Orientaliste Paul Geuthner,
1986), 75 and sources.

[104] For details see Włodzimierz Godlewski, "The Cruciform Church Site in
Old Dongola: Sequence of Buildings from the 6th to 18th Century," *Nubica*
1–2 (1990): 511–33; Włodzimierz Godlewski, "The Role of Dongolese Milieu
in the Nubian Church Architecture," *Themelia: Spätantike und koptologische Studien Peter Grossmann zum 65. Geburtstag*, ed. Martin Krause and Sofia Schaten,
Sprachen und Kulturen des christlichen Orients 3 (Wiesbaden: Reichert, 1998),
127–35. Firsthand information on Nubia was obtained during the mission
organized by the Centre Français des Études éthiopiennes (C.F.E.E., Addis
Ababa) in cooperation with the corresponding center in Sudan (S.F.D.A.S.,
Khartoum) in February 2011. Other participants were Ewa Balicka-Witakowska,
Claire Bosc-Tiessé, Marie-Laure Derat, Jan Retsö, and Robin Seignobos. Éloi
Ficquet, director of C.F.E.E. at the time, Claude Rilly, director of S.F.D.A.S.,
and Włodzimierz Godlewski all generously welcomed us and we would like

Pastophoria in Dongola: Third (earlier church in same place, left) & Cruciform Churches (9th c., right)

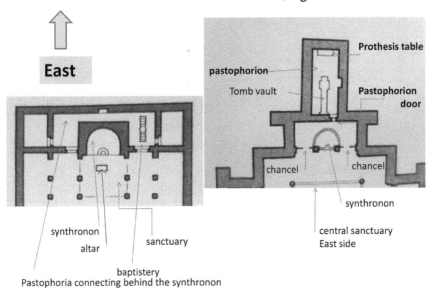

Fig. 16. *(Old) Dongola Cruciform Church, eastern area*

Although Godlewski thought that the table he discovered in the extremity of the eastern branch of the construction was the altar, much as at Bēta Giyorgis at Lālibalā,[105] he agreed in conversation that this was a time when the prothesis was still done in its pastophorion.[106] The very existence of the prothesis room points to a lockable space. That such a room would also provide access to an important tomb is not unexpected. It would hardly have made sense to have had the altar in such a narrow place isolated from the assembly, beyond an off-center door and chancels, with the seats of

to express our gratefulness for their support. I am in particular indebted to Prof. Włodzimierz Godlewski, who kindly guided the group on site and discussed with us the various issues reflected here.

[105] Almost, for at Lālibalā there were, for example, no synthronon, no chancels, no tomb, no doors, no central pillars and dome. Especially, there was no need any more for a pastophorion.

[106] Godlewski, "Dongolese Milieu in Nubian Architecture," 132.

Old Dongola, the Cruciform Church, end 9th cent.

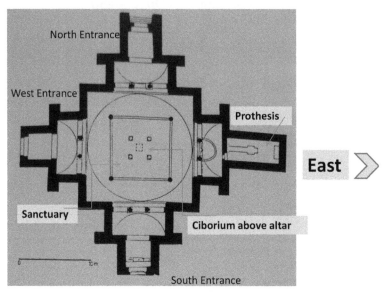

Fig. 17. *(Old) Dongola Cruciform Church, ground plan*

the clergy turned westward toward the center of the large edifice instead of looking toward the altar.

The evidence suggests an interpretation significantly different from earlier interpretations.[107] The east branch of the church is the pastophorion where the prothesis was performed and which also gave access to the tomb. That room is accessed from the church through chancels fixed in the sides of the eastern trifolium, on either side of the synthronon, which occupies the center. The seats of the bishop and presbyters are as usual turned west, looking toward the center of the whole structure, where the altar was found, surmounted by a ciborium, inside an enclosed sanctuary shaped by four columns. The celebrant normally stood to the west of the

---

[107] Cp. Godlewski, "The Cruciform Church," *Nubica* 1–2 (1990): 530–31; William Y. Adams, *The Churches of Nobadia*, vol. 2, BAR International Series 17 (London: Sudan Archaeological Research Society, 2009), 409.

altar, turning eastward.[108] That the ciborium may have been where the golden cross robbed by Baibars hung has no structural implications: such a cross would have been a normal accessory for the sanctuary and altar, its price congruent with the likely royal status of this grand church.

This type of structure is a martyrium, familiar from Palestine, Syria, and Asia Minor, where we find examples that are all older than the church in Old Dongola.[109] The structure points to the great importance for the local church of the two persons buried in the crypt of this Nubian cathedral. And the Holy Sepulcher, too, is a martyrium.

The Cruciform Church was an inspiration for many Nubian churches,[110] and it is not surprising that its influence was felt in Ethiopia when so many travelers of every condition were using the Nile valley as a thoroughfare. Borrowings from Nubia evidently took place at a significant rate, as can be seen in the example of the passage from the *prothesis* door directly to the altar at Gāzēn (East Tegray, ca. eighth century), the west rooms at Mikā'ēl Ambā (East Tegray, AD 1150), and later churches like the monolithic churches at Lālibalā, the porches of Bēta Māryām (turn of the thirteenth century), the cruciform structure of Bēta Giyorgis (thirteenth century), the ambo platforms at Lālibalā (end twelfth to thirteenth centuries) and surroundings, especially at Yemrehanna Krestos (mid-thirteenth century), the synthronon of Gannata Māryām (Lāstā, thirteenth century), and the murals of Māryām Qorqor (AD 1260–1320). The very existence of the prestigious cruciform cathedral of Sus at Old Dongola would have authorized neighboring construction that imitated its central square sanctuary.[111]

---

[108] A last detail: unless the arrangements of chancels made it otherwise, the synthronon / presbyterium would have been separated from the sanctuary, which it is impossible to verify.

[109] Godlewski, "The Cruciform Church," 531.

[110] Godlewski, "Dongolese Milieu in Nubian Architecture," 132.

[111] Literature on the Ethio-Nubian connections is scarce; see, for example, Jean Doresse, "Nouvelles recherches sur les relations entre l'Égypte copte et l'Éthiopie: XIIᵉ–XIIIᵉ siècles: Communication," *Comptes-rendus de l'Académie des Inscriptions et Belles-Lettres* 3 (1970): 557–66; Jean Doresse, Review of "Tamīt

All that remained was to connect the salient points of the periphery of the building to create an octagonal contour, tantamount to drawing a circle. By the end of the fifteenth century or early sixteenth century, Christian Nubia was largely a thing of the past; any impact in Ethiopia would have had to have come earlier. While that impact has not as yet been uncovered in the written sources, it would seem possible in light of the importance of the exchange of the twelfth and thirteenth centuries.

The notion of a martyrium, however, does not seem to have taken root, for it is associated by definition with forms of burial that are not found in Ethiopia, or at any rate not in relation to the circular churches. Moreover, such burials alone cannot explain the systematic transformation of the churches into rotundas or why such a model would have suddenly become the general pattern.

What, then, can be said about the emergence of the circular churches? Such buildings are characterized by a central sanctuary, which, incidentally, systematically integrated Egyptian developments, with the now-lockable sanctuary forming a pastophorion, where the valuable paraphernalia required by the liturgy could be kept secure. The division of the space into three parts is an almost universal feature, but it had no specific ties to the temple in Jerusalem. Although the shape of the church of the Holy Sepulcher may have been the inspiration, that association is undocumented and was not made by visitors such as Alvares or by Ethiopian scholars over the last three centuries or so.

(1964), Missione Archaeologica in Egitto dell'Università di Roma," *Revue d'Égyptologie* 21 (1969): 183–85; Henri de Contenson, "Les fouilles à Haoulti-Melazo en 1958," *Annales d'Ethiopie* 4 (1961): 39–60; Henri de Contenson, "Relations entre la Nubie chrétienne et l'Ethiopie axoumite," in *Proceedings of the Third International Conference of Ethiopian Studies* (Addis Ababa: Institute of Ethiopian Studies, Haile Selassie I University, 1970), 1:17–18; Małgorzata Martens-Czarnecka, "Certain Common Aspects of Ethiopian and Nubian Painting," *Nubica et Aethiopica* 4–5 (1999): 163–76; Bogdan Żurawski, "Nubia and Ethiopia in the Christian Period—Some Affinities," in *Aspects of Ethiopian Art from Ancient Axum to the 20th Century: Proceedings of the Second International Conference on the History of Ethiopian Art, September 1990 Nieborów Poland*, ed. Paul B. Henze (London: Jed Press, 1993), 33–41.

If the round churches were constructed according to popular ways of building south of Tegray—which would have required less architectural skill and made the task easier—the adoption of a circular plan, it has been suggested, would have greatly facilitated the process of rebuilding urgently needed in the wake of the devastation caused by the Muslim *ğihad* of the sixteenth century. The time frame indicated by Castanhoso makes this explanation possible.[112] It can also be argued that contact with the Nubian cruciform cathedral of (Old) Dongola may have been the impetus behind the idea of a central sanctuary in Ethiopian lands.

Yet perhaps the interrelation of the various elements studied above is not even necessary for an explanation of the circular shape of churches. If the circular shape was usual, then perhaps churches had been built in that form for ages in areas far away from centers. They might have remained undocumented because they disappeared from the landscape, for they would have been made of earth and straw and would have been small enough not to require durable foundations. Such was the case in the "historic north," where the rock churches witness to the existence of a network of churches that has now disappeared, except in the case of a few exceptional buildings such as Giyorgis Zāramā or Māryām Nāzrēt, discussed above. In the Amhara region, high-standard rectangular churches would have been the produce of royal initiative and remain visible, even as ruins, but the more usual and widely dispersed places of worship—which might possibly have been circular—would have disappeared. That explanation of the circular church requires no further evidence.

CONCLUSION

The *unicum* manuscript of the Aksumite Collection provides us with crucial late antique liturgical material that goes beyond even our wildest expectations in answering longstanding questions about the nature of the liturgy practiced in Aksumite Christianity. The eucharistic prayer of St. Mark and an actual liturgical edition

---

[112] This idea would also be shared by Deresse Aynachew and Marie-Laure Derat.

of the anaphora found in the *Apostolic Tradition* and known as the Anaphora of the Apostles were indeed available in Ge'ez in the late antique polity of the Aksumites. Additionally, the Aksumite editing of the anaphora is relatively easy to detect. Just as important is that the development and practical nature of the liturgico-canonical documentation can be assessed, and it appears that a historical reality is conveyed in parts of the material.

Two stages of the history of Ethiopian church buildings, each matching a particular liturgical development, have been examined in this essay: the emergence of buildings with several sanctuaries and the emergence of circular churches. The discovery of a large mid-twelfth-century Coptic church at Māryām Nāzrēt has enabled us to explain the appearance of the first Ethiopian church with several sanctuaries and altars, namely, Mikā'ēl Ambā. The existence of the Coptic church at Māryām Nāzrēt also throws light on the active presence and leadership of the Coptic head of the church. Which is not to say that the liturgical rites attached to such architectural evolution did not also undergo earlier development, for changes came earlier in Egypt, and the Coptic hierarchy may have influenced the Ethiopian rite, possibly in the centers first.

Investigation of the appearance of circular churches supports in various ways the identification of the first third of the sixteenth century as the likely time frame. Proposed ties to both the Jerusalem temple and the Holy Sepulcher have proved inadequate. Advances in regard to Nubia have provided an opportunity to consider the liturgical architectonics in the Cruciform Church at (Old) Dongola, an important ninth-century martyrium at the gates of Ethiopia that may have been instrumental in ushering in the central sanctuary for later Ethiopian round churches. The possibility that a round form may have been the standard for buildings in peripheral areas should not be excluded and would make unnecessary recourse to a specific time frame or to a specific initiative from authorities. Remains that would confirm that theory, however, are not extant. While several points of interest have been uncovered on our journey, as is so typical of research, the last word—in this case on the appearance of the round churches—has not yet been uttered. We await another discovery of textual or architectural remains, and preferably of both.

Imagining Early Christian Liturgy

The *Traditio Apostolica*—A Case Study

Maxwell E. Johnson

In his graduate-level Notre Dame courses on liturgical history, James F. White (1932–2004) would ask, at least in his later years, on his midterm examination something like the following: "If Paul Bradshaw and his collaborators succeed in dethroning Hippolytus, what would that mean for the contemporary renewal of Christian worship?" While it remains news to me that Paul Bradshaw, L. Edward Phillips, and I[1] were ever actually engaged in some kind of revolutionary *coup* to "dethrone Hippolytus," I ask a similar type of question today in my own teaching of that same course, namely, "Given the view of contemporary liturgical scholarship that the so-called *Apostolic Tradition*, ascribed to Hippolytus of Rome, is probably neither *Roman*, nor of *Hippolytan* authorship, nor from the early third century, but is rather a composite document reflecting no church in particular, would this have any significance for how it has been or should be used in contemporary liturgical renewal? Would contemporary liturgy be different than it is? Why or why not?"

Between these two distinct ways of asking that question lie two ways of imagining liturgy's past, at least with regard to early, pre-Nicene Christianity, at Rome especially, and in the West in general.

---

[1] See our coauthored volume, *The Apostolic Tradition: A Commentary*, by Paul F. Bradshaw, Maxwell E. Johnson, and L. Edward Phillips, Hermeneia Commentary Series (Minneapolis, MN: Fortress Press, 2002).

The first way of this imagining is well summarized by John F. Baldovin, SJ, in his important 2003 article on this document:

> When I was a student, the commonly accepted opinion on the *Apostolic Tradition* ran something like this: Here we have a church order that gives us data on important ecclesiastical practices from the early-third century. The writer was a presbyter/theologian, named Hippolytus, who opposed Bishop Callistus of Rome over the latter's laxity in readmitting sinners to church fellowship. He thus became a schismatic anti-pope, but was reconciled before his death as a martyr. A conservative, he advocated ancient usages of the Church. A crusty old parish priest unwilling to abide by his bishop's liturgical innovations, he set down in a single document these rather antiquarian rules for liturgy and church conduct.[2]

Hence, it was regularly thought that whatever we might glean from this document even for our own practice today must be authentic and early, if not, quite possibly, even apostolic. So, a world-renowned scholar like Josef A. Jungmann, SJ, in his 1976 book *The Mass*, could conclude with Hans Lietzmann about the famous eucharistic prayer in *Apostolic Tradition* 4 that "what we find there could . . . have been spoken also at the time of the Apostle Paul in Corinth or Ephesus."[3] Or, Cyprian Vaggagini, one of the architects of the eucharistic prayers in the Roman Missal of Paul VI could say with authority: "The anaphora of Hippolytus . . . would seem to give us the usual structure of an anaphora in the early Church."[4] And many of us remember fondly two videos produced by the then Murphy Center for Liturgical Research, now the Notre Dame Center for Liturgy, in the early 1970s. One of these was on the rites of Christian initiation from the *Apostolic Tradition*, with well-placed palm trees around the pool shielding the imagined nakedness of the graduate student "baptismal candidates," and the other

---

[2] John F. Baldovin, "Hippolytus and the *Apostolic Tradition*: Recent Research and Commentary," *Journal of Theological Studies* 64 (2003): 520–21.

[3] Josef A. Jungmann, *The Mass: A Historical, Theological, and Pastoral Survey* (Collegeville, MN: Liturgical Press, 1976), 33.

[4] Cyprian Vaggagini, *The Canon of the Mass and Liturgical Reform* (London: Geoffrey Chapman, 1967), 25.

on the imagined eucharistic liturgy of the time, actually spoken in some form of a Greek retroversion, complete with everyone in a toga. More telling was the filmed panel discussion following the dramatic reenactment of "Hippolytus' Eucharist" in which liturgical scholars of the time were rather adamant in their assertion that because of this document, "We now know what the liturgy was like in the Church at Rome at the beginning of the third century."

It is John Baldovin, who, in the same essay quoted above, also provides for us the beginnings of a second way of imagining liturgy's past by summarizing what can no longer be said with any degree of certainty about this so-called *Apostolic Tradition*. Reflecting on contemporary liturgical scholarship, Baldovin summarizes the current approach, if not yet full consensus, saying:

> Nothing about this [previously held] synthesis is correct. The title of the document in question is not the "Apostolic Tradition." It cannot be attributed to Hippolytus, an author whose corpus of biblical commentaries and anti-heretical treatises is somewhat well known. As a matter of fact it is doubtful whether the corpus of that writer can actually be attributed to a single writer. Finally, our document does not give us certain information about the liturgical practice of the early third century Roman Church.[5]

Inseparably connected to these two ways of imagining liturgy's past with regard to this document is not only a radical change in historiography itself but also in the normative values that may be attached to a historical document in the first place. Hence, in the one case, "dethroning of Hippolytus" represents a frontal assault on the then-common historiographical master narrative of a normative liturgical development and evolution in monolinear continuity from the past to the present, whereas, in the other case, liturgical history is viewed in a more fragmentary, discontinuous, and diversified way, with only some things that emerge as certain or plausible in terms of what we might actually know of this past. As Bryan Spinks has recently said, "One does not have to be absorbed in postmodern mania to recognize that there is something

---

[5] Baldovin, "Hippolytus," 521.

different about how liturgical material is handled now compared with four decades ago."[6]

In this essay I will explore these diverse approaches to the interpretation of this document, and I will do so in three ways. First, in "The *Apostolic Tradition*'s 'Imagined Past' in Twentieth-Century Liturgical Renewal," I will present an overview of what, based on that document, many imagined early Christian liturgy to have been in third-century Rome and how this vision contributed toward shaping the worship books of several major Christian traditions today. Second, in "Re-imagining Liturgy's Past Without 'Hippolytus,'" I will offer an interpretation of what we can say about Christian liturgy in the third century based on other extant and less controversial sources. Third and finally, in "The Role of the *Apostolic Tradition* in Ongoing Liturgical Renewal Today," I will attempt to answer my own question asked at the beginning, namely, whether and how our contemporary liturgical renewal would be different or how it might still become different, given the recent new scholarly assessment of the *Apostolic Tradition*. While in all three sections I am concerned with various liturgical rites, a major focus will be the eucharistic anaphora in *Apostolic Tradition* 4.

It is worth emphasizing that this essay is not so much concerned about contemporary scholarship on this document, which is easily available elsewhere, but about its reception, use, and interpretation for liturgical reform and renewal, based on historiographical suppositions and assumptions.

THE *APOSTOLIC TRADITION*'S "IMAGINED PAST" IN TWENTIETH-CENTURY LITURGICAL RENEWAL

Thanks especially to the editions of Gregory Dix[7] and Bernard Botte,[8] both of whom composed a unified narrative text out of

---

[6] Bryan D. Spinks, "What Is 'New' in the 'History' of Christian Baptismal Liturgy: The Early Centuries," *Studia Liturgica* 42 (2012): 16–42, here 16.

[7] Gregory Dix, *The Apostolic Tradition of St. Hippolytus* (London: Morehouse Press, 1937; 2nd ed., 1968).

[8] Bernard Botte, *La Tradition Apostolique de saint Hippolyte*, 5th ed., LQF 39 (Münster: Aschendorff, 1963, 1989).

the diverse manuscript and linguistic versions of the *Apostolic Tradition* (even filling in from other versions where various *lacunae* appear in the mid-fifth-century Latin version, to create the impression of a unified document), there is no question but that how we imagined much of early Christian liturgy to be was based on this reconstructed document. With regard to Christian initiation, for example, liturgical scholarship assumed that in the early third century, if not earlier, all of the following were standard features: First, the catechumenate at Rome regularly lasted for three years and daily instruction and daily exorcism accompanied it, at least in the final unspecified phase of preparation. Second, there was a prebaptismal anointing with exorcised oil, and a threefold baptismal immersion accompanied by an interrogatory formula, based on a rather full text of what would become the "Apostles' Creed." Third, postbaptismal rites included an anointing by a presbyter with the oil of thanksgiving, an episcopal hand-laying prayer and subsequent anointing, and a culminating reception of the Eucharist, including also a cup or cups of water, milk, and honey. So eager were scholars to see early evidence of "episcopal confirmation" in this text that even though the bishop's hand-laying prayer in the Verona Latin text prayed not for the Holy Spirit but for "grace" and the anointing formula was trinitarian, both Dix and Botte titled this prayer with its anointing "Confirmation," and chose for their source text one of the other much later Coptic, Ethiopic, and Arabic translations of the prayer which did pray for the Holy Spirit. Furthermore, although the document never specified a liturgical season or feast, the fact that immediate preparation for baptism began with a bath on a Thursday and culminated in a vigil presumably on a Saturday night lent itself easily to an interpretation that it must be the Easter Vigil that was intended at the conclusion of what must have been an early Paschal Triduum.

The document also nowhere describes in any detail a eucharistic liturgy, but within the materials provided for the ordination of a bishop in chapter 4, the now-famous eucharistic prayer appears, often called simply "Hippolytus." This prayer has found its way in some form into most of the contemporary worship reforms of mainline churches. Because I shall be concerned with this anaphora frequently throughout this essay, it is printed here according to the mid-fifth-century Verona Latin manuscript, the earliest known manuscript source:

> We render thanks to you, God, through your beloved servant Jesus Christ, whom in the last times you sent to us as savior and redeemer and angel of your will, who is your inseparable word, through whom you made all things and it was well pleasing to you, [whom] you sent from heaven into the virgin's womb, and who conceived in the womb was incarnate and manifested as your Son, *born from the Holy Spirit and the virgin*; who fulfilling your will and gaining for you a holy people stretched out [his] hands when he was suffering, that he might release from suffering those who believed in you; who *when he* was *being* handed over to voluntary suffering, that he might destroy death and break the bonds of the devil, and tread down hell and illuminate the righteous, and fix a limit and manifest the resurrection, *taking bread [and] giving thanks to you, he said: "Take, eat, this is my body that will be broken for you." Likewise also the cup, saying, "This is my blood that is shed for you. When you do this, you do my remembrance." Remembering therefore his death and resurrection*, we offer to you the bread and cup, giving thanks to you because you have held us worthy to stand before you and minister to you. And we ask that *you would send your Holy Spirit in the oblation of [your] holy church, [that]* gathering [them] into one you will give to all who partake of the holy things [to partake] in the fullness of the Holy Spirit, for the strengthening of faith in truth, that we may praise and glorify you through your servant Jesus Christ, through whom [be] glory and honor to you, *Father and Son with the Holy Spirit*, in your holy church, both now and to the ages of ages. Amen.[9]

Even though earlier scholars such as E. C. Ratcliff had argued that the entire anaphora in the document was a later revision of an earlier "Hippolytan" text,[10] and both Ratcliff and Gregory

[9] Bradshaw, Johnson, and Phillips, *Apostolic Tradition: A Commentary*, 38 and 40; for discussion of the contents of this prayer, see pp. 37–48 in that volume. Words in italics indicate sections we consider to be later additions or interpolations.

[10] E. C. Ratcliff, "The Sanctus and the Pattern of the Early Anaphora," *Journal of Ecclesiastical History* 1 (1950): 29–36, 125–34.

Dix viewed the epiclesis of the Holy Spirit on the oblation as a fourth-century interpolation,[11] few really questioned the overall early Roman and/or Hippolytan origins of this anaphora.[12] The judgments of Lietzmann, Jungmann, and Vagaggini referenced above may be taken as generally accepted. The only real issue seemed to be how to make a prayer so seemingly un-Roman fit with what was known of presumably later Roman euchology as exemplified in the Roman *canon missae*. When combined, however, with the description of the mid-second-century Sunday and baptismal eucharistic liturgies in Justin Martyr's *First Apology* 65–67 (widely believed also to be reflective of Roman liturgy), this anaphora with its similar language of praise to the Father, through the Son, in the Holy Spirit, giving thanks "at some length that we have been deemed worthy to receive these things from him,"[13] combines nicely to create the impression that together these two documents give us a fairly reliable and authoritative picture of early Roman eucharistic liturgy.

A similar influential understanding of daily prayer and the rites of ordination in our document have also influenced contemporary usage and interpretation. As is well known, the prayer for the ordination of the bishop in *Apostolic Tradition* 3 [14] was taken over directly into the current Roman Catholic ordination rites, thus replacing the prior Roman prayer for episcopal ordination, because, again, it was believed, at least in part, by Pope Paul VI that the prayer "was written at the beginning of the third century."[15] And while the so-called *Apostolic Tradition* does not really contain Vespers or Evening Prayer as part of its daily *cursus horarum*, the opening dialogue and thanksgiving for the "bringing in of lamps" at the beginning of

[11] See ibid., and n9 above.

[12] With the notable exception of J. M. Hanssens, *La Liturgie d'Hippolyte: Documents et Etudes* (Rome: Libreria Editrice dell'Università Gregoriana, 1970).

[13] Justin, *First Apology*, 65.

[14] For the text see Bradshaw, Johnson, Phillips, *Apostolic Tradition: A Commentary*, 30.

[15] Paul VI, *Apostolic Constitution: Approval of New Rites for the Ordination of Deacons, Presbyters, and Bishops* in *The Rites of the Catholic Church*, vol. 2 (New York: Pueblo, 1980), 45.

the evening congregational supper in chapter 29,[16] extant only in Ethiopian, has been adapted widely in the creation of *Lucernarium* rites in many modern ecumenical versions of "cathedral" Vespers. Given that the document was presumed to reflect the earliest pattern and contents of liturgy at Rome, many contemporary liturgical celebrations have been shaped to a large extent, by, or even come directly from this document: the contemporary Roman Catholic Rite of Christian Initiation of Adults (RCIA) as well as the adult catechumenate in several other churches; the recovery of the "original" Roman eucharistic prayer; the introduction of the *Lucernarium* or Light Service with its thanksgiving at Evening Prayer; and the complete takeover of the prayer for the ordination of bishops in the Roman Catholic liturgy. Therefore, we might say that the *Apostolic Tradition* represents the creation of a fictional document on which many people imagined or projected a fictional past to which we gave normative status for determining our liturgical present.

But liturgical reformers have always done that, have they not? Haven't we almost always sought precedent in the past for something we have already decided to do? In *Quo Primum*, the promulgation of the *Missale Romanum* of 1570, Pope Pius V could not have been clearer in his statement that this new Missal had been restored to the "pristine norm received from the holy Fathers" (*ad pristinam Missale ipsum sanctorum Patrum normam ac ritum restituerunt*).[17] Similarly telling was the title of John Calvin's 1542 "The Form of Prayers and Ecclesiastical Chants with the Manner of Administering the Sacraments and Solemnizing Marriage *according to the Custom of the Ancient Church*." We might note also the fascination with and use of the "Clementine Liturgy" in book 8 of the then-recently discovered *Apostolic Constitutions* among the Non-Jurors in England and Scotland and their liturgical products,

---

[16] For the text see Bradshaw, Johnson, Phillips, *Apostolic Tradition: A Commentary*, 156.

[17] Pius V, *Quo primum tempore*, in *Missale Romanum, Editio Princeps (1570)*, Edizione anastatica, Introduzione e Appendice a cura di Manlio Sodi - Achille Maria Triacca (Vatican City: Libreria Editrice Vaticana, 1998), 3. Pius V's *Quo primum tempore* is included in every altar edition of the pre–Vatican II *Missale Romanum* and can easily be accessed there also.

which eventually influenced the worship materials of the Episcopal Church in the United States.[18]

The contemporary use then of a document like the *Apostolic Tradition* for liturgical renewal should not really appear all that surprising, since the attempt to discover the earliest and most authoritative documents for the right worship of the church is precisely the quest we have been on from the polemical context of the Reformation until only recently. And consistent with this quest, a common interpretation of the current Roman Rite is that with so many more sources available, twentieth-century liturgical reform was able to do what the reforms of Pius V could not do, namely, to come much closer to having restored the "pristine norm received from the holy Fathers."[19] A similar claim was made, of course, for how and why the rest of us were no longer bound to the liturgical products of a Luther or a Cranmer, because we now had better and earlier sources than the Reformers did for our own liturgical products today. You see, we were doing what they would have done had they known what we know now. It is because of how we all viewed history, and this view comes not from some new historiographical methodology but actually reflects a "theology" of history, we might say, namely, a liturgical unbroken and monolinear *Heilsgeschichte*, which assumed earliest is best and provided the norm or at least the precedent for what we should do now. This approach to history was fueled in its beginning stages by the Reformation itself, and then by the liturgical movement, the ecumenical movement, and the concomitant rise in biblical and patristic scholarship, all of which granted a particular normativity to the doctrine and worship of orthodox Christianity in the first millennium. The further back we could go, if not to the New Testament period itself, the better for our contemporary liturgical adaptations and restorations.

What we had not learned yet, as liturgical scholars—never mind whether a document like the *Apostolic Tradition* was third century,

---

[18] See Marion Hatchett, *The Making of the First American Book of Common Prayer* (New York: Seabury Press, 1982), 22ff.

[19] See n17: "*ad pristinam Missale ipsum sanctorum Patrum normam ac ritum restituerunt.*"

apostolic, Roman, and Hippolytan, or not—is that, in the words of Robert Taft:

> The past is always instructive, but not necessarily normative. What we do today is not ruled by the past but by the adaptation of the tradition to the needs of the present. History can only help us decide what the essentials of that tradition are, and the parameters of its adaptation.[20]

The *Apostolic Tradition*, however, was *not* incorporated directly into contemporary liturgical use and renewal without undergoing serious adaptation and revision, and this has not often been noted. That is, even though we all thought in common that we were dealing with the authentic early Roman/Western liturgical tradition, we made sure individually that our own particular theological and/or confessional positions were not challenged too greatly by our use of that document. Here again, the eucharistic prayer provides the best example. In the Roman Rite's adaptation of this prayer in the composition of its current Eucharistic Prayer 2, what remained of the text of *Apostolic Tradition* 4 is limited almost exclusively to what is now the "preface" and a very few other phrases in the introduction to the institution narrative, anamnesis, and now a "second" epiclesis, as indicated below in italics:

> It is truly right and just, our duty and our salvation,
> always and everywhere to give you thanks, Father most holy,
> *through your beloved Son, Jesus Christ,*
> *your Word through whom you made all things,*
> *whom you sent as our Savior and Redeemer,*
> *incarnate by the Holy Spirit and born of the Virgin.*
>
> *Fulfilling your will and gaining for you a holy people,*
> *he stretched out his hands as he endured his Passion,*
> *so as to break the bonds of death and manifest the resurrection.*
>
> And so, with the Angels and all the Saints
> we declare your glory,
> as with one voice we acclaim:

[20] Robert Taft, *The Liturgy of the Hours in East and West: The Origins of the Divine Office and Its Meaning for Today* (Collegeville, MN: Liturgical Press, 1986), xiv–xv.

(SANCTUS)

You are indeed Holy, O Lord,
the fount of all holiness.
Make holy, therefore, these gifts, we pray,
by sending down your Spirit upon them like the dewfall,
so that they may become for us
the Body and Blood of our Lord Jesus Christ.

At the time he was betrayed
and entered willingly into his Passion,
he took bread and, giving thanks, broke it,
and gave it to his disciples, saying:
TAKE THIS . . .
In a similar way, when supper was ended,
he took the chalice
and, once more giving thanks,
he gave it to his disciples, saying:
TAKE THIS . . .
Therefore, as we celebrate
the memorial of his Death and Resurrection,
we offer you, Lord,
the Bread of life and the Chalice of salvation,
giving thanks that you have held us worthy
to be in your presence and minister to you
[astare coram te et tibi ministrare].

Humbly we pray
that, *partaking of the Body and Blood of Christ,*
we may be gathered into one by the Holy Spirit.
Remember, Lord, your Church,
spread throughout the world,
and bring her to the fullness of charity,
together with N. our Pope and N. our Bishop
and all the clergy.
Remember your servant N.,
whom you have called
from this world to yourself.
Grant that he who was united with your Son in a death like his,
may also be one with him in his Resurrection.

Remember also our brothers and sisters
who have fallen asleep in the hope of the resurrection,
and all who have died in your mercy:
welcome them into the light of your face.
Have mercy on us all, we pray,
that with the Blessed Virgin Mary, Mother of God,
with blessed Joseph, her Spouse
with the blessed Apostles,
and all the Saints who have pleased you throughout the ages,
we may merit to be coheirs to eternal life
[aeternae vitae mereamur esse consortes],
and may praise and glorify you
through your Son, Jesus Christ.[21]

As is easily demonstrated, the overall structure of the anaphora
in the *Apostolic Tradition* (like Eucharistic Prayers 3 and 4 in the
current Roman Rite) was remodeled to fit the structure, if not the
contents, of the Roman *canon missae* itself, with the insertion of the
Sanctus, a pre-institution narrative consecratory petition (here an
explicit epiclesis of the Holy Spirit) and intercessions for the living
and the dead. Hence, not even the overall *structure* of the anaphora
of *Apostolic Tradition* 4 was deemed suitable for contemporary
Roman Catholic use, even though it was viewed as *the* earliest and
most authentic eucharistic prayer of the early *Roman* tradition.
Such adaptations continue even now in this prayer. In the 2011
English translation of the third edition of the *Missale Romanum* of
Pope Paul VI, the Latin text in the anamnesis, "*astare coram te et tibi
ministrare*," is translated as "to be in your presence and minister to
you." The previous translation had clearly and accurately rendered
this as "to *stand* in your presence and serve you," but the current
translation chooses "to be" for no other reason than that most of
the liturgical assembly in English-speaking countries is kneeling
at this point. So much in this case for the strict fidelity to the Latin
text as it was mandated by *Liturgiam Authenticam*.[22]

[21] *Roman Missal* (Collegeville, MN: Liturgical Press, 2011), 645–49.

[22] For the text of *Liturgiam Authenticam* and an outstanding critical commentary, see Peter Jeffery, *Translating Tradition: A Chant Historian Reads* Liturgiam Authenticam (Collegeville, MN: Liturgical Press, 2005).

The Anglican tradition—as represented by the 1979 *Book of Common Prayer* in the United States, especially in Eucharistic Prayer B,[23] and by *Common Worship* in Eucharistic Prayer B in England[24]—adapted the anaphora from *Apostolic Tradition* 4 in similar but more direct ways. The Lutheran use of the anaphora in the 1978 *Lutheran Book of Worship* and now the 2006 *Evangelical Lutheran Worship* reflects more directly a particular confessional perspective. Lutherans provide the text as it appears in the Verona Latin manuscript of *Apostolic Tradition*, without the addition of the *sanctus* or other characteristic anaphoral additions, although the institution narrative was expanded and in current usage it often follows *sursum corda*, preface, and *sanctus*. The following text appears in *Evangelical Lutheran Worship*:

> We give you thanks, Father,
> through Jesus Christ,
> your beloved Son, whom you
> sent in this end of the ages
> to save and redeem us
> and to proclaim to us your will.
>
> He is your Word,
> inseparable from you,
> through whom you created all things,
> and in whom you take delight.
>
> He is your Word,
> sent from heaven to a virgin's womb.
> He there took on our nature and our lot
> and was shone forth as your Son,
> born of the Holy Spirit and of the virgin Mary.
>
> He, our Lord Jesus, fulfilled all your will
> and won for you a holy people;
> he stretched out his hands in suffering in order to
> free from suffering those who trust you.

[23] *The Book of Common Prayer* (New York: The Church Hymnal Corporation, 1979), 368–69.

[24] *Common Worship: Services and Prayers for the Church of England* (London: Church House Publishing, 2000), 188–90.

He is the one who,
handed over to a death he freely accepted,
in order to destroy death,
to break the bonds of the evil one,
to crush hell underfoot,
to give light to the righteous,
to establish his covenant,
and to show forth the resurrection,
taking bread
and giving thanks to you, said:
Take and eat: this is my body, given for you.
Do this for the remembrance of me.

In the same way he took the cup, gave thanks,
and gave it for all to drink, saying:
This cup, is the new covenant in my blood,
shed for you and for all people
for the forgiveness of sin.
Do this for the remembrance of me.

Remembering, then, his death and resurrection,
we take this bread and cup
[offerimus tibi panem et calicem],
giving you thanks that you have made us worthy
to stand before you and to serve you as your
priestly people.

Send your Spirit upon these gifts [oblationem] of your church;
gather into one all who share this bread and wine;
fill us with your Holy Spirit to establish our faith in truth,
that we may praise and glorify you
through your Son Jesus Christ;
through whom all glory and honor are yours,
almighty Father,
with the Holy Spirit in your holy church,
both now and forever. Amen.[25]

---

[25] Eucharistic Prayer 11, *Evangelical Lutheran Worship*, Leader's Desk Edition (Minneapolis, MN: Augsburg Fortress Press, 2006), 205. The Latin text is supplied from Hanssens, *La Liturgie d'Hippolyte*, 74.

Even if Lutherans translate *"astare coram te et tibi ministrare"* correctly as "to stand in your presence and serve you," Lutheran theological reluctance to speak the language of offering in the eucharistic prayer serves here to change the entire direction of the prayer with its rendering of *"offerimus tibi panem et calicem"* as "we *take* the bread and cup" and with its substitution of "gifts" for "oblation" in the epiclesis. The text of this same prayer in *Lutheran Book of Worship* was rendered as "we *lift* this bread and cup before you,"[26] much like the 1993 Presbyterian *Book of Common Worship* text, "We *set* before you this bread and cup,"[27] in both cases keeping not only the upward direction of the prayer intact but also retaining the direct object *"tibi"* as well, which the *Evangelical Lutheran Worship* version now glosses over.

Contemporary use made of this eucharistic prayer from *Apostolic Tradition* 4, therefore, tends to reveal that even what we might think of as "common" liturgical use turns out to be not so common after all. And the question must surely be asked why—if we need to change a liturgical source so much to make it fit our preconceived eucharistic theology and inherited euchological patterns—should such a text be deemed appropriate for use at all? In 1980, just two years after the publication of *Lutheran Book of Worship* (LBW), Paul V. Marshall had this to say about the Lutheran translation and usage of this prayer:

> The least satisfying aspect of this translation is the treatment of the anamnesis-oblation. The textual evidence is unanimous for *Offerimus tibi panem et calicem* here rendered "we lift this bread and cup before you." . . . This apparent avoidance of directly sacrificial language raises the question of just what the LBW drafters would consider appropriate language of sacrifice. . . . The alteration of an historic text may be the occasion for those responsible for LBW to ask themselves whether they are not indicating their own difference from the classic tradition. This was the question Ralph Keifer raised,

---

[26] *Lutheran Book of Worship: Minister's Desk Edition* (Minneapolis, MN: Augsburg Fortress Press, 1978), 226.

[27] *Book of Common Worship* (Louisville, KY: Westminster/John Knox Press, 1993), 151.

along with others, when his (Roman Catholic) denomination felt constrained to insert "we offer you his body and blood" into the anaphora of Basil.[28]

So, why would we use a text like this, or any patristic liturgical text, if all of us had to change it to match our own theological positions and presuppositions? I suspect that the answer has to do with the presumed normativity and authenticity of this prayer and of the *Apostolic Tradition* itself. That is, because of what it was assumed to be, everyone had to use it in some form or risk idiosyncratic departure from the ecumenical-liturgical consensus. Nevertheless, even with our ecumenical agreement in "imagining liturgy's past" with regard to this document, we were still able to keep ourselves from allowing our imaginations to run away with themselves. So we made sure in our various adaptations that "Hippolytus" was really Catholic, Anglican, or Lutheran in the way his prayer sounded, was structurally shaped, and "translated" for liturgical use.

RE-IMAGINING LITURGY'S PAST WITHOUT "HIPPOLYTUS"

In his 2002 Aidan Kavanagh Lecture at the Yale Institute of Sacred Music, titled "Liturgy in the Absence of Hippolytus,"[29] Paul Bradshaw drew attention to the challenges raised to contemporary liturgical assumptions and practices when faced with the absence of the earlier foundation provided by the *Apostolic Tradition*. Bradshaw called for a less selective view of history among liturgical scholars, a stronger theological critique of worship practices, attention to ethical issues within that theological critique, and attention to pastoral realities of given situations. But how much does our picture of liturgy in the first three centuries actually change without the *Apostolic Tradition*? With regard to what was assumed to be

---

[28] Paul V. Marshall, "The Eucharistic Rite of the Lutheran Book of Worship," *Worship* 54, no. 3 (1980): 246–56, here 255f.

[29] Paul F. Bradshaw, "Liturgy in the Absence of Hippolytus," Yale Institute of Sacred Music, *Colloquium: Music, Worship, Arts* 1 (September 2004): 1–10.

liturgical practice at Rome, a great deal of course. Together with recent scholarly questions about whether Justin Martyr is reflecting what may be called "Roman" or even "Syrian" practices in his *First Apology*, the disappearance of the *Apostolic Tradition* from third-century Roman consideration means that we now know next to nothing about what the Church at Rome was doing liturgically in the first three centuries. Evidence for Rome now has to wait until we begin to get some pieces in the fourth and more pieces in the fifth century. And while there may be some kind of evolutionary continuity with an earlier period, what we do discover about early Rome's eucharistic prayer, the liturgy of the hours, and the ordination of bishops, displays *no* relationship whatsoever to the contents of the *Apostolic Tradition*. As Mathieu Smyth has recently demonstrated, the anaphora of *Apostolic Tradition* 4 follows a West Syrian or Syro-Byzantine anaphoral pattern and finds its parallels in the East and not with the Roman *canon missae* at all.[30] In fact, much of the Roman *canon missae* may well be earlier than the anaphora in *Apostolic Tradition* 4. With regard to Christian initiation in the *Apostolic Tradition*, with its unique postbaptismal episcopal hand-laying prayer and anointing, the first witness confirming this structure, pun intended, is the *Letter of Innocent I to Decentius of Gubbio* in 416, a liturgical description perhaps even influenced by the fifth-century Latin manuscript of the *Apostolic Tradition*. Furthermore, the first use of the full Apostles' Creed in question and answer form at Rome is in the post–Vatican II baptismal rite for infants in 1969.[31]

That said, outside of early Rome, very little actually changes in what we can know about early Christian worship. Although specifics like the three-year catechumenate, daily exorcism, and what many have wanted to call "confirmation" disappear from our

---

[30] Mathieu Smyth, "The Anaphora of the So-called 'Apostolic Tradition' and the Roman Eucharistic Prayer," in *Issues in Eucharistic Praying in East and West*, ed. Maxwell E. Johnson (Collegeville, MN: Liturgical Press, 2010), 71–98.

[31] W. Kinzig, C. Markschies, and M. Vinzent, *Tauffragen und Bekenntnis. Studien zur sogenannten "Traditio Apostolica", zu den "Interrogationes de fide" und zum "Römischen Glaubensbekenntnis"* (New York: Walter de Gruyter, 1999).

understanding of early third-century initiation rites, the fact of the matter is that many of the details about the catechumenate and the overall pattern of the rites of initiation in our document, with the exception of the unique postbaptismal anointing associated with the bishop, do find parallels in the writings of Tertullian.[32] This is true even for the presence of milk and honey in the first communion of the neophytes. The custom also appears later in the *Verona Sacramentary*, as well as in Egyptian and Ethiopic sources.[33] Similarly, some forms of *Lucernarium* or Lamp Lighting with prayers and hymns of thanksgiving, such as the famous *Phos Hilaron*, at Vespers are certainly documented elsewhere and will continue to be a characteristic of Vespers in what we have called traditionally the "cathedral office." Bishops, presbyters, deacons, and others also were ordained or appointed according to other sources even if, in the absence of the *Apostolic Tradition*, we lack specific early liturgical rites. And, of course, we *do* have other eucharistic prayer texts such as *Didache* 9 and 10, *Addai and Mari*, possibly the anaphoral-type prayer in the *Martyrdom of Polycarp* and the *Strasbourg Papyrus*, none of which contain an institution narrative and all with structural patterns either similar to or different from *Apostolic Tradition* 4. Furthermore, there is evidence, at least in the Christian East, that the anaphora of *Apostolic Tradition* 4 was used in the construction of other eucharistic prayers, as witnessed to by its presence as a source both in *Apostolic Constitutions* 8 and in the *Testamentum Domini*. The anaphora also appears in the Ethiopic version of *Apostolic Tradition* itself, the *only* version apart from the Verona Latin actually to include the anaphora. To this may be added its possible influence on the eucharistic prayer in the Barcelona papyrus.[34] Apart from the Eucharist, Juliette Day

[32] Tertullian, *De Corona* 3.

[33] For sources see E. C. Whitaker, *Documents of the Baptismal Liturgy*, rev. and expanded Maxwell E. Johnson, hereafter: *DBL* (London: SPCK, 2003), 207 (*Verona Sacramentary*); and Maxwell E. Johnson, *The Rites of Christian Initiation: Their Evolution and Interpretation*, rev. and expanded ed. (Collegeville, MN: Liturgical Press, 2007), 69–71, and 301–2.

[34] See Paul Bradshaw, "The Barcelona Papyrus and the Development of Early Eucharistic Prayers," in *Issues in Eucharistic Praying in East and West*, ed.

has suggested that the initiation rites of our document may well have been influential in determining the final shape of those rites in Egypt and Jerusalem.[35]

What actually *does* change, even outside Rome, however, is that the presumed normativity of the *Apostolic Tradition* is no longer the criterion by which liturgical historians and theologians, hopefully, judge the authenticity of other liturgical sources and traditions. That is to say, the so-called "dethroning of Hippolytus" from his normative status in contemporary scholarship has meant and means that the sheer variety of early liturgical sources is no longer to be viewed simply either as confirming or departing from what we "know," supposedly, to be the most ancient and authentic liturgical practice of early Rome as represented in the *Apostolic Tradition*. What this means concretely is that, for example, early Syrian (and possibly Egyptian) patterns of Christian initiation are allowed to stand on their own.[36] This would mean that elements such as the ordination of women, at least as deacons, the use of diverse metaphors for imaging the divine, e.g., invoking the Holy Spirit as "Mother," and other eucharistic prayer texts without narratives of institution (from the Syrian Acts of the Apostles) are to be seen not as idiosyncratic departures from some presumed early third-century (Western) norm but as reflective of one distinct ancient Christian tradition. Furthermore, the loss of the normativity of what we thought was implied in the *Apostolic Tradition* also means that other occasions for initiation than Easter, such as Epiphany or Theophany or even Pentecost, might make a claim for even greater antiquity; and we are free to admit a plurality of theological interpretations of baptism as rich as the diversity of the New Testament images of baptism themselves. It means that alternate patterns for

---

Maxwell E. Johnson (Collegeville, MN: Liturgical Press/Pueblo, 2010), 129–38. For critical edition and commentary see Michael Zheltov, "The Anaphora and the Thanksgiving Prayer from the Barcelona Papyrus: An Underestimated Testimony to the Anaphoral History in the Fourth Century," *Vigiliae Christianae* 62 (2008): 467–504.

[35] Juliette Day, *The Baptismal Liturgy of Jerusalem: Fourth- and Fifth-Century Evidence from Palestine, Syria, and Egypt* (Aldershot: Ashgate, 2007).

[36] For texts, see *DBL* (note 33), 14–25.

daily prayer appear, some two-fold, such as Tertullian's description of morning and evening prayer as *legitimae orations*,[37] and some three-fold, as in Cyprian of Carthage[38] and Origen of Alexandria.[39] The list could be extended further, with alternate patterns appearing for the overall ritual shape and culinary contents of the eucharistic meal,[40] and for the fact that monarchical episcopacy, so important both for Ignatius of Antioch and for the *Apostolic Tradition*, is not necessarily the model followed everywhere already in this period, as witnessed to even later by Jerome for Egypt.[41]

In relationship to this, Paul Bradshaw has noted that: "the supposed appeal to history by liturgical reformers has always been highly selective. We have found in ancient liturgies the things we wanted to find, and ignored and passed over those that did not suit our current needs."[42] But with that selective appeal to the *Apostolic Tradition* now made increasingly suspect, what Robert Taft has referred to as the Bradshaw-Johnson "Neo-Skeptic School of Paleo-liturgiology" makes it increasingly more difficult to "ignore" or "pass over" those elements previously deemed unsuitable. As I like to tell my students at the beginning of my regular course in liturgical history, "We used to know a lot more than we do today about early liturgy." In a similar vein, Bryan Spinks directs our attention to Keith Jenkins, who wrote in *Re-thinking History*:

> The historian's viewpoint and predilections will shape the choice of historical materials, and our own personal constructs determine what we make of them. The past that we "know" is always contingent upon our own views, our own "present." . . . Epistemology shows that we can never really know the past; that the gap between the past and history (historiography) is an ontological one, that is, it

---

[37] Tertullian, *De Oratione*, 24–5.

[38] Cyprian of Carthage, *De Dom. Orat.*, 34–6.

[39] Origen of Alexandria, *De. Oratione*, 12.2.

[40] See Andrew McGowan, *Ascetic Eucharists: Food and Drink in Early Christian Meals*, Oxford Early Christian Studies (Oxford: Clarendon Press, 1999).

[41] Jerome, *Commentary on the Epistle to Titus*, 1.5, 6, and *Epistle to Euangelus*, 146.

[42] Bradshaw, "Liturgy in the Absence of Hippolytus," 7.

is in the very nature of things such that no amount of epistemological effort can bridge it.[43]

Teresa Berger is undoubtedly correct in referring to the underlying suppositions of contemporary liturgical historiography as sharing and reflecting postmodern approaches to historical analyses, which emphasize fragmentariness, discontinuity, difference, and are obviously fueled by a "hermeneutics of suspicion." Berger is equally correct in noting that recognition of the presuppositions behind such a methodological approach does not negate what actually has been discovered and proposed with regard to Christian liturgical origins.[44] Call it "postmodern" or by some other term, if you will, the fact remains that current liturgical historiography continues to build on the comparative methodology of Anton Baumstark,[45] as furthered by the likes of Robert Taft, Gabriele Winkler, Paul Bradshaw, and other practitioners of the craft. As Taft himself has said, in words sounding themselves rather postmodern:

> The process of formation of rites is not one of diversification, as is usually held, but of unification. And what one finds in extant rites today is not a synthesis of all that went before, but rather the result of a selective evolution: the survival of the fittest—of the fittest, not necessarily the best.[46]

Based on the work of the philosopher of science Karl Popper, Taft notes, "Knowledge in a field advances not by the accumulation

[43] Keith Jenkins, *Re-thinking History* (London: Routledge, 1991), 12, 19, as quoted by Spinks, "What Is 'New' in the 'History' of Christian Baptismal Liturgy," 16.

[44] Teresa Berger, *Gender Differences and the Making of Liturgical History: Lifting a Veil on Liturgy's Past* (London/Burlington: Ashgate, 2011), 17.

[45] Anton Baumstark, *Comparative Liturgy*, rev. Bernard Botte, trans. F. L. Cross (London: A. R. Mowbray & Co., Ltd., 1958); Baumstark, *On the Historical Development of the Liturgy*, trans. Fritz West (Collegeville, MN: Liturgical Press, Pueblo, 2011); Fritz West, "A Reader's Guide to the Methodological Writings of Anton Baumstark," *Worship* 88, no. 3 (May 2014): 194–217.

[46] Robert Taft, "How Liturgies Grow: The Evolution of the Byzantine Divine Liturgy, in Taft, *Beyond East and West*, 2nd ed. (Rome, Pontificio Istituto Orientale, 1997), 203f.

of new data but by the invention of new systems; not by hypothesis verification but by hypothesis negation."[47] That is, we read the same data but we wear different interpretative lenses. That is what has happened and what continues to happen in our contemporary approaches to liturgical history.

So, what really changes in early liturgy without the *Apostolic Tradition*? On the one hand, very little in terms of our overall knowledge and understanding in general, that is, outside of claims previously made specifically about early Roman liturgy. And while that change is quite significant, the fact remains that we still have a pretty good overall, albeit fragmentary, sense of the various practices that make up early liturgy across a diversity of ecclesial traditions. What really does change, on the other hand, is the way we now read the liturgical sources we do have, apart from the *Apostolic Tradition*, and the value we place on those sources, no longer for producing norms or precedents to follow but in providing the overall picture we can glean from them.

THE ROLE OF THE *APOSTOLIC TRADITION* IN ONGOING LITURGICAL RENEWAL TODAY

Where does all of this leave us with regard to the role of the so-called *Apostolic Tradition* in liturgical renewal today? There are those who imagine that the current motivating force behind the discipline of liturgical history is a desire not to find a normative document as a precedent but instead to re-create early Christianity's primitive diversity in contemporary practice and remove from today's liturgical books those elements or prayers that are now recognized as later additions or compositions than we previously thought. As a recent example of this, a review of *The Oxford History of Christian Worship*, edited by Geoffrey Wainwright and Karen Westerfield-Tucker,[48] suggested strongly that if readers could read only one chapter of the book it should be chapter 2, that is, my chapter on liturgy in the first three centuries. Why? Because I

---

[47] Taft, "An Essay in Methodology," in *Beyond East and West*, 190.
[48] *The Oxford History of Christian Worship*, ed. Geoffrey Wainwright and Karen B. Westerfield-Tucker (New York: Oxford University Press, 2005).

allegedly demonstrate that the rationale for the 1979 *Book of Common Prayer* of the Episcopal Church "was made of sand and has now fallen apart, so that virtually all the major claims made on behalf of the new liturgies of the 1970s have no solid foundation. Of course, modern bishops and liturgists who have pushed so hard for the adoption of the liturgies of the 1970s and 1980s are not rushing forward to apologize."[49] And they should *not* rush forward to apologize, in my opinion. For no liturgical historian or theologian, to my knowledge, is suggesting, for example, that the multiple versions of the anaphora from *Apostolic Tradition* 4 in various liturgical traditions should not be used anymore since the prayer might not be what scholars thought it was some forty or fifty years ago. And no one is suggesting that the Roman Catholic rites of initiation of adults or the restoration of similar rites for the adult catechumenate in other traditions now need a major overhaul because recent historical scholarship suggests things might not have been this way in early third-century Rome. Similarly, the key question for the ordination of bishops in the Roman Rite is not whether the ordination prayer from the *Apostolic Tradition* is ancient or Roman, but whether it reflects theologically what the Roman Catholic Church today wants to say about the office of a bishop.

Granted, without the hegemony of "Hippolytus" things might have been different. I have suggested elsewhere that if contemporary liturgical reform and theology were to take more seriously the contemporary contributions of historical research on the origins of Christian worship and its sources, the worship books of several Christian traditions today might reflect a much greater diversity in form, content, and style regarding initiation, Eucharist, and the liturgy of the hours, than what actually appears.[50] At the same time, however, if the recognized normative authority of the *Apostolic Tradition* served as a catalyst for liturgical reform, that reform itself

[49] Peter Toon, "One Chapter of One Book, then let it be this. . . ." *Mandate* (June 2006): 13.
[50] See my "Can We Avoid Relativism in Worship? Liturgical Norms in the Light of Contemporary Liturgical Scholarship," *Worship* 74 (March 2000): 135–54.

did not slavishly follow that document in all its particulars. The Roman Rite, for example, did not really need the *Apostolic Tradition* in order to restore the adult catechumenate with its practice of scrutinies on the third, fourth, and fifth Sundays of Lent, with their accompanying *traditions* of the Creed and Our Father, leading to the culminating celebration of baptism, confirmation, and Eucharist at the Easter Vigil, followed by a period of mystagogy. The *Letter of John the Deacon to Senarius*, the *Gelasian Sacramentary*, and *Ordo Romanus XI* already provide an abundance of liturgical materials for Christian initiation in what is the undisputed initiatory tradition of the Church at Rome.[51] And, for that matter, even the preferred single postbaptismal confirmation anointing in the RCIA owes more to the liturgical evidence of the non-Roman, late fourth-century *Mystagogical Catecheses* of Cyril of Jerusalem[52] than it does to the *Apostolic Tradition*, and it is no secret that the current confirmation anointing formula itself, "Be sealed with the Gift of the Holy Spirit," was taken directly and deliberately from the Byzantine Rite.[53] Nor does the current Roman Eucharistic Liturgy, apart from its use of the *Apostolic Tradition* 4 in the composition of Eucharistic Prayer 2, depend on this document in the least. If anything, the current Roman Mass follows closely the overall structure of the seventh-century *Ordo Romanus primus*, a restoration of the Roman Eucharist closer to the time of Pope Gregory the Great in the early Middle Ages, together with diverse liturgical sources from the traditional Roman sacramentaries, including as well both Gallican-Mozarabic (Eucharistic Prayer 3) and Eastern sources (Eucharistic Prayer 4).

The *Apostolic Tradition*, then, may well have been viewed as demonstrating early forms of Roman liturgy, including Christian initiation, but this largely served merely to confirm for liturgical reformers the presumed antiquity and continuity of the Roman liturgical tradition with the earliest centuries. While that claim can

---

[51] For the pertinent texts of these documents in English see *DBL*, 208–51.

[52] Cyril (or John) of Jerusalem, *Myst. Cat.* 3.

[53] *The Rites of the Catholic Church*, vol. 1 (Collegeville, MN: Liturgical Press, 1990), 476–77.

no longer stand uncritically, the liturgical products of these reforms do not really stand or fall as much on the liturgical contents of that document as we have sometimes imagined them to do. The one possible exception here, of course, is the use of the ordination prayer for bishops now in the Roman Rite. But even here, Pope Paul VI's *Apostolic Constitution* approving the new Roman rites for the ordination of deacons, presbyters, and bishops defends the use of this episcopal ordination prayer not only because he believed that it "was written at the beginning of the third century" but also because it appears in West Syrian and Coptic ordination rites (though the text of the prayer in those documents is an expanded version of that text as it appears in the late fourth-century *Apostolic Constitutions* VIII).[54]

Several years ago, at the beginning stages of our research leading eventually to our commentary on the *Apostolic Tradition*, I said in a conversation with Jaroslav Pelikan that this document was not apostolic, and probably not early third century, Hippolytan, or Roman. Pelikan responded humorously to the effect that: "yes, but it might still be a tradition." And he was correct. For what contemporary liturgical reformers have done with this document is not all that far removed from how others viewed it as authoritative for use in their own liturgical compositions in the past. Clearly, the compilers of the *Apostolic Constitutions, Canons of Hippolytus*, and the *Testamentum Domini* found therein elements of a "liturgical tradition" well worth using, even if that meant changing things here and there to suit their own contextual liturgical and theological needs. In fact, these church orders are themselves necessary, along with the other sources of the *Apostolic Tradition*, in determining the very contents of that document in the first place. Similarly, the continued presence of elements from the *Apostolic Tradition* in later Eastern liturgical sources merely underscores its widespread influence there if not in the West.

---

[54] Paul VI, *Apostolic Constitution: Approval of New Rites for the Ordination of Deacons, Presbyters, and Bishops*, in *The Rites of the Catholic Church*, vol. 2 (New York: Pueblo, 1980), 45. See Paul Bradshaw, *Rites of Ordination: Their History and Theology* (Collegeville, MN: Pueblo, 2013), 185.

We saw earlier already that the eucharistic prayer was, in fact, used in the construction of other Eastern anaphoras in the fourth and fifth centuries. Such a process continued well into the Middle Ages, at least in the under-studied Ethiopian Rite where the *Ethiopian Anaphora of the Apostles*, which might be as late as a fourteenth-century composition, reflects clearly a synthesis of the eucharistic prayer of *Apostolic Tradition* 4 with another anaphoral pattern, quite probably Egyptian in overall structure.[55] Although there are several things we do not yet know about this prayer, including the time of its composition, the current shape and contents of this anaphora provide a concrete historical parallel to what we ourselves have done with the anaphora of *Apostolic Tradition* 4 within our own diverse liturgical traditions today. This demonstrates that the use made of *Apostolic Tradition* 4 in the current Roman tradition in its own composition of Eucharistic Prayer 2 is not decidedly different from what appears to have been done before, that is, the use of *Apostolic Tradition* 4 as a source in the construction of other anaphoral texts. Such an approach is in fact consistent with what *Apostolic Tradition* 9 says about liturgical prayer, i.e., that the anaphora itself was but a "model" for eucharistic praying rather than a normative text to be recited by the bishop.

Therefore, even without the presuppositions about this prayer and the entire *Apostolic Tradition* widely held by twentieth-century liturgical reformers as early third century, Roman, and Hippolytan (if not even apostolic), the text has commended itself throughout the ages as an anaphora worthy of liturgical use and adaptation—at least outside of Western Christianity. And if the Ethiopian

---

[55] Trans. from *The Liturgy of The Ethiopian Church*, trans. Marcos Daoud, rev. Marsie Hazen (Cairo: The Egyptian Book Press, 1959), 69–76. A critical edition of the Ethiopian text is in process by Reinhard Meßner and Martin Lang. See their study, "Ethiopian Anaphoras. Status and Tasks in Current Research Via an Edition of the Ethiopian Anaphora of the Apostles," in *Jewish and Christian Liturgy and Worship: New Insights into Its History and Interaction*, ed. Albert Gerhards and Clemens Leonhard, Jewish and Christian Perspectives 15 (Leiden/Boston: Brill, 2007), 185–206. The view of Meßner and Lang may have to be revised in the light of the Askumite Collection; see the essay by Emmanuel Fritsch in this volume.

Church in its *Anaphora of the Apostles* might adapt this prayer by integrating it into an overall Egyptian or Coptic anaphoral structure, there is no reason why the Roman Catholics cannot do the same with regard to the structure of the Roman canon, or why the rest of us can't use the text in diverse manners in our own liturgical books. The issue, like the use of the prayer for the ordination of bishops in the Roman Rite (noted above) is not whether the anaphora in *Apostolic Tradition* 4 is ancient or Roman, but whether it reflects what we believe theologically a eucharistic anaphora is to pray and proclaim today. Obviously many in the Christian East concluded from the fourth to the fourteenth centuries that it was surely appropriate theologically at various times to answer yes.

CONCLUSION

So, have contemporary liturgical historians, in "dethroning Hippolytus," actually called into question the twentieth-century liturgical reform by demonstrating that it was based on "sand and has now fallen apart, so that virtually all the major claims made on behalf of the new liturgies of the 1970s have no solid foundation?" Hardly! Yet that foundation is perhaps more appropriately viewed as theological and/or pastoral today rather than strictly historical. If at one time liturgical historians appeared to give normative and prescriptive judgments regarding the documents on which they worked, they do not work that way anymore. As I have noted elsewhere,[56] archeologists do not dig beneath the surface of sites where many generations of peoples have lived and expose the different layers of habitation in order to persuade humans today to return to the conditions of prehistoric dwellings. Nor are liturgical historians bent on excavating the various strata of the past in order to restore some sort of imaginary primitive purity to contemporary rites. The gradual development of liturgical practice involved the positive refinement and enrichment of earlier ways of thinking, speaking, and acting, even if it also tended to bring along with it elements

[56] See my "Introduction" to *Issues in Eucharistic Praying in East and West: Essays in Liturgical and Theological Analysis*, ed. Maxwell E. Johnson (Collegeville, MN: Liturgical Press/Pueblo, 2010), xiv–xv.

of impoverishment and distortion.[57] It is, however, only when we have a clearer picture of the stages of development that we are in a position to make any judgments about which of these trends were of genuine lasting value and which represented a loss of something significant from earlier times.

But it is not up to liturgical historians to reform the liturgy! All the liturgical historian can do is to unpack as carefully and clearly as possible the richness and diversity of the liturgical traditions as they actually appear in history. There may, indeed, be losses of significant elements from earlier times that should be restored. But that is not a judgment to be made by the liturgical historian. Rather, what legitimate liturgical authorities in the various churches do with the results of liturgical history in service to liturgical reform and renewal is something altogether distinct.

[57] See Paul F. Bradshaw, "The Homogenization of Christian Liturgy— Ancient and Modern: Presidential Address," *Studia Liturgica* 26 (1996): 1–15.

Liturgical Historiography and Gender Obliviousness

Re-Dressing an Imagined Past

Teresa Berger

The scholarly search for how gender differences have shaped liturgical practices is a contemporary quest. The writing of liturgical history before the mid-twentieth century was, for the most part, gender-oblivious. That is to say, it imagined a past in which gender differences had little relevance in what mattered both for the practice and for the study of worship. In what follows, I sketch the emergence of an alternative way of writing liturgical history, namely, one that makes gender-attentiveness an integral part of its scholarly inquiry. I situate this particular scholarly inquiry within larger historiographic shifts in the twentieth century. My overall aim is to render compelling a gender-attentive narrative of liturgy's past, not only as a historiographic imperative but also as a resource for our contemporary cultural context, in which new ways of both doing and theorizing gender have emerged with force. Although the history of the liturgy may at first glance seem an unlikely collaborator for contemporary concerns, the fact that gender differences have shaped liturgical life over centuries is important for today: rendering visible this genealogy in Christian worship has much to offer at a point in time when gender differences are sources of conflict in many ecclesial communities.

In order to comprehend how profoundly gender differences shaped and continue to shape Christian worship, one first has to recognize gender as an elemental marker of all liturgical practices.

Gender is such an elemental marker because the basic materiality of Christian worship is the bodily presence of worshippers. This bodily presence of worshippers is the primary object of inquiry, the "text" of liturgical studies. To date, however, this text of the worshippers' bodily presence has insufficiently been explored as gendered. (This claim does not pre-judge what kind of gendering processes are active at any given point in time. The claim does, however, assume that some form of gendering is present in all cultural formations.) Gender differences are occluded even in recent works explicitly dedicated to bodies at worship or to human beings as liturgical subjects.[1] The same occlusion has marked liturgical historiography until quite recently. Although gender differences were deeply inscribed into the very fabric of liturgical practices, liturgical history writing began to face this reality in earnest only in the second half of the twentieth century, largely following the emergence of broader gender-attentive historiographies. The development is worth sketching in some detail.

TWENTIETH-CENTURY MASTERS OF LITURGICAL HISTORIOGRAPHY

In the first half of the twentieth century, a number of distinct emphases emerged in the work of liturgical historiography. These emphases are largely connected with the names of a handful of great "masters" who shaped the field lastingly. Historical inquiry into the liturgical past had emerged in earnest during the nineteenth century, in tandem with broader cultural trends. Among these trends were the rising prominence of history writing overall, the growing importance of historical inquiry in ecclesial contexts, and the discovery and publication of a number of crucial early Christian texts. Liturgical historiography attended to its work with the standard historical, exegetical, and philological approaches of the time.

---

[1] See, for example, *Bodies of Worship: Explorations in Theory and Practice*, ed. Bruce T. Morrill, et al. (Collegeville, MN: Liturgical Press, 1999); and *Liturgical Subject: Subject, Subjectivity, and the Human Person in Contemporary Liturgical Discussion and Critique*, ed. James G. Leachman (Notre Dame, IN: University of Notre Dame Press, 2009).

One particularly influential mode of scholarly investigation of liturgy's past emerged with the work of Anton Baumstark (1872–1948) and his program of *liturgie comparée*, comparative liturgical historiography. Baumstark, a classical and oriental philologist, sought to elucidate liturgical developments by comparative analysis across ritual families, East and West. He possessed not only strong philological skills but also a keen interest in questions of methodology. One chapter in his *Comparative Liturgy*, for example, sought to describe "The Laws of Liturgical Evolution."[2] The influence of contemporary developments in evolutionary biology on Baumstark's thinking was marked.[3] Gender differences, on the other hand, were largely irrelevant in Baumstark's historiography (although by no means in his personal life[4]). For liturgical historiography in the twentieth century, Baumstark's theorizing of liturgical change—namely, in linear or evolutionist terms—came to have almost naturalizing power. A historical narrative was imagined whose unfolding required the identification of individual liturgical elements that became stepping stones for later progress.[5]

Evolutionary thinking also undergirded a liturgical historiography that focused on the in-depth analysis of one specific rite, seeking to explain how this rite came to have its present form.

---

[2] Anton Baumstark, *Liturgie comparée* (first published as a book in French in 1939). The English edition by F. L. Cross, *Comparative Liturgy*, is a translation of the third edition of the French book as revised by Bernard Botte (Westminster, MD: The Newman Press, 1958). I am here referring to chapter 2 of the English version of the book.

[3] See Fritz West, *The Comparative Liturgy of Anton Baumstark*, Alcuin Club/GROW Joint Liturgical Studies 31 (Bramcote: Grove Books, 1995).

[4] Baumstark was married, fathered fourteen children, and in 1935 resigned from his university post—despite his National Socialist commitments and party support—rather than face crushing evidence for his long-term homosexual practices. See Michael Grüttner, *Biographisches Lexikon zur nationalsozialistischen Wissenschaftspolitik* (Heidelberg: Synchron, 2004), 19, and Helmut Heiber, *Universität unterm Hakenkreuz*, Teil I: *Der Professor im Dritten Reich. Bilder aus der akademischen Provinz* (München: K. G. Saur, 1991), 465–72.

[5] For an analysis of the weaknesses of this linear model, see Nathan D. Mitchell's description of "Tree versus Crabgrass" in his *Meeting Mystery: Liturgy, Worship, Sacraments*, Theology in Global Perspective Series (Maryknoll, NY: Orbis Books, 2006), 6–22.

The preeminent exponent of this form of liturgical historiography was Josef Andreas Jungmann, SJ (1889–1975), best known for his magisterial *Missarum Solemnia* (1948). The author sought to offer a narrative of the evolution—the "genetic" development—of the Roman Mass. This historiography had a clear and present purpose, namely, the demonstration that the Mass had developed not only with continuity but also with much change. Such historicizing underwrote a progressive project, ultimately that of liturgical reform.[6] As with Baumstark, the material basis of Jungmann's analysis was almost exclusively that of liturgical texts, interpreted with the exegetical tools of his time, especially philological ones. Gender analysis obviously was not a scholarly tool available at the time (neither does gender analysis unleash its power most clearly when applied to liturgical texts in isolation). It is thus unsurprising that in the one thousand pages of *The Mass of the Roman Rite* women appeared but a dozen times, and mostly in passages that narrated their liturgical presence as problematic, marginal, or absent. Neither did men who were "only men" make much of an appearance in this liturgical historiography, nor were priests seen as having a gendered particularity of their own. Gender history would later reveal such (seemingly) ungendered histories of the liturgy as quite particular representations of the past. These histories were text- and event-centered institutional chronicles of male elites. Such history writing quite "naturally" bypassed liturgical sites that did not conform to the preestablished scholarly paradigm. In this way, liturgical historiography projected on the object studied what its own interpretive strategies and investigative procedures required: a narrative of liturgy's past largely untroubled by gender.

These interpretive strategies functioned with limited success, however, a pointer in and of itself to the power of gender in liturgy's past. One can after all not really write a history of the Eucharist—to name just one example—without confronting the fact that gender has been inscribed into its very celebration, if only through

[6] For more on this point, see Rudolf Pacik, "Josef Andreas Jungmann: Liturgiegeschichtliche Forschung als Mittel religiöser Reform," *Liturgisches Jahrbuch* 43 (1993): 62–84.

constraints on the gender of the presider. Indeed, as some studies had already intimated at the time, the historical narrative of eucharistic practices was profoundly shaped by gender differences. Peter Browe, SJ (1876–1949), for example, had studied rituals surrounding the celebration of Mass, from *viaticum* to eucharistic visions to magic practices involving hosts. Gender as a factor in these liturgical practices surfaced in Browe's work on the frequency of eucharistic reception among saintly women and men in the Middle Ages.[7] Browe had to confront the gender-specific unevenness of his sources at the outset of his study; he noted that while some information existed about women's reception of communion, there was little on the eucharistic reception of "men who were only men" (Thelma Fenster).[8] In other words, Browe's sources proved to be gender-asymmetric: the literature about saintly men was overwhelmingly about those who became priests and were thus noted for *presiding* at Mass, while other men remained largely invisible. Saintly women on the other hand did not preside at eucharistic celebrations, or at least were not narrated as such.[9] What the example of Peter Browe's work does show is that liturgical historiographies could attest the power of gender—even if that was not their intention. It is worth noting that Browe also wrote a book on "medieval sexual ethics," whose focus really was on gender-specific liturgical taboos and pollutions.[10] And in 1936, Browe published his research on the history of castration—only at first sight a seemingly arcane subject. Browe's history writing had a contemporary

[7] Peter Browe's disparate studies on the Eucharist have been edited in one volume, *Die Eucharistie im Mittelalter. Liturgiehistorische Forschungen in kulturwissenschaftlicher Absicht*, ed. Hubertus Lutterbach and Thomas Flammer, Vergessene Theologen 1 (Münster: LIT Verlag, 2003), see his essay "Die Kommunion der Heiligen im Mittelalter," 199–209, here 199f.

[8] See Thelma Fenster's "Why Men?," in *Medieval Masculinities: Regarding Men in the Middle Ages*, ed. Clare A. Lees, et al., Medieval Cultures 7 (Minneapolis, MN: University of Minnesota Press, 1994), ix–xiii, here x.

[9] Browe acknowledges the existence of female clerics in earlier centuries, ibid., 119, see n46.

[10] Peter Browe, *Beiträge zur Sexualethik des Mittelalters*, Breslauer Studien zur historischen Theologie 23 (Breslau: Verlag Müller & Seiffert, 1932).

purpose. He notes in the introduction recent legislation both in Nazi Germany and in North America(!) that allowed for the sterilization of certain parts of the population.[11] Browe's work is a stark reminder of how the historians' questions of the past are shaped, for better and for worse, by their own times.

Another example for the limited success of gender-oblivious liturgical historiography comes in the work of Dr. Josephine Mayer. Mayer, a teacher who was active in the liturgical movement and committed to expanding the roles of women in the Roman Catholic Church, focused her historiographic work in the 1930s on early Christian texts that witnessed to women's ministries as deaconesses, widows, and consecrated virgins. She edited a collection of these texts in 1938 in the series *Florilegium Patristicum*,[12] An essay of hers on women deacons, written for a broader audience, appeared in the same year in a prominent Catholic journal.[13] For Mayer too, her historiographic work was undertaken with a clear and present purpose: she concluded her studies of early Christian texts by advocating a restored diaconate for women, with a sacramental ordination no less.

Another influential approach to liturgical historiography in the twentieth century is linked to the name of an Anglican Benedictine monk and scholar Gregory Dix (1901–1952). In his vastly influential *The Shape of the Liturgy*, he sought to identify, in the eucharistic shape of the early church, a "standard or model" that could guide the liturgical reforms of the Church of England at the time.[14] His

---

[11] Peter Browe, *Die Geschichte der Entmannung. Eine religions- und rechtsgeschichtliche Studie*, Breslauer Studien zur historischen Theologie Neue Folge 1 (Breslau: Verlag Müller & Seiffert, 1936), 1.

[12] *Monumenta de viduis diaconissis virginibusque tractantia*, ed. Josephine Mayer, Florilegium Patristicum, Fasc. XLII (Bonn: Peter Hanstein Verlag, 1938). Mayer's work on early Christian women's ministries did not happen in a vacuum; there had been a flurry of publications related to the subject for at least two decades. Mayer credits in particular the work of Fr. Adolf Kalsbach (1888–1974) for her own work. Kalsbach had published his dissertation on the ministry of deaconesses in the early church in 1922.

[13] Josephine Mayer, "Vom Diakonat der Frau," *Hochland* 36 (1938/39): 98–108.

[14] Gregory Dix, *The Shape of the Liturgy*, with an introduction by Simon Jones to the 2005 edition (New York: Continuum, 2005), here 208.

basic methodological strategy was to move beyond a narrow focus on texts to an analysis of "ritual patterns."[15] It was in a common pattern or "shape," rather than verbal contents that Dix thought to locate the earliest, core, shared expression of Christian worship. As in Jungmann's work, in Dix's also, gender differences appeared to be irrelevant. Pouring over early Christian texts at roughly the same time as Josephine Mayer, Dix mentioned deaconesses only once in over seven hundred pages, and that merely in a discussion of ministerial headgear!

Before I turn to how these dominant ways of writing the history of the liturgy came under sustained scrutiny in the second half of the twentieth century, it is worth stressing that liturgical historiography always moved (and continues to move) in tandem with broader developments, including intellectual and cultural trends. Any sketch of the development and changes in liturgical history writing needs to attend carefully to this fact and render it visible as an integral part of all history writing rather than as accidental or in and of itself problematic.

CRITIQUING THE MASTERS' NARRATIVE

In the second half of the twentieth century, historical inquiry as a scholarly discipline erupted. Innovative and alternative ways of writing the past emerged, especially from the many variants of social history, whether the French Annales school, Marxist history, or local histories. What all these had in common was a critical analysis of conventional historiography. This historiography was faulted for its exclusionary focus on particular sites (elite institutions) and a few historic agents (elite or "hegemonic" males), a focus that had produced a host of historiographic occlusions, e.g., the men who were only men, women, non-elites, etc. The scholarly discipline of liturgical studies did not remain untouched by these developments in historiography, although in general it sought to maintain the strengths of earlier methodologies while nodding toward newer approaches. Change came slowly and through

---

[15] Ibid., xxix–xxxiii.

broader methodological shifts. Four of these shifts proved to be particularly important. The first concerns a broadening of the material object of historical analysis. The study of liturgy's past came to be seen as requiring more than the study of liturgical texts. A deepened appreciation of liturgy as a multitextured practice emerged, in which not only words but also material culture, bodies, voices, and instruments—to name just a few—played a role.

Writing a history of worship thus came to involve a study of practices rather than an analysis of liturgical texts alone. With this first shift, the narrow focus on elite (male) institutions and their textual productions was broken open, making room for more diverse liturgical agents. Second, liturgical texts themselves came to be read afresh, e.g., as a form of "living literature" with a quite complicated relationship to the past to which they witnessed. For example, a rubric forbidding women to baptize might now be read as pointing to an actual practice as much as to its envisioned ending. Third, the narrow (and at heart: early modern) boundedness of the term "liturgy" began to give way to an older, more comprehensive understanding of liturgical practices. This understanding included not only the key sacramental rites but also ecclesial rituals more broadly, among them processions, blessings, domestic liturgical practices, and feasts and fasts as these shaped everyday life.[16] Once again, both women and "men who were only men" became more easily visible through this shift. Lastly, the context of worship, that is its situated-ness in the material realities of lived life including particular social and cultural givens, increasingly came to the fore in liturgical scholarship. Here too, the importance of gender differences for liturgy's past became more readily visible, since gender codes are an elemental part of cultural context and formations.

None of the four shifts just described took place in liturgical historiography alone. On the contrary, these developments were fueled

---

[16] See, for example, C. Clifford Flanigan, "Liturgy as Social Performance: Expanding the Definitions," in *The Liturgy of the Medieval Church*, ed. Thomas J. Heffernan and E. Ann Matter (Kalamazoo, MI: Medieval Institute Publications, 2001), 695–714.

by wide-ranging shifts in intellectual knowledge production, especially by the twentieth-century anthropological and linguistic turns. For liturgical studies in the second half of the twentieth century this meant a definite broadening of scholarly tools of analysis. Fields and subfields from within the social sciences—such as cultural anthropology, semiotics, sociology, performance theory, ritual studies, and ethnography—began to supplement the more traditional ancillary disciplines of liturgical studies. In accordance with this trend, two newer histories of Christian worship self-identify as social histories.[17] Neither of them, however, employs gender as a category of historical analysis, although both seek to attend to women as liturgical agents. Tellingly, "men" as the relational "other" of women remain mostly invisible, as does the category gender itself.

ADDING WOMEN TO THE WORK OF LITURGICAL HISTORIOGRAPHY

Given all these developments in the field of history writing, what about gender analysis as a conversation partner for liturgical historiography? As regards the writing of history, second-wave feminist scholarship generated critical insights into the working of traditional historiography, a wealth of groundbreaking studies of women of the past, and a much greater visibility and recognition of particular women-identified historical sites (e.g., female convents). An interest in women's voices and feminist theory, as these emerged in the early 1970s, also found a place in liturgical studies, most prominently in its pastorally oriented work. The impact of women's history and feminist historiography on the writing of liturgical history was less pronounced.

Before I sketch this impact in more detail, a larger point needs to be made. It is this: To think that women began to make liturgical

[17] Martin D. Stringer, *A Sociological History of Christian Worship* (New York: Cambridge University Press, 2005); Frank C. Senn, *The People's Work: A Social History of the Liturgy* (Minneapolis, MN: Fortress Press, 2006). Robert Taft's work has also increasingly drawn on the interpretive strategies of social history, see for example his *Through Their Own Eyes: Liturgy as the Byzantines Saw It* (Berkeley, CA: InterOrthodox Press, 2006).

history only in the late 1960s would be a grave mistake. Such a misconception can only be sustained by limiting the critical engagement with liturgy to the practice of professional academic research. Reflections on and critical engagement with worship, however, are as old as the first Christian gatherings. These gatherings obviously included many women (although we know very little about these women's engagement with, never mind their reflections on, worship). Yet through the centuries, there are witnesses to women's reflections on liturgical practice, from Egeria's travelogue to the Holy Land in the late fourth century to the ninth-century Frankish noblewoman Dhuoda's written instructions on the recitation of the psalms; from Hildegard of Bingen and Teresa of Avila's rich reflections on liturgy to the work of Josephine Mayer in the 1930s on women deacons in the early church. The emergence of women's voices in liturgical studies in the second half of the twentieth century has to be seen within this larger trajectory. What was new was the fact that women, who had begun to enter the academy during the twentieth century, now also gained access to the scholarly discipline of liturgical studies. The first doctorate in liturgical studies at a Roman Catholic faculty, at least in Europe, came in 1965, when Irmgard Pahl defended her dissertation at the University of Munich. The importance of this moment reaches well beyond the entry of female bodies into a field of scholarly inquiry traditionally linked with priestly ordination and/or a religious vocation. This entry meant access to a particular material practice, with its own scholarly protocols and possibilities, including sustained access to libraries and archives, academic networks, employment opportunities, and professional status and voice. The beginnings of liturgical scholarship in conversation with women's history and feminist theory lie here.

A first witness, in print, to this conversation appeared in 1990 in a volume titled *Liturgie und Frauenfrage*.[18] Roughly half of the essays were dedicated to historical inquiries. The approach was

---

[18] *Liturgie und Frauenfrage. Ein Beitrag zur Frauenforschung aus liturgiewissenschaftlicher Sicht*, ed. Teresa Berger and Albert Gerhards, Pietas Liturgica 7 (St. Ottilien: EOS-Verlag, 1990).

basically one of "adding women" to the traditional history of liturgy's past. The volume combined this historiographic work with a clear and present vision. A second part focused on issues such as inclusive language, women in the lectionary texts, and images of women in the Masses for women saints. Two monographs soon followed which analyzed in depth two very different moments in liturgical history using the interpretive lenses of women's history. The magisterial study *Famula Dei* examined the liturgical lives of women's communities in Romano-Merovingian Gaul and showed that the center of daily life in these communities was a liturgy the women themselves shaped and celebrated under the liturgical presidency of their abbess.[19] *Liturgie und Frauenseele* focused on the early twentieth-century liturgical movement and investigated the (considerable) presence of women in this movement.[20] Six years later, in a turn to methodological questions, *Women's Ways of Worship* sought to introduce gender analysis more broadly to the study of liturgy's past, in order to bridge the growing rift between the conventional historical narrative and the ever-growing study of women's history. The subtitle of the book, *Gender Analysis and Liturgical History*, already laid claim to the broader field of gender studies, while the book's focus remained on one particular aspect of gender identity, namely, "women." Other work in this vein followed, for example, Susan White's *A History of Women in Christian Worship*.[21] The approach's importance is by no means exhausted for liturgical historiography. Katharine Harmon's recent book on women in the North American liturgical movement is a case

[19] See Gisela Muschiol, *Famula Dei. Zur Liturgie in merowingischen Frauenklöstern*, Beiträge zur Geschichte des alten Mönchtums und des Benediktinerordens 41 (Münster: Aschendorff, 1994).

[20] Teresa Berger, *"Liturgie und Frauenseele." Die Liturgische Bewegung aus der Sicht der Frauenforschung*, Praktische Theologie Heute 10 (Stuttgart: Kohlhammer Verlag, 1993).

[21] Susan J. White, *A History of Women in Christian Worship* (Cleveland, OH: The Pilgrim Press, 2003). Despite the grand title, the focus lies on post-Reformation, English-speaking, literate, North Atlantic, Protestant women.

in point.[22] Another, quite different witness to the importance of "adding women" to the historical narrative is the volume *Ancient Christian Worship* by Andrew McGowan. Seeking to integrate "social, historical, and theological" perspectives, McGowan weaves attention to the liturgical practices of early Christian women—or the glimpses that the sources offer—into his book as a whole.[23]

FROM "ADDING WOMEN" TO "DOING GENDER"

Gender theory emerged out of both the deepening insights and the increasing difficulties produced by the vibrant growth of women's studies and feminist scholarship; it now comprises a broad range of diverse and complex scholarly projects. With the emergence of gender history, analyses of sexual difference—that is: gender, gender systems, and gender hierarchies as these have marked the past—came alive.[24] The expansion and shift are usually linked to the beginnings of third-wave feminism. Influenced by postmodern, especially Foucauldian thought and the "linguistic turn," third-wave feminism moved away both from essentializing categories ("women's experience") and from meta-narratives ("women's oppression"), the weaknesses of which its own vibrant scholarship had rendered visible. Three new foci of analysis emerged and became critical to the workings of gender history. The first was an insistence on "difference." This insistence inscribed into the notion of gender the recognition that relational others are fundamental to the construction of a category in the first place. To put this con-

[22] Katharine E. Harmon, *There Were Also Many Women There: Lay Women in the Liturgical Movement in the United States, 1926–59* (Collegeville, MN: Liturgical Press, 2012).

[23] See Andrew B. McGowan, *Ancient Christian Worship: Early Church Practices in Social, Historical, and Theological Perspective* (Grand Rapids, MI: Baker Publishing Group, 2014). The index significantly underrepresents that attention.

[24] On gender history as a scholarly field of inquiry, see Claudia Opitz, *Um-Ordnungen der Geschlechter: Einführung in die Geschlechtergeschichte*, Historische Einführungen 10 (Tübingen: Edition Diskord, 2005), and Laura Lee Downs, *Writing Gender History, Writing History* (New York: Oxford University Press, 2004). Johanna Alberti, *Gender and the Historian* (New York: Longman, 2002) maps the writings of historians of women from the late 1960s to the turn of the century.

cretely: one cannot invoke "women" without acknowledging that its meaning is constituted by what women are not, namely, men. Difference, in other words, reigns in gendering processes. Not surprisingly, detailed analyses of gender differences—whether between women and men, or between men and women of differing sexualities, or of different genders beyond the traditional binary—became a dominant concern. These gender differences were acknowledged to be socially constructed. The older distinction between sex (as supposedly "natural" and based in biological fact) and gender (as culturally constructed) had been rendered unworkable. This was the case not least because the biological differentiation of the sexes came to be understood as more complex than a differentiation of two sexes.[25] As the seemingly natural category "women," which had anchored much of women's history, crumbled under the weight of evidence that the underlying binary division was neither universal nor stable but rather negotiated differently in different historical contexts, further fields of inquiry emerged. Obviously, feminist historiography itself did not simply stop with the emergence of gender theory. Rather, it fine-tuned its tools, usually along the theoretical lines of gender theory, with the subject matter continuing to be a particular female gendering process (e.g., adolescent girls, or lesbian women).[26] Among the newly emerging fields, the most prominent were the study of masculinities, sexuality studies, and queer theory.

The study of masculinities is the most obvious complement to women's studies, especially in the field of history. Traditional historiography, which had already come under criticism for its women-specific blind spots, was now seen as also occluding the "millions of men who were only men."[27] The study of masculinities began to focus on these occluded subjects. From this search for the histories of "non-hegemonic males" the study of masculinities has

[25] For more on this see Anne Fausto-Sterling, *Sexing the Body: Gender Politics and the Construction of Sexuality* (New York: Basic Books, 2000), 51–54.

[26] The field has been mapped well in a reader; see *The Feminist History Reader*, ed. Sue Morgan (New York: Routledge, 2006).

[27] Fenster, "Why Men?"

evolved into an inquiry into all the manifold historical formations of masculinity. The Christian tradition, with its own formations of masculine identities, has been a quite fertile field of inquiry.[28] Sexuality studies emerged out of a different, although related, recognition, namely, that a person's gender and a person's sexual practices are not necessarily coterminous. This scholarly field of inquiry consequently focused on sexual desires and *practices* rather than on gender-identified labels. It has produced a wealth of studies, many of which are dedicated to nondominant sexualities and cultures—e.g., gay, bisexual, or intersexed—without however leaving hetero-normative sexualities unmarked.[29] Queer theory, usually linked in one way or another with the 1990 publication of Judith Butler's book *Gender Trouble*, emerged in the challenge to, and the undoing of, the distinction between sex as a stable biological reference point and gender as a cultural construct. For Butler, all gender identities were constructed in performance, and for those who followed in her footsteps, "doing gender" became the signpost for the scholarly inquiry into fundamentally unstable gender identities. Queer theory as it emerged from these roots has been committed particularly to alternative performances of gender identity, which challenge what has been constructed as (hetero-) normative. The term has, however, also expanded in meaning and can now refer more broadly to nonconventional readings of gendered practices.

So much for the focus on gender *differences* as it came to the forefront in gender history. The other two foci, briefly, are the insistence on intersectionality and the emphasis on an oppositional understanding of power in gender relations. The insistence on "intersectionality" focused attention on the interrelatedness of various markers of difference such as gender, social class, ethnicity, and age. The emphasis on an oppositional understanding of power

---

[28] For an overview, see the reader *Men and Masculinities in Christianity and Judaism: A Critical Reader*, ed. Björn Krondorfer (London: SCM Press, 2009).

[29] A good overview is provided by Robert A. Nye, "Sexuality," in *A Companion to Gender History*, ed. Teresa A. Meade and Merry E. Wiesner-Hanks, Blackwell Companions to History (Malden, MA: Blackwell Publishing, 2004), 11–25.

first emerged in Joan W. Scott's seminal essay "Gender: A Useful Category of Analysis," in which the author famously described gender as a "primary way of signifying relationships of power."[30] Scott's claim inscribed into gender analysis a basically oppositional understanding of power in gender hierarchies. This understanding has since been critiqued on the basis that gender is not always and everywhere practiced in oppositional binaries.[31]

THE TASK OF GENDERING LITURGICAL HISTORY WRITING

How can this complex field of gender history be brought to bear on the writing of liturgy's past? The key challenge and the main task here are to write gender back into the "facts" of liturgical history. What is construed as the facts of the past is after all theory-specific—that is to say, dependent on the kind of questions asked of witnesses to the past. Highlighting gender in the questions asked is not about discarding the writing of liturgical history to date but about "un-dressing" its gender-oblivious narrative and that narrative's explanatory and authorizing power. Methodologically, such reconfiguration happens by bringing the tools of gender history to the discipline of liturgical historiography. Two steps stand out, familiar from other scholarly disciplines that have effectively gendered their historiographic work. First, the traditional interpretive strategies that have informed the writing of liturgical history have to become the subject of critical analysis. Critical questions must be raised about traditional liturgical historiography and its explanatory power: What is occluded in this history writing, given that what comes to be authorized as facts of liturgical history is always theory-specific? What assumptions about gender (or the unimportance of gender) are written into the liturgical record as we know it? How has gender-oblivion shaped our image of liturgy's past? These questions help to destabilize the

[30] Joan Wallach Scott, "Gender: A Useful Category of Historical Analysis," *American Historical Review* 91 (1986): 1053–75, here 1067.

[31] See Jeanne Boydston, "Gender as a Question of Historical Analysis," *Gender and History* 20 (2008): 558–83.

givenness of inherited ways of writing liturgical history and to ask what has been occluded or rendered unintelligible in such history writing. The second step in restoring gender to liturgical history follows from this. If a critical engagement with the interpretive strategies that produced the traditional narrative is the first step, then the second is to reconceive the narrative of the past in more nuanced, gender-attentive ways. For such a "re-dressing" of liturgy's past, a set of methodological principles and interpretive strategies is needed, based on the insights of gender history and now to be put to work for the writing of liturgy's past. In many ways, principles earlier identified for the writing of women's liturgical history continue to be applicable here. I am thinking in particular of an expanded set of sources, a broadened understanding of what constitutes liturgical sites, and a fresh look at conventional periodizations.[32] The one methodological principle that demands more sustained attention, not surprisingly, is the understanding of gender itself. As will be obvious from the sketch of the development from women's history to gender history above, the category gender needs, first, to be freed from primarily meaning women, and, second, unmoored from dominantly signifying binary gender models.

First, gender is not a synonym for women. Gender difference is nothing if not a relational category, and it has to be displayed as such. In terms of the writing of liturgical history, for example, not only women but also "men who were only men" have been written out of this history. Traditional liturgical historiography with its attention to elite males and their textual productions rendered invisible not only women but also millions of "men who were only men." A gender-attentive liturgical historiography, then, cannot leave men's cultures unmarked and invisible, as if women alone were gendered. In fact, gender history can never treat "women" as if that category can stand on its own and was not constituted by its relational other, men.

---

[32] See Teresa Berger, *Women's Ways of Worship: Gender Analysis and Liturgical History* (Collegeville, MN: Liturgical Press, 1999), 5–26.

The second point elaborates the previous point. Gender applies not only to masculinity and femininity but also to all gendering processes and identities, including those that subdivide one of the sides of the traditional binary, e.g., virgins and widows, or those that defy the binary, as intersexed persons do. A gender-attentive rereading of the liturgical past thus will have to attend to, for example, the presence of eunuchs in Byzantium or castrati singers in the West, and how holy virgins and celibate priests embodied gendering processes that complicate a simple binary notion of gender. Attention as to how all gendered identities such as these intersect with liturgical life reveals a liturgical past much more intricate than one shaped exclusively by two sides of an oppositional binary, men and women.

All this goes to say that gender is not a stable universal. Rather, gendering processes are invariably complex, configured differently in diverse historical places and times. The importance of intersectionality is worth repeating here. Gender never stands alone but is always inflected by other markers of difference, such as ethnicity and race, age, and ecclesial affiliation, to name just a few. Moreover, the lived experience of gender is forever shifting, as the human body is transformed by the life cycle and its cultural codes. In restoring gender to the writing of liturgy's past, one therefore has to assume multiple constructions of gender and gendering processes. The task, then, is to historicize, not to essentialize, gender differences as these mark liturgical practices. This set of methodological principles can guide the re-dressing of liturgical history writing in gender-attentive garb. I have offered an example of such work in my 2011 book *Gender Differences and the Making of Liturgical History*.[33] The invitation expressed in this book to others to take up this scholarly labor still stands. Much remains to be done. For this essay, however, the time has come to turn to our own times.

---

[33] See Teresa Berger, *Gender Differences and the Making of Liturgical Tradition: Lifting a Veil on Liturgy's Past*, Ashgate Liturgy, Worship and Society Series (Burlington, VT: Ashgate, 2011).

I claimed at the outset of this essay that gender-attentiveness in liturgical history writing ultimately gestures toward more than the past alone. That is to say, making gender a critically important set of questions for liturgical historiography is not solely about liturgy's imagined past. There is also a contemporary ecclesial commitment embedded in the endeavor to re-dress the occlusions of conventional historiography. Rendering visible the complex ways in which liturgical life has always been shaped by changing gender constructions opens a much-needed space for nuanced reflections in a world where gender differences continue to be alive and well in worship. The workings of gender trouble are evident across a broad spectrum of ecclesial communities today. This fact is related, at least in part, to the crumbling of traditional gender systems in most cultures over the last century. The development has deeply affected all cultural practices, those of Christian worship included. Some churches, for example, have now authorized rituals for the blessing of same-sex unions, largely following the growing cultural acceptance of same-sex marriages in Europe and North America. Other churches are ordaining openly transgender priests, also following in the footsteps of a widening cultural visibility of transgender lives. The largest Christian churches worldwide (Roman Catholic and Eastern Orthodox, as well as the Oriental churches) continue to maintain the nonordination of women yet find this position increasingly hard to render intelligible in today's world. A few faith communities aim for more "masculine" worship experiences so as to counter a perceived feminization of worship that they see expressed, for example, in the preponderance of "girly" worship songs. At the same time, feminist concerns over liturgical language continue to mark some communities, while others are now working on making their worship services more welcoming for those with nonbinary gender identities. Even where gender is not a visible troublemaker in Christian worship, its power continues to hide in plain sight. Some churches rooted in more traditional contexts retain spatial arrangements in the sanctuary that separate women and men. On the other side of the ecclesial spectrum are contemporary high-tech evangelical worship services that are buoyed by a phenomenon aptly described as "boys and their worship toys."[34] Clearly, the workings of gender in Christian worship today span a broad spectrum of quite dissimilar features. These dissimilarities are mostly rooted in widely divergent temporalities of ecclesial life and cultural context. At the core of these dissimilar features, however, lies one reality, namely, that worship as an embodied and therefore gendered practice takes place within specific cultural contexts and their particular gender systems, codes, and hierarchies.

What a gender-attentive narrative of liturgy's past offers to the present is a genealogy for contemporary struggles and questions. This genealogy comes clothed as a liturgical history filled with gender differences as both a fundamental given and also constantly deliberated. Unearthing the contours of this genealogy is a vital task for historians of liturgy as well as a compelling project in service of the church's life and witness today.

[34] James Fenimore, "Boys and Their Worship Toys: Christian Worship Technology and Gender Politics," Journal of Religion, Media and Digital Culture 1, no. 1 (2012), http://jrmdc.com/papers/boys-and-their-worship-toys -christian-worship-technology-and-gender-politic/.

Part 3

Liturgy's Past/s: Broadening the View

Gregorian Chant's Imagined Past, with Yet Another Look at the Roman Lenten Repertoire

Harald Buchinger

The Second Vatican Council's *Constitution on Sacred Liturgy* asserts that "the Church acknowledges Gregorian chant as distinctive of the Roman liturgy; therefore, other things being equal, it should be given pride of place in liturgical services."[1] Despite all efforts, in 1963 only quixotics could seriously believe in a universal renaissance of Gregorian chant, and in fact such a project was a quite recent phenomenon: the council's statement came only sixty years after Pius X's programmatic motu proprio *Tra le sollecitudini* on sacred music and one hundred years after the first appearance of a critically restored Roman chant book, though at that point only on private initiative. Both the scholarly investigation and the performance of chant have ever since gone along with a generous dose of imagination, and since reconstructions of the past often

---

[1] *Sacrosanctum Concilium* 116; English translation: *Documents on the Liturgy 1963–1979: Conciliar, Papal, and Curial Texts* (Collegeville, MN: Liturgical Press, 1982), 24. Fundamental for every study of Gregorian chant is David Hiley, *Western Plainchant: A Handbook* (Oxford: Clarendon, 1993), with comprehensive bibliographies; for a reduced but updated introduction, see Hiley, *Gregorian Chant*, Cambridge Introductions to Music (Cambridge: Cambridge University Press, 2009); for an extremely succinct outline, Harald Buchinger, "Gregorianik: Das Kernrepertoire," in *Der Gottesdienst und seine Musik*, vol.1: *Grundlegung: Der Raum und die Instrumente. Theologische Ansätze. Hymnologie: Die Gesänge des Gottesdienstes*, ed. Albert Gerhards and Matthias Schneider, Enzyklopädie der Kirchenmusik 4/1 (Laaber: Laaber, 2014), 133–52.

were guided by a vision for the future, a historical inquiry is not a mere retrospective, but a contribution to ideology critique.

After a brief résumé of the presuppositions underlying modern ecclesial legislation of the Roman Catholic Church, a second section will recapitulate how an imagined past of Gregorian chant served its implementation in the early Middle Ages. The last—and most detailed—part of this essay shall investigate traces of a tension between imagination and reality within the core repertoire itself: it appears that even at the time when the Mass proper was redacted, substantial components did not match the actual conditions of their liturgical context.

PART 1: IMAGINING CHANT'S FUTURE: PRESUPPOSITIONS OF MODERN RESTORATION AND ECCLESIAL LEGISLATION

Sanctioning Modern Practice or Reviving Medieval Tradition? The Controversial Restoration of Gregorian Chant

The restoration of Gregorian chant is a project of nineteenth-century historicism. Though some forms of Latin liturgical monody were maintained in many places, even in reformed contexts, until the end of the Old Order after the French Revolution, the dissolution of the Holy Roman Empire with its ecclesial institutions in the wake of the Napoleonic wars, and the secularization in the last decade of the eighteenth and the first decade of the nineteenth centuries, restoration of medieval chant was an attempt at reanimating a virtually extinct practice, which could hardly tie up to continuous use, and if so, only to a profoundly transformed shape.[2]

---

[2] On the *Graduale de tempore juxta ritum Sacrosanctae Romanae Ecclesiae* (Rome: Medicaea, 1614); *Graduale de sanctis . . .* (Rome: Medicaea, 1614) (repr. ed. Giacomo Baroffio, Manlio Sodi, and Eun Ju Kim, Monumenta Studia Instrumenta Liturgica 10–11 ([Vatican City: Vaticana, 2001]), see Raphael Molitor, *Die nach-tridentinische Choral-Reform zu Rom. Ein Beitrag zur Musikgeschichte des XVI. und XVII. Jahrhunderts*, 2 vols. (Leipzig: Leuckart, 1901–1902 [repr. Hildesheim: Olms, 1967]); Theodore Karp, *An Introduction to the Post-Tridentine Mass Proper*, part 1: *Text*; part 2: *Music Examples*, Musicological Studies & Documents 54 (Middleton, WI: American Institute of Musicology, 2005). The post-medieval history of the Gregorian Office chant has not yet been written;

Renewed interest in medieval, especially Roman, liturgy arose in the context of Restauration and ultramontanism;[3] it took much of its motivation from historicism and romantic interest in medievalism, and it went along, on the one hand, with pedagogical and popularizing Enlightenment concerns that ultimately would lead to the plea for active participation and, on the other hand, with the rise of critical methods of modern philological and historical sciences.

Although partially restored chant books were published in France toward the middle of the century, it was not before 1863 that a somewhat critical edition of a gradual by Michael Hermesdorff, music director of the cathedral of Treves, appeared; in its second edition it was even complemented with neumes.[4] It is well known that the following decades were dominated by a fierce struggle between two parties that represent different models of nineteenth-century Catholicism: on the one hand, conservative Bavarians centered in Regensburg mistook the appearance of post-Tridentine Catholicism for the Tradition of the Church and fought successfully for the *Editio Medicaea* of 1614/15; in 1868, the publisher Friedrich Pustet earned a thirty-year pontifical privilege for printing an update of this modern edition[5] that had its melodies profoundly revised according to the taste of the time by students of Giovanni Pierluigi da Palestrina.[6]

On the other hand, the proponents of a restoration of melodies according to the oldest available sources, headed by the monks of

---

at least in many convents, medieval books or their copies appear to have remained in use for a long time.

[3] Katherine Bergeron, *Decadent Enchantments: The Revival of Gregorian Chant at Solesmes*, California Studies in Nineteenth-Century Music (Berkeley, CA: University of California Press, 1998).

[4] Michael Hermesdorff, *Graduale juxta usum Ecclesiae Cathedralis Trevirensis dispositum . . .* (Trier: Grach, 1863); Hermesdorff, *Graduale ad normam cantus S. Gregorii . . .* (Trier: Grach, 1876–1882). On earlier liturgico-/musico-political, scholarly, and practical endeavors, especially in France, see Hiley, *Western Plainchant*, 622f.

[5] *Graduale de tempore et de sanctis juxta ritum Sacrosanctae Romanae Ecclesiae* (Regensburg: Pustet, 1871).

[6] See above, n2.

Solesmes, collected, compared, and in part edited key manuscripts;[7] their efforts culminated in the Vatican edition of 1908, the melodies of which have since remained normative. Encouraged by Vatican II's *Sacrosanctum Concilium* 117, however, several grassroots initiatives of the last decades have provided elements of a "more critical" edition, the principles of which remain disputed, since controversial visions of the origin and history of Gregorian chant are implied.[8]

"The Distinctive Chant of the Roman Liturgy": Explicit Assertions and Implicit Assumptions

In addition to an undifferentiated application of the term "Gregorian" to various genres of Office and Mass, sometimes including even dialogues and acclamations, ecclesial legislation of the twentieth century has been led by anachronistic convictions: (1) the designation as "Gregorian" conveys an attribution of the composition or redaction to Pope Gregory the Great (which in some documents is depicted in detail[9]), thus claiming (2) late antique Roman origin not only of the texts but also of the melodies. The ultimate goal of its promotion is (3) universal use, which implies (4) its suitability also for small settings such as parishes (even in rural contexts[10]), wherefore (5) prospective clerics "from their

[7] Pierre Combe, *The Restoration of Gregorian Chant: Solesmes and the Vatican Edition* (Washington, DC: The Catholic University of America Press, 2003); originally published as *Historie de la Restauration du Chant Grégorien* (Solesmes: Abbaye, 1969).

[8] Andreas Pfisterer, "Ziele und Methoden in der Geschichte der Choralrestauration," *Beiträge zur Gregorianik* 49 (2010): 61–74. The efforts documented in *Beiträge zur Gregorianik* since vol. 21 (1996) led to the improved yet still disputable *Graduale novum. Editio magis critica . . .* vol. 1: *De dominicis et festis*, ed. Christian Dostal and others (Regensburg: Con Brio; Vatican City: Vaticana, 2011).

[9] Pius XI, *Divini cultus sanctitatem*, prologue (1928), *Acta Apostolicae Sedis* 21 (1929): 36; translated by Robert F. Hayburn in *Papal Legislation on Sacred Music 95 A.D. to 1977 A.D.* (Collegeville, MN: Liturgical Press, 1979), 329: "In the shrine of the Lateran . . . Gregory the Great, after collecting and adding to the monumental musical legacy of the Fathers, had so wisely established his great Schola to perpetuate the true interpretation of liturgical chant."

[10] Pius X, *Tra le sollecitudini* 8, 27 (1903), *Acta Sanctae Sedis* 36 (1903–1904): 338f.; translated by Hayburn, *Papal Legislation*, 230f.

earliest years are to be taught Gregorian Chant."[11] For this purpose, Dom André Mocquereau (1849–1930)—though originally a zealous promoter of paleographical studies—created the "Solesmes method," which would afford execution by non-specialists;[12] his admirer Justine Ward (1879–1975) extended the goal to children.[13] Gregorian chant was imagined as a universal sound mark of the Roman tradition; its promotion was directed by a claim for uniformity to an extent that even in Catholicism never had become effective before the nineteenth century, when most of the remaining local usages, especially in France and Germany, were replaced by the Roman Rite. As late as 1955, Pius XII decreed in his encyclical *Musicae sacrae disciplina* that

> if in Catholic churches throughout the entire world Gregorian chant sounds forth without corruption or diminution, the chant itself, like the sacred Roman liturgy, will have a characteristic of universality, so that the faithful, wherever they may be, will hear music that is familiar to them and a part of their own home. In this way they may experience, with much spiritual consolation, the wonderful unity of the Church. This is one of the most important reasons why the Church so greatly desires that the Gregorian chant traditionally associated with the Latin words of the sacred liturgy be used.

Everything else was deemed "quite definite exceptions."[14] In a certain sense and apart from the peculiarities of modern curial diction, such claims and the underlying views are ultimately taken in by Carolingian ideology.

---

[11] *Divini cultus sanctitatem* 1, *Acta Apostolicae Sedis* 21 (1929): 36f. Translated by Hayburn, *Papal Legislation*, 329; implicitly cf. already Pius X, *Tra le sollecitudini* 8, 27 (as in n10).

[12] André Mocquereau, *Le nombre musical grégorien ou rythmique grégorienne. Théorie et pratique* 2 vols. (Rome: Desclée, 1908; 1927).

[13] Dom (Pierre M.) Combe, *Justine Ward and Solesmes* (Washington, DC: The Catholic University of America Press, 1987); Justine Ward, *Music Fourth Year: Children's Manual Gregorian Chant According to the Principles of Dom André Mocquereau*, Catholic Education Series (Washington, DC: Catholic Education, 1923).

[14] *Musicae sacrae disciplina* 3, *Acta Apostolicae Sedis* 48 (1956): 16. Translation by Hayburn, *Papal Legislation*, 351, § 45f.

PART 2: IMAGINING CHANT'S PAST: THE MAKING OF "GREGORIAN" CHANT

A Multi-Media Strategy: Promoting "Gregorian" Chant in the Early Middle Ages

Egbert, archbishop of York from 735 to 766, apparently first recurs to customs that "our teacher, blessed Gregory, in his antiphoner and Mass-book transmitted in order and script (or: in orderly and written form) through our preceptor, blessed Augustine"; he even claims to have seen the respective books in Rome.[15] Although caution is demanded by the apparent bias of the text and the general bond of the Anglo-Saxon church to Pope Gregory, Egbert's claim is not totally absurd, since he was ordained deacon in Rome. Whatever the case, from the later eighth century, it became very common to attribute both the chant book and the sacramentary of the papal liturgy to Gregory;[16] corresponding prologues were attached to the "Gregorian" sacramentary, as it was therefore called, and to a number of chant books.[17] Details of these texts may point to non-Roman origins (when Gregory is addressed "Roman pope") and be anachronistic (especially when the *schola cantorum* is mentioned), and, indeed, all of these manuscripts were written centuries after Gregory and outside of Rome in order to promote the acceptance of the Roman liturgy beyond the area of its original use. Though it has been hypothesized that originally Gregory

[15] *De institutione catholica dialogus* 16, Patrologia Latina 89, 441 B; C / *Councils and Ecclesial Documents Relating to Great Britain and Ireland*, vol. 3, ed. Arthur West Haddan and William Stubbs (Oxford: Clarendon, 1871), 411f.

[16] References in Harald Buchinger, "Gregor der Große und die abendländische Liturgiegeschichte: Schlüssel- oder Identifikationsfigur?," in *Psallite sapienter. A 80 éves Béres György köszöntése / Festschrift zum 80. Geburtstag von Georg Béres*, ed. István Verbényi (Budapest: Szent István Társulat, 2008), 113–54, see esp. 136–38.

[17] Bruno Stäblein, "'Gregorius Praesul', der Prolog zum römischen Antiphonale. Buchwerbung im Mittelalter," in *Musik und Verlag. Karl Vötterle zum 65. Geburtstag am 12. April 1968*, ed. Richard Baum and Wolfgang Rehm (Kassel: Bärenreiter, 1968), 537–61; James McKinnon, "Gregorius presul composuit hunc libellum musicae artis," in *The Liturgy of the Medieval Church*, ed. Thomas J. Heffernan and E. Ann Matter, Medieval Institute Publications (Kalamazoo, MI: Western Michigan University Press, 2001), 673–94.

II (715–731) may have been referred to,[18] the Carolingians clearly thought of the Pope Gregory the Great (590–604).

The later ninth century even furnished an etiological legend: in the latest of several vitae of Gregory, John the Deacon († 880/882), traveler between Rome and the Carolingian court, narrates in detail how his hero ordered stational liturgy, redacted sacramentary and lectionary, and took care of the book and the institutions for the cultivation of Roman chant:

> After the manner of the most wise Solomon, the exceedingly diligent Gregory, motivated by the compunction of musical sweetness, compiled a centonate antiphoner of chants, a task of great usefulness. He also founded the *schola cantorum*, which still sings in the holy church of Rome according to its original instructions. And he built two dwellings for the *schola*, with the proceeds from some plots of land: one near the steps of the basilica of St. Peter the Apostle, and another near the lodgings of the Lateran palace, where even today are preserved with fitting reverence, the bed on which Gregory lay while singing, the switch with which he threatened the boys, as well as the authentic antiphoner.[19]

The etiological goal and the ideological context of this hagiographical narration are all the clearer since the earlier lives of Gregory are absolutely silent about any liturgical activity. John also tells that he was familiar with the iconography of the dove, which the deacon Peter is quoted as having seen above Gregory's head,[20] though he does not yet apply it to the inspiration of the pope's liturgical activity.

In fact, at exactly the same time, around 870, the first examples of sacramentaries that use this iconography in their author's

---

[18] Stäblein, *Gregorius Praesul*, 552; McKinnon, *Gregorius presul*, 690–92.

[19] *S. Gregorii Magni Vita* 2, 6, Patrologia Latina 75, 90 C. Translation by James McKinnon in *Source Readings in Music History*, ed. Oliver Strunk, rev. Leo Treitler, vol. 2: *The Early Christian Period and the Latin Middle Ages*, ed. James McKinnon (New York: Norton, 1998), 69. On the anachronistic character of this account, see the literature quoted below in n50.

[20] *Vita* 4, 69, Patrologia Latina 75, 222 A.

depiction occur[21]—the Carolingian propagation of Roman liturgy was supported by a multimedia effort that continued well into later centuries; the oldest extant fully notated Office antiphoner, the famous codex of Hartker, St. Gall, Stiftsbibliothek 390 (ca. 1000), legitimates not only the text but also the music itself by delineating its descent from the inspired pope in word and image.[22]

Imagination became even more suggestive when from the tenth century on another level was added to the advertising strategy: the prologue of the antiphoner did not remain a metaliturgical text, but was set to music and sung as a trope before the first piece of "this little book of musical art," which "Gregory composed for the schola cantorum according to the circle of the year": the introit of the first Sunday of Advent.[23]

These concentrated efforts yielded considerable success: the spread of "Gregorian" chant from Sicily to Norway and from the Atlantic coast to the eastern confines of Latin influence certainly is one of the most impressive achievements of cultural history, although one has to regret that it was accomplished at the cost of an extensive eradication of non-Roman Western chant repertoires. For more than a millennium, at least the texts of "Gregorian" chant remained normative in most of occidental Christianity.[24]

---

[21] Sacramentary of Charles the Bald, Paris, Bibliothèque nationale Ms. lat. 1141, ca. AD 870, fol. 3r (http://gallica.bnf.fr/ark:/12148/btv1b53019391x/f15. item); A. Thomas, "Gregor I. der Große," *Lexikon der christlichen Ikonographie* 6 (1974): 432–41, esp. 434.

[22] P. 13, opposite the prologue, http://www.e-codices.unifr.ch/de/doubleview /csg/0390/13/.

[23] Stäblein, *Gregorius Praesul*, esp. 548f., nos. 7 and 10; pp. 556–61. The Italian trope *Sanctissimus namque Gregorius* appears also in the 1908 Vatican edition of the Graduale Romanum.

[24] The great number of polyphonic compositions on the quasi-canonical texts of the Mass and Office proper certainly betrays its importance for Western cultural history of many centuries; vernacular contrafacta also illustrate the popularity of certain pieces. Nevertheless, it would certainly be a rewarding field of historical research to investigate the factual impact of Gregorian chant beyond a small elite whose spirituality was shaped by Latin liturgy (the possibly most interesting sources of lay spirituality, the Books of Hours, contain only a little choice of the liturgical diet, deprived of its melodic shape). A medieval counterpart of Ramsay MacMullen's—however controversial—*Second*

Between the Extremes: Elements of a Historical Reality Check

The Time Frame: Mid-Fifth to Mid-Eighth Centuries

There are very little really firm historical data for the creation of the Roman Mass proper.[25] Since its received musical forms and elaborate style clearly are unsuitable for popular use and require trained specialists, the *terminus post* definitely is Leo I (440–461), who attests congregational participation in psalmody, most likely by singing a refrain;[26] perhaps this psalmody as such was not introduced at all into Roman liturgy until Celestine I (422–432).[27]

Church: Popular Christianity A.D. *200–400*, Society of Biblical Literature Writings from the Greco-Roman World Supplement Series 1 (Atlanta: Society of Biblical Literature, 2009), waits to be written; but see Arnold Angenendt, *Geschichte der Religiosität im Mittelalter* (Darmstadt: Primus, ³2005 = 2nd rev. ed. 2000 [¹1997]).

[25] The case of the Office is much more difficult: manuscripts occur only later, their content is much more disparate, and creativity continued through the whole Middle Ages and beyond. In turn, it is not clear if continuity of the transmitted forms (especially the practice of alternate psalmody and the concrete shape and use of antiphons) goes back behind the Carolingian era; among the most recent contributions, see Michel Huglo, "Recherches sur la psalmodie alternée à deux chœurs," *Revue Bénédictine* 116 (2006): 352–66, and Andreas Pfisterer, "Überlegungen zur Frühgeschichte der Psalmodie," in *Theorie und Geschichte der Monodie 4. Bericht der Internationalen Tagung Wien 2006*, ed. Martin Czernin and Maria Pischlöger (Brno: Tribun, 2012), 429–37, with references to the earlier bibliography. The dominance of the Roman psalter (and not the Gallican version of the Vulgate) in antiphons taken from the book of Psalms at least suggests pre-Carolingian origin.

[26] Tractatus 3, in *Sancti Leonis Magni . . . Tractatus*, ed. Antonius Chavasse, Corpus Christianorum, Series Latina 138 (Turnhout: Brepols, 1973), 10: Ps 109 (110):4; the verse is used as gradual responsory in the later Roman Mass antiphoner on feasts of popes: *Antiphonale Missarum Sextuplex*, ed. René-Jean Hesbert (Rome: Herder, 1985 = Brussels: Vromant, 1935), 236: Index s. v. *Juravit Dominus*.

[27] The interpretation of *Liber pontificalis* 1, 45, ed. L. Duchesne, Bibliothèque des Écoles Françaises d'Athènes et de Rome (Paris: de Boccard, 1981 = 1955), 88f.; 230, is controversial: Peter Jeffery, "The Introduction of Psalmody into the Roman Mass by Pope Celestine I (422–432): Reinterpreting a Passage in the *Liber Pontificalis*," *Archiv für Liturgiewissenschaft* 26 (1984): 147–65; Joseph Dyer, "*Psalmi ante sacrificium* and the Origin of the Introit," *Plainsong and Medieval Music* 20 (2011): 91–121.

Absolute *terminus ante* is the import of Roman chant into the Carolingian realm under Pepin III (751/752–768) in the 750s;[28] not much later the first manuscripts occur.[29] The astonishing stability,[30] with the almost perfect liturgical concordance and the textual agreement of Frankish and (later) Roman manuscripts in the core of their repertoire,[31] demonstrates that the texts and their liturgical order that were disseminated in the wake of the Carolingian reform are to be identified with the repertoire that was taken over from Rome.[32] Further corroboration comes from the use of the Roman psalter version instead of the "Gallican" Vulgate, which became the norm under the Carolingians,[33] and from other non-Vulgate elements in the chant texts.[34]

That the Bible version was not substituted in the reception process is a strong argument for the supposition that the texts were

---

[28] Helmut Hucke, "Die Einführung des Gregorianischen Gesanges im Frankenreich," *Römische Quartalschrift* 49 (1954): 172–87.

[29] *Antiphonale Missarum Sextuplex.*

[30] Most early manuscripts show an awareness of the Roman heritage when they render later accretions of the repertoire—especially chants for processions which were not taken over from Rome—in the appendix; only in a second stage are they integrated at the respective liturgical place in the corpus of the books.

[31] Philippe Bernard, "Les chants du propre de la messe dans les répertoires 'grégorien' et romain ancien. Essai d'édition pratique des variantes textuelles," *Ephemerides Liturgicae* 110 (1996): 210–51; Bernard, "Les variantes textuelles des chants du propre de la messe dans les répertoires 'grégorien' et 'romain ancien'," *Ephemerides Liturgicae* 110 (1996): 445–50; but see Andreas Pfisterer, *Cantilena Romana. Untersuchungen zur Überlieferung des Gregorianischen Chorals*, Beiträge zur Geschichte der Kirchenmusik 11 (Paderborn: Schöningh, 2002), 127f., n349.

[32] Daniel J. DiCenso, "Sacramentary-Antiphoners as Sources of Gregorian Chant in the Eighth and Ninth Centuries" (PhD dissertation, University of Cambridge, 2011), however, draws attention to the differences and problems of a too homogeneous view.

[33] Joseph Dyer, "Latin Psalters, Old Roman and Gregorian Chants," *Kirchenmusikalisches Jahrbuch* 68 (1984): 11–30.

[34] Petrus Pietschmann, "Die nicht dem Psalter entnommenen Meßgesangstücke auf ihre Textgestalt untersucht," *Jahrbuch für Liturgiewissenschaft* 12 (1932): 87–144; Pfisterer, *Cantilena Romana*, 221–32.

intimately connected to music at the point of their import;[35] the extremely high degree of melodic conformance of manuscripts when music was first notated in different regions from the early tenth century on insinuates a common origin, which is to be sought in early Carolingian times.[36]

Carolingian cantors seemingly did not have the competence (or the intention) to compose new pieces; apart from very few contrafacts,[37] the formulaic genre of the Tract, and the immense creativity in the relatively young repertoire of Alleluias,[38] no substantial extension of the Mass proper took place after it was taken over from Rome, though within that corpus pieces of allegedly non-Roman origin can be identified.[39] Frankish cantors did not produce new antiphons for introit and communion, and though Office responsories continued to be created, this was not the case with the Gradual responsories of the Mass.[40]

---

[35] Texts sung on formulaic melodies like the verses of the introit and communion psalmody are more prone to be updated, all the more as they were often not written out in full in early manuscripts; Emmanuela Kohlhaas, *Musik und Sprache im gregorianischen Gesang*, Beihefte zum Archiv für Musikwissenschaft 49 (Stuttgart: Steiner, 2001), 53, also observes occasional alterations in the verses of Gradual responsories.

[36] Kenneth Levy, "Charlemagne's Archetype of Gregorian Chant," in Levy, *Gregorian Chant and the Carolingians* (Princeton, NJ: Princeton University Press, 1998), 82–108 [= *Journal of the American Musicological Society* 40 (1987): 1–30], even posits a notated antiphoner at that early date; the formal independence of the various regional kinds of neumes is the main argument against this view.

[37] Most famous examples of contrafacts are the chant pieces of the Mass of the Trinity.

[38] Karlheinz Schlager, *Alleluia-Melodien*, 2 vols., Monumenta monodica medii aevi 7–8 (Kassel: Bärenreiter, 1968; 1987).

[39] Olivier Cullin and Michel Huglo, "Gallikanischer Gesang," *Die Musik in Geschichte und Gegenwart*, 2nd ed., vol. 3 (1995): 998–1027; Kenneth Levy, "Toledo, Rome, and the Legacy of Gaul," in Levy, *Gregorian Chant*, 31–81 [= *Early Music History* 4 (1984): 49–99]. In addition to the common "Gregorian" heritage, regional traditions especially of southern Italy and Aquitaine contain pieces which in many cases are remnants of earlier local repertoires.

[40] Indeed, the compositional logic of graduals is difficult to understand, and it seems that the documented musical shape—in spite of being a responsorial

Instead of new compositions in existing forms, categorically new genres were introduced when contemporary spirituality of the early Middle Ages claimed its right of expression soon after the import of "Gregorian" chant; they did not change or substitute the quasi-canonical heritage from Rome but were interpolated, prepended, or attached to the existing forms as tropes and sequences;[41] and when new feasts were introduced, existing chants were assigned to new occasions.[42]

Nevertheless, contemporary literary sources and the comparison with later Roman manuscripts coercively demonstrate that the adoption of Roman chant in mid-eighth-century Metz went along with considerable stylistic modification; only the outcome of this creative process can be identified with "Gregorian" chant as it was disseminated in the Carolingian reform. Divergent stories are told in early medieval sources to account for the discrepancies:[43] according to the above-mentioned Roman deacon John, distortion was due to the "native brutishness" of Frankish cantors, "for Alpine bodies, which make an incredible din with the thundering of their voices, do not properly echo the elegance of the received melody, because the barbaric savagery of a drunkard's gullet, when it attempts to sing the gentle cantilena with its inflections and reper-

----

form and regardless of the formulaic elements which can be observed in certain melodic groups—is transmitted already in a detrital state.

[41] Hiley, *Western Plainchant*, 172–273; Michael Klaper, "Zwischen Alt und Neu: Die Erweiterung des Repertoires," in *Der Gottesdienst und seine Musik*, vol. 1: *Grundlegung: Der Raum und die Instrumente. Theologische Ansätze. Hymnologie: Die Gesänge des Gottesdienstes*, ed. Albert Gerhards and Matthias Schneider, Enzyklopädie der Kirchenmusik 4/1 (Laaber: Laaber, 2014), 153–76.

[42] Creativity seems to have ceased already in the course of the seventh century in Rome: Peter Jeffery, "Rome and Jerusalem: From Oral Tradition to Written Repertory in Two Ancient Liturgical Centers," in *Essays on Medieval Music in Honor of David G. Hughes*, ed. Graeme M. Boone, Isham Library Papers 4 (Cambridge, MA: Harvard University Press, 1995), 207–47, on 214–18. While Office chants were created throughout the Middle Ages, the Mass propers of newly introduced feasts drew on the received repertoire.

[43] Hucke, *Einführung*; Susan Rankin, "Ways of Telling Stories," in *Essays on Medieval Music in Honor of David G. Hughes*, ed. Graeme M. Boone, Isham Library Papers 4 (Cambridge, MA: Harvard University Press, 1995), 371–94.

cussions, emits, by a kind of innate cracking, rough tones with a confused sound like a cart upon steps."[44] Frankish sources, in turn, created the counterideology that the Roman cantors taught their colleagues "as differently and corruptly as they could possibly contrive."[45]

What really happened is shrouded in mystery, and how the Frankish version of "Gregorian" chant and the high medieval Roman version of (perhaps misleadingly so-called) "Old Roman" chant relate to their common ancestor, that is, to what was sung in mid-eighth-century Rome, remains what Willi Apel has named "the central problem of Gregorian chant."[46]

Before or After Gregory I? The Schola Cantorum and the Formation of the Repertoire

It is still disputed when the Roman chant repertoire itself received its shape. Not only does the performance of the various genres require trained specialists; but the astonishing congruence of sources for the Mass antiphoner suggests that a coherent group was responsible for its redaction. The earliest detailed source for the Roman Mass, *Ordo Romanus 1*, presupposes both the evolved musical forms—including the schola chants that accompany the liturgical action at the three "soft points" (to use Robert Taft's words)[47] of introit, offertory, and communion—and the respective institution of professional singers, the schola cantorum with its

[44] *Vita* 2, 7, Patrologia Latina 75, 90 D–91 A; English translation slightly adapted from McKinnon in Strunk, *Source Readings*, 69.

[45] Notker Balbulus, *Gesta Karoli Magni* 1, 10, ed. Hans F. Haefele, Monumenta Germaniae Historica. Scriptores Rerum Germanicarum Nova Series 12 (Berlin: Weimann, 1959), 14; English translation: McKinnon in Strunk, *Source Readings*, 72.

[46] Willi Apel, "The Central Problem of Gregorian Chant," *Journal of the American Musicological Society* 9 (1956): 118–27.

[47] Robert F. Taft, "How Liturgies Grow: The Evolution of the Byzantine Divine Liturgy," in *Beyond East and West: Problems in Liturgical Understanding*, 2nd. ed. (Rome: Pontifical Oriental Institute, 2001; ¹1997), 203–32 [= *Orientalia Christiana Periodica* 43 (1977): 355–78], 204.

officials.[48] The final state of this *ordo* does not antedate the late seventh century,[49] which is the period in which the schola cantorum also emerges in historical sources.[50] Not much later, the production of new music must have ceased definitely: when eucharistic celebrations on Thursdays of Lent were introduced under Gregory II (715–731), all propers were composed of existing pieces.[51]

James McKinnon therefore suggestively argued that the Roman Mass proper was redacted by the schola cantorum in the later seventh century and thus significantly after Gregory I.[52] There is no hint at a group of professional singers in the writing of this pope;[53] instead, he still seems to know "lector chant" only,[54] though he sowed the seed for the professionalization of singers by decreeing

[48] *Ordo Romanus 1*, ed. Michel Andrieu, *Les "Ordines Romani" du haut moyen âge*, vol. 2 : *Les textes (Ordines I–XIII)*, Spicilegium Sacrum Lovaniense 23 (Louvain: Spicilegium Sacrum Lovaniense, 1960 = 1948), 67–108.

[49] *Ordo Romanus 1*, 105, ed. Andrieu 101, mentions the *Agnus Dei*, which is said to have been introduced by Sergius I (687–701) in the *Liber Pontificalis* 86, 14, ed. Duchesne 1, 376.

[50] Joseph Dyer, "The Schola Cantorum and Its Roman Milieu in the Early Middle Ages," in *De musica et cantu. Studien zur Geschichte der Kirchenmusik und der Oper. Helmut Hucke zum 60. Geburtstag*, ed. Peter Cahn and Ann-Katrin Heimer, Musikwissenschaftliche Publikationen. Hochschule für Musik und Darstellende Kunst Frankfurt/Main 2 (Hildesheim: Olms, 1993), 19–40; Dyer, "Boy Singers of the Roman Schola Cantorum," in *Young Choristers, 650–1700*, ed. Susan Boynton and Eric Rice, Studies in Medieval and Renaissance Music (Woodbridge: Boydell & Brewer, 2009), 19–36; Christopher Page, *The Christian West and Its Singers: The First Thousand Years* (New Haven, CT: Yale University Press, 2010), 243–59. The aforementioned Sergius I started his career as a singer according to *Liber Ponitificalis* 86, 1, ed. Duchesne 1, 371.

[51] Jeffery, *Rome and Jerusalem*, as quoted in n42.

[52] James McKinnon, *The Advent Project: The Later-Seventh-Century Creation of the Roman Mass Proper* (Berkeley, CA: University of California Press, 2000); for a critical view, see Andreas Pfisterer, "James McKinnon und die Datierung des gregorianischen Chorals," *Kirchenmusikalisches Jahrbuch* 85 (2001): 31–53, and the reviews by Joseph Dyer in *Early Music History* 20 (2001): 279–309, Susan Rankin in *Plainchant and Medieval Music* 11 (2002): 73–82, and Peter Jeffery in *Journal of the American Musicological Society* 56 (2003): 169–79.

[53] Buchinger, *Gregor der Große*, 115–32.

[54] McKinnon, *Advent Project*, 62, credits Dom Jean Claire with the creation of the terminology.

that deacons should not exercise the office of cantors any more: "I hold that the psalms and other readings (!) should be performed by subdeacons or, if necessary, by minor orders."[55]

While these are strong indications that the formation of the repertoire took place after this pope, there are in turn also hints that musical creativity faded not too much after him:[56] feasts that were introduced in the course of the seventh century get few new pieces but mostly recycle existing material;[57] the last feast that has a completely new set of proper chants is the dedication of St. Mary *ad martyres*,[58] the former Pantheon, which was conducted under Boniface IV (608–615),[59] though the proper need not have been composed at this occasion.[60]

Room and Need for Imagination: Unresolved Questions

Leaving aside the even more complicated situation of Office chant, there is thus no consensus when the texts of the Roman Mass proper were composed, and the origin of its melodies is likewise an open question. The existing shape of both is at any rate the result of significant change. Historical imagination, though, is no mere speculation: on the one hand, inference can be made from the

[55] The decree of the Roman synod of 595 is edited as *Epistula* 5, 57a in *Gregorii I papae registrum epistolarum* 1/2, ed. Ludovicus M. Hartmann, Monumenta Germaniae Historica. Epistolae 1/2 (Berlin: Weidmann, 1891), 363; discussion and further references in Buchinger, *Gregor der Große*, 133.

[56] Cf. the critics quoted in n52; arguments for an early date are conveniently summarized by Andreas Pfisterer, "Gregorianischer Gesang," in *Lexikon der Kirchenmusik*, ed. Günther Massenkeil and Michael Zywietz, Enzyklopädie der Kirchenmusik 6/1 (Laaber: Laaber, 2013), 458–67, on 463f.

[57] Jeffery, *Rome and Jerusalem*, as quoted in n42.

[58] *Antiphonale Missarum Sextuplex*, 118f., no. 100.

[59] *Liber pontificalis* 69, ed. Duchesne 1, 317.

[60] McKinnon, *Advent Project*, 11f., epitomizes the arguments brought forward in his "The Emergence of Gregorian Chant in the Carolingian Era," in *Antiquity and the Middle Ages: From Ancient Greece to the 15th Century*, ed. James McKinnon, Man & Music. A Social History (Houndmills: Macmillan, 1990), 88–119, on 107–9: (1) the dedication feast of *Maria ad Martyres* is missing from several early sources of the Roman liturgy; (2) the church was renovated under Gregory III (731–741; cf. *Liber pontificalis* 92, 12, ed. Duchesne 1, 419), which may have been the occasion for the composition of a proper.

textual and musical forms of the received repertoire; on the other hand, analogies are provided by comparative liturgy. Peter Jeffery has drawn attention to the fact that developments that can be assumed to have occurred in Rome are testified by the sources that document the history of the liturgy in Jerusalem between the fifth and the eighth centuries.[61]

The Formative Period of the Roman Repertoire

While it is not clear whether the chants that accompany the movements of introit, offertory, and communion ever were congregational song in the Roman liturgy,[62] the "lector chant" of the gradual must have undergone a number of significant transformations: (1) the response underwent the transition from congregational to choral singing; (2) the concomitant evolution of the musical forms of both, the response and the psalmody itself (from simple "lector psalmody" with elementary congregational responses to elaborate responsories), resulted (3) in considerable abbreviation and the reduction of the psalmody to a single verse; (4) the musical development went along with the professionalization of the office of cantor.[63] In Jerusalem, this process took place between the period documented by the Armenian Lectionary (417–439) and that of the Georgian Lectionary (sixth/seventh c.?);[64] valuable insights also

---

[61] Jeffery, *Rome and Jerusalem*.

[62] *Ordo Romanus 1* (as quoted in n48) is the earliest clear evidence for these schola chants; on the controversial testimony of the *psalmi ante sacrificium* mentioned in *Liber pontificalis* 1, 45, see n27.

[63] See also Michel Huglo, "Le Répons-Graduel de la Messe. Évolution de la forme. Permanence de la fonction," *Schweizer Jahrbuch für Musikwissenschaft. Neue Folge* 2 (1982): 53–77 [repr. in Huglo, *Chant grégorien et musique médiévale*, Collected Studies Series 814 (Aldershot: Ashgate, 2005), no. 3]; James McKinnon, "The Fourth-Century Origin of the Gradual," *Early Music History* 7 (1987): 91–106 [repr. in McKinnon, *The Temple, the Church Fathers and Early Western Chant*, Collected Studies Series 606 (Aldershot: Ashgate, 1998), no. 9].

[64] While the Armenian Lectionary, *Le codex arménien Jérusalem 121*, ed. Athanase Renoux, Patrologia Orientalis 36/2 = 168 (Turnhout: Brepols, 1971), regularly seems to provide full psalms to go with both, the response (*kc'urd*; Renoux translates "antienne") of the responsorial psalm as well as with the Halleluja, the evidence of the Georgian Lectionary, *Le grand lectionnaire de*

come from historical sources like the sixth-/seventh-century narration of the abbots John and Sophronius with Nilus that testifies to the professionalization of ordained psalmists while at the same time referring to participation of the congregation in pieces of proper chant.[65]

Peter Jeffery has furthermore shown a path to bridging the gap between patristic hints at the use of psalms and some of the choices made in the existing Roman chant repertoire[66]—certainly a rewarding field of further research.

The Creative Reception in the Frankish Realm

It has already been mentioned that the exact character of the transformation that resulted when Frankish cantors received the Roman chant in the mid-eighth century remains "the central problem of Gregorian chant"[67] because one can only speculate about the Roman music of that time; at any rate it is astonishing that in spite of the declared will to implement the Roman way of singing

---

l'Église de Jérusalem (V^e–VIIIe siècle), ed. Michel Tarchnischvili, Corpus Scriptorum Christianorum Orientalium 188f.; 204f. = Scriptores Iberici 9f.; 13f. (Louvain: CorpusSCO, 1959–1960), appears ambivalent: hints at continuous use of the former practice are complemented with clear indications that a gradual reduction of both forms to selected verses was widely accomplished: Helmut Leeb, Die Gesänge im Gemeindegottesdienst von Jerusalem (vom 5. bis 8. Jahrhundert), Wiener Beiträge zur Theologie 28 (Vienna: Herder, 1970), 50–99, esp. 53–62 and 82–87. At the same time, non-biblical troparia were introduced; they are preserved in the older Georgian Iadgari.

[65] Robert F. Taft, "The βηματίκιον in the 6/7th c. Narration of the Abbots John and Sophronius (BHGNA 1438w): An Exercise in Comparative Liturgy," in Crossroad of Cultures: Studies in Liturgy and Patristics in Honor of Gabriele Winkler, ed. Hans-Jürgen Feulner, Elena Velkovska, and Robert F. Taft, Orientalia Christiana Analecta 260 (Rome: Pontificio Istituto Orientale, 2000), 675–92, on Augusta Longo, "Il testo integrale della 'Narrazione degli abati Giovanni e Sofronio' attraverso le 'ἑρμηνεῖαι' di Nicone," Rivista di studi bizantini e neoellenici 12–13 = Nuova serie 2–3 (1965–1966): 223–67, esp. 253f.; 263.

[66] Peter Jeffery, "Monastic Reading and the Emerging Roman Chant Repertory," in Western Plainchant in the First Millennium: Studies in the Medieval Liturgy and Its Music, ed. Sean Gallagher, et al. (Aldershot: Ashgate, 2003), 45–103.

[67] See n46.

(*cantilena Romana*), the creative process of transforming the latter to what was then disseminated as "Gregorian" chant took place.

It therefore can be summarized that notwithstanding all efforts at unification and universalization since Carolingian times the tradition of chant is neither continuous nor monolithic and that the reconstruction of its past is inextricably linked to both imaginations of its past and visions of its possible or desired future.

PART 3: IMAGINATION AND REALITY: PAST AND PRESENT IN THE GREGORIAN CORE REPERTOIRE

Not only does the scholarly reconstruction of the creation of the Roman chant proper leave ample room for historical imagination, but chant itself may also contain elements of imagination, traces of which shall be investigated in pieces of the Easter cycle, especially of Lent, probably the most famous test area of research into the historical stratigraphy of Roman liturgy.[68]

"All You That Thirst, Come to the Waters": Catechetical and Mystagogical Elements in the Roman Chant Repertoire of the Lenten Period

Even more than in other rites, the celebration of Easter in the Roman liturgy is centered on the process of Christian initiation: references to baptism determine not only the selection of readings and the formulation of prayers but also the choice of chant pieces from the preparatory period of Lent over the core celebration of baptism in the Paschal Vigil into the mystagogical time of the Easter season.

Ordo Romanus 11

Most explicit is *Ordo Romanus 11*, the oft-copied key source for initiation in the Roman Rite, which is generally thought to retain

---

[68] Harald Buchinger, "On the Early History of Quadragesima: A New Look at an Old Problem and Some Proposed Solutions," in *Liturgies in East and West: Ecumenical Relevance of Early Liturgical Development; Acts of the International Symposium Vindobonense I, Vienna, November 17–20, 2007*, ed. Hans-Jürgen Feulner, Österreichische Studien zur Liturgiewissenschaft und Sakramententheologie 6 (Vienna: LIT, 2013), 99–117 = *Studia Liturgica* 43 (2013): 321–41, with reference to the earlier bibliography.

guidelines for Roman presbyters who were in charge of the preparation for baptism in the later sixth or seventh centuries (although the extent of Frankish revision is unclear, and any dating before the ninth century, from which the earliest manuscripts survive, remains hypothetical and open to revision);[69] it gives a detailed order especially for the seven scrutinies of the elect, inserting them into the Liturgy of the Word of several occasions during Lent. Two moments are accentuated by reference to special readings and pieces of chant.

The first emphasized date is the first scrutiny. At the formal commencement of the catechumenate at which the names of the baptismal candidates are inscribed, Ezekiel 36:25-29 is read; from the same pericope comes also the characteristic introit *Dum sanctificatus fuero*, with its typological references to water, cleansing, and spirit, as well as the motif of gathering the people, which is so dear to Roman baptismal theology: "When I shall be sanctified in you, I shall gather you from all countries, and I shall pour out clean water over you, and you shall be cleansed from all your filthiness, and I shall give you a new spirit" (Ezek 36:23-26).[70] It is noteworthy

[69] Andrieu, *Ordines*, 417–47; translated by E. C. Whitaker, *Documents of the Baptismal Liturgy*, rev. Maxwell E. Johnson (Collegeville, MN: Liturgical Press, 2003), 244–51.

[70] *Ordo Romanus 11*, 8. 28, ed. Andrieu 419; 424. The introit *Dum sanctificatus fuero* is assigned to Wednesday of the fourth (!) week of Lent by the Mass Antiphoner (*Antiphonale Missarum Sextuplex*, 76f., no. 63), as is the reading from Ezek 36 (Antoine Chavasse, *Les lectionnaires romains de la Messe au VIIe et au VIIIe siècle. Sources et dérivés*, Spicilegii Friburgensis Subsidia 22, 2 vols. [Fribourg: Éditions universitaires, 1993], 2, 13).

The (gradual) responsory *Aspiciam vos* mentioned by *Ordo Romanus 11*, 28 is unknown to the Roman Mass Antiphoner; its text from Lev 26:9 occurs only as Verse to the Office responsory *Ecce ab austro* in minority traditions of the second Sunday of Advent: *Corpus Antiphonalium Officii*, ed. Renatus-Joannes Hesbert, Rerum Ecclesiasticarum Documenta. Series maior: Fontes 7–12 (Rome: Herder, 1963–1979), 4, 147, no. 6570. Likewise, the Gospel pericope Matt 11:25-30 provided by *Ordo Romanus 11*, 31, ed. Andrieu 425, is not attested in Lent by the Roman Gospel lectionaries (it appears only in the Comes Murbach on the fifth Sunday after Epiphany: Chavasse, *lectionnaires*, 2, 26).

The collect *Da quaesumus, domine, electis*, and the prayer over the gifts *Miseratio tua* mentioned by *Ordo Romanus 11*, 9. 33, ed. Andrieu 420; 425, are used

161

that the clergy (*clerus*) is said to sing the antiphon, not the choir (*schola*), as is the case in the key sources of the Roman Mass;[71] is this a hint at a relatively early date?

The other emphasized date is the third scrutiny, at which the Gospel, the Symbol, and the Lord's Prayer are handed over. The first reading is taken from Isaiah 55:2-7, a text that recurs repeatedly in the process of initiation and is read again at the Paschal Vigil. Significantly the pericope does not start with the exhortation of verse 1, *Omnes sitientes venite ad aquas*, "All you that thirst, come to the waters," but—quite suitably to the occasion of the "opening of the ears" and the handing over of the Gospel—with the later part of verse 2, which calls for "hearing" (*audite audientes me*). Very convenient are the two gradual responsories. The first is *Venite fili* from Psalm 33 (34): "Come, children, listen to me, and I will teach you the fear of the Lord"; meaningful is also the choice of verse 6 (instead of the more usual first verse) of the psalm as verse, "Come to him and receive enlightenment [*illuminamini*]," which is certainly inspired by the metaphorical designation of baptism as "enlightenment." The ecclesiological dimension is stressed by the second responsory *Beata gens* from Psalm 32 (33):12: "Blessed is the nation whose God is the Lord, the people whom he has chosen as his heritage."[72]

---

on the third Sunday of Lent "which is celebrated for the scrutinies of the elect" in the Old Gelasian Sacramentary 26, 193f.: *Liber sacramentorum Romanae aeclesiae ordinis anni circuli (Cod. Vat. Reg. lat. 316/Paris Bibl. Nat. 7193, 41/56)*, ed. Leo Cunibert Mohlberg, Rerum Ecclesiasticarum Documenta. Series maior: Fontes 4 (Rome: Herder, 1960), 32f.

[71] *Ordo Romanus 1*, 44. 50, ed. Andrieu 81; 83.

[72] *Ordo Romanus 11*, 42f., ed. Andrieu 427f. A reading of Isa 55:1-11 is consigned to Saturday of the fourth week of Lent by the Lectionaries (Chavasse, *lectionnaires*, 2, 14), of Isa 55:6-11 to the first Tuesday after Quadragesima Sunday (ibid., 2, 13); Isa 54:17–55:11 is read at the Paschal Vigil (ibid., 2, 14), while in the chant repertoire, Isa 55:1—which is not read according to *Ordo Romanus 11*, 42—is the text of the introit *Sitientes* on Saturday of the fourth week of Lent (*Antiphonale Missarum Sextuplex*, 80f., no. 66). The combination of Col 3:9 and Rom 10:18 used by *Ordo Romanus 11*, 43, as epistle of the day does not appear in the Roman lectionaries. The two gradual responsories *Venite fili* and *Beata gens* are part of the proper designed for Wednesday of the fourth week

Although *Ordo Romanus 11* is one of the earliest extant comprehensive orders for the Roman catechumenal liturgy, it certainly
does not preserve its original shape. The few pieces that are
quoted, not only of chant, but also of readings and prayers, do
not match precisely any other existing source,[73] and the number
of seven scrutinies contradicts all earlier testimonies. Most significantly, it mirrors the decay of adult initiation; though sumptuous
rituals of the classical catechumenate are performed, there is repeated evidence that the regular candidates for baptism were little
children who are not active subjects of the liturgy but, for example,
are carried in and out or left under supervision and who cannot
respond themselves to questions.[74]

In fact, the sequence of seven scrutinies prescribed in *Ordo Romanus 11* is generally interpreted as the result of secondary developments: earlier testimonies refer to three scrutinies as the minimum
in Roman practice;[75] since the third, fourth, and fifth Sundays of
Lent are said to be "celebrated for the scrutinies of the elect" in
the Gelasian sacramentary, it is widely assumed that originally

---

of Lent in the Roman Mass antiphoner (*Antiphonale Missarum Sextuplex*, 76f.,
no. 63; both pieces return—alternatively, not cumulatively as in Lent—on the
seventh Sunday after Pentecost ibid. 180f., no. 179), part of which is also the
introit *Dum sanctificatus fuero* mentioned above (n70: Wednesday of the third
week in *Ordo Romanus 11* and of the fourth week in the Antiphoner).

[73] See above, n70 and n72.

[74] Bruno Kleinheyer, *Sakramentliche Feiern*, part 1: *Die Feiern der Eingliederung
in die Kirche*, Gottesdienst der Kirche. Handbuch der Liturgiewissenschaft 7,1
(Regensburg: Pustet, 1989), 107; cf., among others, *Ordo Romanus 11*, 62–64. 73.
95–98, ed. Andrieu 434f.; 441; 445f.

[75] Yves-Marie Duval, *La décrétale "Ad Gallos Episcopos": son texte et son auteur*,
Supplements to Vigiliae Christianae 73 (Leiden: Brill, 2005), 38, can. 4, 11,
mentions a "third scrutiny" towards the end of the fourth century; around one
century later, ca. 500, the *Epistula Iohannis Diaconi ad Senarium* 2, in André Wilmart, "V. Reg. lat. 69 (fol. 116-122). Un florilège carolingien sur le symbolisme
des cérémonies du baptême, avec un Appendice sur la lettre de Jean Diacre,"
in Wilmart, *Analecta Reginensia. Extraits des manuscrits latins de la reine Christine
conservés au Vatican*, Studi e Testi 59 (Vatican City: Biblioteca Apostolica Vaticana, 1933), 153–79, on 171, speaks of three scrutinies. Translated by Whitaker
in *Documents*, 205; 208.

those were the dates for these catechumenal rites.[76] Only when they lost their importance after infant baptism had become the rule would the scrutinies have been deferred from the Sundays to less prominent weekdays; at the same time, their number would have been increased. Corroboration for this hypothesis has mainly been sought in the distribution of chants in the Roman Mass proper, which therefore shall be examined in the next step.[77]

Antiphonale Missarum

HISTORICAL STRATA

Although the concordance of the various manuscripts is almost perfect in the season of Lent,[78] the liturgical disposition in the Mass antiphoner contains conspicuous inconsistencies that allow insights into historical developments and changes, the analysis of which has become standard knowledge since the first half of the twentieth century.[79] Most fundamental is the fact that the series of Lenten communion antiphons starts on (only later so-called) Ash Wednesday with Psalm 1 and runs in continually ascending order until Psalm 26 (27) on Friday before Passion Sunday. Two irregularities grant further discernment. Firstly, Thursdays are skipped, which implies that the series must have been established before Gregory II (715–731), who is credited with having introduced the

---

[76] *Gelasianum Vetus* no. 26–28, ed. Mohlberg 32; 36; 39; but see Dominic E. Serra, "New Observations about the Scrutinies of the Elect in Early Roman Practice," *Worship* 80 (2006): 511–27, with references to earlier research.

[77] Further hints come on the one hand from the fact that the prayers mentioned at the first scrutiny by *Ordo Romanus 11* agree with those given for the third Sunday of Lent in the Gelasian sacramentary (see n70), while on the other hand the assignment of readings does not concur with existing lectionaries (see n70 and n72).

[78] Hesbert, *Antiphonale Missarum Sextuplex*, XLVI.

[79] After Hesbert, *Antiphonale Missarum Sextuplex*, XLVI–LVI, and many others, see most recently and thoroughly Dyer Joseph, "The Chronology of the Lenten Weekday Communions," in *"Quod ore cantas, corde credas". Studi in onore di Giacomo Baroffio Dahnk*, ed. Leandra Scappaticci, Monumenta studia instrumenta liturgica 70 (Vatican City: Vaticana, 2013), 277–91. Both contain illustrative tables.

164

celebration of Mass on Lenten Thursdays by the papal chronicle;[80] at this occasion, pieces of the existing repertoire were used to fill the gaps—perhaps a sign that the period of creativity in the production of Roman chant had ended in the first third of the eighth century.[81] Secondly, five psalmodic pieces are replaced by antiphons taken from the Gospel of the day: Saturday of the second week by Luke 15, and Friday and Saturday of the third week as well as Wednesday and Friday of the fourth week by a series from chapters 4, 8, 9, and 11 of John.[82]

CAUSE AND DATE OF THE SHIFT

Since three of them are considered pericopes of catechetical import and are employed on Sundays of Lent in non-Roman Western liturgies,[83] the hypothesis has found broad acceptance in the last century that also in Rome the Johannine readings about the water of eternal life (John 4), the healing of the blind-born (John 9), and the resurrection of Lazarus (John 11) may originally have belonged

[80] *Liber pontificalis* 91, 9, ed. Duchesne 1, 402.

[81] Cf. n42 and n51.

[82] *Antiphonale Missarum Sextuplex*, 66f., no. 52; 72f., no. 58f.; 78f., no. 63; 80f., no. 65; for the Gospel lectionary evidence, see Chavasse, *Lectionnaires*, 2, 28.

[83] A. Rose, "Les grands évangiles baptismaux du Carême romain," *Questions liturgiques et paroissiales* 43 (1962): 8–17; Balthasar Fischer, "Der patristische Hintergrund der drei großen johanneischen Taufperikopen von der Samariterin, der Heilung des Blindgeborenen und der Auferweckung des Lazarus am dritten, vierten und fünften Sonntag der Quadragesima," in *I simboli dell'iniziazione cristiana. Atti del I° Congresso Internazionale di Liturgia. Pontificio Istituto Liturgico, 25–28 Maggio 1982*, ed. Giustino Farnedi, Studia Anselmiana 87 = Analecta liturgica 7 (Rome: Pontificio Ateneo S. Anselmo, 1983), 61–79. From the Old Spanish rite comes the *Liber commicus*, ed. Justo Pérez de Urgel and Atilano González y Ruiz-Zorrilla, Monumenta Hispaniae Sacra. Serie liturgica 2–3 = Consejo superior de ivestigaciones cientificas: Escuela de estudios medievales. Textos 13; 28 (Madrid: Bermejo, 1950; 1955), 1, 124–44; 210–12; 299–301; on the lectionaries of the Ambrosian Rite of Milan, see Patrizia Carmassi, *Libri liturgici e istituzioni ecclesiastiche a Milano in età medioevale. Studio sulla formazione del lezionario ambrosiano*, Liturgiewissenschaftliche Quellen und Forschungen 85 = Corpus ambrosiano-liturgicum 4 (Münster: Aschendorff, 2001), 304; 318; 325, for the Beneventan evidence, René-Jean Hesbert, "Les Dimanches de Carême dans les manuscrits romano-bénéventains," *Ephemerides Liturgicae* 48 (1934): 198–222.

to Lenten Sundays on which scrutinies were celebrated; in the wake of the decline of adult initiation, they would have been transferred to weekdays.[84]

The fact that this shift must have occurred after the introduction of (Ash) Wednesday instead of the first Sunday of Lent as the commencement of the fast (*caput ieiunii*) gives a cue for a not too early date of this process: though it is unclear when exactly (Ash) Wednesday was established, it is definitely unknown to Leo I (440–461), and even Gregory I (590–604) clearly calculates the fast beginning with Sunday (i.e., the first Sunday of Lent).[85]

A coherent reconstruction is complicated by the fact that in Rome different liturgical orders coexisted; the distinction between pontifical and presbyteral celebrations (of which we do not know how uniform their tradition has to be imagined[86]) is particularly relevant in the process of initiation, since the regular Lenten scrutinies were probably presided by presbyters and not by the pontiff (from whose sacramentary they are missing),[87] whereas the early

---

[84] The theory advanced above all in numerous works of Antoine Chavasse was summarized and to a certain extent criticized already by Josef Andreas Jungmann, "Die Quadragesima in den Forschungen von Antoine Chavasse," *Archiv für Liturgiewissenschaft* 5 (1957): 84–95, and integrated into a partly new model by Maxwell E. Johnson, "From Three Weeks to Forty Days: Baptismal Preparation and the Origins of Lent," *Studia Liturgica* 20 (1990): 185–200 [repr. in *Living Water, Sealing Spirit: Readings on Christian Initiation*, ed. Maxwell E. Johnson (Collegeville. MN: Liturgical Press, 1995), 118–36, and *Worship: Rites, Feasts, and Reflections* (Portland, OR: Pastoral, 2004), 199–213]; cf. also Serra, *Observations*.

[85] Winfried Böhne, "Beginn und Dauer der römischen Fastenzeit im sechsten Jahrhundert," *Zeitschrift für Kirchengeschichte* 77 (1966): 224–37, with reference to *Homilia* 16, 5, in Gregorius Magnus, *Homiliae in evangelia*, ed. Raymond Étaix, Corpus Christianorum, Series Latina 141 (Turnhout: Brepols, 1999), 113f.

[86] Sources of the presbyteral liturgy are scarce. The established characterization of the Old Gelasian Sacramentary as the Roman presbyteral presiders' book is achieved by way of exclusion: it comes from Rome but obviously is not the book used in the stational liturgy of the pontiff. However, the extant witnesses bear traces of ruptures; even the "Old Gelasian" sacramentary contains episcopal functions and material of alleged Gallican provenance.

[87] I owe this argument to an unpublished paper of Dominic E. Serra on "The Purpose of the Lenten Scrutinies" presented at the 2014 Annual Meeting of

manuscript testimonies for both the Roman Gospel lectionary and Mass-antiphoner suggest an origin in the papal liturgy because of their stational indications.

While the secondary assignment of the Lenten Gospel communions is evident from the fact that they interrupt the psalmodic series, the causal nexus to the development of the catechumenate and the date of the intervention remain disputed: it is an obvious flaw of the traditional hypothesis that the number of four Johannine plus one Lukan Gospel communions does not match the number of originally three scrutinies; furthermore, their musical character has led James McKinnon to challenge the received knowledge and propose an alternative explanation: for him, the simple syllabic style of these communions does "not just resemble Office antiphons; they *are* Office antiphons."[88] In McKinnon's view, the Gospel communions are not old pieces of the Mass proper that were replaced from other occasions but part of a late attempt at creating Communion chants for the characteristic Gospel pericopes; they were "borrowed, apparently, to fill out the communion repertory as expeditiously as possible at a point in the history of the Advent project when . . . the Office antiphons . . . fulfilled the

---

the North American Academy of Liturgy; he is also preparing a monograph on initiation in the Roman liturgy. The "authentic" Gregorian sacramentary contains only the prayers for the opening of the catechumenate, the handing over of the Gospel (at which occasion Antoine Chavasse, "Aménagements liturgiques, à Rome, au VIIᵉ et au VIIIᵉ siècle," *Revue Bénédictine* 99 [1989]: 75–102, on 94f. [repr. in idem, *La liturgie de la ville de Rome du Vᵉ au VIIIᵉ siècle. Une liturgie conditionnée par l'organisation de la vie* in urbe *et* extra muros, Studia Anselmiana 112 = Analecta Liturgica 18 (Roma: Pontificio Ateneo S. Anselmo, 1993), 109–46, on 135f.], hypothesized that Gregory's Homilia 19 may have been preached; cf. below, n94), and the final scrutiny on Holy Saturday (*Sacramentarium Gregorianum* 80–83, 356–61: *Le Sacramentaire Grégorien. Ses principales formes d'après les plus anciens manuscrits*, ed. Jean Deshusses, Spicilegium Friburgense 16 [Fribourg: Éditions universitaires, 1971], 180–83), but not the regular exorcism as described by the Gelasian sacramentary and *Ordo Romanus 11*; in turn, the annunciations of the location where the next scrutiny is to be held according to *Ordo Romanus 11*, 37. 39. 78. 80, ed. Andrieu 426f.; 442, presuppose some kind of stational liturgy also in the baptismal preparation presided by a presbyter.

[88] McKinnon, *Advent Project*, 338.

---

aesthetic and devotional aims of those members of the schola cantorum responsible for the communion cycle."[89]

The classical model with its earlier dating has recently been vindicated in a most thorough and careful study by Joseph Dyer: he finds that the two additional Gospel pericopes of Luke 15 (the prodigal son) and John 8 (the woman caught in adultery) "fit preparation for baptism passably well"; furthermore, that "Gregory the Great (590–604) early in his pontificate preached on the 'new' non-scrutiny Gospel for the fifth Sunday of Lent (Jn 8,46–59)" seems to prove that "the reorganisation certainly took place before the end of the sixth century."[90] However, caution is required in face of the headings that assign Gregory's homilies to particular liturgical dates. Already Georg Pfeilschifter warned that they may reflect a secondary alignment with later liturgical customs,[91] and exactly this may particularly be the case with some Lenten homilies: the newest critical edition does not maintain the assignment of Homily 18 to "Passion Sunday"[92] (which was suspicious anyway, since that designation is otherwise first attested in the eighth-century manuscripts of the "Gregorian" Sacramentary and the ninth-century Antiphoner of Compiègne and is therefore unlikely to go back to the days of Gregory I[93]). The liturgical assignment of the immediately following Homily 19 is particularly instable; the hypothesis has been made that its original occasion may have been

[89] Ibid.

[90] Dyer, *Chronology*, 289.

[91] Georg Pfeilschifter, *Die authentische Ausgabe der 40 Evangelienhomilien Gregors des Großen. Ein erster Beitrag zur Geschichte ihrer Überlieferung*, Veröffentlichungen aus dem kirchenhistorischen Seminar München 4 (Munich: Lentner, 1900), 100–103.

[92] The critically established title of *Homilia* 18, ed. Étaix 136, gives no date, but only the station *in basilica beati Petri apostoli*; ibid., LX, the editor holds the assignment to the fifth Sunday of Lent as "all but certain" because of the coincidence of Gospel pericope and station with the earliest lectionaries; cf. Chavasse, *lectionnaires*, 2, 28. Since the series of Johannine readings is disturbed anyway, the prehistory of the order transmitted in the manuscripts remains obscure.

[93] *Sacramentarium Gregorianum* 66, ed. Deshusses 160 (the heading is text-critically instable); *Antiphonale Missarum Sextuplex*, 81, no. 67 (Compiègne only).

the catechumenal Opening of the Ears in Lent and was only secondarily identified as Septuagesima Sunday.[94]

However this hypothesis is to be judged, Gregory's place in the history of Lent remains unclear, his elaborate calculation of fast-days beginning with the first Sunday remaining the relatively firmest piece of evidence—which would speak in favor of a later date of the development of the Lenten weekday Mass proper, since the earliest stratum of the latter clearly presupposes a beginning on (Ash) Wednesday, which is not yet attested in Gregory's preaching.

INITIATION IN THE RECEIVED REPERTOIRE

Regardless of these questions of age and the possible prehistory, the baptismal implications of John 9 on Wednesday of the fourth week in the established Roman Mass Antiphoner are apparent both from the liturgical context and from a detail of the communion itself: firstly, the proper of the day includes three of the four pieces quoted by *Ordo Romanus 11* for the catechumenal masses;[95] secondly, the formulary has a second gradual responsory, which is characteristic of scrutiny Masses; thirdly, the culmination of the piece is a characteristic addition to the résumé of the Gospel text taken from John 9:11: "The Lord made mud with his spittle, and he anointed my eyes; and I went, and washed, and came to see, *and I came to believe in God*"—thus explicating the metaphorical dimension which constitutes the catechetical value of the story.

The case is much less certain at the other possible dates for scrutinies: Neither Saturday of the second week (with the gospel of the prodigal son) nor Friday of the third week (with John 4) has any

---

[94] On *Homilia* 19, ed. Étaix 143, see Chavasse, *Aménagements liturgiques*, as quoted above in n87; cf. Buchinger, *Gregor*, 121. Étaix, Corpus Christianorum, Series Latina 141, LXIV, discusses the manuscript evidence of assignations not only to Septuagesima and the church of St. Laurent but also to the latter saint's feast day, as well as to St. Peter's, St. Paul's, and St. Mary's *ad presepe*. None of them is considered original by the editor; furthermore, the insertion of Homily 19 on Matt 20:1-16 in the series of homilies is instable.

[95] *Antiphonale Missarum Sextuplex*, 76–79, no. 63: Introit *Dum sanctificatus fuero* and Gradual responsories *Venite filii* and *Beata gens*; *Ordo Romanus 11*, 8. 42f., ed. Andrieu 419; 427f.; cf. above, n70 and n72.

other piece of chant with a clear catechetical dimension,[96] and both occasions come before the third week of Lent, which is indicated by the Gelasian Sacramentary and *Ordo Romanus 11* as the beginning of the period of ritual preparation for baptism. Friday and Saturday of the fourth week, in turn, may be somewhat related to baptismal themes: though the occasional occurrence of a second gradual on both dates is not too firm a basis to build a solid case,[97] the gospel and communion from John 11 on Friday may be chosen for catechetical reasons, though this is difficult to prove. This is also true of the introit of the following Saturday: "You, that thirst, come to the waters" from Isaiah 55 is not only part of a reading of the Paschal Vigil which is clearly chosen in view of its baptismal typology explicated also by the subsequent oration;[98] it is also the verse immediately preceding the reading provided by *Ordo Romanus 11* for the great catechumenal liturgy of the opening of the ears and the handing over of creed and the Lord's Prayer.[99] The communion antiphon of the day, "The Lord is my shepherd . . . he has led me to refreshing waters," comes from Psalm 22 (23) and thus is part of the original series of ascending psalmodic pieces;

[96] Dyer, *Chronology*, 288, however, draws attention to the fact that on Saturday of the second week "the introit includes the phrase 'sapientiam praestans parvulis' and the offertory is *Illuminans oculos*, which may well have a connection to the scrutinies." Following Hartmann Grisar, *Das Missale im Lichte römischer Stadtgeschichte. Stationen, Perikopen, Gebräuche* (Freiburg: Herder, 1925), he also suggests "that the content of the readings . . . determined the choice of stational church in some instances. S. Lorenzo in Lucina [the station on Friday of third week, when John 4 was read; H. B.] was located next to a famous well" (ibid.). Though "the connection with Susannah of the Old Testament and the Roman church of the same name dedicated to a martyr (Saturday of the third week) is a purely fortuitous one" (ibid.), it gives a sufficient reason for the choice of the Gospel pericope (and respective communion antiphon) John 8 (the woman caught in adultery), typologically opposed to the first reading from Dan 13 about Susannah being wrongly accused of the same crime.

[97] *Antiphonale Missarum Sextuplex*, 78–81, no. 65 (Senlis only); 66 (Rheinau only); for the alleged antiquity of the use, see ibid., LV.

[98] Chavasse, *Les lectionnaires*, 2, 14; *Sacramentarium Gregorianum* 84, 369, ed. Deshusses 184; *Sacramentarium Gelasianum Vetus* 43, 436, ed. Mohlberg 71.

[99] See above, n72.

at the same time, it is most suitable for the evocation of baptismal associations in light of its patristic understanding[100] (we might also wonder which reason came first).

Other pieces related to baptism can only be listed briefly: at the Paschal Vigil, Psalm 41 (42) is a particularly interesting piece because it was treated as a reading with subsequent collect before it ultimately became depreciated to a processional chant on the way to the baptistery;[101] of eminent mystagogical import are the introits of the Easter octave, during which some communions likewise have baptismal implications.[102]

The existing Roman chant repertoire conveys clusters of associations with the process of Christian initiation that, however, appear only as the debris of historical shiftings. The quest for baptismal themes in the Gregorian repertoire thus leads into some of the most debated questions of early liturgical history: on the one hand, the origin, character, and development of Lent; on the other hand (and related to the first question), the transition from adult

[100] Jean Daniélou, "Le Psaume 22 dans l'exégèse patristique," in *Richesses et déficiences des anciens Psautiers latins*, Collectanea Biblica Latina 13 (Rome: Abbaye Saint-Jérôme / Vatican City: Vaticana, 1959), 189–211; Daniélou, "Le Psaume 22 et les étapes de l'initiation," in Daniélou, *Études d'exégèse judéo-chrétienne (Les Testimonia)*, Théologie historique 5 (Paris: Beauchesne, 1966), 141–62.

[101] *Antiphonale Missarum Sextuplex*, 98f., no. 79; *Sacramentarium Gregorianum* 84, 370–72, ed. Deshusses 185; *Sacramentarium Gelasianum Vetus* 43, 442, ed. Mohlberg 72; cf. Hansjörg Auf der Maur, *Feiern im Rhythmus der Zeit*, part 1: *Herrenfeste in Woche und Jahr*, Gottesdienst der Kirche. Handbuch der Liturgiewissenschaft 5 (Regensburg: Pustet, 1983), 93; Harald Buchinger, "Reformen der Osternachtfeier. Eine Fallstudie römischer Liturgiegeschichte," in *Operation am lebenden Objekt. Roms Liturgiereformen von Trient bis zum Vaticanum II*, ed. Stefan Heid (Berlin: Bebra, 2014), 277–302, on 283; the tract *Sicut cervus* was drawn in with the subsequent procession from the twelfth century on: *Bernhardi cardinalis et Lateranensis ecclesiae prioris Ordo officiorum ecclesiae Lateranensis* 147, ed. Ludwig Fischer, Historische Forschungen und Quellen 2–3 (Munich: Datterer, 1916), 63; *Liber politicus* 42, in *Le Liber censuum de l'église de Rome*, ed. Paul Fabre and L. Duchesne, Bibliothèque des Écoles Française d'Athènes et de Rome, 2nd series 6/5 (Paris: Fontemoing, 1905), 151.

[102] *Antiphonale Missarum Sextuplex*, 100–107, no. 81–87.

to infant initiation. In sum, apart from the historically documented introduction of certain feasts in the Roman calendar, Lent is perhaps the only season that allows insights into the chronological development of the chant repertoire. The rupture lines of historical processes not only reveal a differentiated stratigraphy; they also pose fundamental questions: did certain rites and liturgical pieces ever have a real and relevant Sitz im Leben, or are there elements that right from their first occurrence are the product of historical reminiscence of clerics, monks, and other members of the religious elite who were edifying themselves with an imagined past?

Reminiscence or Actuality? Initiation of Adults in Late Antique Rome

Decline of Adult Initiation: Documents and Date
In spite of the dominance of baptismal themes in the celebration of the Easter cycle, it is not clear how long the initiation of adults was an actual reality in the life of the Roman church: sources are scarce,[103] and the existing texts are ambiguous not only because the age of the traditions that were codified in early medieval manuscripts often remains a question of guess.

Terminus ante: It has already been mentioned that *Ordo Romanus 11* bears undeniable traits that the developed ritual of initiation conserves an obsolete state of liturgical development in the seventh or even sixth century; the "infants" are little children who cannot fulfil the various rites themselves.

Terminus post: Clear references to initiation of adults come from the later fourth century,[104] and a letter of Leo I (440–461) still speaks not only of scrutinies and exorcisms of the elect but also of their

---

[103] Stefan Heid, "Die Taufe in Rom nach den frühen römischen Märtyrerlegenden," *Rivista di Archeologia Cristiana* 89 (2013): 217–52, complements the overview given by Victor Saxer, *Les rites de l'initiation chrétienne du IIe au VIe siècle. Esquisse historique et signification d'après leurs principaux témoins*, Centro Italiano di Studi sull'Alto Medioevo 7 (Spoleto: Centro Italiano di Studi sull'Alto Medioevo, 1988), 567–624, and Everett Ferguson, *Baptism in the Early Church: History, Theology, and Liturgy in the First Five Centuries* (Grand Rapids, MI: Eerdmans, 2009), 760–69.

[104] Most explicitly, among others, see bishop Siricius' *Epistula ad Himerium* 2, 3, *Patrologia Latina* 13, 1135 A (AD 385).

"sanctification through fasting" and their "instruction through frequent preaching,"[105] which would make little sense in the case of minors.

It is not known when this practice declined.[106] At the beginning of the sixth century, John the Deacon expounds the traditional liturgy to his addressee Senarius, but it seems that the catechumenal rites have begun to lose their existential relevance; it is probably not an exception any more "that all these things are done even to infants, who by reason of their youth understand nothing."[107]

When Roman liturgy was codified and exported towards the early Middle Ages, the Easter cycle had definitely become an empty husk even if infants were baptized: the liturgical rites of Lent with its pieces which originated from the preparation for baptism, of the Paschal Vigil with its dominant baptismal imprint, and of the Easter octave as the week of mystagogy all remained in substance a sequence of initiatory rites as they emerge from sources of the late fourth and early fifth centuries, but did not celebrate an existential process of the baptizands any more.

Initiation and Chant: Actuality or Imagination?

The historical situation allows two possible interpretations. First, traditional wisdom holds that the liturgical material, including prominent pieces of chant, go back to the golden age of flourishing liturgy at the heyday of patristic liturgical development; they would thus conserve traditional meaning. Actual initiation of adults would be the real Sitz im Leben of a number of pieces of the Easter cycle. One may ask, however, why that should be true particularly for Gospel communions when unbaptized were

---

[105] *Epistula* 16 *ad episcopos Siciliae* 6, Patrologia Latina 54, 702 B: *electi secundum apostolicam regulam et exorcismis scrutandi et ieiuniis sanctificandi et frequentibus sunt praedicationibus imbuendi.*

[106] Heid, *Taufe*, draws the attention to accounts of missionary baptism in Roman martyrs' legends of the fifth/sixth centuries, which in his view retroject their authors' liturgical experience of adult initiation into the era of the persecutions (235).

[107] *Epistula Iohannis Diaconi ad Senarium* 7, ed. Wilmart, *florilège*, 175; English translation: Whitaker, *Documents*, 211.

dismissed before the eucharistic part of Mass. Secondly, not only if the chant repertoire was redacted and to a certain extent created only in the century after Gregory the Great, but even if that would have been the case in the century before his pontificate, chant would not be a vehicle of reminiscence but rather a medium of imagination: the sheer memory of the meaningful process of initiation would have shaped the repertoire at a point in liturgical history when this process had no existential relevance any more for most of its subjects. Imagination would have been an inner momentum of this liturgical creativity as such.

Medieval Incongruity and Modern Reform: The Creative Potential of Liturgical Conservatism

It may be a paradox of the Roman chant repertoire that it evokes a liturgy that probably was more imagination than reality even at the time of its redaction; as such, however, it conserved or, to put it perhaps more adequately, to some extent created the ritual memory of baptismal catechesis and mystagogy in a time when the rites of Christian initiation usually were administered to unconscious objects rather than self-aware subjects of the liturgical celebration.

The scholarly imagination of historical processes of change in late antique Roman liturgy, however, paved the way for a development that has been hailed as one of the greatest ecumenical achievements of recent liturgical renewal:[108] the instauration of initiation of adults after the Second Vatican Council was not a mere repristination but a creative act, inspired by a scholarly reconstruction—or rather, imagination—of patristic liturgy. Even if pieces like the Gospel communions *Qui biberit aquam* from John 4 and *Videns dominus* from John 11 never were sung at a real scrutiny in antiquity, their existence inspired beautiful and meaningful new prayers

---

[108] David R. Holeton, "Ecumenical Liturgical Consensus: A Bumpy Road to Christian Unity; Presidential Address," *Studia liturgica* 38 (2008): 1–16; Susan K. Roll, "'The RCIA Was the Appetizer': Ten Issues Affecting the Future of Adult Christian Initiation," in *Initiation chrétienne et la liturgie / Christian Initiation and the Liturgy. Hommage au Prof. Em. Dr. Jozef Lamberts / In Honour of Prof. Em. Dr. Jozef Lamberts*, ed. Lambert Leijssen, Textes et études liturgiques / Studies in Liturgy 22 (Leuven: Peeters / Abdij Keizersberg, 2008): 87–103.

of the current rites of initiation,[109] thus proving that medieval con-
servatism was productive in modernity, which in turn suggests
that Tradition is much too precious to be left to traditionalists.

[109] Cf. Serra, *Observations*, esp. 526f.

"It Is the Lord's Passover"

History, Theology, and Memory in the Liturgy of the Lord's Supper in Reformation Zurich

Bruce Gordon

Few acts of the Reformation provoked more controversy or proved more influential than the introduction of the liturgy for the Lord's Supper in Zurich on Maundy Thursday, 1525.[1] By decree of the city magistrates virtually every trace of the Mass was extirpated, including altars, vestments, and Latin, bringing to expression in worship Zurich's departure from the Catholic Church.[2] As the old priesthood was guided out the door, the spoken word and silence replaced instrumental and sung music.[3] Those who gathered for the service in the Grossmünster found themselves in a church whose walls had been whitewashed the previous year and whose religious art had been returned to affluent donors in the city to adorn their homes.[4]

---

[1] Zwingli's first liturgical work was introduced in 1523. During his career as a Reformer, liturgy remained central to his work. After the new service in 1525, revisions were offered in 1529 and 1531.

[2] Bruce Gordon, *The Swiss Reformation* (Manchester: Manchester University Press, 2002), 46–85.

[3] Markus Jenny, "Reformierte Kirchenmusik? Zwingli, Bullinger und die Folgen," in *Reformiertes Erbe: Festschrift für Gottfried W. Locher zu seinem 80. Geburtstag*, 2 vols., ed. Heiko A. Oberman, Ernst Saxer, Alfred Schindler, and Heinzpeter Stucki (Zurich: Theologischer Verlag, 1992–93), 1:187–205.

[4] On iconoclasm in Zurich, see Lee Palmer Wandel, *Voracious Idols and Violent Hands: Iconoclasm in Reformation Zurich, Strasbourg, and Basel* (Cambridge,

Yet in that Holy Week of 1525, discerning eyes and ears would have been alert to the degree that the old order was still present in the new. In both the new Reformed liturgy and the principles of church discipline that shaped the emerging ecclesiastical institutions, innovation and tradition were carefully interwoven, although seams remained visible.[5] In the heady days of the 1520s, reform was a delicate balance of scripturally inspired ideals, the search for biblical and historical continuity, and political and social realities.[6] As Paul Collerton has argued, no beginnings are absolutely new, regardless how radical. Recollection is an essential part of all change.[7] And as Finnish sociologist Tuula Sakaranaho has added, "Thus every religion is, in one way or another, a 'reproduction' of prevailing traditions."[8]

Certainly, the dramatic break with the past was everywhere evident. The consecration of the Host, denounced as idolatrous by the Reformers, no longer formed the climax of liturgical drama in the

---

UK: Cambridge University Press, 1995). Further, Victoria George, *Whitewash and the New Aesthetic of the Protestant Reformation* (London: Pindar Press, 2012).

[5] The recent literature on liturgy and worship in Reformation Zurich is rather mixed. There has been little appreciation of the rich tradition of liturgy from which Zwingli drew. See Ralph Kunz, *Gottesdienst Evangelisch-Reformiert: Liturgik und Liturgie in der Kirche Zwinglis* (Zurich: Pano, 2001); Alfred Ehrensperger, *Gottesdienst: Visionen-Erfahrungen-Schmerzstellen* (Zurich: Theologischer Verlag Zürich, 1988). The classic works remain invaluable: Hermann Waldenmaier, *Die Entstehung der evangelischen Gottesdienstordnung Süddeutschlands im Zeitalter der Reformation* (Leipzig: Komissionsverlag von Rudolf Haupt, 1916); F. Schmidt-Clausing, *Zwingli als Liturgiker* (Göttingen: Vandenhoeck & Ruprecht, 1952); J. Schweizer, *Reformierte Abendmahlsgestaltung in der Schau Zwinglis* (Basel: Reinhardt, 1954); Fritz Schmidt-Clausing, *Zwinglis Liturgische Formulare* (Frankfurt: Verlag Otto Lembeck, 1970).

[6] I have pursued this theme at greater length in Bruce Gordon with Luca Baschera and Christian Moser, "Emulating the Past and Creating the Present: Reformation and the Use of Historical and Theological Models in Zurich in the Sixteenth Century," in *Following Zwingli: Applying the Past in Reformation Zurich*, ed. Luca Baschera, Bruce Gordon, and Christian Moser (Farnham: Ashgate, 2014), 1–40.

[7] Paul Connerton, *How Societies Remember* (Cambridge, UK: Cambridge University Press, 1998), 13, cited in Tuula Sakarahaho, "Religion and the Study of Social Memory," *Temenos* 47 (2011): 140.

[8] Sakarahaho, "Religion and the Study of Social Memory," 140.

community. The aesthetic of the late medieval cult and its culture of intercession were replaced by what the Reformers claimed to be worship drawn wholly from Scripture. In the case of Zurich, the triumph of the new order was given spatial expression by the removal of the pulpit to the nave, creating one of three visual focal points, the other two being the baptismal font standing where the rood screen once separated priests from laity and the table for the Lord's Supper.[9] Within the familiar architecture of the building, new sites of memory were created with strong links to the past. Through iconoclasm, an act of forgetting, those sites stood in contentious relationship to the past in which they were located. The Grossmünster in Zurich, the location of the first Reformed celebration of the Eucharist, was a site of contestation where remembering and forgetting were inseparable as the Reformers sought to impose a different sacred narrative on the community.

From the first moment of liturgical reform in the city, compromise and continuity formed equal parts of the zeal for change. A congregant, be it a woman standing on the left of the nave or a man on the right, would have found herself or himself in a service led by clergymen separated from the laity by their position at the front of the church. The new pastorate was distinguished by black preaching gowns, beards (recommended), and caps, and by their place at the table and in the pulpit: all primary liturgical spaces were reserved for those ordained into the preaching office. Only the ministers stood around the elements, while the people remained on their feet or kneeling, waiting to receive the Supper.

According to Zwingli's 1525 liturgy, while the Lord's Supper might no longer involve the consecration of the Host, the words of institution over the plate of bread and cup of wine were to be

---

[9] The literature on sacred space in the Reformation is expanding rapidly, but particularly relevant to our interests is the work of Christian Grosse. See his *Les rituels de la Cène. Le culte eucharistique réformé à Genève (XVIᵉ–XVIIᵉ siècles)*, Travaux d'Humanisme et Renaissance 443 (Geneva: Droz, 2008), and his "Places of Sanctification: The Liturgical Sacrality of the Genevan Reformed Churches, 1535–1566," in *Sacred Space in Early Modern Europe*, ed. Will Coster and Andrew Spicer (Cambridge: Cambridge University Press, 2005), 60–80.

recited only by the presiding pastor.[10] Even in preaching, the central rite of worship, the pastor was elevated above the people, marking out his special office as prophetic—an office also distinguished by knowledge of the Bible and its languages.[11] The ghost of the old priesthood still walked the walls like Hamlet's murdered father, whispering, "Remember me."

This essay explores the ways in which the Zurich Reformers negotiated a historical and theological relationship with the past to establish the authentic lineage for their worship while drawing freely from the liturgical traditions of the church. All too frequently, the use of the past by Protestant Reformers has been characterized as "invention," but the label is misleading.[12] The place of memory in early modern society lay in the unshakable belief that all truth claims had to be rooted in history.[13] Engagement with the past was selective, yet memory was understood as a repository of truth accessible and applicable to the present.

In their reading of the church fathers and scholastic authors, the Protestant Reformers, like their Catholic and more radical counterparts, drew selectively from these sources. We know that many leading figures frequently did not engage ancient or medieval authors in the original texts but relied on florilegia and the works of others to provide choice passages. In historical writing and liturgy the approach was similar, evidenced by the preference for certain *auctoritates* and sources above others. Zwingli and his

[10] Bruce Gordon, "Transcendence and Community in Zwinglian Worship: The Liturgy of 1525 in Zurich," in *Continuity and Change in Christian Worship*, ed. R. N. Swanson (Bury St. Edmonds: Boydell Press, 1999), 139–40.

[11] Peter Opitz, "The Authority of Scripture in the Early Zurich Reformation (1522–1540)," *Journal of Reformed Theology* 5 (2011): 296–309.

[12] With a slightly unfortunate title for a good book, Esther Chung-Kim, *Inventing Authority: The Use of the Church Fathers in Reformation Debates over the Eucharist* (Waco, TX: Baylor University Press, 2011).

[13] Judith Pollmann and Erika Kuijpers, "Introduction. On the Early Modernity of Modern Memory," in *Memory before Modernity: Practices of Memory in Early Modern Europe*, ed. Erika Kuijpers, Judith Pollmann, Johannes Müller, and Jasper van der Steen (Leiden: Brill, 2013), 6.

contemporaries had a deep sense of time and temporal distance.[14] They understood that neither history nor the ancient sources of the church were static. The interaction of the Reformers with the authorities of the past entailed constant negotiation and reassessment: at different moments, different sources or authors were most applicable, although they were always to be read in light of Scripture, the essential hermeneutical principle. Hence there was a degree of freedom in the use of ancient material, which could depend on contemporary needs.

We must place liturgy within the framework of memory, history, and reform because the Reformers understood worship as an essential part of the historical identity of a community, as a principal means by which a community remembered, and as ritual enacting an embodiment of memory. But as text or embodied act, liturgy did not stand alone. A fuller consideration of the subject needs to place liturgy alongside sermons, devotional literature, drama, and theological tracts, for example. All these forms of literature were aspects of a culture of remembrance, commemoration, and identity.

Attention to the early liturgical changes in Zurich reveals the mindset of the Reformers on the nature of religious change in the first years of the Reformation. The 1520s witnessed a recalibration of the present in terms of a past imagined to provide many different examples—the virtuous kings of Israel and a golden age of the "early church," for example—and with an implicit acknowledgment of the validity of medieval reform movements. As Elizabeth Castelli has written of early Christian martyrological texts, the task of Christian historians was to form collective memory by creating continuity over temporal and geographical distance.[15] The purpose of early Christian authors, as of Protestant Reformers, was to plot a trajectory with a teleology understood in light of the divine will.

Against their Catholic opponents, the Protestant Reformers understood the necessity of winning the struggle for the past in order

---

[14] Paulina Kewes, "History and Its Uses," in *The Uses of History in Early Modern England*, ed. Paulina Kewes (San Marino, CA: Huntington Library, 2006), 3.

[15] Elizabeth A. Castelli, *Martyrdom and Memory: Early Christian Culture Making* (New York: Columbia University Press, 2004), 25.

to claim the legitimacy of contemporary changes.[16] They scoured the ancient sources available to them to support their claims, and the results were not simply proof-texting, though they may seem so to our eyes.[17] Rather, the Reformers' approach is best understood as a conscious and shrewd study of texts determined by contextual, polemical, and theological concerns that were not easily separated. The practical needs and demands of their reading of church history must not be mistaken for mere pragmatism or apology; above all, the Reformers looked to history and theology to find material that both supported the arguments and ecclesiology of the Reformation and stood the test of "sola scriptura."[18]

The argument, held by both confessional proponents and critics of the Reformers, that the Reformation was entirely *de novo* does little justice to the theological, historical, and liturgical lines of continuity in the sixteenth century. But the radical nature of change in the 1520s must not be underestimated, and when Zwingli penned his liturgies in 1523 and 1525, he was fully aware that he was creating forms of worship that had never existed previously. Yet, as we shall see, liturgical creativity for Zwingli was not license for innovation: he understood reform as a means to recover the Hebrew and early Christian origins of worship. His approach, however, requires our careful attention to the manner in which he interpreted

[16] The classic work on Protestant history writing remains A. G. Dickens and J. M. Tonkin, *The Reformation in Historical Thought* (Oxford: Basil Blackwell, 1985). See also Alexandra Kess, *Johann Sleidan and the Protestant Vision of History* (Aldershot: Ashgate, 2008); Irena Backus, *Historical Method and Confessional Identity in the Era of the Reformation (1378–1615)* (Leiden: Brill, 2003); Patrick Collinson, "Truth and Legend: The Veracity of John Foxe's Book of Martyrs," in *Clio's Mirror: Historiography in Britain and the Netherlands*, ed. A. C. Duke and C. A. Tamse (Zutphen: De Walburg Pers, 1985), 31–54.

[17] See Backus, *Historical Method*; Gillian Evans, *Problems of Authority in the Reformation Debates* (Cambridge, UK: Cambridge University Press, 1992); Leif Grane, Alfred Schindler, and Markus Wriedt, eds., *Auctoritas Patrum: Contributions on the Reception of the Church Fathers in the 15th and 16th Century* (Mainz: Philipp von Zabern, 1993); and Anthony N. S. Lane, *John Calvin, Student of the Church Fathers* (Grand Rapids, MI: Baker Books, 1999).

[18] The most accessible overview of Zwingli's theology is Peter Stephens, *The Theology of Huldrych Zwingli* (Oxford: Oxford University Press, 1986).

historical and theological continuity. When we consider the new liturgical formulae within the context of space and action, a window opens onto the nature of the Reformation itself, in which the present was beholden to the past. At the same time, the needs of the present reshaped that past.

The formation of the 1523 and 1525 liturgies in Zurich was a bold expression of historical imagination.[19] Efforts have been made to link Zwingli's form of worship with late medieval offices such as the 1502 *Manuale curatorum* of Ulrich Surgant in Basel, but the evidence is not conclusive.[20] Zwingli's principles of reform, which have been by no means fully explored, derived from his desire to embrace the biblical narrative of salvation in covenantal form. As Gottfried Locher remarked more than sixty years ago, the covenantal reading of biblical history was the great contribution of Zurich to Reformed thought.[21] In other words, Zwingli interwove Scripture and prayer, together with physical movement and visual effect, to place worshipers in a salvation history of the Israelites that was fulfilled in the cross.

The overlapping engagements with the past integral to the formation of a liturgy of the Lord's Supper in Zurich manifested Zwingli's central concern that the worship of the church stand in continuity with an imagined golden age, a time when the church was pure. In the crossfire of theological debate and an extraordinary personal experience, the Reformer came to understand how the new liturgy created during the years 1523–1525 was an authentic expression of the Last Supper and, even more, of the covenantal relationship with God. A story was told that made the Reformation a crucial moment in salvation history yet linked to the past by

---

[19] Lee Palmer Wandel, "Envisioning God: Image and Liturgy in Reformation Zurich," *Sixteenth Century Studies* 24 (1993): 21–40.

[20] See the critique in Roland Diethelm, "Bullinger and Worship: 'Thereby does one plant and sow the true faith,'" in *Architect of Reformation: An Introduction to Heinrich Bullinger, 1504–1575*, ed. Bruce Gordon and Emidio Campi (Grand Rapids, MI: Baker Academic, 2004), 136.

[21] Gottfried W. Locher, *Zwingli's Thought: New Perspectives* (Leiden: Brill, 1981), 114.

authentic worship in which believers had an immediate and intimate encounter with both the ancient Israelites and Christ.

Here we shall explore the historical and theological girders of Zurich ideology as well as the prophetic quality manifested in a remarkable dream of Zwingli's. And finally, we shall turn to how the defense of Zwingli and the historical account of his grounding of the tradition became defining markers of identity for the Zurich church, by looking briefly at the history of the conflict over the Lord's Supper written by Ludwig Lavater in Latin in 1563 (and published in German in 1564).[22]

RECOVERING HISTORY

Zwingli believed that the Reformation occupied a particular and special moment in history, a moment of divine intervention when evil had reached full fruition in Christian lands.[23] Like Luther, Zwingli was persuaded that the depredations of his age, such as the moral chaos in the Swiss lands attributed to the mercenary service and the calamitous state of the church, were not simply regrettable occurrences but evidence of the eschatological reality of Antichrist's presence in the world. Indeed, it was the age of Antichrist. Humanity had abandoned God and was wholly given over to sensuous desires—manifested, among other ways, in the plague of syphilis. Zwingli was a fierce critic of what he saw as the moral turpitude of his age, when all things stood in opposition to the

[22] I use the German translation of 1564: *Historia oder Gschicht von dem Ursprung und Fürgang der grossen Zwyspaltung, so sich zwüschend D. Martin Luthern an eim und Huldrychen Zwinglio am anderen Teil, auch zwüschend anderen Gelerten von wägen dess Herren Nachtmals gehalten hat und noch haltet, von dem Jar des Herren 1524 an biss uff das 1563. & c / anfangs in Latin durch Ludwigen Lafatern, Dieneren der Kirchen zuo Zürych, beschriben, letstlich in tütsche Spraach verdolmätschet. . . .* Getruckt zuo Zürych: durch Christoffel Froschower, anno 1564. Manfred Vischer, *Bibliographie der Zürcher Druckschriften des 15. und 16. Jahrhunderts* (Baden-Baden: V. Koerner, 1991), C 746; *Verzeichnis der im deutschen Sprachbereich erschienenen Drucke des 16. Jahrhunderts* (VD 16), L 823.

[23] See Gottfried W. Locher, "Huldrych Zwingli's Concept of History," in Locher, *Zwingli's Thought,* 95–120. See also Bruce Gordon, "The Changing Face of Protestant History Writing," in *Protestant History and Identity in Sixteenth-Century Europe,* 2 vols., ed. Bruce Gordon (Aldershot: Scolar, 1996), 1:1–22.

revealed Word of God. Yet, for those who believed, for those who lived in faith, it was an age of a different triumph, for Christ had risen again, the Word of God had been loosed upon the earth and proclaimed by prophets such as the German Reformers.

Drawing on Augustine and other patristic authors, Zwingli began to articulate his vision of a godly society.[24] At the first disputation in Zurich, in 1523, he declared that customs of the church had to give way to truth, setting up a dichotomy between past and present that served his immediate polemical purposes but that was by no means the Reformer's final word on the nature of religious change. That he had every intention of preserving existing forms of the church became evident within months. In August of the same year, Zwingli introduced his *De canone missae epichiresis*, in which he made clear his repudiation of any sense that the Mass was a sacrifice on the altar.[25] The Lord's Supper, he wrote, was a memorial and thanksgiving. Yet although he made significant alterations to the Canon, Zwingli retained a considerable amount of the liturgy, such as worship in Latin, although the Bible was read in German. The compromise suited no one, including Zwingli, but reflected the hybrid nature of reform that inflected change in Zurich. As with liturgical reform, institutional reform and doctrinal reform also required a balancing act involving tradition and innovation, a canny set of decisions about how far one could go, as well as a desire to remain within the established practices of the Western church.

Zwingli's approach to the past naturally molded his reading of church history, where he made a clear distinction between the absolute authority of the Word of God and the "relative" authority of

[24] On Zwingli's use of Augustine, see Christian Moser, "Ulrich Zwingli," in *The Oxford Guide to the Historical Reception of Augustine*, vol. 3, ed. Karla Pollmann (Oxford: Oxford University Press, 2013), 1926–30.

[25] "De canone missae epichiresis," 29 August 1523, *Huldreich Zwinglis sämtliche Werke* (Corpus Reformatorum 88–93.5; Berlin, Leipzig, and Zurich: 1905–91) (henceforth cited as Z, with volume number) vol. 2, 556–608. See Johannes Voigtländer, *Ein Fest der Befreiung: Huldrych Zwinglis Abendmahlslehre* (Neukirchen-Vluyn: Neukirchener Theologie, 2013), 43–49.

history, that is, of human events.[26] Yet his choices could seem random. For example, on the basis of tradition he recognized the first four ecumenical councils of the church and placed the appearance of Antichrist in the church from about 500 CE, when, he believed, human doctrines began to prevail over Scripture. Zwingli offers little guidance to help us understand his historical arguments.[27] Without doubt, history was crafted by the Reformer to provide a source of authority for his doctrinal positions. This disposition was also integral to his reading of ancient texts.

To engage with Zwingli's understanding of the reciprocal relationship between past and present, we need to turn to his scholarly labors. The picture becomes distinctly mixed. Like his contemporaries, Zwingli drew widely from the fathers, whom he had first encountered in the library of the monastery of Einsiedeln, without any clear designation of who they were. He never referred to them as "patres ecclesiae," but simply as "patres" or "veteres."[28] He went to great lengths to procure the latest editions of the fathers for his library, which has remained intact. But he was less interested in the authenticity of ancient figures than in adopting their interpretive methods for his own use.[29] If one takes the example of Augustine, the eight volumes of whose works Zwingli owned and extensively annotated, the method of reading is instructive. The Reformer drew heavily from passages that supported his idea of a spiritual eating of the bread and wine and ignored those less congenial to his theology.[30]

Zwingli provides a good example of the extent to which the Reformers relied on medieval sources for their arguments. In the case of the Zurich Reformer, of central importance was canon law, from which he drew arguments that shaped his understanding of history and where he found material for his position on the

[26] Locher, "Huldrych Zwingli's Concept of History," 96f.
[27] Ibid.
[28] Irena Backus, "Ulrich Zwingli, Martin Bucer and the Church Fathers," in *The Reception of the Church Fathers in the West: From the Carolingians to the Maurists*, ed. Irena Backus, 2 vols. (Leiden: Brill, 1997), 2:629.
[29] Ibid., 2:639.
[30] Ibid., 2:631.

marriage of priests, fasting, and the papacy.[31] Canon law was not only authoritative but also the source of essential passages from the fathers for use in theological and historical arguments.

As Irena Backus has argued, Zwingli had considerable reverence for tradition as expressed in written texts but not for oral tradition.[32] In this respect, the church fathers, above all Augustine, occupied a place just below Scripture. Sola scriptura, the heart and soul of the Reformation, was nuanced by the place of patristic material in the tradition of the church. We need, however, to be attentive to what the Zurich Reformer believed he was doing. His arguments remained focused on the biblical text, and his use of Augustine was both polemical and proof that the written corpus of Christian doctrine supported his position.[33] Reading of the fathers was intended to help the identification of doctrine in the Word, though such activity necessarily involved the choice of one ancient source over another. The Bible held the place of honor, while the patristic authors enabled the construction of theology. The relationship between the two, however, was often murky, as the Reformers' opponents were quick to notice. Zwingli's method was to find in the fathers support for his reading of Scripture.[34] The Bible was read through the exegetical and institutional forms of the early church, which were, in turn, studied in light of the Bible.

DREAMING REFORM

The Zwingli of Reformation textbooks is generally the "humanist Reformer," with little in the way of a distinctive personality in comparison to the volcanic Luther. While that particular discussion need not detain us here, of considerable interest is the Reformer's emerging sense of personal authority in the period leading up to the liturgy of 1525. Our consideration of Zwingli's construction of the past takes us to a remarkable moment in his life rarely mentioned in scholarly literature. In his 1563 account of the dispute

---

[31] Ibid., 2:640.
[32] Ibid.
[33] Ibid., 2:643.
[34] Ibid., 2:644.

over the Lord's Supper, Ludwig Lavater, minister and son-in-law of Heinrich Bullinger, Zwingli's successor as the head of the Zurich church, provides brief mention of a 1525 incident in which Huldrych Zwingli claimed to have had a dream in which the true nature of the Lord's Supper was revealed to him.[35]

Lavater's account comes from Zwingli's own words, found in his 1525 treatment of the Lord's Supper, *Subsidium sive coronis de eucharistia*.[36] Zwingli emphasizes his belief in the power of dreams as a medium of God's Word, in the utter graciousness of a saving God, and in his singular calling as a prophet. No less than Luther, Zwingli was wholly convinced that God had called him at a particular moment in history to bring about the revival of the church.[37]

One is unprepared for the sudden appearance of a dream sequence in the *Subsidium*. Indeed, Zwingli opens his story with a recognition that what is to follow will be dismissed by many, and he was opposed to any suggestion that dreams might offer any additional or alternative form of revelation. Following a series of arguments on the Lord's Supper that had largely appeared in previous writings, he suddenly and tantalizingly reveals that he is about to recall an experience that he knows will open him to ridicule but that must be told as a matter of conscience. The imagined debate concerned the correct interpretation of "est" in "hoc est enim corpus meum." In the dream, Zwingli had been arguing that "est" was to be understood as "significat," but opposition to his view was fierce, and Zwingli was struggling to hold his ground. His opponents could produce a great deal of supporting material from Scripture, including the parables, where "est" clearly did not mean "signify."

---

[35] Lavater, *Historia oder Gschicht von dem Ursprung*. sig. Biiir–v. The literature on dreams in the Reformation is limited; see Alec Ryrie, "Sleeping, Waking, and Dreaming in Protestant Piety," in *Private and Domestic Devotion in Early Modern Britain*, ed. Jessica Martin and Alex Ryrie (Farnham: Ashgate, 2012), 73–92.

[36] "Subsidium sive coronis de eucharistia," Z 4:483–84.

[37] See Martin Hauser, *Prophet und Bischof: Huldrych Zwinglis Amtsverständnis im Rahmen der Zürcher Reformation* (Fribourg: Universitätsverlag, 1994).

Zwingli speaks of his dream. He writes,

> Undoubtedly, no easy task was before me, namely to cite an exam-
> ple for my mode of interpretation, derived from no parable. I began
> to think over it, to look for it everywhere; in vain! I could find noth-
> ing. The 13th of April was at hand; I tell the truth (willingly, would I
> keep silent, for I know well many will make a mock of it; but it is
> God's finger, my conscience constrains me to speak) early in the
> morning, before the break of day, I dreamed that I, yet full of cha-
> grin, was once more attacked in battle with the under-clerk, and so
> beaten that I could discover no way of escape, and my tongue re-
> fused to do its office.[38]

Zwingli continues by speaking of the anguish of his dream and
his wish to dismiss the event as belonging to the deceitful night,
but he has learned that such is God's power that God can act by
any means God chooses. Nevertheless, he is foggy on some of the
details and reminds his reader that what he recounts was a dream.

By means of a staging device (μηχανή or machina) an admonisher
(monitor) appeared—Zwingli adds that he does not know whether
the person was in black or white—who rebuked the Reformer, calling him a coward ("ignavus").[39] The force of the figure's language
is arresting, for he did not hesitate to insult the Reformer, who was
doing his best to contend with his opponent. Why was he a coward? According to the story, Zwingli's foolishness and weakness lay
in his failure to consult the Word of God. With Zwingli rendered
mute, only the dramatic appearance of the admonisher resolved the
confrontation between the two men. The mysterious figure barked
at Zwingli to respond to his opponent ("respondes ei") that in Exodus 12:11 is written, "Est enim Phase" (It is the Lord's Passover).[40]

How did this line from the second book of Moses enable Zwingli
to prevail? A moment of revelation, Zwingli continues, caused him

---

[38] The translation of this passage is from Johann Jakob Hottinger, *Life and
Times of Ulric Zwingli*, trans. T. C. Porter (Harrisburg: Theo F. Scheffer, 1859),
305.
[39] Z 4:483.
[40] Ibid.

to wake and spring from his bed to consult his Septuagint, which confirmed the visitor's reading. Zwingli undertook to preach on the passage, thereby teaching those who doubted that "est" means "significat."[41] The Passover meal (Lord's Supper) was celebrated at Easter in Zurich as never before, according to Zwingli, and no one looked back to the garlic and oil of Egypt (Num 11:4), that is, the Mass.[42] The dream led Zwingli in his writings to his narrative of the first Reformed celebration of the Lord's Supper in Zurich, which he described as a "Passover."

The strategic placing of the dream in the midst of one of Zwingli's most important texts on the Lord's Supper has several dimensions worthy of attention. The scene is a crucial moment in establishing the authority of Zwingli and his teaching, perhaps in response to the supernatural elements in Luther's *vita*. The occurrence of the dream just before Easter and the introduction of the new liturgy provided divine sanction of reform, while the text in Exodus confirmed Zwingli's view of the meal as an act of remembrance of God's deliverance of the Israelites and Christ's gathering with his disciples in the Upper Room.

Who exactly was the unnamed adversary of Zwingli's dream? We might presume he was one of Zwingli's local opponents, but on the larger stage the figure could be a reference to Martin Luther, who robustly contested Zwingli's interpretation of "est." The admonisher or counselor who appeared via a theatrical machine intended to make him appear divine is harder to identify, but what is not in doubt is that the person spoke the truth by directing Zwingli to the crucial passage in Exodus.

Zwingli's own role is significant. He was frozen in the face of his opponent, unable to speak; he had no answers in the debate. In the German version later recounted by Lavater, the emphasis is on Zwingli's failure to answer. In this state of paralysis Zwingli was rebuked, told to say something that the admonisher seemed to suggest that Zwingli should have known. The Zurich Reformer therefore presented himself in the dream account as having failed.

---

[41] Ibid., 484.
[42] Ibid.

He was unable to deal with his adversaries on the human level; he was only able to speak when the admonisher, possibly the Holy Spirit, came to him and provided revelation from the Word.

The resolution came with the connection between the Lord's Supper and the Passover meal of the Israelites. That link is what Zwingli needed to know in order to be able to refute his adversary, what he needed to know to explain to those who doubted the nature of the Eucharist. That the admonisher pointed Zwingli to a passage from the Pentateuch reinforced the covenantal nature of the sacrament. The Eucharist in Zurich found its narrative in the story of the Israelites' liberation from Egypt. The historical memory of the meal of thanksgiving became the framework of the liturgy.

Zwingli's response was to awaken from his dream and immediately confirm the revelation in Scripture, in this instance in the Septuagint ("Locum apud Septuaginta primum undique circumspicio"). Zwingli had a high view of the Greek translation of the Old Testament as an inspired text, and he valued it above the Hebrew Masoretic text.[43] Once the verity of the admonisher's words had been established, Zwingli moved to preach, to the proclamation of the Word. The link between inspiration and homiletic exposition is conveyed in the order of the story. True preaching, by which Zwingli's authority was confirmed, immediately resulted in the establishment of certainty: those students who did not understand the nature of the Lord's Supper or the parable had "the mist lifted from their eyes."

Zwingli devoted considerable attention to the character of the Passover as a means of interpreting the Lord's Supper.[44] The key texts were Matthew 26:29 and the passage of the dream, at Exodus 12:11. Particularly, the Exodus passage took him to an understanding of the Passover as a harbinger of Christ's sacrifice, for the Son of God is the true Passover lamb. The Passover meal was a reminder, a symbol, of God's saving action. Just as the Passover was

---

[43] On Zwingli and the Septuagint, see Henning Reventlow, *Epochen der Bibelauslegung*, vol. 3 (Munich: Beck, 1997), 111f.

[44] See Voigtländer, *Ein Fest der Befreiung*, 87–88.

celebrated before the avenging angel brought death to the Egyptians, so too was it celebrated by Christ before his crucifixion. The meal was a celebration of memory, a commemoration of salvation that had become a thanksgiving for God's having sent his son into the world.

The remarkable dream sequence was not a mere curiosity in the life of Huldrych Zwingli, for it offers us a perspective on the emerging sense of historical authority in Zurich worship. The role of memory was crucial. Dreams are unreliable, as Zwingli says, and they take place at night, a time full of danger and disorder.[45] Zwingli was aware that what he remembered from the dream would be treated by many as mere delusion, and he was himself skeptical until confirmation was found in Scripture. Zwingli demonstrated awareness of the danger or fragility of memory as a means of reform. Memory can only be legitimated through the prophetic interpretation of Scripture. Memory, for Zwingli, therefore, became the possession of a few. In his later reference to the dream, in accord with the words of Castelli, Lavater engages in "narrativising of the past and a careful linking of particular stories to larger, cultural master narratives."[46]

SACRAMENT AND MEMORY

From 1523 Martin Luther had voiced powerful opposition to Zwingli's reading of crucial New Testament passages relating to the Lord's Supper.[47] The successors of the German Reformer

[45] On the fear of night in the early modern world, see Craig Koslofsky, *Evening's Empire: A History of the Night in Early Modern Europe* (Cambridge and New York: Cambridge University Press, 2011).

[46] Castelli, *Martyrdom and Memory*, 30.

[47] The literature on the Wittenberg-Zurich struggle is vast. The classic study is Walther Köhler, *Zwingli und Luther: Ihr Streit über das Abendmahl nach seinem politischen und religiösen Beziehungen* (Gütersloh: C Bertelsmann, 1953). Notable recent contributions are Stephen Strehle, "Fides aut Foedus: Wittenberg and Zurich in Conflict over the Gospel," *Sixteenth Century Journal* 23 (1992): 3–20; Amy Nelson Burnett, *Karlstadt and the Origins of the Eucharist Controversy: A Study in the Circulation of Ideas* (Oxford: Oxford University Press, 2011); and Armin Buchholz, *Schrift Gottes im Lehrstreit: Luthers Schriftverständnis und Schriftauslegung in seinen drei grossen Lehrstreitigkeiten der Jahre 1521–1528*

continued the polemic, responding with outrage to the 1549 *Consensus Tigurinus*, struck between Heinrich Bullinger and John Calvin, in which Zurich and Geneva reached a level of agreement on the Eucharist. The Lutheran assault fell largely on Zwinglian Christology, which was named both Nestorian and Arian. Luther had charged that Zwingli had improperly separated the two natures of Christ by denying any bodily presence in the world after the resurrection. Later, Bullinger faced the accusations of Johannes Brenz and others that the Zurich church subordinated the Son to the Father, even reducing Christ to the status of a prophet, as did the Muslims.

The roots of that controversy lay in the first years of the Reformation, when Zwingli's eucharistic theology emerged with his liturgical innovations. In the white heat of the conflict over the Lord's Supper that engulfed the Reformation during its first half-dozen years, Zwingli devoted more time and ink to the Eucharist than to any other subject, and his position deepened. His central arguments, however, are easily retrieved. For Zwingli, all theology derived from one essential truth, the utter simplicity and sovereignty of God.[48] The Reformer saw the error of the late medieval church as lying in an idolatrous relationship between the material and the divine. He sought to separate God's absolute goodness from what is human sinfulness. Such an Augustinian view would find consensus among most of the Reformers, but Zwingli's next move proved highly controversial. He refused to admit that any material object could be a conduit of divine grace. In other words, the bread and wine were symbols of God's saving grace in Christ, but the liturgical action could have nothing to do with rendering the elements channels of God's gifts. The same applied to water in the rite of baptism.

(Basel: Brunnen Verlag, 2007). Also, John A. Maxwell, "Luther, Zwingli, and Calvin on the Significance of Christ's Death," *Concordia Theological Quarterly* 75 (2011): 91–110; Thomas Kaufmann, "Luther and Zwingli," in *Luther-Handbuch*, ed. Albrecht Beutel (Tübingen: Mohr-Siebeck, 2005), 152–61, and Amy Nelson Burnett, "The Social History of Communion and the Reformation of the Eucharist," *Past and Present* 211 (2011): 77–119.

[48] See Voigtländer, *Ein Fest der Befreiung*.

In his account of John 6:51, "whoever eats this bread will live forever" (NIV),[49] Zwingli writes:

> Christ is not speaking here of sacramental eating; for he is only so
> far salvation unto us as He was slain for us; but he could be slain
> only according to the flesh and could be salvation bringing only ac-
> cording to his divinity. In this way, then, is Christ the food of the
> soul, because the soul, seeing that God spared not his only begotten
> son but delivered him to an ignominious death in order to restore us
> to life, becomes sure of the grace of God and of salvation.[50]

The crux of the matter was Christ's words "this is my body,"
which Zwingli famously interpreted to mean "this signifies
my body." The Reformer's purpose was to establish that Christ
commanded the faithful to eat the bread and drink the wine in
remembrance of him, for Zwingli named the Lord's Supper a commemoration of Christ's death that does not, as a ritual, expiate sins.
That role belongs to Christ's death alone. The people were to give
thanks and proclaim the Good News of Jesus Christ. Luke 22:20
speaks of "the new covenant in my blood," and Zwingli interpreted the passage thus: "for in this we commemorate the blessing
that Christ's death and the shedding of his blood have brought us,
and enjoying these blessings we are grateful unto the Lord God for
the testament that he has freely bestowed upon us."[51]

The celebration of the Lord's Supper is the response of the community to God's actions, a response under the guidance of the
Holy Spirit to Christ's words "do this in remembrance of me."
The foundation of the communal response is God's action in Jesus
Christ. It was on account of this response that Zwingli spoke of
the Lord's Supper as "commemoratio."[52] Memory takes the people
back to the crucifixion with the words of institution. These words
are linked to the symbols of the bread and the cup, which serve the

---

[49] Scripture quotations in this essay are taken from the *New International
Version*.
[50] Z 3:779.
[51] Z 3:800.
[52] Z 3:785.

people's weak faith. The Lord's Supper is a bringing to mind or re-visualizing of Christ's death on the cross.

Crucial to this understanding of the sacrament is what is meant by memory and remembering. Zwingli, particularly in his later writings, spoke of a "fidei contemplatio," a faithful meditation that moves from the external symbols of Christ to an inward sense of "our Christ." The "fidei contemplatio" was key to understanding Zwingli's view of remembrance and how Christ was present in the bread and wine in both his natures.[53] For Zwingli, the whole of Christ was present at the celebration of the Lord's Supper. He was hesitant to speak in terms of presence because of associations with the Mass, but he was clear that with reference to real presence, Christ was present in his divinity. The precise manner in which the Holy Spirit works in the Lord's Supper was not a subject on which Zwingli wished to speculate. He preferred to argue that the Spirit could not be limited to or restrained by the institutional church. It could move and act as it wished, without any damage to God's relationship with humanity.

The relationship between sign and signified in Zwingli was delicately balanced. The bread and wine did not become the body of Christ—those qualities remain with the Son. Everything that happened did so through the Holy Spirit, through whom the bread and wine, as symbols or images, reveal the similarity to the body and blood. At the same time, however, God is not in any respect bound to that relationship between symbol and reality. Zwingli wanted to preserve the reality of the symbolic relationship while maintaining the absolute freedom of God. The combination of the outward form and the inner reality of faith confirmed by the Holy Spirit reminded men and women of God's promises and encouraged them in the faith. The Lord's Supper was a celebration of God's saving action and of his continuing love toward his chosen.

[53] The expression "fidei contemplatio" is used in the *Fidei ratio* of 1530, see Z 6.2:806.

At Easter 1525, the Zurich council introduced a new order of service for the Lord's Supper. The letter of the pastors that opened the order offered an account of the principles by which liturgical reform were undertaken. The pastors, likely Zwingli, described the new worship as a liberation from "darkness" and "a long imprisonment" as in the time of Hezekiah (2 Kgs 18:4) and Josiah (2 Chr 34:3-7), when the children of Israel recovered the Easter Lamb with the help of God.[54]

Some people, Zwingli wrote, might accuse the Zurichers of having done too much in revising the ceremony of worship, while others believed their efforts to be too little. Be that as it may, the pastors argued that there was considerable latitude within the church, and that each congregation should decide what was best for itself. Such flexibility, however, was sharply confined by the absolute necessity of not returning to the idolatry of the Mass, which damaged the church as a sign of apostasy. The boundary between true and false worship for the Zurich Reformers was marked by the doctrine of transubstantiation, which was the highest form of desecration.

To begin, Zwingli cast the liturgical act of 1525 as a recovery of the Lord's Supper, employing a verb of aggression, "conquer," that suggests a forceful act.[55] Zwingli was creating a form of worship previously unknown. No longer, as in 1523, was he framing Reformed worship around the canon of the Mass. In 1525 Zwingli dispensed with any pretense of continuity with the Mass in order to place his emphasis on the covenantal relationship of the Zurich church with the ancient Israelites. The dream narrative had pointed to Exodus and the link of the Eucharist with the Lord's Supper, providing the Reformer with a usable past for his changes.

In the letter accompanying the liturgy for the Lord's Supper of 1525, the biblical narrative is taken from 2 Chronicles 34, where young King Josiah purged the worship of the land, removing idols and cutting down the altars of Baal. Similarly, Hezekiah, in

---

[54] "Aktion oder Brauch des Nachtmahls" Z 4:13.
[55] Ibid.

2 Kings, "did what was right in the eyes of the Lord," and destroyed images and altars, including the bronze serpent of Moses. Creative in Zwingli's account was his seamless linking of these stories to something they naturally do not mention explicitly, the claiming of the "Easter Lamb" and his rightful establishment as the sacred meal.[56] Zwingli's christological reading of the text forms the backbone to the practice of Reformed theological thought and the creation of liturgical drama.

For Zwingli, ceremony ("cermonien") is only partially a neutral act. Indeed, it can vary from place to place—within the limits of avoiding idolatry—but worship cannot be without structure, and the Reformer was acutely aware that Scripture offered few guidelines.[57] In his first liturgical reforms of 1523, as we have seen, Zwingli had stayed close to the canon of the Mass, replacing certain elements and retaining others. In 1525, however, he opted for an entirely new order of worship, although he wished to avoid charges of innovation. "We therefore think it best," he wrote, "to prescribe as little ceremonial and churchly custom as we can for our people's use of this Supper—which is also a ceremony, but instituted by Christ—lest we yield again, in time, to the old error."[58] An important interplay of terms in the address helps us to follow Zwingli's distinctions. Most significant is the distinction between practice (or use) ("Bruch") and ceremony ("Ceremonien"), which is indicated by the presence of the former term in the title and the absence of the latter. The "use of this Supper" refers to the historical fact that the sacrament was implemented by Christ at the Last Supper. It has the force of both divine command and historical continuity, for the Supper was a Passover meal, linking the sacrament to the salvation story of Israel.

Ceremony, in contrast, does not have divine warrant and, therefore, it can be adapted to human circumstance. Zwingli speaks of

---

[56] Ibid.

[57] Z 4:14.

[58] The translations of the 1525 liturgy are from Bard Thompson, *Liturgies of the Western Church* (New York and Scarborough, Ont: Meridian Books, 1961), 149. I have lightly revised the translations in accordance with the original German.

ceremony as a concession to "human weakness" ("menschlichen blödikeit") so that the essential sacramental act, the "practice" or "action," is not performed in a "lifeless" manner and without shape.[59] Therefore, "we have authorized such ceremonies," he claims, "for the action—as appointed here which we have deemed beneficial and appropriate to enhance in some degree the spiritual memorial of the death of Christ, the increase of faith and brotherly love, the reformation of life, and the prevention of the vices of the human heart."[60]

Ceremony is the outward form of true religion, but Zwingli did not pose a dichotomy between ceremony and action.[61] The latter did not rely on the former, for the author of the sacrament is Christ himself, and the focus of memory was on the words of institution. However—and this point was crucial to Zwingli's understanding of Reformation in all its forms (institutional, doctrinal, etc.)—the action of the Lord's Supper did not have an established form in terms of performance in the church. Essential are the bread, wine, and the words, but otherwise there is considerable latitude.

Such interpretive space was where Reformation took place and where it established narrative. Further, when he came to ceremony, Zwingli acquired a degree of authority, arguing that he and his fellow ministers had decided what constitutes a sufficient level of liturgical practice. The basis of their decision, he argued, was an assessment of how much ceremony was required to promote piety among fallen humans. Zwingli made a subtle though determined shift from "Aktion" as a divine act to ceremony as the product of a human authority—in this case, of Zwingli himself.

In his 1525 letter accompanying the liturgy, Zwingli made a series of theological and historical moves that framed the evolving character of the Zurich Reformation. He innovated by creating a form of liturgy for the Lord's Supper that had no clear historical

---

[59] Ibid.
[60] Ibid.
[61] On Zwingli on the nature of "religion," Gordon, "Emulating the Past," 16–19, and J. Samuel Preus, "Zwingli, Calvin, and the Origin of Religion," *Church History* 46 (1977): 186–202.

precedent, although vague references to early Christianity are present. At the same moment, the Reformer provided a historical and theological lineage by linking the new ceremony directly to Christ in the Upper Room and, by extension, to the Passover meal of the Israelites. Just as the Zurich churches had been stripped and whitewashed a year earlier, so too Zwingli had purposefully abandoned all forms of medieval worship. He wanted no trace to remain, particularly of music, though as he wrote in the letter, "we have no wish to condemn the additional ceremonies of other churches—singing and such—for perhaps they are suitable for them and beneficial to their devotion."[62]

In the preface that follows the letter, Zwingli provided a model of the liturgy, of how it should take place. He opened with his boldest theological statement about the nature of reform: the liturgy that he presented is distinguished by having been purged of "everything that does not conform to the divine Word."[63] He then set the new liturgy against history, for the Word of God shows that Christ's Supper was "seriously abused" for "a long time." Zwingli saw his reforms as redeeming time, cleansing the polluted history of the church. Crucially, at no point in the *Aktion* did he refer to the Supper as a sacrament. Rather he describes "this memorial" as "a thanksgiving and a rejoicing before Almighty God for the benefit which He has manifested to us through His Son."[64]

The location of Zwingli's imagined ideal liturgy was the Grossmünster in Zurich, where the people were to gather in the nave, men on the right and women on the left. During the sermon, unleavened bread and wine were placed on a plain table in front of the people. The elements were to be presented on simple wooden dishes in order that the eye not be distracted from the bread and wine as symbols of faith. After the words of institution had been clearly recited, the elements were distributed among the people, most of whom would have been standing. At the completion of the

---

[62] Bard, *Liturgies of the Western Church*, 149–50.
[63] Ibid., 150.
[64] Ibid.

service the people came together in a prayer of thanksgiving. Such practice, according to Zwingli, was to take place four times a year.

The structure of the 1525 liturgy was relatively simple. After opening prayers and a reading of 1 Corinthians 11, the people were admonished against the unworthy reception of the bread and wine, at which point the men and women recited the Gloria antiphonally, saying the Amen together. At the conclusion of the Gloria the faithful were read passages from John 6, principally verses 47 ("Very truly I tell you, the one who believes has eternal life") and 63 ("The Spirit gives life; the flesh counts for nothing. The words I have spoken to you—they are full of the Spirit and life"). The pastor then kissed the Bible and proclaimed, "Praise and thanks be to God. He willeth to forgive all our sins according to his holy Word."

Following the confession of sin, the men and women sang the *Apostolicum* antiphonally, after which the invitation and admonition to the Supper were pronounced, which warned against "anyone [who might] pretend to be a believer who is not, and so be guilty of the Lord's death." The people knelt for the Lord's Prayer and a prayer said by the pastor beseeching God that the people might live "purely as becomes the body."

The words of institution were read at the table over unleavened bread and wine. The pastors served themselves first, before the servers took the elements to the people, who knelt to receive. The bread and wine were passed among the people in silence, which was their response to the gift of God. Following reception, Psalm 113 was recited, once more antiphonally. At the conclusion of this psalm, the benediction was pronounced and the people departed.

The reading of Psalm 113 at the end was particularly significant because of its association with the Passover, where it formed part of the Hallel. It was to be recited on joyous occasions, such as the first night of Passover, and its inclusion in the worship of the 1525 and 1529 liturgies was an intentional link between the Lord's Supper and the Passover meal, one which again placed the people of Zurich in the salvation history of the Israelites.

The 1525 liturgy, and its slightly revised 1529 form, focused the people on their obligation to live holy lives within the community while constantly reminding them that salvation is a gracious gift of God, thus linking together ethical obligations of the earthly and heavenly cities.[65] For Zwingli, the community is the body of Christ not because of any liturgical action but because of the divine promises. Liturgy for Zwingli, therefore, had ambivalence, as did the elements: liturgy was nothing in and of itself and served only to point people to higher realities, yet it was indispensable as a means to stir memory and thanksgiving. Liturgy shaped the emotions and senses, while reflecting social, political, and gender distinctions.

What takes place in worship is entirely directed by the Holy Spirit. The memory of the people, that is, those whom God has elected, is recalled by the Holy Spirit to the divine promises: that God's election and mercy is their salvation; that they alone must confess their sins; that God was gracious to them in the death and resurrection of Christ; and that they must trust that they are his people.

The Lord's Supper liturgy of 1525 emphasized the communal nature of the sacrament but was also a means of bringing the whole community together.[66] In the liturgical act in which the bread and wine were placed on the table as common elements, Zwingli stressed the link between the Supper in the church and the bread of the household. Both church and home are sacred spaces, sites of sacred memory. This bond was an essential part of the memory of Passover so important to Zwingli's theology and liturgy. The ordinariness of the bread and wine in the communion service emphasized the historical nature of the event, linking the Last Supper to the present moment. Christ is present in both.

ZWINGLI'S MEMORY AND CRAFTING
HISTORICAL NARRATIVE

In this essay I have argued for an expansive approach to memory and the past as central to liturgical change in Zurich. During the 1520s, Zwingli sought to create a new historical and theological

---

[65] Voigtländer, *Ein Fest der Befreiung*, 205–6.

[66] This argument is effectively made in Palmer Wandel, "Envisioning God," 34–39.

narrative for the community and did so through selective use of the past. In the liturgy of 1525, that narrative, with all its attendant tensions, was ritually enacted, creating new sites of memory. But within six years Zwingli was dead, a martyr for some.

It fell to a later generation to turn Zwingli's pioneering work into a historical narrative of the life of the church in the polemical battles of the 1550s and 1560s. Zwingli the master reformer became himself the object of myth. In the work of Ludwig Lavater, Heinrich Bullinger's son-in-law and head of the Zurich church in the 1570s, we see how Zwingli's own efforts at memory formation became the creation myth by which the Zurich church derived its identity as the true Body of Christ. As the Reformers of later generations sought to navigate their way through the heated polemics of the ongoing sacramentarian struggles, they provided selective accounts of Reformation history in order to create a link with an authentic past.

Lavater contended in his 1664 *Historia oder Gschicht von dem Ursprung und Fürgang der grossen Zwyspaltung* that he was offering an accurate history of the sixteenth-century conflict between the Lutherans and the Swiss churches over the Lord's Supper, while at the same time defending the memory of Zwingli and his teaching on the sacrament. Lavater's brief formed a significant challenge. He sought to reconcile scholarly and apologetic needs by providing an account of the debate that would be accepted by fellow churchmen and humanists for its objectivity and distance, while at the same time, he actively sought to counter Lutheran polemic against Zwingli and Lavater's church of the 1560s. In his treatment of the sacrament of the Lord's Supper and the liturgy of the Zurich church, Lavater was dealing with multiple pasts. First, he asserted the fidelity of the reform of worship to the rituals of the early church, arguing for a purity of inheritance that owed little to non-biblical sources. Second, he sought to demonstrate the theological orthodoxy and moral rectitude of Zwingli, who as the founding Reformer was a synecdochal figure for the Zurich church.

Lavater laid out his approach to these formidable tasks in the preface to his *History*. He began his treatment of the controversy by establishing his position as a scholar of integrity, a scholar who had examined all the sources faithfully to pursue several key questions. Above all, he asked, why did the churches split on the nature of the sacrament, and, more specifically, why did some follow Zwingli while others turned to Luther? In many places, he observed, Zwingli's teaching had been suppressed, while in others it flourished openly.

Lavater underscored the contradictory nature of events, arguing that no simple explanation was to be found. For his part, he openly admitted that he was writing from the perspective of the Swiss Confederation, and that while numerous books had been written on the Eucharist controversy, none had explained the "Zwinglian" position.[67] The story was perverted for different reasons, with some authors either lacking the texts or allowing themselves to write from hearsay.

In contrast, Lavater claimed to understand the positions of both parties. His hope was that he would be able to unite the two sides through the work of his book. His history was intended to set the record straight and thereby be a basis for future conversations. Such was the character of his book, he noted, that no one needed doubt its veracity.[68] He has only written about those things that he has been able to establish as true. To achieve this goal of accuracy, he recorded, he has made use of the work of other historians, such as Johannes Sleidanus.[69] Lavater's greatest hope remained that he would bring into the light all events, whether open or concealed, that pertained to his subject, just as would happen on the Last Day at the appearance of Christ the Savior.

Despite his claims to accuracy, Lavater did not hesitate to declare his allegiances—he adheres to the doctrine of the Eucharist proclaimed by the Swiss churches.[70] His fidelity to the Swiss doctrine of the Eucharist was not held on account of any love of Zwingli or hatred of Luther, for he declared that both were called to serve

---

[67] Lavater, *Historia oder Gschicht von dem Ursprung*, sig. Aiir–v.
[68] Ibid., sig. Aiiv.
[69] Ibid., sig. Aiiir.
[70] Ibid.

with body and life the true God.[71] The Lord's will was not that the conflict between the two men should arise, but rather that they should be reconciled in order to battle together the "Widerschriften reych." For the sake of argument, Lavater wrote, he uses the terms "Zwinglian" and "Lutheran" to distinguish the two positions, although he knows that God-fearing people do not name themselves after humans; they take the name of Christ alone.[72]

Above all, Lavater wrote, he wished his book to be useful and fruitful, and that posterity should have a full account or history of the controversy. The lesson one will learn is how out of a relatively minor affair a great division within the church arose.[73] One will also learn that only by considerable courage and labor can the matter be settled. For Lavater, the whole purpose of his book was to examine the roots of the conflict between the Zwinglians and Lutherans and to make that information as clear as possible. He was, however, not able to free himself from a polemical stance, for he maintained that the Swiss churches spared no effort to end the division, although both sides produced printed works that fanned the flames of controversy.[74]

Lavater took the sixteenth-century art of history writing to present what he claimed to be an objective account of the eucharistic struggle, but his real intention was, as we have noted, to provide a useable past for the present. Central to that narrative was the rectitude of Huldrych Zwingli, Reformer and martyr. Lavater placed himself in the text as a follower of the Christlike Zwingli. The layered discourses about the Lord's Supper in Zurich involved varied aspects of memoria.

CONCLUSION

The Zurich liturgy for the Lord's Supper of 1525 was a creative moment of historical memory, a radical act of change embedded in the traditions from which it emerged. Zwingli's engagement

---

[71] Ibid.
[72] Ibid.
[73] Ibid., sig. Aivv.
[74] Ibid., sig. Aivr.

with the past was shaped by his discovery of the link of the sacrament to the Passover meal and Last Supper. With that revelation he could create a form of worship in which Christ's instituting words—"This is my body"—could be understood in a figurative manner. The idea of "commemoratio" at the center of worship was the transformation of the faithful to an immediate encounter with the risen Christ through the intercession of the Spirit. Past and present converged in worship framed by sites of memory that included an aesthetic of whitewashed walls, table and elements, text, and silence. In a newly established ritual, the people reenacted the history of salvation, the liberation of the Israelites from Egypt, and Christ's sacrifice on the cross. The distinctive version of the Christian story comprised a rich mixture of local and universal elements specific to the chaotic years of the mid-1520s and the ideas of a particular reform.

The imagined pasts central to discourses of theology, reform, and worship need to be examined as parts of a whole, as a way of understanding the fraught and fragile world of religious change. Engagement with liturgy and the expression and embodiment of memory and change awaits the attention of Reformation scholars.

On the Wrong Side of History?

Reimagining William Whittingham,
Dean of Durham, 1563–1579

Bryan D. Spinks

A frequent saying among some contemporary politicians, as exemplified by President Obama of the United States, is that an opponent is or will find himself/herself "on the wrong side of history." In his first inaugural address, Obama stated, "To those who cling to power through corruption and deceit and the silencing of dissent, know that you are on the wrong side of history, but that we will extend a hand if you are willing to unclench your fist." Later, Obama declared that Vladimir Putin, president of Russia, was on the wrong side of history for supporting the Assad regime in Syria. He also said that Bashar Assad, president of Syria, was on the wrong side of history.[1] According to Fred Shapiro, editor of *The Yale Book of Quotations*, the phrase

---

[1] Ben Yagoda, "Is Obama Overusing the Phrase 'the Wrong Side of History'? Are We All?," http://www.slate.com/blogs/lexicon_valley/2014/04/17/the_phrase_the_wrong_side_of_history_around_for_more_than_a_century_is_getting.html, April 17, 2014. For British prime minister David Cameron's being accused of being on the wrong side of history by Nile Gardiner in the *Telegraph*, October 25, 2011, see http://blogs.telegraph.co.uk/news/nilegardiner/100112617/david-cameron-is-on-the-wrong-side-of-history-as-eu-referendum-rebels-strike-a-blow-for-british-freedom/ and by Sayeeda Wasi in the *Daily Sabah*, 15 November 2014, see http://www.dailysabah.com/europe/2014/11/15/former-british-minister-uks-palestine-policy-on-wrong-side-of-history.

"wrong side of history" appeared in more than 1,800 articles in 2013, compared to 1,485 in the previous year, and only 524 in 2006. The first use of that phrase that Shapiro found occurred in a 1908 review in the *Spectator*, and he has noted that nine years later a sermon assured soldiers that their German opponents "are on the wrong side of history and they cannot but fail."[2]

This phrase raises an interesting question: who or what determines what the "right" side of history is? Is it the prevailing system or conviction or orthodoxy in hindsight, or is there some ethical content that determines "right" and "wrong"? Michael Brick has commented that sometimes history does seem to favor things that are hard to describe as absolute moral victories for universal good, such as global warming. He noted, however, that the phrase "on the wrong side of history" has evolved into a culturally emblematic rhetorical device as the soft bullet of utter dismissiveness.[3] This paper explores the implications of the phrase with particular focus on the historical perception of William Whittingham, who was dean of Durham from 1563 to 1579. Although no one seems to have actually used this particular phrase in reference to Whittingham, it is certainly implied in the disparaging remarks that have been made about his legacy at Durham Cathedral.

William Whittingham was born in Chester in either 1520 or 1524.[4] He entered Brasenose College at the University of Oxford at the age of sixteen and became a fellow of All Souls College, and then a student (i.e., fellow) of Christ Church College. He later traveled for study at Orléans and Paris in civil law. In 1552 he arrived

---

[2] Shapiro is quoted by Michael Brick in "'Wrong Side of History' Seems to Be on the Right Side of It," *Daily Intelligencer*, December 6, 2013, http:// nymag.com/daily/intelligencer/2013/12/wrong-side-of-history-is-on-right -side-of-it.html.

[3] Ibid.

[4] Mary Anne Everett Green, ed., *Life of Mr. William Whittingham, Dean of Durham* (London: Camden Society, 1870); J. Hay Colligan, *The Honourable William Whittingham of Chester (?1524–1579)* (London: Simpkin Marshall, 1934); Richard Hunter, "William Whittingham: A Study of His Life and Writings, with Especial Reference to the Geneva New Testament" (PhD dissertation, University of Pennsylvania, 1953).

in Geneva. He returned to England in May 1553, but following the accession of Mary, two months later, he chose exile rather than return to the Catholic fold. That, however, was not before he was one of several scholars who petitioned for the Italian reformer Peter Martyr Vermigli to be allowed to leave the country. In 1554, Whittingham journeyed to Germany and with other exiles settled in Frankfurt. This was the beginning of the liturgical disputes and divisions that are recorded in *A Brief Discourse of the Troubles Begun at Frankfort*, published in 1574. This work has often been attributed to William Whittingham, but Patrick Collinson argued that the author was in fact Thomas Wood and subsequently suggested that John Field had edited the material.[5] Recently discovered transcripts of what are thought to be letters by Christopher Goodman have suggested a new chronology of the events that are recorded in *A Brief Discourse*.[6]

A Brief Discourse reports that

> in the year of our Lord 1554, and the 27th of June, came EDMUND SUTTON, WILLIAM WILLIAMS, WILLIAM WHITTINGHAM, and THOMAS WOOD, with their companies, to the City of Frankfort in Germany; the first Englishmen that there arrived to remain and abide.[7]

Valerand Poullain, minister of the French congregation in Glastonbury, England, had arrived in Frankfurt and had been granted the use of the church of the White Ladies. The newly arrived English exiles were also permitted to worship in that church, sharing it with Poullain's congregation, though "it was with this commandment,

---

[5] Patrick Collinson, "The Authorship of a Brieff Discours off the Troubles Begonne at Franckford," *Journal of Ecclesiastical History* 8 (1958): 188–208; Patrick Collinson, "John Knox, the Church of England and the Women of England," in *John Knox and the British Reformations*, ed. Roger A. Mason (Aldershot: Ashgate, 1998), 74–96, here 95.

[6] Timothy Duguid, "The 'Troubles' at Frankfurt: A New Chronology," in *Reformation & Renaissance Review* 14 (2012): 243–68; "Letters from Exile: New Documents on the Marian Exile 1553-9," www.marianexile.div.ed.ac.uk.

[7] E. Arber, ed., *A Brieff Discours of the Troubles at Frankfort 1554–1558 A.D.* (London: Elliot Stock, 1908), 23.

That the English should not dissent from the Frenchmen in Doctrine and Ceremonies: lest they should thereby minister occasion of offence."[8] In fact, as Beth Quitslund has observed, between July 1554 and the end of March 1555, ensuing struggles produced four separate liturgies at Frankfurt.[9]

At first, the English-speaking congregation followed the 1552 Prayer Book rites but with *ad hoc* modifications that conformed these rites to those of Poullain's congregation—through, for example, the omission of versicles and responses and the litany as well as the pastor's not wearing a surplice. They also agreed to sing metrical psalms as was the custom of the Reformed churches. Several letters were sent to English exiles in other cities explaining the action that had been taken. The advice that was received from those in Strasbourg and Zurich was to adopt the full 1552 rite, out of solidarity with those who were now suffering in England. Richard Chambers came to Frankfurt to urge full use of the Prayer Book, but when he could not prevail, he returned to Zurich. In November 1554, John Knox arrived in Frankfurt and was appointed minister of the congregation. Knox felt unable to use the Communion rite from the 1552 Prayer Book. At the end of November, Chambers, together with Edmund Grindal, returned to Frankfurt, where he urged the congregation once more to adopt the full English liturgy, though "not . . . to have it so strictly observed but that such Ceremonies and things, which the country [Germany] could not bear, might well be omitted; so that they might have the substance and effect thereof."[10] Knox and Whittingham questioned what was meant by "the substance." It was proposed that the congregation use the liturgy of Geneva, which had been translated into English and published by William Huycke in 1550. Knox, however, refused to use either the Geneva Rite or the English Rite. Knox and others drew up a summary of the English liturgy and sent it to Calvin in Geneva for his judgment. Eventually, "after

[8] Ibid., 24.

[9] Beth Quitslund, *The Reformation in Rhyme: Sternhold, Hopkins and the English Metrical Psalter, 1547–1603* (Aldershot: Ashgate, 2008), 118.

[10] Arber, A *Brieff Discours*, 39.

long debating to and fro, it was concluded, That Master KNOX, Master WHITTINGHAM, Master GILBY, Master FOX, and Master T. COLE, should draw forth some Order meet for their state and time. Which thing was by them accomplished and offered to the Congregation, being the same Order of Geneva, which is now in print."[11]

Though many liked this liturgy, those who wanted the English Prayer Book were not satisfied, and in the end another way was taken by the congregation. Knox, Whittingham, Parry, and Lever were appointed to devise an order to end all strife and contention. A new order was duly agreed on, some of which was taken from the English Prayer Book, with other things "put to, as to the state of that Church required."[12] In the past this "Liturgy of Compromise" has been identified with the liturgy contained in a manuscript in the British Library, Egerton 2836. Robin Leaver has argued that in fact the text of the compromise order has been lost and that Egerton 2836 represents the fourth liturgy, which was mainly the work of Richard Cox.[13] The narrative of *A Brief Discourse* explains that in late March 1554, Richard Cox and others arrived from England and that these newcomers began to break with the agreed new order and to use more portions of the English Prayer Book. As events unfolded, Cox drew the magistrates' attention to Knox's published views on Catholic rulers, and as a result, Knox was expelled and journeyed to Geneva. Leaver believes that Egerton 2836 was drawn up as a compromise that Cox negotiated between the remaining English congregation and the French. Whittingham apparently could not accept the Coxian liturgy, and he and others eventually joined Knox in Geneva. There, with Knox as minister of the English-speaking congregation, the order referred to as "now in print" was adopted, the work with the title *The Form of Prayers and Ministration of the Sacraments, etc., Used in the English Congregation at Geneva; and Approved by the Famous and Godly Learned Man,*

[11] Ibid., 52.

[12] Ibid.

[13] Robin Leaver, *The Liturgy of the Frankfurt Exiles 1555* (Bramcote: Grove Books, 1984).

John Calvin, together with a collection of metrical psalms often referred to as *The Geneva Form of Prayers*.

Whittingham left Geneva in 1560. Many of his former fellow exiles had departed earlier and many were rewarded with key positions in the Elizabethan church. James Pilkington, who at various times had been in Zurich, Geneva, and Frankfurt, was rewarded with the bishopric of Durham; Adam Holyday, who had been a member of the Geneva congregation, was appointed to the seventh prebendary stall of Durham Cathedral. Edmund Grindal, who had been in Strasbourg and was a mediator at Frankfurt, became bishop of London. Richard Cox was to become bishop of Ely; John Jewel and Edwin Sandys, who had both been at Strasbourg and then Zurich, were appointed bishop of Salisbury and bishop of Worcester, respectively. No immediate preferment was offered to Whittingham. With the help of Sir Edward Horsey, he obtained a chaplaincy with the forces of Ambrose Dudley, Earl of Warwick, at Le Havre. Warwick was charged with keeping the town out of the hands of the French. Whittingham served him well as chaplain, go-between, spy, and soldier, and Warwick wrote to William Cecil, Elizabeth's Secretary of State, that Whittingham deserved great thanks from the queen.[14] As a military chaplain, Whittingham appears to have been able to avoid using the Book of Common Prayer as set, and it is possible he used prayers from *The Form of Prayers*, since it agreed with the Reformed liturgical forms in use at Le Havre. He wrote to Cecil explaining why he did not follow the Prayer Book form. Whatever Whittingham's scruples concerning the Prayer Book, he was able to overcome them sufficiently to be able to accept the position of dean of Durham, where his old friend James Pilkington was bishop, through the patronage and advocacy of Robert Dudley.

Rites of Durham, being a description or brief declaration of all the ancient monuments, rites, & customs belonging or being within the monastical church of Durham before the suppression was written in 1593

---

[14] *Calendar of State Papers, Foreign Series, of the Reign of Elizabeth, 1562*, ed. Joseph Stevenson (London: Longmans, Green, Reader & Dyer, 1867), 476, no. 1081.

and was probably compiled by William Claxton, squire of Wyn-yard. He seems to have had the close assistance of someone who knew the pre-Reformation cathedral and its rites and ceremonies, and the most likely candidate is George Clyff, the last monk of Durham, who retained his prebend's stall until his death in 1595. In *Rites of Durham* Whittingham was accused of destroying an image of St. Cuthbert and of removing two holy water stoups to his kitchen, where he used them for washing fish and meat.[15] The author noted, "He could not abyde any auncyent monuments, nor nothing that appteyned to any godly Religiousnes or monas-ticall life."[16] A manuscript note in an eighteenth-century edition of this work dubbed Whittingham "A Great Villain of the Geneva Gang."[17] Whittingham had married Catherine Jacquemayne of Orléans in Geneva in 1556 and according to the author of *Rites of Durham*, the dean's wife burned the precious banner of St. Cuthbert.[18] This image of Whittingham as an arch-iconoclast seems to be the source used by a later history of Durham, in which he is described as "a most devoted Calvinist" and "a Puritan Dean."[19] William Hutchinson, in *The History and Antiquities of the County Palatine of Durham*, concluded that Whittingham was "guilty of much profanation on the pious monuments and sacred remains in this church."[20] Hutchinson added that the dean "was a violent opposer of measures touching the sacerdotal vesture, and used all his influ-ence with the earl of Leicester therein."[21] Whittingham was alleged

[15] J. T. Fowler, G. Bates, and J. Mickleton, eds., *Rites of Durham: Being a Description or Brief Declaration of all the Ancient Monuments, Rites, & Customs Belonging or Being within the Monastical Church of Durham before the Suppression. Written 1593* (Durham and London: Surtees Society, 1903), 61, 68.

[16] Ibid., 60.

[17] Ibid., 169.

[18] Ibid., 26.

[19] J. L. Low, *Historical Scenes in Durham Cathedral* (Durham: Andrew & Co., 1887), 99, 108.

[20] William Hutchinson, *The Histories and Antiquities of the County Palatine of Durham*, vol. 2 (Newcastle: Hodgson & Robinson, 1787), 145.

[21] Ibid., 143. The tale is also told by Eamon Duffy in his *Saints, Sacrilege and Sedition* (London: Bloomsbury, 2012), 247, though his point is that the author/compiler (Claxton) was a conformist.

to have wandered the streets of Durham in Geneva cap and gown and to have declined to wear the appointed vesture for Communion in the cathedral. When the rules were pressed on him, he finally gave his assent, but he apparently avoided wearing a cope for Communion by never celebrating Communion in the cathedral again. In 1577, Whittingham found himself accused of a number of violations and abuses, including drunkenness and adultery, and was the subject of an official visitation in 1578 headed by Edwin Sandys, archbishop of York. The main accusations, though, were that he had neither the proper university degree nor valid ordination to hold the deanship. He died before the proceedings were concluded. Whittingham's monument was destroyed by the Scots in 1640 and recalling the dean's iconoclasm regarding Cuthbert's cult, Hutchinson wryly noted that it "met with the same fate as he had treated others."[22]

The author of *Rites of Durham*, nostalgic for the pre-Reformation cathedral, clearly disapproved of Whittingham's destruction. Looking back from the perspective of later Anglican tradition as re-imaged after the Restoration and also in the wake of the Tractarian revival, Whittingham might well be regarded as someone who was on the wrong side of Anglican history. Today English cathedrals and churches that boast remains of saints' tombs find themselves popular places for private devotion. Durham Cathedral's current redecoration of the feretory that houses St. Cuthbert's tomb and the revival of devotion to the saint naturally cast all those responsible for the cult's destruction as iconoclastic and very un-Anglican. In light of the outcome of the Elizabethan vestment controversy and the nineteenth-century revival of pre-Reformation vestments, Whittingham's stance on the surplice and the cope seems both petty and equally wrong sided.[23] Finally, by later Anglican standards, his nonepiscopal ordination would disqualify him from holding any clerical office in the Church of England. A recent collection of studies on Durham Cathedral continues the culture of disapproval, with references to Whittingham as a "radical" whose

---

[22] Hutchinson, *Histories and Antiquities*, 2:146, 150.

[23] John Henry Primus, *The Vestments Controversy* (Kampen: J. H. Kok, 1960).

"vigorously Calvinistic" stance was probably responsible for the destruction of the memorial brasses of ten bishops and eight priors.[24]

The accusations of iconoclasm, disdain of vesture, and "irregular" ordination need to be seen in context. Elizabeth's Royal Articles of 1559, for the visitors, enquired whether "in their churches and chapels all images, shrines, all tables, candlesticks, trindals or rolls of wax, pictures, paintings, and all other monuments of fegned and false miracles, pilgrimages, idolatry, and superstition be removed, abolished, and destroyed."[25] Destruction of "popish images" that had been restored under Mary had proceeded very quickly in London and the Southern Province, but the North was more conservative and more resistant to Protestantism. In the diocese of Durham, Whittingham's former fellow expatriate James Pilkington appointed clergy and enlisted support specifically for stamping out items that he and the other first-generation Elizabethan bishops regarded as popish survivals. When Edmund Grindal was translated from London to be archbishop of York in 1570, he was still having to root out rood lofts and ordered John Beckwith of Swinton to transport "certain superstitious monuments and images" to Richmond marketplace and personally burn them.[26] Whittingham was obeying the archdiocesan and diocesan articles and policies and destroyed objects that seemed to have been overlooked when the shrine of St. Cuthbert was destroyed years before his arrival at Durham. In Durham Cathedral, he did exactly what Bishop Pilkington was doing throughout the diocese, and none of their actions were as destructive and iconoclastic as had been the demolition of St. Cuthbert's shrine in 1539. Indeed, remarkably, for

---

[24] David Brown, ed., *Durham Cathedral: History, Fabric and Culture* (New Haven, CT: Paul Mellon Centre for Studies in British Art and Yale University Press, 2015), 84, 232. For a sympathetic treatment see Geoffrey Moorhouse, *The Last Divine Office: Henry VIII and the Dissolution of the Monasteries* (Katonah, NY: BlueBridge, 2008).

[25] W. H. Frere and W. M. Kennedy, *Visitation Articles and Injunctions of the Period of the Reformation*, vol. 3 (London: Longman, Green & Co., 1910), 2.

[26] Patrick Collinson, *Archbishop Grindal 1519–1583* (Berkeley, CA: University of California Press, 1979), 203.

all his Geneva experience, Whittingham did not destroy more of the surviving fabric of Catholicism of the cathedral.

As regards vesture, bishops Pilkington, Grindal, Sandys, and Jewel all regarded the surplice and episcopal rochets as popish attire that they had been thus far unable to abolish, but they hoped that such vesture would in due course fall into disuse. Clergy such as Thomas Upcher, near Colchester, and Richard Greenham of Oakington, Cambridge, were allowed to dispense with the surplice.[27] Whittingham shared the disappointment and frustration of Grindal and Jewel but nevertheless appears to have conformed after 1566.[28] If his iconoclasm and dislike of the surplice and cope puts Whittingham on the wrong side of Anglican history, then most of the first Elizabethan bishops and those who held high preferment in the Church of England should join him there. Elizabeth's furnishing of her Chapels Royal and the advancing ceremonial stemming from them undermined the official view on ornaments and vesture, and many of her leading churchmen viewed the queen as on the wrong side of Scripture and divine providence for the English nation. Thomas Sampson complained to Peter Martyr in 1560:

> What can I hope, when three of our lately appointed bishops are to officiate at the table of the Lord, one as priest, another as deacon, and a third as subdeacon, before the image of the crucifix, or at least not far from it, with candles, and habited in the golden vestments of the papacy: and are thus to celebrate the Lord's supper without any sermon?[29]

[27] Ibid., 172; John H. Primus, *Richard Greenham: The Portrait of an Elizabethan Pastor* (Macon: Mercer University Press, 1998), 56–61; Kenneth L. Parker and Eric J. Carlson, *"Practical Divinity": The Works and Life of Revd Richard Greenham* (Aldershot: Ashgate, 1998), 16.

[28] As expressed in a letter to Christopher Goodman of 12 November 1566, cited in Jane Dawson, *John Knox* (New Haven, CT: Yale University Press 2015), 260.

[29] Thomas Sampson to Peter Martyr, 6 January 1560, *The Zurich Letters, Comprising the Correspondence of Several English Bishops and Others* (Cambridge: Parker Society, 1846), 63.

John Jewel commented to Martyr,

> The doctrine is every where most pure; but as to ceremonies and maskings, there is a little too much foolery. That little silver cross, of ill-omened origin, still maintains its place in the queens's chapel. Wretched me! this thing will soon be drawn into a precedent.[30]

Jewel's fears proved prophetic and were brought to fruition with the ceremonial of the Durham House or "Laudian" divines, for whom the ceremonial of the Chapels Royal was to be that of cathedrals and, ideally, parish churches too.[31]

What of the charges of mismanagement and the doubts over the validity of Wittingham's ordination? David Marcombe has suggested that this attack was payback from some of those who had reason to dislike Whittingham.[32] Ralph Lever, one of the prebends of Durham seems to have become disaffected over the division of profits from leases and their distribution among the prebendaries. Thomas Wilson had expected the deanery in 1563 and now, as secretary of state, was able to find reason for removing Whittingham, spurred on by his hopes of being the next dean and of making financial gain from leasing coal mines. On succeeding Grindal as archbishop of York and after Grindal's suspension from duties as archbishop of Canterbury in 1577, Edwin Sandys may have seized a chance to settle an old score. Sandys and Cox had attempted to freeze and preserve the Edwardian church of 1553 among the English exiles. Whittingham, Knox, and others who resided in Geneva had chosen instead to make further reforms along lines that seemed to them in 1556 the obvious continuation of Cranmer's trajectory. Sandys and Cox had opposed such further reforms.

---

[30] Ibid., 69.

[31] Bryan D. Spinks, "Durham House and the Chapels Royal: Their Liturgical Impact on the Church of Scotland," *Scottish Journal of Theology* 67 (2014): 379–99.

[32] David Marcombe, "A Great Villain of the Geneva Gang? William Whittingham, Dean of Durham: A Reassessment," in *Conflict and Disaster at Durham* (Durham: Friends of Durham Cathedral, 2003), 1–13. See also David Marcombe, "The Dean and Chapter of Durham, 1558–1603" (PhD dissertation, University of Durham, 1973).

Furthermore, after the Admonition to the Parliaments of 1572 and Thomas Cartwright's argument for *de jure divino* Presbyterian polity, there seems to have been scrutiny of those who had been ordained in foreign Reformed churches. The Articles of Subscription of 1571 had stated that anyone

> which does or shall pretend to be a priest or minister of God's holy word and sacraments, by reason of any other form of institution, consecration, or ordering, than the form set forth by Parliament in the time of the late king of most worthy memory, King Edward VI, or now used in the reign of our most gracious sovereign lady, before the feast of the Nativity of Christ next following, shall in the presence of the bishop or guardian of the spiritualities of some one diocese where he has or shall have ecclesiastical living, declare his assent, and subscribe to all the articles of religion.[33]

Although this practice was primarily aimed at those ordained in England during the reign of Mary, the words "minister of God's holy word and sacraments" referred to those ordained in Protestant exile communities. Proof of ordination and subscription was all that was required.

For proof of his ordination, Whittingham produced two certificates. The first, dated July 8, 1578, declared that "it pleased God by lot and election of the whole English congregation there orderly to choose Mr. William Whittingham . . . unto that office of preaching the word of God and ministering his sacraments."[34] It was signed by eight members of the former Geneva congregation, including William Williams and John Bodley, and the commissioners agreed that most of the witnesses were known to be very honest men. The second certificate, dated November 15, 1578, was presented because there had been objections to the words "lot and election" in the first certificate; in this second certificate these words were replaced by the term "suffrages."

---

[33] The Subscription (Thirty-Nine Articles) Act (1571), 13 Elizabeth, Cap. 12, in *Documents Illustrative of English Church History*, ed. Henry Gee and William John Hardy (New York: Macmillan, 1896), 478.

[34] Cited in Marcombe, "Dean and Chapter of Durham," 255.

Archbishop Sandys believed that the ordination in Geneva had been irregular and thus was invalid. Marcombe has conjectured that although Whittingham underwent ordination in Geneva, the congregation was depleted and thus unable to follow the requirements as laid down. Marcombe notes, "There were probably no ministers to examine him or present him to the congregation, for example, and he may well have only been 'chosen' in the broadest sense of the word."[35] *The Form of Prayers* of the English congregation in Geneva gave a distinct process for choosing ministers, which included examination by ministers and elders, presentation to the congregation, and election by the whole congregation after eight days. Since the ministers (Knox and Goodman) had left for Scotland, it would have been difficult to fulfill these requirements, making Marcombe's position plausible. The visitation commissioners became deeply divided, with Matthew Hutton, dean of York, suggesting that since Whittingham had been ordained in Geneva, he was more a minister than Archbishop Sandys, who apparently had been ordained by the Latin medieval rite.[36] Whittingham appealed to the Privy Council, but he became ill and died before the issue had been resolved. As to his degrees, according to the Brasenose College register, Whittingham was granted his bachelor of divinity degree in July 1563 and his doctor of divinity degree in February 1567; he was thus fully qualified to hold the office of dean.[37]

While the context of Whittingham's iconoclasm and the apparently bogus nature of the accusations against the dean may mitigate his popular image, other important information produces a different impression altogether. Ignored by *Rites of Durham* are the facts that the dean was a musician, retained the organ, and

---

[35] Ibid., 256.

[36] There is in fact no record of his ordination, but it seems to have taken place prior to the 1550 ordinal. Patrick Collinson, "Edwin Sandys (1519?–1588), Archbishop of York," *Oxford Dictionary of National Biography* (Oxford: Oxford University Press, 2004; online ed., January 2008), http://www.oxforddnb.com/view/printable/24649.

[37] Charles Heberden, ed., *Brasenose College Register, 1509–1909* (Oxford: Clarendon, 1909), 9.

acquired music from the Chapel Royal for the cathedral. Wittingham also recorded his work in the cathedral:

> First, in the Morning at Six of the Clock the Grammar Schoole and
> Song Schole with all the Servants of the House, resort to Prayers into
> the Church. Which Exercise continueth almost half an Houre. At
> nyne of the Clock we have our ordinary Service; and likewise at
> three after none. The Wednesdays and Fridays are appointed to a
> general Fast with Prayers, and Preaching of God's Word. The Sun-
> daies and Holydays before none we have Sermons; and at after none
> the Catechisme is expounded.
>
> Because we lak an able Scholemaster I bestow daily three or Four
> Hours in teaching the Youth, till God provide us of some that may
> better suffice.[38]

Whittingham was also instrumental in helping to defeat the Northern Rebellion in 1569.

There is, however, another less frequently told history of Whittingham that might encourage us to imagine him rather differently
than did the author of *Rites of Durham* and subsequent critics such
as Hutchinson. Posterity seems to have conveniently forgotten the
enormous influence that Whittingham had on devotional life in
England and Scotland. There is evidence that in 1559 a number of
London congregations were using *The Form of Prayers* in anticipation of its becoming the Elizabethan liturgy, but it was not to be,
and attempts in Parliament in 1584 and 1587 to replace the *Book of
Common Prayer* with *The Form of Prayers* failed. The story in Scotland, however, was very different.

The Form of Prayers, together with a metrical Psalter, was re-
printed in 1556, 1558, and 1560.[39] In *The First Book of Discipline* of the
Church of Scotland, which was drawn up in 1560, the section "Of

---

[38] John Strype, *The Life and Acts of Matthew Parker* (London: 1711), 135.

[39] William Fuller had special copies of the French Bible, a New Testament,
and *The Forme of Prayers* finely bound as a present for Queen Elizabeth,
though in the end he did not present them; see Karl Gunther, *Reformation
Unbound: Protestant Visions of Reform in England 1525–1590* (Cambridge: Cambridge University Press, 2014), 115.

Sacraments" noted, "And albeit the order of Geneva, which is now used in some of our Churches, is sufficient to instruct the diligent Reader how both these sacraments may be rightly ministered, yet for an uniformitie to be kept, we have thought good to adde this as superaboundant."[40] This liturgy is also referred to elsewhere, for the catechism and the order for every Sunday, as well as for the singing of psalms "together with common hearts and voyces to praise God."[41] In the fifth session of the 1562 General Assembly, it was concluded that "ane uniforme ordour salbe takin or keipit in the administratioun of the Sacraments and solemnization of mariages and burialls of the dead, according to the Booke of Geneva."[42] An act of the December 1564 General Assembly ordained "that everie Minister, Exhorter, and Reader, sall have one of the Psalme Bookes latelie printed in Edinburgh, and use the order contained therein in Prayers, Marriage, and ministration of the Sacraments."[43] The reference is to Robert Lekpreuik's 1564 and 1565 editions, published as *The Form of Prayers and ministration of the Sacraments, &c. used by the English Church at Geneva, approved and received by the Church of Scotland.*

Although in subsequent accounts this liturgy has been referred to as Knox's liturgy, it is clear from *A Brief Discourse* that the liturgy was a collaborative work of Knox, Whittingham, Gilby, Fox, and Cole. And there is good reason to think that Whittingham was the major player in this project. The preface of the Geneva edition of 1556 was written in February, and since Knox did not arrive back in Geneva until September, Robin Leaver suggests that the preface was probably the work of Whittingham.[44] The preface is addressed thus: "To our Bretherne in Englande, and els where which love Jesus

<hr />

[40] James K. Cameron, ed., *The First Book of Discipline* (Edinburgh: The Saint Andrew Press, 1972), 30–31.

[41] Ibid., 182, 187.

[42] Thomas Thomson, *Acts and Proceedings of the General Assembly of the Kirk of Scotland from 1560*, First Part: *1560–1577* (Edinburgh, 1839), 30.

[43] Ibid., 54.

[44] Robin Leaver, *Ghoostly Psalmes and Spiritual Songes: English and Dutch Metrical Psalms from Coverdale to Utenhove 1535–1566* (Oxford: Clarendon, 1991), 226.

Christe unfaynedly. Mercie, and peace."[45] Its context is England, and it noted that with the Marian restoration of Catholicism, false prophets had been sent forth with lies in their mouths to deceive England. It cited the cities of Emden, Wesel, and Frankfurt as having godly churches and noted that the freedom they had been given in the city of Geneva meant that the congregation was no longer being negligent in reforming "that religion, which was begone in Englande,"[46] a process that entailed removing ceremonies that had no warrant in Scripture. The preface also stressed the importance of singing the psalms, and Whittingham had a major hand in composing and rewriting the metrical psalms that were published with the liturgy.

It is clear that the compilers of *The Form of Prayers* in 1556 had at least three Reformed liturgies as paradigms and sources: Valerand Poullain's *Liturgia Sacra*, published for his Stranger Church in Glastonbury, England, and used by that church in Frankfurt; William Huycke's English translation of Calvin's Geneva liturgy; and Jan Laski's *Forma ac ratio*, issued for use by the Stranger Churches in London that were under Laski's superintendency. In addition, *The Form of Prayers* drew on the 1552 *Book of Common Prayer*—a number of obvious verbal parallels were listed by Geoffrey Cuming.[47] It also utilized some material from a liturgy that Knox had authored for use in Berwick-upon-Tweed in 1550.[48] The material for Sunday worship opened with a confession, from a choice of two. The first was based on Daniel 9, which may have been suggested by the *Forma ac ratio* and was taken from the Wesel Psalter of 1555–1556, where it is attributed to Bishop Miles Coverdale.[49]

[45] *The Forme of Prayers and Ministration of the Sacraments etc.,* . . . (Geneva: John Crespin, 1556), STC/1490:06, p. 3, accessed via Early English Books Online, http://eebo.chadwyck.com.

[46] Ibid., 11.

[47] Geoffery J. Cuming, "John Knox and the Book of Common Prayer: A Short Note," *Liturgical Review* 10 (1980): 80–81.

[48] Bryan D. Spinks, *From the Lorde and the Best Reformed Churches: A Study of the Eucharistic Liturgy in the English Puritan and Separatist Traditions 1550–1633* (Rome: CLV Edizioni Liturgiche, 1984).

[49] Robin Leaver, "Coverdale and the Anglo-Genevan liturgy of 1556," *Mededelingen van het Instituut voor Liturgiewetenschap Rijks-universiteit Groningen* 18 (1984): 30–34.

The 1564 edition of *The Form of Prayers*, printed by Lekpreuik, omitted the preface, which was replaced by a calendar with an explanation by William Stewart. Coverdale's confession of sin was removed from the public service and placed in private household prayers. The Scottish edition added two other confessions of sin: the first was titled "An other Confession and Prayer Commonly used in the Church of Edinburgh, on the day of commune prayers"; the second was entitled "A Confession of sinnes, and petitions made unto God in the tyme of our extreame troubles, and yet commonly used in the Churches of Scotland, before the sermon," though the opening sentences were inspired by Coverdale's confession. The Scottish edition also included further prayers from Calvin's rite, and it is quite possible that Knox was involved in the Scottish emendations. The Communion service was without change, as were the marriage and baptismal rites. Thus the 1556 liturgy was bequeathed to and altered only slightly for use in the Church of Scotland.

With five compilers listed for the 1556 liturgy, why single out Whittingham as the major editor? In her recent biography of John Knox, Jane Dawson observes that although Knox was involved in the Frankfurt drafts of *The Forme*, the assembling and publishing of the 1556 edition occurred when Knox was back in Scotland.[50] The probability of Whittingham's editorial polishing of the rite is founded on his other projects where his literary skills are clearly demonstrated: the metrical Psalter, the Geneva New Testament of 1557, and the Geneva Bible of 1560. The Communion service of *The Form of Prayers* of 1556 followed Calvin's rite closely, but unlike Calvin's version, it included a prayer of thanksgiving, or eucharistic prayer, which gave thanks for creation and salvation in Christ. Part of this prayer was taken from Knox's Berwick liturgy, but Knox's original rough phraseology had been greatly improved by someone with better mastery of the English tongue.

> **Berwick:** Omnypotent and everlasting God, whome all creatures do know and confesse thee to be Governor and Lorde, but we thy

---

[50] Dawson, *John Knox*, 151.

creatures, created to thyne own image and similitude, ought at all tymes to feare, adore, love and prayse thye godlye Majestie—fyrst for owr creation, but principally for our redemption when we were dead and lost to sin.[51]

Form of Prayers: O Father of mercye and God of all consolation, seinge all creatures do confesse thee, as governor, and lorde, it becometh us the workmanship of thyne own hands, at all tymes to reverence and magnifie they godli maistie, first that thou haste created us to thyne own Image and similitude: but chieflye that thou haste delievered us from everlasting death and damnation into the which Satan drewe mankind by the meane of synne:[52]

Whittingham certainly had that mastery of language, as shown by his other compilations and editorial work.

Metrical psalmody has a complex history, and in the English-speaking world the lead was taken by Miles Coverdale and Thomas Sternhold.[53] Sternhold, a mid-level civil servant, published nineteen metrical psalms in 1547/48 under the title *Certayne Psalmes*. He died in 1549, but eighteen more of his compositions were posthumously published together with the original nineteen by Edward Whitchurch under the title *Al such psalms of David as Thomas Sternehold late grome of [the] kings Maiesties Robes, didde in his life time draw into English Metre*. This book included a further seven psalms by John Hopkins. Both these Psalters were probably intended for private use rather than public worship, though public worship would prove their destiny. With the death of Edward VI and the accession of Mary, English-language metrical psalmody was on hold in England, but it began to take on a more prominent role in the worship of the English groups that fled to the Continent.

---

[51] Text in Peter Lorimer, *John Knox and the Church of England* (London: Henry S. King, 1875), 290.

[52] Cited from William D. Maxwell, *The Liturgical Portions of the Genevan Service Book* (Westminster: Faith Press, 1965), 124–25.

[53] Leaver, *Ghoostley Psalmes*; Quitslund, *Reformation in Rhyme*; Timothy Duguid, "Sing a New Song: English and Scottish Metrical Psalmody from 1549–1640" (PhD dissertation, University of Edinburgh, 2011). See Timothy Duguid, *Metrical Psalmody in Print and Practice: English "Singing Psalms" and Scottish "Psalm Buiks," c. 1547–1640* (Farnham: Ashgate, 2014).

New compositions were made in Wesel, but it was from those in Frankfurt that a wider and more lasting contribution came. *A Brief Discourse* records that when granted use of the church used by Poullain, in their worship the people were required to "sing a Psalm in metre in a plain tune; as was, and as is accustomed in the French, Dutch, Italian, Spanish, and Scottish, Churches."[54] Though initially *Al such psalms* was probably used, Whittingham revised the poetry and added new compositions of his own. He was an accomplished linguist, and he also knew Hebrew. The fruits of his skills were included in the 1556 *Form of Prayers*. There were now fifty-one psalms and also a metrical version of the Ten Commandments. Whittingham contributed versions of Psalms 23, 51, 114, 115, 130, 133, and 137. In the 1558 edition, Whittingham contributed further additions—Psalms 37, 50, 67, 71, 119, 121, 124, 127, and 129. With reference to the 1556 edition, Quitslund has noted:

> The primary prose source of all the psalms is the Great Bible, as it was for both Sternhold and Hopkins. Each of the new texts shows verbal traces, however, of the French metrical psalms by Clémont Marot and Theodore Beza, most likely from the 1551 version, *Pseames octantetrois de Dauid mis en rime Francoise*. The Ten Commandments amounts, in fact, to a loose translation of Marot's version, though influenced by the language of the Great Bible.[55]

Leaver has suggested that since initially the Frankfurt exiles had agreed to use forms similar to those used by the French congregation, a versification of the Ten Commandments was required and was composed by Whittingham to fill this need.[56] Timothy Duguid notes how Whittingham's translations were guided by the current situation of the exiles.[57] Thus verses 3 and 4 of Psalm 137 read:

> Then they to whome we prisoners were
> said to vs tauntinglie,
> nowe let vs heare your hebrewe songes

[54] Arber, *A Brieff Discours*, 25.
[55] Quitslund, *Reformation in Rhyme*, 144.
[56] Leaver, *Ghoostley Psalmes*, 220.
[57] Duguid, "Sing a New Song," 34; *Metrical Psalmody*, 22.

and pleasaunte melodie.
Alas sayde we, who can once frame
his sorrowfull hart to synge:
the praises of our louyng god,
thus vnder a strange kynge?

Whittingham also rewrote some of Sternhold's and Hopkins's verses. Observing that since Whittingham had a near-monopoly on the composition of the new English metrical psalms for the first two years of the Anglo-Scots church, and thus he should be assumed to have been responsible for the rewrite, Quitslund notes:

> Overall, the 1556 Genevan edition of the psalter replaces about 26 per cent of Sternhold's language, and supplies 16 additional quatrains that do not correspond to anything in Stenrhold's originals. Only one psalm (Ps.123) escapes with no emendation. The changes to Hopkins's versifications are much less dramatic, amounting to less than 8 per cent of the language and only one additional quatrain.[58]

The final quatrain of Psalm 49 gives a good example:

Sternhold	Whittingham
A foolish man whom riches hath,	Thus man to honor God hath called,
to honor thus preferred	yet doth he not consider:
That doth not know and understand	But like brute beasts so doth he live,
Is to a beast compared	which turn to dust and powder.

The Anglo-Genevan Psalter did not incorporate all the 150 psalms. The Psalter of 1556 provided fifty-one psalms, and that of 1558 contained sixty-seven. The Psalter was expanded again in 1560, with twenty-five further psalms by William Kethe. In England, the printer John Day published editions of these partial metrical Psalters, and as a step toward a full Psalter, in 1562 he published a collection entitled *The residue of all Davids Psalmes in metre, made by*

---

[58] Quitslund, *Reformation in Rhyme*, 156.

John Hopkins and others. Amongst the "others" was Thomas Norton. In that same year Day also published a full Psalter under the title *The whole booke of Psalmes, collected into Englysh metre by T. Starnhold, I. Hopkins, & others.* Though some of Whittingham's compositions were replaced by those of John Hopkins and *The Whole Book of Psalmes* is regarded as having a more Edwardian and London flavor than the Geneva Psalter, nevertheless Day kept Whittingham's revisions of the original Sternhold versions.

Day's edition included some hymns and canticles in meter, but perhaps most important is the third section of this metrical Psalter, which Quitslund believes demonstrates the continuities between Day's finished metrical Psalter and the aspirations of the Marian exile communities. This last section contained prayers for use in the home, but nearly all were selected from *The Form of Prayers.* Day used the household prayers as found in the 1561 edition of *The Form of Prayers,* which had already been adapted to make the prayers suitable for Elizabethan England. Two prayers from the public Sunday liturgy had been incorporated into these household forms and were reproduced by Day. In considering a description of the book as "a model of selfhood based upon the struggle to achieve confessional purity," Quitslund has aptly commented on Day's Psalter: "Though in support of the Elizabethan Church, the materials with which it sought to create such a selfhood were in large part those that had been created to sustain the godly during the Marian diaspora."[59] While England was never to have *The Form of Prayers* as its public liturgy, English pious households could and did share with the Scots in the same household prayers, which included two prayers from the Sunday public worship of the Anglo-Geneva community.

The Scottish Psalter that was contained in the 1564 Lekpreuik edition of *The Form of Prayers* seems to have taken as its base the 1561 edition of the *Form of Prayers.* In his important study Duguid has commented:

[59] Ibid., 235.

In contrast to the Day volumes, however, the motives of the Scottish *Forme of prayers* were driven by the religious and political beliefs of the [General] Assembly. While they could have chosen to follow the intentionally English *Whole booke*, Scots instead chose to continue where the Genevan editions had left off, which was a decision that was undoubtedly influenced by Knox and his colleagues. Indeed, these men sought to make Scotland a transplanted version of the Anglo-Genevan community, so they chose to use the more complete edition of the *Forme of prayers* as the foundation for the Scottish *Forme of prayers*, reprinting each psalm text and tune as they appeared in the 1561 edition. This would explain the textual differences between the Day and Lekpreuik editions, especially the reduced number of Hopkins' texts that appear in the latter.[60]

The Scottish Psalter incorporated the work of Scottish compilers Robert Pont and John Craig. The Psalter retained sixteen of Whittingham's psalms, however, and all of his rewriting of Sternhold's and Hopkins' psalms. Thus, thanks to Whittingham, the two nations shared a good number of psalm texts in common.

The Geneva New Testament was published in 1557, and its compilation and preface are anonymous. It is generally agreed that the evidence points to both being the work of Whittingham.[61] To be sure, this is not a totally new translation, as the compiler has drawn on Tyndale's and Coverdale's versions and the Great Bible. Much of the 1557 text would be utilized by the King James Bible of 1611. For example, Tyndale translated Luke 15:8 as:

> Ether what woman havynge x grotes, yf she loose one, doth not lyght a candell, and swepe ye housse . . .

The 1557 Geneva New Testament has:

> Either what woman having ten pieces of silver, if she lose one, doth not light a candle, and sweep the house . . .

---

[60] Duguid, "Sing a New Song," 128; cf. *Metrical Psalmody*, 87–88.

[61] Richard Edward Hunter, "William Whittingham: A Study of His Life and Writings, with Especial Reference to the Geneva New Testament" (PhD dissertation, University of Pennsylvania, 1953).

And the King James Version has:

> Either what woman having ten pieces of silver, if she lose one piece,
> doth not light a candle, and sweep the house . . .

The 1557 English New Testament provided summary arguments concerning the texts as well as notes and also chapter and verse numbers, and this publication was a prelude to the 1560 Geneva Bible. This translation is certainly not the work of one man. Whittingham seems to have been the general editor, but the author of the contemporary life of Whittingham stated that Miles Coverdale, Christopher Goodman, Anthony Gilby, and William Cole were associated with the project.[62] Whittingham and Gilby were both Hebraists. David Daiches has commented, "The Hebrew scholarship of the Geneva Bible translators is attested by . . . the clear fact that in many instances they restored the literal meaning of the Hebrew text which had been obscured. . . . Further, there is strong evidence for concluding that the Geneva Bible translators were the first of the English translators to make considerable use at first hand of the Hebrew commentary of David Kimchi."[63]

Many of the exiles in Geneva returned to England in 1559, but it would seem that Whittingham delayed his return to England in order to see the Bible through the press. It contained an introduction addressed to Elizabeth and would become the most popular version in use until the King James Version eventually displaced it in the English-speaking devotional psyche. It was printed in London in 1575 and Edinburgh in 1579, and it was the preferred preaching text of Lancelot Andrewes, Joseph Hall, and John King, and the version used by Richard Hooker and William Shakespeare.[64] It was even more popular for family and individual reading in both England and Scotland. The Scottish printing of

[62] Mary Anne Everett Green, ed., *Life of Mr. William Whittingham, Dean of Durham* (London: Camden Society, 1870), 9–10.

[63] David Diaches, *The King James Version of the English Bible* (Chicago: University of Chicago Press, 1941), 179, 180.

[64] Naseeb Shaheen, *Biblical References in Shakespeare's Plays* (Newark, DE: University of Delaware Press, 1999), 27.

1579, approved by the General Assembly and usually known as the Bassandyne Bible, was a reprint of the second edition of 1561 and contained a preface praising James VI for having authorized its publication and noting that by the king's authority it had been ordered, "That this holy book of God should be set forth, and printed of new within your own realme, to the end that in every parish kirk there should be at least one thereof keeped, to be called the Common Book of the Kirk."[65] An act of the Scottish Parliament made it mandatory for every householder worth 300 marks of annual rent and every yeoman and burgess worth £500 stock to have a Bible in the vulgar tongue in their homes under a penalty of ten pounds—the Geneva Bible was the preferred version.[66]

We return to where this essay began: What constitutes being on the wrong or right side of history? On which side should Whittingham be placed?

In 1560 Whittingham, together with a good number of Elizabethan bishops and churchmen who had also experienced Continental Reformed worship, imagined a reformed Church of England that would be a product of divine providence. By 1572 it was clear to many that this vision would not be fulfilled. In that sense Whittingham was on the wrong side of Elizabethan Anglican history, and in the light of the metamorphosis of the Anglican tradition through the Tractarian movement, Whittingham can be regarded as being on the wrong side of subsequent Anglican history too, other than perhaps that of the diocese of Sydney, Australia.[67] Yet this dean of Durham bequeathed not only to his own church but also to the Church of Scotland prayers, metrical psalm texts, and a vernacular Bible that together constitute a considerable ecumenical liturgical and literary legacy. Since the Geneva Bible is still alluded to every time certain of Shakespeare's plays are performed, it

[65] *Acts and Proceedings of the General Assemblies of the Kirk of Scotland*, vol. 2 (Edinburgh: Bannatyne Club, 1840), 443.

[66] *The Records of the Parliaments of Scotland to 1707*, ed. K. M. Brown and others, 1579/10/21, http://www.rps.ac.uk/trans/1579/10/21.

[67] Muriel Porter, *The New Puritans: The Rise of Fundamentalism in the Sydney Anglican Church* (Melbourne: University of Melbourne Press, 2007).

would seem that Whittingham is on the right side of English cultural histories.

Whittingham was buried in Durham Cathedral. Unlike the tomb of St. Cuthbert, his site of interment is not marked by pilgrims or lighted candles. The place is now unknown, and even if it were, any such devotion would have been anathema to him.[68] Perhaps, however, it would be on the right side of history to dedicate a new memorial in the cathedral to this creative Elizabethan dean whose literary and liturgical work was used on both sides of the border. From this historical perspective, William Whittingham is one of the most remarkable and influential deans that Durham has had.

---

[68] For a splendid view of recent devotions at Cuthbert's tomb on St. Cuthbert's Day, see illustration 264 in Brown, *Durham Cathedral*, 313.

Liturgy's Past
on the American Frontier

Melanie C. Ross

When we hear the phrase "American Evangelicalism," many of us picture a scenario like the one this participant describes:

> Recently, out of curiosity, I went to a service at a famous megachurch. This church had it all: the hustle and bustle of important people; the man with a flashlight and walkie-talkie who met us at the door and briskly ushered us to our seats; the dimly lit auditorium with its brightly coloured stage; the use of words like "vision" and "awesome"; the advertising segments (last week's sermon was available on DVD for only $14.95). There was exuberant music performed by handsome musicians and voluptuous singers; a give-your-life-to-Jesus altar call; and throughout all this, the ubiquity of what Peter Berger has called "the Protestant smile."[1]

Evangelicalism is essentially a spiritual movement found mainly in Protestant churches. It is doctrinally conservative in the sense that it holds to the central beliefs of both the ancient creeds and the sixteenth-century Reformation confessions. The movement, however, lacks a central authority or clear boundaries: generally speaking, Evangelicals put their spiritual experience before their church organization or a denominational confession of faith. In fact, sociologists have identified the growth of nondenominational Prot-

---

[1] Ben Myers, "Megachurch Worship: Supersize Me!" http://www.faith-theology.com/2009/08/megachurch-worship-supersize-me.html.

estantism as one of the most significant developments in American religion in the past fifty years. Consider how the pastor of a mega-church in Nashville explains the demographic of his congregation: "There's so many people here that, if somebody else asked what denomination they are, they might still say Baptist or Lutheran or whatever, because that's where they still feel their roots are, but they attend church here, and it's just a part of the body of Christ—we're not big on the label thing."[2] Of course, as Nancy Ammerman points out, the very act of refusing an external denominational label can result in high levels of commitment. She suggests that just as "claiming a Catholic or Lutheran identity provides a recognizable place on the religious map, we are now recognizing the space occupied by non-denominational churches and according it a kind of ironically 'denominational' identity."[3] Evangelicals are not entirely indifferent to tradition, but for many, it is a tool to use and not an object to revere. As Gerald Bray wryly notes, "If you can show an evangelical that he has something to learn from Augustine, Aquinas, or John Calvin, he may be interested in them, but in evangelical circles the great saints of the past are liable to find themselves competing with modern preachers like Mark Driscoll or Tony Campolo for attention."[4]

This raises an interesting methodological question: to what authorities do nondenominational evangelical Christians turn when they consult the past to imagine the future? To get at the difficulties inherent to this question, I begin with a brief case study of the 1977 "Chicago Call: An Appeal to Evangelicals."

A CASE STUDY: "THE CHICAGO CALL:
AN APPEAL TO EVANGELICALS"

In May of 1977, evangelical visionary leader Robert Webber gathered a group of forty-five evangelical leaders together in

[2] Quoted in Nancy T. Ammerman, *Pillars of Faith: American Congregations and Their Partners* (Berkeley, CA: University of California Press, 2005), 217.

[3] Ibid.

[4] Gerald L. Bray, "Evangelicals: Are They the Real Catholics and Orthodox?," in *Evangelicals and the Early Church: Recovery, Reform, Renewal*, ed. George Kalantzis and Andrew Tooley (Eugene, OR: Cascade Books, 2012), 223.

Chicago. These individuals were either associated with Christian colleges and conservative seminaries, pastors, people working in publishing and news media, or prominent members of their church community. All shared the same convictions: namely, that "evangelical Christianity was suffering from a reduction of the historic faith and practice," and that it was time for the "free-spirited, anti-institutional Christianity of the 'Jesus generation'" to grow to fuller maturity.[5] The fruit of their three-day gathering was the first draft of the "Chicago Call," an eight-point manifesto which urged Evangelicals toward greater continuity with the historic church, increased attention to sacraments, fidelity to Scripture as interpreted in light of the best insights of historical and literary study, and visible ecumenical unity.

In its day, the Call sparked interest in both ecclesial and national circles. *Newsweek* devoted an entire religious section to the document, and major Christian journals, including *Christianity Today*, *Christian Century*, and *New Oxford Review* gave the statement a positive evaluation. Evangelicals, it seemed, were "dissatisfied with their inherited identities as sectarian Christians," and hoped "to recover what their forefathers rejected."[6]

Nearly forty years later, can we judge the Chicago Call to have been successful? Commentators are divided. On one end of the spectrum are those who believe that the Call inspired significant evangelical liturgical renewal. They observe that more and more traditionally evangelical congregations are "experimenting with advent candles, sampling practices associated with Lent, and marking Holy Week with special services."[7] Monasticism has also captured the evangelical imagination, a trend that has resulted in "retreats at Catholic monasteries, recovery of Celtic spirituality, and observance of the divine hours."[8] Many of today's Evangelicals number among their ancestors not only John Wesley and Billy

---

[5] Ibid., 223.

[6] Kenneth L. Woodward, with Frank Maier, "Roots for Evangelicals," *Newsweek* (May 23, 1977), 76.

[7] Chris Armstrong, "Monastic Evangelicals," at http://www.christianitytoday .com/ct/2008/february/23.28.html.

[8] Ibid.

Graham but also "everyone from the early church's Tertullian and Clement of Alexandria, to the medieval church's Bernard of Clairvaux and Hugh of St. Victor, to the Reformers and the Puritans."[9] At the other end of the spectrum are those who say the Call had no effect on evangelicalism whatsoever. In 1987, ten years after the Call was issued, the journal *Touchstone* asked several leaders who participated in the drafting to evaluate its success. On the basis of these interviews, the journal reports, "One thing became clear very quickly: there was not much of a direct impact on people outside of the participants themselves, outside their own circles and ministries. The massive conglomerate that makes up Protestant Evangelicalism scarcely felt a tremor."[10]

Critics suggest that one reason for the Call's failure is that it "glossed over the question of how particular elements from the past should be affirmed or repudiated."[11] This is because two divisions became apparent at the conference. Some sought to preserve what was Catholic and to subordinate the Reformation, looking to the undivided church of the first five centuries for doctrine and authority. Others believed the church must incorporate the contributions of the Reformation, particularly toward worship and doctrine. They regarded the Reformation as a "tragic necessity." In the end, the Callers emphasized that the catholic evangelicalism they sought was inclusive to the Reformation: "to recover catholicity we do not have to jettison our Protestant heritage, but exactly *recover its finest models*."[12] About a half-dozen of the original signers themselves, however, eventually left Protestantism.[13] Armed with this

---

[9] Ibid.

[10] Michael F. Gallo, "*The Chicago Call* Ten Years Later," *Touchstone* (Winter 1988), at http://www.touchstonemag.com/archives/article.php?id=02-02-007-f.

[11] Gary J. Dorrien, *The Remaking of Evangelical Theology* (Louisville, KY: Westminster John Knox Press, 1998), 173.

[12] Robert Webber, "Behind the Scenes: A Personal Account," in *The Orthodox Evangelicals: Who They Are and What They Are Saying*, ed. Robert E. Webber and Donald G. Bloesch (Nashville, TN: Nelson, 1978), 25.

[13] The most prominent were Thomas Howard, formerly of Gordon College, who would convert from his twenty-five-year membership in the Anglican

knowledge, many of the Call's critics rallied around David Wells's scathing critique of the manifesto: "This may be a time of small happenings [in the evangelical world] . . . but a mass pilgrimage into the world of Anglo-Catholicism is not, with all due respect, what we need right now. Indeed, it is not what we need at any time."[14] The truth probably lies in the middle. One contemporary evangelical pastor explained his congregation's dilemma to me this way: "We're having Ash Wednesday services. We're having sermons on the creed. We recognize that historically, the evangelical church has at times been anti-intellectual and liturgically thin. It's not a problem to say that we threw the baby out with the bathwater, and that now, in a later generation, we're trying to get back some of the things we lost. But we're not going directly back to the early church, or the patristic era, or to Luther and Calvin. That's impossible."[15] In short, many Evangelicals want to recover deeper historical roots but are uncertain about several key issues such as: Who has the authority to imagine the past? How do we understand the Reformation in the history of Protestantism? What practical implications will historical recovery have on weekly worship practices?

TWO NINETEENTH-CENTURY CASE STUDIES

In what follows, I will pose these three questions to two prominent leaders in nineteenth-century American theology: Alexander Campbell of the Restoration Movement and John Nevin of the Mercersburg Movement. I turn to the nineteenth century because it was a time of unique challenges and sectarian divisions on the American frontier:

> Although nine of the thirteen colonies had "establishments"—tax-supported Christian churches—a new situation developed in the colonies that had never existed before. No single Christian group be-

---

Church to Roman Catholicism, and Peter Gillquist, formerly of Thomas Nelson Publishing, who would lead his flock into the Eastern Orthodox Church.

[14] David F. Wells, "Reservations about Catholic Renewal in Evangelicalism," in Webber and Bloesch, *The Orthodox Evangelicals*, 214.

[15] Quoted in Melanie C. Ross, *Evangelical versus Liturgical? Defying a Dichotomy* (Grand Rapids, MI: Eerdmans), 10.

came dominant over all the colonies. The Puritans dominated New England, but there were also small numbers of Baptists, Anglicans, Quakers, Deists, Lutherans, Catholics, and Unitarians there. The Anglicans were most numerous in the southern colonies, but all manner of dissenters were also found there. The middle colonies had accumulated the largest numbers of Christian diversity, representing in significant numbers a variety of Christian expressions. And, of course, non-Christian religion also existed, including, for example, Judaism and a wide variety of Native American spirituality. Consequently, no one Christian denomination could be the church of the colonies. We take that situation for granted, but it was unique for its time.[16]

Furthermore, evangelistic efforts were something of a free-for-all. As the Mennonite theologian John Howard Yoder quipped: "There were no ethics in the battle for the souls of the pioneers. Baptists were obliging enough to immerse any stray Methodists they could find; mounted Methodist circuit-riders were glad to rope and brand Calvinistic sheep with the marks of Arminius and Wesley. . . . In this complete freedom to be different, Americans pulled sectarianism to the end of its rope."[17]

Two significant theologians of this time period were Alexander Campbell (d. 1866) and John Williamson Nevin (d. 1886). Both men forged their understandings of church in conscious opposition to the assumptions of revivalistic Protestantism. Both believed that revivalistic Protestant theology stressed individual spiritual new birth at the expense of the corporate church. And both intentionally invoked theologies of history in their search for a corrective. The two theologians, however, approached the task of liturgical reform from opposite directions. Campbell sought to counteract sectarian divisions by democratizing Christianity, placing power in the hands of the people. He urged people to reject the authority and traditions

[16] Mark G. Toulouse, Gary Holloway, and Douglas A. Foster, *Renewing Christian Unity: A Concise History of the Christian Church* (Abilene, TX: ACU Press, 2011), 25.

[17] John Howard Yoder, "Christian Unity in Nineteenth-Century America," in *A History of the Ecumenical Movement, 1517–1948*, ed. Ruth Rouse and Stephen Charles Neill (Philadelphia, PA: Westminster Press, 1954), 232.

of their churches and to read and interpret the Bible for themselves. Nevin deplored anti-intellectualism and lack of systematic theological analysis and developed a far more scholarly proposal.

After a brief analysis of the work of both individuals, I will conclude with a discussion of why these nineteenth-century controversies might be instructive for twenty-first-century Evangelicals who want to imagine the future by drawing on the past.

ALEXANDER CAMPBELL AND THE RESTORATION MOVEMENT

Restorationism was a nineteenth-century movement that sought to unify Christians under one body and return to apostolic Christianity. The pioneers of this movement did not see themselves as establishing new denominations; rather, they sought to disassociate from denominationalism and restore primitive Christianity. Two groups, which independently developed similar approaches to the Christian faith, were particularly important. The first, led by Barton W. Stone, began at Cane Ridge, Kentucky, and called themselves simply "Christians." The second began in western Pennsylvania and Virginia (now West Virginia) and was led by Thomas Campbell and his son, Alexander Campbell; they used the name "Disciples of Christ." Both groups sought to restore the whole Christian church on the pattern set forth in the New Testament and eventually came together in 1832. In what follows, I will focus on the thought of Alexander Campbell.

Who Has Authority?

Alexander Campbell was deeply troubled by divisions among Christians and traced the problem back to human opinions that were codified in creeds and systematic theologies. Campbell chastised "religious philosophers of the Bible"—including Calvin, Arminius, and Wesley—for developing a theological vocabulary that had had less to do with "Bible facts" and more to do with human theories and speculation.[18] If not theologians or "religious philosophers of the Bible," then who has authority? Campbell strongly believed that it

[18] Richard Thomas Hughes, *Reviving the Ancient Faith: The Story of Churches of Christ in America* (Grand Rapids, MI: Eerdmans, 1996), 32.

came from the bottom-up (laypeople) rather than the top-down (ministers, ecclesiastical leaders, elites). In this sense, Campbell's religious movement shared striking parallels with the new American political system. In 1809, Alexander Campbell's father, Thomas, produced his *Declaration and Address*—a religious document that some historians interpret as analogous to the 1776 "Declaration of Independence." Just as Thomas Jefferson challenged citizens to a bold new adventure in self-government, so the Campbells proposed a similar adventure in Christian thinking. Now that the citizens of America had accomplished political reform by casting off old forms of tyranny, it was left to the citizens of the heavenly kingdom to throw off all forms of ecclesiastical oppression, including the oversight of clergy and the theological norms of creeds and confessions. Nathan Hatch summarizes the ethos of the movement well: Campbell and his followers demanded "a new kind of institutional church premised on the self-evident principles of republicanism, and a new form of biblical authority calling for the inalienable right of common people to interpret the New Testament for themselves."[19]

A word of caution is in order here: we must guard against an overly simplistic understanding of Campbell's theological position. A superficial reading of Campbell—one that focuses narrowly on popular slogans such as "No Creed but Christ" or "No Book but the Bible"—will produce a distorted view of his teaching. Campbell knew quite well that merely insisting on "the Bible alone" was not enough; he therefore insisted that the Bible in and of itself is of "no value" without "fixed and certain principles of interpretation."[20] Campbell thus proceeded to develop seven rules of interpretation and published them in at least three different works.[21] Here are a number of his rules in paraphrase:

[19] Nathan Hatch, "The Christian Movement and the Demand for a Theology of the People," in *Reckoning with the Past: Historical Essays on American Evangelicalism from the Institute for the Study of American Evangelicals*, ed. D. G. Hart (Grand Rapids, MI: Baker Publishing, 1995), 156.

[20] Cited in M. Eugene Boring, *Disciples and the Bible: A History of Disciples Biblical Interpretation in North America* (St. Louis: Chalice Press, 1997), 85.

[21] Alexander Campbell, *The Christian System in Reference to the Union of Christians and Restoration of Primitive Christianity as Plead by the Current Reformation*,

- Responsible interpretation of any text requires understanding where the biblical book is placed within Scripture as a whole, when it was written and to whom, and reasons the writer chose to address the specific topics in the book.

- Biblical texts have various levels of authority for Christians. . . . New Testament texts carry more weight for Christians because the new covenant in Christ supersedes the covenants found in the Old Testament. The words of some biblical writers are more prescriptive for Christians than the words of other biblical writers.

- To understand a text properly, the interpreter must pay attention to syntax, grammar, and the history and meaning of words. Responsible Bible study must include careful word studies, examination of parallel passages, and an awareness that some texts are to be interpreted literally while others are not.

- In order to receive the full benefits of Scripture study, the interpreter must approach the text open to the possibility that God will speak. Humility is crucial. God, not our own wisdom, is the center of all faithful interpretation.[22]

In Campbell's view, the Bible was not so much a book of theology as a kind of technical blueprint, laying out in precise detail the outlines both of primitive theology and the primitive church.[23]

Campbell's thought was shaped by early modern Enlightenment presuppositions, especially Francis Bacon's method of induction, as filtered through the Scottish "Common Sense" Realist philosophers. According to this method, one simply collects all the perti-

---

2nd ed. (Bethany, VA: Alexander Campbell, 1839; repr. St. Louis: Christian Publishing Co., 1890), 95–99; Campbell, *The Christian System*, 2nd ed. (St Louis: Christian Publications, 1839; repr. Joplin, MO: College Press Publishing Co., 1989), 3–6; Campbell, *The Millennial Harbinger* (Bethany, VA: Alexander Campbell, 1846), 13–24. Cf. Boring, *Disciples and the Bible*, 85f.

[22] These summaries come from *Listening to the Spirit: A Handbook for Discernment*, ed. William Paulsell (St. Louis: Chalice Press, 2001), 21–24.

[23] See Richard Thomas Hughes, *Reviving the Ancient Faith*, esp. 30–32.

nent facts on a given topic and then draws the proper conclusion on the basis of those facts.[24] When Christians of goodwill agreed on a viable method, Campbell was certain they could not help but conclude that Scripture taught a single, coherent doctrine of salvation and a logical pattern for the worship practices of the church.

The Role of the Protestant Reformation and Historical Development

In a series of articles on "A Restoration of the Ancient Order of Things," published in the *Christian Baptist* between 1825 and 1829, Campbell attempted to lay out the original pattern of the church. At the beginning of this series, he acknowledged the debt Christians had to all past reformers, including those of the Protestant Reformation. Nevertheless, Campbell argued that the Protestant Reformers had not done enough. Too often, the Reformation had substituted one set of human opinions for another. Campbell believed the Roman pope had been replaced by numerous "little popes" of Protestantism, and that "creeds, manuals, synods and councils, soon shackled the minds of men."[25] The process of reformation which Luther began had faltered, and Christianity was still in dire need of reform. Only a restoration of the ancient order found in the New Testament could heal the divisions of Christianity. William Richardson points out that for Campbell, restoration of the apostolic order never meant that the church had disappeared in history: "Campbell was neither ignorant nor disdainful of the history of the church between New Testament times and his own and often referred to that history as affording examples of common understanding of the meaning of Scripture. But development in the life of the church could not be accorded normative value."[26]

Campbell's attitude toward ecumenical creeds is a case in point. Campbell saw value in creeds as positive statements of faith but

---

[24] Ibid., 31.

[25] Alexander Campbell, *Christian System*, vii. See also Mark Weedman, "History as Authority in Alexander Campbell's 1837 Debate with Bishop Purcell," *Fides et Historia* 28 (1996): 17–34.

[26] W. J. Richardson, "Ecumenical Perspectives in the Thought of Alexander Campbell," *Restoration Quarterly* 40 (1998): 160.

deplored the fact that creeds justified and maintained divisions among the churches. Campbell frequently drew on creeds to explain and defend orthodox trinitarian theology. In particular, he liked the Apostles' Creed as a brief summary of the apostolic faith: "in every word true."[27] Campbell's concern was that creeds not be used as tests of orthodoxy to judge whether a Christian was worthy of belonging to a particular denomination or receiving communion. According to Campbell, the only "term of communion" is assent to the biblical confession that "Jesus is the Christ, the Son of the living God (Matt 16:16)."[28] Since all creeds contained more than this simple fact, Campbell considered them divisive and counterproductive to Christian unity and eucharistic hospitality.[29]

Liturgical Implications

Thomas Campbell famously stated that "Nothing ought to be received into the faith or worship of the Church, or to be made a term of communion among Christians, that is not as old as the New Testament." Since no detailed rite for worship is prescribed in the New Testament, Alexander Campbell turned to Acts 2:42, which briefly mentions the substance of Lord's Day gatherings in the primitive church in Jerusalem: apostolic teaching, the breaking of bread, fellowship, and prayers (to which he added the hymned praise elsewhere attested in the New Testament). Campbell conceded that there was no strict directory of all the details for worship; yet he also believed that Scripture supplied discernible parameters. In *The Christian System* (1839) Campbell described a service of worship he had attended that he thought worthy of emulation and consistent with the ancient order. The service set out the following components:

---

[27] Alexander Campbell, *Millennial Harbinger* (1855), 74.

[28] Campbell, *The Christian System*, 121.

[29] See William Tabbernee, "Alexander Campbell and the Apostolic Tradition," in *The Free Church and the Early Church: Bridging the Historical and Theological Divide*, ed. D. H. Williams (Grand Rapids, MI: Eerdmans, 2002), 163–80.

(1) opening hymn

(2) gospel reading

(3) prayer of thanksgiving followed by a congregational "Amen"

(4) New Testament epistle reading

(5) hymn

(6) invitation to the table

(7) simple administration of bread and wine by an elder

(8) hymn

(9) prayer of supplication

(10) readings from Old Testament and New Testament and remarks from the people for edification

(11) "spiritual songs"

(12) apostolic benediction by the presider[30]

Not everyone on the American frontier was happy with Campbell's New Testament worship hermeneutic. In March 1826, Joseph Hostetler, a German Baptist, wrote Campbell a letter in which he commended Campbell for being "so great an advocate for primitive Christianity," but he wondered how Campbell could disregard the commands for footwashing, the kiss of charity, and triune immersion. In his response to Hostetler and other critics, Campbell studied each New Testament passage in its context to determine what was "essential" (a common practice that seemed to be required of all the churches) and what was "circumstantial." Campbell's treatment of the subject must have satisfied Hostetler, for in the early 1830s Hostetler and fifteen German Baptist churches in southern Indiana and Kentucky became a part of Campbell's Restoration Movement. Other contemporaries, however, including the architects of the Mercersburg Movement, would not be as easily satisfied.

[30] Paul M. Blowers and Bruce E. Shields, "Worship," in *The Encyclopedia of the Stone-Campbell Movement*, ed. Douglas A. Foster, et al. (Grand Rapids, MI: Eerdmans, 2005), 787.

The most prominent spokesmen for the Mercersburg Movement were Philip Schaff, a church historian from Germany, and John Williamson Nevin, an American who joined the German Reformed Church after teaching theology in Presbyterian seminaries for a number of years. During the time when American churches were being swept away by revival, these men drew on European Reformed traditions to criticize revivalism and offer an alternative vision for the church. My comments will focus on the writings of John Nevin, who emphasized mystery, historical rootedness in creeds and confessions, and the authority of the church and its ministers.

Nevin was critical of Alexander Campbell's theology on several accounts. First, Nevin pointed out that nearly all of the competing Christian churches on the American frontier laid claim to Scripture as their final authority. In Nevin's words, "It sounds well, to lay so much stress on the authority of the Bible, as the only text-book and guide of Christianity. But what are we to think of it, when we find such a motley mass of protesting systems, all laying claim so vigorously to one and the same watchword?"[31] Contra Campbell's appeal to Francis Bacon and the scientific method, Nevin pointed out that the Bible "never speaks of itself as being either a system of divinity or confession of faith."[32] Rather than a text, Christianity was meant to rest on a *living* authority, beginning in Jesus Christ. Finally, Nevin critiqued that Campbell and his fellow Restorationists carelessly dismissed history as having nothing to contribute to the life of the contemporary church: "The idea of a historical continuity in the life of the Church, carries with it no weight whatever for the sect consciousness. It is felt to be as easy to start a new Church, as it is to get up a new moral or political association under any other name."[33] With this brief background, we turn to a consideration of the same three questions from Nevin's perspective:

---

[31] Charles Yrigoyen, Jr., and George H. Bricker, eds., *Catholic and Reformed: Selected Theological Writings of John Williamson Nevin* (Pittsburgh, PA: Pickwick Press, 1978), 137.

[32] Ibid., 244.

[33] Ibid., 146.

Nevin and Schaff deplored the anti-intellectualism they saw in the freewheeling market place of religious ideas on the American frontier. In Philip Schaff's colorful assessment, "Anyone who has, or fancies that he has, some inward experience and a ready tongue, may persuade himself that he is called to be a reformer; and so proceed at once, in his spiritual vanity and pride, to a revolutionary rupture with the historical life of the church, to which he holds himself immeasurably superior." Nevin firmly believed in the church's authority, which was steeped in learning and tradition. His thought was comprised of three interlocking doctrines: (a) Christology, (b) ecclesiology, and (c) sacraments. At a time when most American Protestants were focusing on what Christ did (atonement) or said (doctrine), Nevin wanted to push the emphasis back to the foundation of who Christ is in his very being as the God-Man. According to Nevin, nothing Christ did or said has any meaning apart from the hypostatic union of the divine and human natures in his very person. In Nevin's words, "Christianity . . . is a *Life*."[34]

Nevin's Christology was based on Paul's image of the first and second Adam. Just as humanity is identified with Adam in his sin, so too are we identified with Christ, who assumed human nature and brought it into union with the Godhead. The result is a "mystical union" of our humanity with Christ's glorified humanity. In Brooks Holifield's summary: [This] "was the unity of the human and the divine toward which all of creation had struggled. It introduced into the world a "divine supernatural order of existence" that elevated human nature to a new level, higher than it could ever have achieved through mere natural progress."[35] In terms of Nevin's ecclesiology, the church is the primary means of communicating Christ and, thus, the salvation of humanity. The church was a single whole—not because all its members adhered to a uniform set of

---

[34] John W. Nevin, *The Mystical Presence and Other Writings on the Eucharist* (Philadelphia, PA: United Church Press, 1966), 222.

[35] E. Brooks Holifield, *Theology in America: Christian Thought from the Age of the Puritans to the Civil War* (New Haven, CT: Yale University Press, 2005), 476.

doctrines or practices, but because it is the continuation of Christ's life on earth through the agency of the Holy Spirit. The reality of the church's organic union with Christ also dramatically affected how Nevin understood the church's sacraments. A full treatment of Nevin's sacramentology is beyond the scope of this paper. Suffice it to say that it was his understanding of the organic union between Christ and the church that led to his elevation of the Lord's Supper as the focal point of the church's life. In the Eucharist, the Body of Christ on earth is brought into contact with the life-giving substance of its heavenly food: the very divine/human life of the glorified, incarnate Christ himself. Nevin accordingly states concerning the Eucharist that "it may be regarded as in some sense central to the whole Christian system. For Christianity is grounded in the living union of the believer with the person of Christ; and this great fact is emphatically concentrated in the mystery of the Lord's Supper."[36]

There is much more that can (and should) be said about Nevin's rich theology. I hope, however, that the contours I have sketched here will be sufficient to help us examine Nevin's theology of historical development.

The Role of the Protestant Reformation and Historical Development

Nevin almost decided to convert to Catholicism. In 1851–1852, he published a series of articles on "Early Christianity" and "Cyprian" that convinced him of the continuity between early Christianity and Catholicism. Brooks Holifield explains, "The conclusion Nevin drew from his studies was that the early church looked "very different from modern Protestantism." It knew nothing of "the Bible and private judgment" as the rule of faith; it accepted the primacy of the Roman pontiff . . . it affirmed asceticism, celibacy, relics, miracles, purgatory, the veneration of saints, prayers for the dead, submission to the church, and faith in the sacraments as supernatural mysteries."[37] Nevin ultimately remained in the

---

[36] John Williamson Nevin, *The Mystical Presence and the Doctrine of the Reformed Church on the Lord's Supper*, ed. Linden J. DeBie (Eugene, OR: Wipf & Stock, 2012), 47.

[37] Holifield, *Theology in America*, 480.

Reformed Confession, but in his writing he never jettisoned the history of Catholicism.

Nevin's challenge was to figure out how to align Protestantism within the history of the church while justifying its break with Rome. He did this through a theory of organic development that depended on the link between Christology and ecclesiology. Nevin took seriously the principle set forth in Matthew 28:20, where Jesus tells his disciples, "Lo, I am with you always, even unto the end of the world." Nevin writes, "How utterly at war [is this] with the notion of a quickly apostatizing and totally failing church." Unlike Campbell, who saw the birth of the Reformation as a sixteenth-century phenomenon, Nevin stressed that the Reformation was a conservative reform that emerged organically as a development. Put differently, Nevin located the history of the Protestant church within the general flow of Christian history from its inception with the Apostles and early church fathers. The church is always moving forward, while at the same time bonded to that which came before. This conviction of Nevin's leads directly to a discussion of the liturgical implications of his thought.

Liturgical Implications

In 1848, the General Synod of the German Reformed Church expressed its desire to revise its liturgy. The resulting liturgy had a difficult and conflicted gestation period, too complex to detail here at length. Ultimately this liturgy, commonly called the *Order of Worship* and referred to as the 1866 Mercersburg Liturgy, was adopted by the General Synod of 1866 by a margin of seven votes. Nevin and Schaff were the chief architects of this liturgy, which attempted to reintroduce to the Reformed tradition a eucharistic liturgy more in keeping with the classic Western shape, including a full eucharistic prayer.

The Mercersburg orientation of the committee charged with this liturgical work was clear from its statement of liturgical principles. The intention was to look not only to the sixteenth century for guidance but also, and with greater rigor, to the early church. The statement read: "The liturgical worship of the Primitive Church, as far as it can be ascertained from the Holy Scriptures, the oldest ecclesiastical writings, and the liturgies of the Greek and Latin Churches of the third and fourth centuries, ought to be made, as much as possible, the general basis for the proposed Liturgy."[38] This did not mean that the Reformation was necessarily defective, because, as the committee also explained, the "merit of the Reformation" was not to produce new liturgies but to hand down older ones translated into the vernacular, "purifying them from certain additions," "reducing them to greater simplicity," and "subordinating them to the preaching of the Gospel."[39]

In his extensive study of the Mercersburg Liturgy, Jack Maxwell determined that in the process of formation, at least twenty-seven antecedent liturgies were consulted, and of some of those, there were multiple editions and revisions. Some striking characteristics of the Mercersburg Liturgy include

- its basis on a theology of the incarnation of Jesus Christ and a strong Calvinistic ecclesiology,
- its strong emphasis on the unity of the Christian church,
- its strong emphasis on the sacraments, the demand for balance between Word and Sacrament in Lord's Day worship, and an insistence on weekly Eucharist.[40]

Nevin was not advocating a simple "return" to sixteenth-century eucharistic liturgies. As Nathan Mitchell has argued, Nevin and Schaff avoided sixteenth-century Reformed liturgies because they realized their eucharistic theology had gone beyond "all that is possible to engraft on Protestantism, even in our German

[38] Quoted in Jack Maxwell, "The Liturgical Lessons of Mercersburg: An Examination of the Issues which Emerged during the Mercersburg Liturgical Controversy with a View toward Establishing Procedural and Theoretical Principles for Liturgical Committees in the Reformed Tradition" (PhD dissertation, Princeton Theological Seminary, 1969), 126.

[39] Ibid., 126.

[40] Jack Martin Maxwell, *Worship and Reformed Theology: The Liturgical Lessons of Mercersburg* (Pittsburgh, PA: The Pickwick Press, 1976), 199–200.

246

Reformed version of it,"[41] as Nevin had put it.[42] Nevin and the Mercersburg theologians did not intend to "Roman Catholicize" Reformed worship. Instead, "they were seeking to develop a sacramental theology compatible with their vision of 'radical catholicity' and with their re-interpretation of the Reformation itself. . . . The Mercersburg search for a 'catholic' liturgy was not based on an archeological nostalgia for quaint and curious forms from the past. It was based on the conviction that Christianity had something vital to do with the 'inward history' of humanity as a whole."[43]

Nevin and Schaff's attempt to recover the real presence in the Eucharist was by and large a failure. They were unable to sway the opinions of the American Protestant theologians. From 1848 to 1850 Nevin engaged in a public debate with Charles Hodge over the doctrine of the real presence. Despite Nevin's forceful rebuttal, the memorialist position became the dominant understanding in American Protestantism. Nevertheless, the Mercersburg theologians were among the finest American scholars and churchmen of the mid-nineteenth century and left an enduring body of work. Their Reformed-Catholic synthesis, their recovery of classical sacramental and liturgical theology and practice, their efforts to promote the visible unity of the church in the face of American sectarianism, their arguments in defense of the Reformation and its organic connection with earlier eras of church history, their desire to center all of theology around the person of Christ, and their attempts to deal squarely with the ecclesiastical problems of their day all make them worthy of study.

CONCLUSION

In many ways, the desire to return to ancient Christian liturgy and thought makes sense—going back to the beginning and starting

[41] James Hastings Nichols, *Romanticism in American Theology: Nevin and Schaff at Mercersburg* (Eugene, OR: Wipf & Stock, 2007), 300, prints the text of Nevin's letter.

[42] Letter to Schaff, December 3, 1835 (Library of the German Reformed Church, Franklin and Marshall College, Lancaster, PA).

[43] Nathan D. Mitchell, "Church, Eucharist, and Liturgical Reform at Mercersburg: 1843–1857" (PhD dissertation, University of Notre Dame, 1978), 416.

afresh is a practical corrective. Contemporary twenty-first-century Evangelicals share the strong primitivist bent of the nineteenth-century Stone-Campbell movement: they prefer to think of their faith as indistinguishable from the faith of Christ's apostles. Elesha Coffman makes the point metaphorically: the goal of the Chicago Call, like that of all restorationist movements, "was to burrow beneath the tangle of ecclesial branches and tap into 'common roots,' unifying Christians rather than staking out a new plant to compete for the sun." But one cannot tap the roots of Christianity without first "boring through the gnarls and burls and wormholes and growth rings of the tree."[44] This is why, in his encouragement to evangelicals who desire to dive more deeply into history, D. H. Williams cautions:

> Clearly, the ancient Christians had ways of expressing themselves and their times that are unfamiliar to us today. Moreover, there are some foreign aspects of the patristic church to which evangelicals are unaccustomed. . . . Contrary to the view that the early fathers represent a sort of proto-Protestantism, evangelicals will find and should find some wholly unique features of the patristic church that will not be easily squared with their free church perspective. A reader may look in vain to find a teaching or a practice in the early church that offers a precedent for a contemporary religious teaching or practice. The intention of the early church was not to be user-friendly, much less seeker-sensitive, but it does offer the means for transformation if the seeker will seek, knock, and ask.[45]

In his recent biography of John Nevin, Reformed theologian D. G. Hart observes:

> As creative, historically aware, and thoughtful as the Mercersburg Theology may have been, Schaff and especially Nevin were guilty of introducing forms and ideas that were foreign to German Reformed congregations. . . . To try to give the German Reformed Church

---

[44] Elesha Coffman, "*The Chicago Call* and Responses," in Kalantzis and Tooley, *Evangelicals and the Early Church*, 119, 123.

[45] D. H. Williams, *Evangelicals and Tradition: The Formative Influence of the Early Church* (Grand Rapids, MI: Baker Academic, 2005), 182.

greater unity by turning to the ancient church, while laudable in theory, was clearly too much too soon. More importantly, it violated the very notion of organic historical development that Nevin and Schaff promoted. At one level, Nevin's liturgy was as novel as Finney's "new measures" because it veered so widely from the experience of German Reformed pastors and church members in the United States.[46]

Nevin's contemporary, John Bomberger vehemently argued that popular reception by the laity is one of the most important criteria by which the value of a liturgy should be assessed. Failure here can override even the best theological, historical and aesthetic considerations.

On the flip side, popular theologies have value, and academics must do a better job studying and appreciating them. I draw on an analogy from Jesuit scholar Michel de Certeau. Imagine an architectural model of a city enclosed under glass, perhaps with tiny human figures added to the scene for scale. From this bird's-eye view, there is a particular logic to the city: it is "laid out, legible, resolved. One can see how things relate to each other, put certain markers in place, take in distances across the city in a single sweep."[47] Now imagine the same city from the street-level perspective of a pedestrian. Pedestrians may take shortcuts or wander aimlessly rather than following the utilitarian layout of street grids. Their outlook continually changes as they walk, "deftly avoiding traffic, sidestepping and negotiating their way around obstacles, ignoring the honking, but noticing the displays on the sidewalk, passing by, reaching toward and generally 'muddling through' on their way to work."[48] In short, pedestrians "reappropriate" the city of architects and planners according to their own interests and rules.

[46] D. G. Hart, *John Williamson Nevin: High-Church Calvinist*, American Reformed Biographies (Phillipsburg, NJ: P & R Publishing, 2005), 199.

[47] Quoted in Fran Tonkiss, *Space, the City and Social Theory: Social Relations and Urban Forms* (Cambridge, UK: Polity Press, 2005), 127.

[48] Robert R. C. H. Chia and R. Holy, *Strategy without Design: The Silent Efficacy of Indirect Action* (Cambridge, UK: Cambridge University Press, 2009), 148.

As with pedestrians, so too with congregations. While there is nothing wrong with drafting or consulting academic liturgical blueprints (the kind both Nevin and Robert Webber have produced), "pedestrian" theologies of worship are negotiated from within a local context that includes "the church's history, both local and worldwide; the background beliefs and the economic and social status of its members; recent developments among its leadership; [and] styles of argumentation in theology." Pedestrian theologies of worship do not transfer wholesale from one context to another. As John Witvliet observes, "In one congregation, a new Gen X service might arise out of genuine spiritual renewal and a desire for deeper worship. In another, it might signal a desire for a less demanding form of worship." Though they may be nontransferable, local theologies need not be myopic. Local communities are impelled to move outward: they must "make some contribution to the way in which the whole of the Christian church understands itself, either by affirming what is already known in the tradition or by extending it to new circumstances." This is a challenging agenda, to say the least. But the relationship between liturgical history, liturgical practice, and liturgical theology must necessarily be a complex one. If the future lies in the past, it will take a great deal of wisdom to learn from both the strengths and the limits of all phases of history.

Hymnals as Theological Texts

The Case of Civil War Publications

Karen B. Westerfield Tucker

From the sixteenth century onward, Protestant Christians have known the value of a printed metrical compendium of doctrine and devotion for the formation and expression of the Christian faith.[1] Books could include translations or paraphrases of the Psalms (characteristic especially of the Reformed tradition), or they might contain versifications of Scripture or freely composed texts. These resources could be used for gatherings of the community, with family and small-group worship, and for personal prayer and meditation.

In the preface to his voluminous *Collection of Hymns for the Use of The People Called Methodists* (1780), John Wesley wrote that this book was "large enough to contain all the important truths of our most holy religion, whether speculative or practical" and that the contents were not "carelessly jumbled together, but carefully ranged under proper heads, according to the experience of real Christians." The book was "in effect a little body of experimental [experiential] and practical divinity."[2] Thus the value of hymnbooks is not just that they conveniently contain the repertoire of words—and sometimes music—to be used for Christian worship and devotions. By their contents and by the method of their organization, these

---

[1] A version of this paper was presented at the Yale Institute of Sacred Music's colloquium in February 2015.

[2] John Wesley, *The Works of John Wesley*, vol. 7, ed. Franz Hildebrandt and Oliver A. Beckerlegge (Nashville, TN: Abingdon Press, 1983), 73–74.

books also teach the faith of the church—and, in the case of denominationally authorized books, convey the particular doctrines or theological emphases of that branch of the Christian tradition. Here, between two covers, the *lex orandi* and the *lex credendi* stand together. Because hymnals are intended for the congregation, they are, in effect, the liturgical and theological books of the people, who are thus enabled to articulate their praise and thanksgiving, their lament and hope. Since these books are literally "at hand," their contents—the words of hymns and the theological shape of the entire collection—can (ideally) be more readily assimilated and "owned." What is "confessed with the lips" therefore can reflect *and* shape what is "believed in the heart" (Rom 10:9).

Hymnals may be configured or constituted in a variety of ways, such as books on a single theological subject (e.g., the Eucharist, the mission of the church, and earth care), multiple-themed books of varying organizational patterns (e.g., alphabetical, following the shape of a denominational liturgy, or according to the sequence of the liturgical year), and polemical books (e.g., antislavery and temperance hymnals, and more recent protest collections). Another category includes books designed for a specific constituency, whether for liturgical or extraliturgical use. Within this type stand the hymnals that were produced by tract societies, denominational publication boards, and private authors, North and South, for the military during the American Civil War. This genre will serve as a window on the broader question of the liturgical, spiritual, and theological function of hymnals.

CIVIL WAR HYMNALS IN CONTEXT

In the immediate and subsequent generations following the War between the States, studies were published on the religious life of Civil War military and on the spiritual revivals in the camps that intensified throughout the course of the war. Some of these studies were by chaplains or others who were there, such as J. William Jones's *Christ in the Camp*[3] and A. S. Billingsley's two books

---

[3] J. William Jones, *Christ in the Camp: Or, Religion in the Confederate Army* (Richmond: B. F. Johnson, 1887; repr. Harrisonburg, VA: Sprinkle Publications, 1986).

From the Flag to the Cross and *Christianity in the War*.[4] Later studies often examined the sociological and theological emphases evident in military religious life and analyzed possible differences in the Union and Confederate contexts; Gardiner H. Shattuck's *A Shield and Hiding Place*[5] and Steven Woodworth's *While God Is Marching On*[6] serve as good examples. Each of these examinations made at least some mention of the role of colporteurs—agents who distributed religious literature—or designated missionaries in supplying hymnals along with Bibles, religious tracts, and church-related newspapers to the men in uniform, who used them for religious meetings, private devotions, curious reading, and as a remedy for boredom. Colporteurs came most notably from Baptist, Episcopal, Methodist, and Presbyterian church organizations or represented nondenominational and interdenominational colportage and tract associations.[7] A tract published in 1862 by Henry Keeling included hymns that were designed to define, encourage, and sustain the mission of the colporteurs who serviced the Confederacy. Both the first and final stanzas of the hymn entitled "The Commission" in Keeling's tract summarized the colporteurs' purpose: "Go forth my friends, and find / Where e'er a wanderer strays, / And seize him in your arms, and bind, / And bring to wisdom's ways."[8]

---

[4] A. S. Billingsley, *From the Flag to the Cross: Or, Scenes and Incidents of Christianity in the War* (Philadelphia, PA: New-World Publishing, 1872); and *Christianity in the War: Containing an Account of the Sufferings, Conversions, Prayers, Dying Requests, Last Words, and Deaths of Soldiers and Officers in the Hospital, Camp, Prison, and on the Battle-field. Also, An Account of Distinguished Christian Men and Their Labors in the War* (Philadelphia, PA: Claxton, Remsen & Haffelfinger, 1872).

[5] Gardiner H. Shattuck, Jr., *A Shield and Hiding Place: The Religious Life of Civil War Armies* (Macon, GA: Mercer University Press, 1987).

[6] Steven E. Woodworth, *While God Is Marching On: The Religious World of Civil War Soldiers* (Lawrence, KS: University Press of Kansas, 2001).

[7] See, for example, William W. Bennett, *A Narrative of the Great Revival Which Prevailed in the Southern Armies During the Late Civil War Between the States of the Federal Union* (Philadelphia, PA: Claxton, Remsen & Haffelfinger, 1877), 71–85. See also George C. Rable, *God's Almost Chosen Peoples: A Religious History of the American Civil War* (Chapel Hill, NC: University of North Carolina Press, 2010), 131–35.

[8] Henry Keeling, *The Colporteur's Commission: A Tract for the Times, in Several Scriptural Hymns* (Richmond: n.p., 1862), 1.

Keeling's use of the term "wanderer" in this repeated stanza undoubtedly carried a double meaning and reflected the twofold interests of ecclesiastical bodies, parachurchly organizations, and concerned individuals (especially chaplains). First, the dissemination of hymnbooks and other religious literature, whether in the North or the South, was part of a wider program of evangelism to convert those "wanderers" who had never heard the Gospel story or who had in calmer and less threatening times turned a deaf ear to it. "Shall we provide for the *casket* and take no thought for the *jewel* which it contains?" queried Samuel Walley, president in 1861 of the Bible Society of Massachusetts.[9] Second, there was a fear for what military life, commonly regarded as morally corrupt, might present to those who confessed the faith either fully or marginally. The General Assembly of the Presbyterian Church in the Confederate States of America in 1862 explicitly warned its ministers and members in the Confederate Army against the temptations of profanity, desecration of the Sabbath, intemperance, and gambling that would be found in the camps.[10] Knowing that even the devout were prone to wander, churchly agencies and private individuals strove to make religious literature freely available so that wandering hearts might instead be bound to God. To that end, donations were sought, with the soldiers themselves numbering highly among the contributors. Even in the South, which lagged behind the North in providing facilities for the printing and binding of books, hymnals and other religious materials were systematically produced. In 1862, the General Association of the Baptist Churches in Virginia disseminated 13,845 copies of a collection entitled *Camp Hymns*.[11] The Soldiers' Tract Association of the Methodist Episcopal Church, South, formally organized in March 1862, received $95,457 in 1863 that allowed 45,000 copies of their *Soldier's Hymn-Book* to be distributed; the next year,

[9] Bible Society of Massachusetts, *Annual Report* 52 (1861): 12, cited in Shattuck, *A Shield and Hiding Place*, 22.

[10] General Assembly of the Presbyterian Church in the Confederate States of America, *A Pastoral Letter of the General Assembly of the Presbyterian Church to the Ministers and Members of Its Congregations in the Confederate Army* (Richmond, VA: Presbyterian Committee of Publications, 1862), 5–8.

[11] Bennett, *A Narrative of the Great Revival*, 73.

70,000 copies of the hymnbook were circulated.[12] In contrast, by the end of the war the United States Christian Commission, organized in November 1861, had given out 1,370,000 hymnbooks.[13]

Not every soldier received a hymnal or brought with him one used at home, so the hymnals that were available were sought after and well used. John N. Henry of the Forty-Ninth New York acknowledged borrowing for devotional reading a hymnbook belonging to the chaplain of the Seventh Maine.[14] The Reverend J. H. Harris, a colporteur who visited one of the Confederate camps, was gratified that the men spoke "in the highest praise of the little camp hymn-books."[15] Because of the limited number of hymnals at hand and also on account of the differences in the hymnbooks used, it was often necessary for worship to line out the hymns one or two stanzas at a time so that all could participate, whether in small groups or in large assemblies.[16] Hymns were sung enthusiastically at these gatherings and outside them as well, with the singers relishing both text and tune. The Reverend Charles Parker of Waterbury, Vermont, encamped in 1864 near the Second Vermont in Culpepper County, Virginia, commented in a letter to his wife that the men's singing was "with a will—ready—strong—earnest."[17] In at least one northern regiment, Wednesday night was designated for singing practice.[18]

[12] Jones, *Christ in the Camp*, 161, 612.

[13] Billingsley, *From the Flag to the* Cross, 333. On the United States Christian Commission, see James O. Henry, "The United States Christian Commission in the Civil War," *Civil War History* 6 (1960): 374–88.

[14] John Michael Priest, ed., *Turn Them Out to Die Like a Mule: The Civil War Letters of John N. Henry, 49th New York, 1861–1865* (Leesburg, VA: Gauley Mount Press, 1995), 275 (September 5, 1863).

[15] Jones, *Christ in the Camp*, 184.

[16] For an account of lining out, see Thomas D. Cockrell and Michael B. Ballard, eds., *A Mississippi Rebel in the Army of Northern Virginia: The Civil War Memoirs of Private David Holt* (Baton Rouge, LA: Louisiana State University Press, 1995), 232–33.

[17] Jeffrey D. Marshall, ed., *A War of the People: Vermont Civil War Letters* (Hanover, NH: University Press of New England, 1999), 208.

[18] Horatio B. Hackett, *Christian Memorials of the War: Or, Scenes and Incidents Illustrative of Religious Faith and Principle, Patriotism and Bravery in our Army* (Boston: Gould and Lincoln, 1864), 124.

Diaries and journals kept by combatants from both sides document the occurrence of spontaneous singing by individuals and groups. The Old Hundredth set to Thomas Ken's "Doxology" ("Praise God from Whom All Blessings Flow") was apparently popular with some Union divisions, and they sang it with deep feeling, even, as the reporter notes, "without any apparent occasion for it and without the least suspicion of irony."[19] Hymns frequently mentioned by combatants in both the North and the South included several by Charles Wesley—"A Charge to Keep I Have" and "Jesus, Lover of My Soul" to name just two—as well as "How Firm a Foundation," "Safely through Another Week," and many others. A few of these same journals record the repertoire of hymns and spirituals offered by the Black soldiers. Particularly notable is the account of Colonel Thomas Wentworth Higginson, who later would highlight these songs in an essay on "Negro Spirituals" published in the *Atlantic Monthly*. One song in particular caught his ear one night near Beaufort, South Carolina, in January 1863, which he later would describe as a "flower of poetry":

> I know moon-rise, I know star-rise,
> Lay dis body down.
> I walk in de moonlight, I walk in de starlight,
> To lay dis body down.
> I'll walk in de graveyard, I'll walk through de graveyard,
> To lay dis body down.
> I'll lie in de grave and stretch out my arms;
> Lay dis body down.
> I go to de judgment in de evenin' of de day,
> When I lay dis body down;
> And my soul and your soul will meet in de day
> When I lay dis body down.

---

[19] Harold Adams Small, ed., *The Road to Richmond: The Civil War Memoirs of Major Abner R. Small of the Sixteenth Maine Volunteers; Together with the Diary Which He Kept When He Was a Prisoner of War* (Berkeley, CA: University of California Press, 1939), 145.

On the words "I'll lie in de grave and stretch out my arms," Higginson commented in his essay, "Never, it seems to me, since man first lived and suffered, was his infinite longing for peace uttered more plaintively than in that line."[20] This song and other spirituals were not included in print songbooks specified for black soldiers, and indeed if there were such special collections they apparently have not been preserved. Hymnals from denominations such as the African Methodist Episcopal Church were, however, in print and available—and likely circulated among the literate. Indeed, a hymn explicitly identified as coming from the African Methodist Episcopal Church's hymnbook—with the first line "Hark! Listen to the trumpeters" and also known by the title "Enlisting Soldiers"—appears in the book *Enlisting Soldiers* published in Philadelphia between 1863 and 1865 by the Supervisory Committee for Recruiting Colored Regiments.

Thus for many in the camp, hymn singing was an expression of faith and trust. Hymn singing, however, could sometimes be simply a diversion that demonstrated little spiritual commitment. Commented Union fighter John Beatty in response to soldiers singing "We are going home, we are going home, to die no more" in front of his tent: "Were they to devote as much time to praying as they do to singing, they would soon establish a reputation for piety; but, unfortunately for them, after the hymn they generally proceed to swear, instead of prayer, and one is left in doubt as to what home they propose to go to."[21]

Sunday gatherings and prayer meetings, when they could be held, were the usual occasion for group hymn singing, and multiple hymns figured as standard parts of the formal or informal liturgy. In some units, the Sunday meeting was called together by

[20] Thomas Wentworth Higginson, "Negro Spirituals," *The Atlantic Monthly* 19, no. 116 (June 1867): n.p.; cited from http://www.theatlantic.com/past /docs/issues/1867jun/spirit.htm. See also Christopher Looby, ed., *The Complete Civil War Journal and Selected Letters of Thomas Wentworth Higginson* (Chicago: University of Chicago Press, 2000), 86.

[21] John Beatty, *Memoirs of a Volunteer, 1861–1863*, ed. Harvey S. Ford (New York: W. W. Norton, 1946), 150. On the "charm of music," see Hackett, *Christian Memorials of the War*, 127.

the company's band playing a hymn tune.[22] Entire regiments might assemble for worship and form a square facing inward around officers, band, and singers. "Usually some 90 or 100 [singers] come out," wrote Captain William Y. W. Ripley of the First Vermont Infantry to his wife, Kelie. "Last Sunday we sang a hymn set to 'Home Sweet Home.' Many of the singers & others wept freely— They are none the less men for that."[23] A familiar hymn sung at the conclusion of a service with sermon and celebration of the Lord's Supper that was held in a clearing on the banks of the Rapidan River (Virginia) took on special significance:

> Then [the old chaplain] gave out the hymn:
> How firm a foundation ye saints of the Lord
> Is laid for your faith in his excellent word.
>
> Everyone sang with a will. We could feel the Spiritual presence of our Lord as a kind of heart manifestation of His love. The men all stood at "Attention" with shoulders back and heads up, as though they were receiving a command from their Superior Officer. I never heard such singing in my life. I looked around at the glowing faces of these seasoned warriors who seemed to be receiving some kind of inspiration, and a new hope, and the impulse of sublime courage. The hymn ended the service, the men lit their pipes and, in small groups, went their different ways without words.[24]

Prayer meetings might take on the shape of an ecclesiastical liturgy: dioceses of the Protestant Episcopal Church in the Confederate States of America published services of morning and evening prayer with accompanying collects and occasional prayers, to

---

[22] Private David Holt commented that the band's hymn playing also served the practical function of announcing the day of the week—a useful purpose, since soldiers often lost track of time. See Cockrell and Ballard, *A Mississippi Rebel*, 231. For a study of music used in a specific region during the Civil War, see James A. Davis, *Music along the Rapidan: Civil War Soldiers, Music, and Community during Winter Quarters, Virginia* (Lincoln, NE: University of Nebraska Press, 2014).

[23] Letter of Captain William Y. W. Ripley of Rutland, Company K, First Vermont Infantry, to his wife, Kelie (Cornelia), May 26, 1861, in Marshall, *A War of the People*, 29; cf. Hackett, *Christian Memorials of the War*, 127.

[24] Cockrell and Ballard, *A Mississippi Rebel*, 233.

which were also attached hymn texts, not all of which were part of the standard hymnal.[25] Or the service might exhibit more of a "free" character typical of a Methodist or Baptist service or of a revivalistic camp meeting. A recollection of a prayer meeting held on April 3, 1863, in the camp of the Twenty-Second Massachusetts Regiment demonstrates the style of meeting as well as the place and variety of hymns in the context of corporate worship.

A Sibley tent, warmed by an army cooking-stove, lighted by three candles, and furnished with a long mess-table, was the "upper-room." One real chair, and several real boxes, chests, etc., furnished seats for twenty or more soldiers. A strange minister, fresh from home, had the meeting in charge. With no ado about agreeing on the tune and "pitching" it, some one began the service, when a hymn was called for, by striking up the words, "Nearer, my God, to thee." Then the minister prayed; and before he could find his passage for reading, they started off with "My days are gliding swiftly by," singing two stanzas. Then was read the account of the blind beggar Bartimeus, and how Jesus healed him, and how he followed the Master afterward. A few words were spoken, showing how poor our estate is by nature, sitting by the way-side of life, and how blind we are to our own good and God's glory, till we call on Jesus. Then somebody began to sing, "I love to steal awhile away," and almost all joined, singing but one verse. This was followed by a prayer, short and fervent. Then came an exhortation from a weather-worn soldier of the Cross and the government. "Jesus, lover of my soul," next filled the tent and died away on the hill-side and among the pines in which the regiment has so charming a location.

---

[25] For example, *The Order for Daily Morning and Evening Prayer, according to the Use of the Protestant Episcopal Church in the Confederate States of America, together with the Ante-Communion Office and a Selection of Occasional Prayers from the Various Offices of the Book of Common Prayer* (Atlanta, GA: R. J. Maynard, 1863). See also the Diocesan Missionary Society, Protestant Episcopal Church in Virginia, *Prayer Book for the Camp* (Richmond, VA: MacFarland & Ferguson, 1863), which also included the burial rite; two years later, the Missionary Society brought out *The Army and Navy Prayer Book* (Richmond, VA: Charles H. Wynne, 1865), which more optimistically included the confirmation rite instead of the burial office.

Here one rose simply to testify, as he said, that he loved Jesus. He did not use five sentences, but it was all testimony. Then came a prayer for loved ones at home, the family, the church, the Sabbath school and prayer-meeting; and so still were all, that you would have supposed the praying man to be alone in the tent. The voice trembled somewhat, and if we wiped away a tear or two when he said amen, we were not ashamed to be seen doing it, for some others did so. Our thoughts went home also,—how could we help the tear?

And then, as if some of them in the chances of battle might miss the earthly home, a verse was sung beginning, "Sweet fields beyond the swelling flood."[26]

Next followed a practical talk about following Christ in the army. The good ideas were briefly, bluntly put, and full of the love of the Lord Jesus. Then a stanza went swelling out among the pines again: "Come we that love the Lord."

An exhortation was now addressed to any who had not enlisted under the Captain of our Salvation, and it was pressed home by the sweet words and, then, familiar air, "O happy day that fixed my choice."

Now one kneels down on the clay floor, and prays in the first person singular. It was a short broken prayer, probably by the brother who, they said, had lately learned to pray, and in that tent. We have all heard such prayers, and none ever affected us so much. An exhortation followed by a sailor on the difficulties of being a Christian in the army. He showed how they tried to do that at sea, and illustrated it by an incident.

Then came the hymn, "Thus far the Lord hath led me on."

The minister here remarked that if we would follow Christ successfully we must keep in the ranks, and own to everybody at proper times, that Christ is our Captain. Following him by side-marches and obscure paths exposes us to the lurking enemy.

Now the hour was almost gone and so followed the doxology, "Praise God from whom all blessings flow," and the benediction.[27]

---

[26] From the hymn "There Is a Land of Pure Delight."
[27] Hackett, *Christian Memorials of the War*, 45–47.

The hymnic repertoire for this worship event was probably drawn from several hymnals and from memory: several specifically "camp" hymnals that could have been used in this setting do not include every one of the hymn texts mentioned. For this service, texts by Isaac Watts were drawn on most frequently, with additional texts by English poets Sarah Flower Adams, Philip Doddridge, and Charles Wesley, and by American-born writers Phoebe Brown and David Nelson. The inclusion of American poets here is reflective of the increasing tendency in this period to look more to indigenous writers while still embracing the favorites imported from across the Atlantic.

Hymns and hymnals of the camp went with the sick and wounded fortunate enough to be transported to hospital. Eyewitness accounts and reminiscences speak of chaplains and attendants singing hymns to comfort their wards, and death scenes—recorded as much for their evangelical capacity as for the historic record—describe invalids "singing themselves to heaven." In one report, a dying soldier sang the trinitarian, single-stanza hymn "Great Jehovah, we adore thee," after which the chaplain read to him two hymns. Between each stanza of "Nearer, My God, to Thee," the man exclaimed, "Oh, Lord Jesus, thou art coming nearer to me!" and with "Just as I am—without one plea," he repeated, "O Lamb of God, I come." Soon afterward, this Christian soldier "fell asleep in Jesus."[28]

THE CONTENTS OF CIVIL WAR HYMNALS

The political and social circumstances that prompted the production of special hymnals for Civil War soldiers and sailors, and the evangelical concerns that gave rise to revivals in the camp, are external indicators that give hints about the contents of these pocket-sized books. Studies have often made assumptions about the theological and social thrusts of the material in the hymnals based primarily on these external indicators. The hymnals, however, can speak for themselves in revealing the purpose behind

[28] Bennett, *A Narrative of the Great Revival*, 182–83.

each compilation and thereby provide further—and concrete—evidence of the function expected of these little books and, more broadly, of the religious consciousness and values expressed in the crisis of the period.

The theological and spiritual agendas of Civil War hymnals—and their practical application—can be exposed by examining an author's or editor's intention as expressed in a foreword. Few hymnbooks printed words addressed to the reader, choosing instead to let the hymn texts speak for themselves. Commitment or adherence to Christ in the face of spiritual and physical warfare was the principal purpose stated in prose prefaces that were supplied. A Chicago publication put it directly: "The circumstances that now surround you are different from any previous ones, and your peril is much greater. . . . You need a strong friend. Such an one is Jesus. Will you have him?"[29] The succinct statement that began *Hymns for the Camps*, published in Raleigh, North Carolina, by the General Tract Agency, was cast in eschatological terms: "God grant that every one who shall read or sing these hymns may join that great multitude, that glorious choir, that shall at last surround the throne on high."[30] J. R. MacDuff, in his *Soldier's Textbook*, comprising Scripture quotations, prayers, and twenty hymn texts, took a pastoral approach of consolation: "These Bible-truths . . . can prove messengers of peace and consolation in the hospital-ward or in the bivouac, as well as amid the homes of your happy fatherland. . . . Should these few peaceful notes of the 'Gospel-trumpet' inspire one drooping spirit among you with confidence or hope, forgive the feebleness of the effort on my part, and to God give all the glory!"[31]

Consistent with the twofold interest of general religious publications during the war, the strengthening or maintenance of moral character through the use of hymns was a second purpose identi-

---

[29] *The Soldier's Hymn Book* (Chicago: Young Men's Christian Association, 1861, 1864), n.p.

[30] *Hymns for the Camps*, 2nd rev. ed. (Raleigh: Strother & Marcom, 1862), 3.

[31] J. R. MacDuff, *The Soldier's Text-Book: Or, Confidence in Time of War* (Boston: American Tract Society, 1861), 3–4.

fied, either explicitly or subtly. The first entry in Episcopal priest and Tennessee regimental chaplain Charles T. Quintard's *Confederate Soldier's Pocket Manual of Devotions* (with forty-four hymns) was a statement on the "Duties of a Christian," with the advice that a man should always practice those duties and regularly call himself to account.[32] Baptist chaplain Frederic Denison let the ordering of hymn texts speak for itself in the two collections of hymns he wrote for the New England regiments he served: the first entry in both was a temperance hymn.[33] Partisan sympathies along with the call to "Christian" behavior were made clear in the anonymously edited *Hymns, Religious and Patriotic, for the Soldier and the Sailor*:

> Soldiers and Sailors of the Loyal States!
> You are in arms to avenge an insulted flag, to crush a most atrocious rebellion, and to reëstablish the supremacy of the Constitution throughout the length and breadth of the land. A more sacred cause never sounded its call to battle. Those who answer to this call can not be too careful to maintain a tone of moral sentiment in keeping with the dignity of their errand. Prayer, accompanied by the reading of God's word, is, of course, the best panoply of the soul, whether at home or abroad, on the land or on the sea; and next to prayer, perhaps, we may reckon the strains of sacred and patriotic song. That strains may every where be heard resounding in our camps, and on board our ships, is the fervent wish of the compilers of this little collection of Hymns and Songs.[34]

Even when compilers provide no prose statement, theological and spiritual agendas are made evident by the systematic or thematic

---

[32] C. T. Quintard, *The Confederate Soldier's Pocket Manual of Devotions* (Charleston, SC: Evans & Cogswell, 1863), 3; cf. the opening statement in Quintard's *Balm for the Weary and the Wounded* (Charleston, SC: Evans & Cogswell, 1864), 3–4.

[33] Frederic Denison, *Army Hymns: Written for the First Regiment New England Cavalry* (Providence, RI: A. Crawford Greene, 1861), n.p., and Denison, *Army Hymns: Written for the Third Regiment Rhode Island Heavy Artillery* (Providence, RI: A. Crawford Greene, 1863), n.p. In both of these collections, the temperance hymn appears before page 1.

[34] *Hymns, Religious and Patriotic, for the Soldier and the Sailor* (Boston: American Tract Society, 1861), n.p.

assignments of the hymns. A formal table of contents or the use of running heads over sections of hymn texts provides a clear indication of organizational intention. Comparison of the headings and subjects in a denominationally produced hymnal for the soldiers with those in the standard book authorized by the same denomination (from which the smaller books were usually drawn) also reveals theological emphases. A single hymn could (and often did) take up multiple theological themes and thus might be placed in different thematic categories depending on the primary meaning it was expected to offer. For example, in three of the Civil War collections, John Newton's hymn "Approach, My Soul, the Mercy-Seat" is variously categorized under "The Sinner,"[35] "Worship,"[36] and "Prayer."[37] Thus the peculiar rationale for the inclusion of the thirty-eight hymns in *Camp Hymns in Alphabetical Order*[38] must be left as a matter for speculation.

Of the twenty-two collections examined, only a few present either a table of contents or an index of subjects. Three books produced in the South—the *Soldier's Hymn Book* of the South Carolina Tract Society (1862), the Presbyterian *Army Hymn-Book* (1863), and the *Hymns for the Camp* of the General Tract Agency (1864)—provide tables of contents that, though different in heading and sequence, have striking similarities, thereby revealing a commonality of purpose. The hymns placed first in the books, perhaps for easy access, are intended for "Worship"—Sunday and daily, corporate and private. Hymns that are designated for the "Sabbath" (i.e., those that speak directly to the nature and purpose of Sabbath and Sabbath worship) or for "Morning" and "Evening" may fall

[35] *The Soldier's Hymn Book* (Charleston, SC: South Carolina Tract Society, 1862), 78.

[36] *The Army Hymn-Book* (Richmond, VA: Presbyterian Committee of Publications, 1863), no. 1.

[37] *Hymns for the Camp* (Raleigh, NC: Biblical Recorder, 1864), 31. There are references in Jones's *Christ in the Camp* to "Camp Hymns" and "Hymns for Camp" that may in turn refer to this collection (see, for example, pp. 157 and 175).

[38] *Camp Hymns in Alphabetical Order* (Charleston, SC: S. C. Colportage Board, [1860s]).

here or elsewhere. Hymns that focus on the person and work of Jesus Christ come next, followed (in different sequences) by hymns meant to warn, identify sin, and call to penitence; hymns to express penance and remorse; and hymns to offer assurance and celebrate the Christian life. In recognition that the faithful still face trials and sorrows and yet must offer a Christian witness, hymns on these themes are then set out, with hymns on dying and readiness for death coming last. Texts on "Heaven" conclude this system, which is principally organized according to the "way" of salvation. Consistent with this scheme, the largest groupings of hymns in these three books fall under the subjects of worship, the saving Christ, calls to conversion, practice of the Christian life, and death/heaven. Noticeably, but not surprisingly, absent are categories on the Trinity, the church, the sacraments, the Christian year, and the second coming of Christ, subjects that historian Stephen Marini has observed are absent from the majority of evangelical hymn collections produced in America up to 1860.[39]

Examination of two books produced in the North—the only ones available with subject indexes; no hymnals with tables of contents were available in the collections examined—reveals similarities and differences between them and also with the three samples from the South. *Hymns, Religious and Patriotic* and *Hymn Book for the Army and Navy*[40] both have an evangelistic emphasis, evident by categories that lay out the way of salvation. In a somewhat unusual move, *Hymns, Religious and Patriotic* lists the subjects of "God," "Christ," and "Holy Spirit" (with the largest percentage under "God"), whereas *Hymn Book for the Army and Navy* (like the Southern books previously mentioned) only identifies hymns on "Christ" and "Holy Spirit." "Worship" is a major category for *Hymns, Religious and Patriotic* but is only an incidental one in

---

[39] Stephen Marini, "Hymnody as History: Early Evangelical Hymns and the Recovery of American Popular Religion," *Church History* (2002): 282–84.

[40] *Hymn Book for the Army and Navy* (New York: American Tract Society, 1860). This publication was issued through the United States Christian Commission and, according to A. S. Billingsley, a former Union chaplain, was the hymnal he most often used (*From the Flag to the Cross*, 96).

Hymn Book for the Army and Navy. In a marked distinction from the Southern books, these two contain an explicitly named category of "Patriotism"; the South Carolina Tract Society's *Soldier's Hymn Book* provides a broad category of "Our Country at War," whereas the other two books carry no such designation. The presence of this category, however, should suggest not that a sense of Christian patriotism was stronger in the North than in the South, but that in the North there was possibly a greater willingness to conflate church and nation. Ironically, the North and the South employed several of the same hymns for "our country" (e.g., "My Country, 'Tis of Thee" and "God Bless Our Native Land").

The contents of three books for the military published by denominations in the South were substantially drawn from their standard hymnals. The aforementioned Presbyterian book borrows hymn texts familiar from Presbyterian books already in circulation but uses headings different from those other books and "recategorizes" many of the texts under new designations. Nonetheless, by examination of headings and of the percentage of hymns under a particular heading in relation to the total number of hymns in the collection, it is possible to evaluate theological emphasis and purpose. A comparison of the *Army Hymn-Book* with these other books reveals the intention of the compilers to supply the soldiers with a larger proportion of hymns for use in worship and with hymns that articulate the evangelical emphasis on invitation, conversion, and Christian hope in the face of death and in anticipation of heaven. These same subjects are present in the older books, but at a smaller overall percentage than in the *Army Hymn-Book*. The same trend of intensification can be seen in the Methodist Episcopal Church, South's *Soldier's Hymn-Book* when compared with that same denomination's 1847 hymnal.[41] Although no table of contents or subject index is provided in the *Soldier's Hymn-Book*, the hymns in this book follow in almost exact progression those in the denominational standard, which does have a table of contents. In the military book, hymns under "Being and

---

[41] *A Collection of Hymns for Public, Social, and Domestic Worship* (Charleston, SC: John Early for the MECS, 1847).

Perfections of God" are reduced in favor of augmenting those on the "Mediation of Christ," and hymns under "Sabbath," "Gospel Call," and "Penitential Exercises" are increased percentage-wise. In an interesting shift, hymns under the broad category of "Christian Experience" are reallocated so that in the *Soldier's Hymn-Book* more fall under the subheading "Justification and New Birth" and fewer appear under "Entire Sanctification and Perfect Love," perhaps indicating that inquirers rather than professors were anticipated to be the greater number among the readership. No hymns under the 1847 hymnbook's categories of "Special Occasions" (including the subhead "National Solemnities") are found in the *Soldier's Hymn-Book*, and only two hymns—on the Sabbath—come from the general heading "Institutions of Christianity." The result of the reworking of these two denominational standards into new books for the camp is that denominational identities are lost (save for the naming of the publisher) and that these books carry no marked distinction from the nondenominational books.

Such evangelistic emphases might be expected in books of Baptist, Presbyterian, and Methodist sponsorship. But similar characteristics can be found in books issued directly or indirectly under the auspices of the Protestant Episcopal Church of the Confederate States of America. The hymns in *The Order for Daily Morning and Evening Prayer* (1863) progress according to the sequence of those in the *Hymns of the Protestant Episcopal Church in the United States* published in 1827[42] and thus may be linked with the categories stipulated in the older book. The hymns in the *Army and Navy Prayer Book* published in 1865 by the Diocesan Missionary Society of the Protestant Episcopal Church of Virginia do not imitate the order but clearly draw from the 1827 collection for the first thirty-six hymns. The remaining eleven hymns, marked as "Additional," come from the songs popular in the camp and found in other books (e.g., "There Is a Fountain, Filled with Blood," "Just as I Am, without One Plea," "Alas! And Did My Saviour Bleed," etc.), with one exception, "Lord, Dismiss Us with Thy Blessing,"

[42] *Hymns of the Protestant Episcopal Church in the United States* (Philadelphia, PA: S. F. Bradford, 1827).

which is the only one from the 1827 book's category "The Church." There is an increase in hymn offerings in both Episcopal books under the designations "Redemption," "Invitation and Warning," "Christian Duties and Affections," and "The Christian Life." Missing are hymns under the headings "Creation" and "Providence" (the latter a surprise, given the popularity of the theme recorded in sermons of the period and in the diaries and letters of the soldiers)[43] and a decrease in the number of hymns under "Church," "Festivals and Fasts," and "Ordinances and Special Occasions." Inexplicably, there is a reduction as well in the categories of "Death," "Judgment," and "Eternity." Such an evangelistic emphasis in the hymnody offered by the Protestant Episcopal Church might be explained by the urgencies of war; selections of the hymns in Episcopal chaplain Charles T. Quintard's *Confederate Soldier's Pocket Manual of Devotions* come from the 1827 book but more often from the evangelical corpus of song already popular in the camp. Many of the hymns already in the 1827 book are shared, however, with the more obviously "evangelical" collections: it contains sixteen of the seventy-one "core" hymn texts identified by Stephen Marini in his essay "Hymnody as History" as the most frequently published in evangelical hymnals.[44] Such a finding raises questions about whether boundaries may be set on the category "evangelical" during this period in American history.

All of the Civil War hymnals examined contain representatives from Marini's "core," which helps to identify them with a broadly evangelical agenda. But they also share many hymns that are not a part of this "core." Among them are hymns that utilize militaristic metaphors and allusions inspired by Ephesians 6:10-20 and 2 Timothy 4:7, such as "Soldiers of Christ, Arise," "The Soldiers Are Gath'ring from Near and From Far," and "The Christian Warrior, See Him Stand."[45] Such formulations allowed the combatants to "own" the texts in a particular way and to internalize the conflict

[43] Woodworth, *While God Is Marching On*, 27–39.

[44] For the core list, see Marini, "Hymnody as History," 280–81.

[45] Isaac Watts's "Am I a Soldier of the Cross," popular in the Civil War collections, is fourth among often-published hymns and ranks in Marini's core.

as one in conformity to the will of God. Hymns that exploited the image of "home"—which could be interpreted both as return to family and as rest with God—were widely popular, as were hymns that spoke of the "land of pure delight" immune from the ravages of war. These texts and also the act of singing had the power to transport the war weary to a better place. Recounted one soldier, "Surely nothing has such power to make us forget earth and its round of troubles as these sweet old church songs, familiar from earliest childhood and wrought into the most tender memories, until we come to regard them as a sort of sacred stream on which some day our souls will float away happily to the better country."[46]

The hymnals for the soldiers and sailors often included the "lighter" texts more commonly associated with the camp meeting and with the Sunday School collections that were popular with the young. Many of the songs absent from authorized denominational hymnals intended for formal corporate worship that are included in the 1864 publication *The Southern Zion's Songster: Hymns Designed for Sabbath Schools, Prayer, and Social Meetings, and the Camps* (with "camps" probably meaning "camp meetings" but not excluding military "camps") are also found in the books intended for the forces.[47] Newly popular texts and original texts (with refrains or choruses) that expanded the long-established repertoire of Watts, Wesley, and the Baptist writer Anne Steele were put to use in some of these books and give first evidence of the type of texts that would flourish in the 1870s under the category of Gospel song. It is possible that the Civil War collections are a bridge between the older style of psalm and hymn singing inherited from English songwriters and a new style that was distinctly American.

CIVIL WAR HYMNALS: SOME OBSERVATIONS

What is striking about the Civil War hymnals is their theological and functional homogeneity. Crossing the Mason-Dixon Line did not bring with it any major distinctions in the hymnbook the

[46] Beatty, *Memoirs*, 67; cf. Jones, *Christ in the Camp*, 243.
[47] *The Southern Zion's Songster*, compiled by the editor of the North Carolina Christian Advocate (Raleigh: N. C. Advocate Publishing Co., 1864).

soldiers carried in their breast pocket or haversack. Hymnals were scavenged from the bodies of enemy soldiers and taken up for devotional purposes or for casual reading by their finders. Such a point was not lost on many of the soldiers and their chaplains— and nor was the reality that the men in the two armies shared a common repertoire of hymns. Confederate veteran J. M. Beadles recalled that at the baptism in the Rapidan River of a soldier from General Lee's army in November 1863, members of the Union army encamped on the opposite bank joined with them in singing "There Is a Fountain Filled with Blood" while both armies remained at peace.[48] In writing about a visit to the home of a Presbyterian clergyman in Virginia, Captain William Wheeler of the Thirteenth New York Battery noted:

> But after the political discussion had waged for some time, we opened the piano, and we had some of the old hymns after the old style, "Ariel," "Greenland's Icy Mountain," "Italian Hymn," etc., which did me good, and then we stayed with them to evening worship. . . . It is strange that opinions and sentiments about the war can be so violent one moment, and the next, all the disputants have their heads close together about one hymn book, or are kneeling at one family altar.[49]

The Baptist Confederate chaplain William Jones observed that "the soldiers who opposed them with constancy and valor, many shedding their lifeblood on the field, were partakers of like precious faith with themselves." To Jones it was "a happy thought that in the two confronting camps, often at the same hour, there rose with voice and heart the common strain, 'All hail the power of Jesus' name!'"[50] Yet Chesley Mosman of Illinois found no comfort in his enemy's worship of the same God and their similar corpus of song. "We can hear the Johnnies singing, 'Come thou font [sic] of every

---

[48] "A Unique Incident," *Confederate Veteran* 25 (1917): 471.

[49] William Wheeler, *Letters of William Wheeler of the Class of 1855, Y. C.*, Printed for Private Distribution ([Cambridge, MA]: [H. O. Houghton], 1875), 421.

[50] Jones, *Christ in the Camp*, 14.

blessing,'" he wrote, "[b]ut how could [God] tune their savage 'hearts to sing thy praise' [?]"[51]

The commonalities of the hymnic repertoire were sometimes painfully evident as men, blue and gray, lay wounded and dying at battle's end. One account after the Battle of Shiloh, in April 1862, gives the words of a mortally wounded man describing his experience in the lonely night:

> "I could not help singing that beautiful hymn:—
> 'When I can read my title clear
> To mansions in the skies,
> I'll bid farewell to every fear,
> And wipe my weeping eyes.'
> And though I was not aware of it till then," said he, "it proved there was a Christian brother in the thicket near me. I could not see him, but was near enough to hear him. He took up the strain from me; and beyond him another, and then another, caught the words, and made them resound far and wide over the terrible battle-field of Shiloh. There was a peculiar echo in the place, and that added to the effect, as we made the night vocal with our hymns of praise to God."[52]

The hymnals testify to a common cause in the North and the South—the salvation and sanctification of those in the field. That cause also transcended the denominational boundaries that were sometimes fiercely delineated and defended during this period. "Denominationalism was swallowed up in the great interests of the soul," claimed A. S. Billingsley.[53] Prior to the 1860s, evangelical hymnody had been widely shared among the churches, except perhaps among the Lutherans, who tended to have a limited

---

[51] Arnold Gates, ed., *The Rough Side of War: The Civil War Journal of Chesley A. Mosman, 1st Lieutenant, Company D, 59th Illinois Volunteer Infantry Regiment* (Garden City, NJ: Basin, 1987), 260.

[52] Hackett, *Christian Memorials of the War*, 19. A variation on this same episode is recounted in Frank Moore, *Anecdotes, Poetry and Incidents of the War: North and South, 1860–1865* (New York: Printed for the Subscribers, 1866), 245 (found also under the title *The Civil War in Song and Story, 1860–1865*), but the same hymn stanza by Isaac Watts is indicated.

[53] Billingsley, *From the Flag to the Cross*, 96.

English-hymn vocabulary, preferring instead English translations of German and Scandinavian hymns. During the war, the evangelical purpose at hand perpetuated such blending and reinforced it by drawing on hymns (older and newer) that played down doctrinal differences in favor of the more general Gospel message. Such generalization also helped to blur the distinctions between denominational and nondenominational books, as had already occurred in the interdenominational prayer-meeting movement of the 1850s, thus helping to promote (wittingly or unwittingly) a Christian civil religion.

On the reception of a hundred hymnbooks, a chaplain ministering in Washington to the sick and wounded thanked the sender and acknowledged that the books would undoubtedly be useful and "do much good."[54] The hymnals produced for soldiers filled multiple needs for their owners and their producers, and the evidence is that they did do much good. For readers today, these little books are still useful in that they provide concrete testimony to the religious milieu and the theological agendas operative at critical junctures in American history and give evidence of the hymnbook as a theological textbook for the people and by the people.

[54] Hackett, *Christian Memorials of the War*, 168.

Part 4

The Presence and Future of Liturgy's Past/s

The Changing Shape of Liturgy

From Earliest Christianity
to the End of Late Antiquity

Wendy Mayer

When we refer to the changing shape of liturgy in the same breath as the writing of liturgical history, as the other chapters in this volume highlight, it is not only liturgy itself as it was performed in all its glorious diversity in the past that changes over time but also our perception of it. Reflecting on precisely how and why we approach liturgy's past in the way that we do is thus an important exercise, to which I contribute this overview of some of the key changes in approach to the study of liturgy in the past that have emerged in recent decades.[1] Throughout my survey and analysis I shall assume that study of the history of the structure of liturgical rites, their content, and their textual sources—the dominant approach of the past—remains fundamental to the field and will in the future continue to be a focus.[2] But

---

[1] My thanks go to Teresa Berger, Bryan Spinks, and the Yale Institute of Sacred Music for inviting me to reflect intentionally on the changes that have been taking place in our approach to liturgy in these formative centuries, many of which have influenced my own work both consciously and subconsciously. Some of the insights presented here came to me only as I was preparing the original keynote lecture; many of the questions I ask have deepened as a result of the other papers presented, their respondents and the questions posed by the audience.

[2] As an example of how this approach continues to define liturgical studies as a field, see the contents of Bert Groen, Steven Hawkes-Teeples, and Stefanos

that is not what interests me here. My focus in this reflection is on how changes in the study of history and new developments in the sciences are currently influencing how we approach liturgy and how this in turn is expanding the way that we view liturgy in these historical periods. Looking at liturgy from these alternative angles raises some very interesting questions. While my focus will also be on Christian worship in the first eight or nine centuries (with a strong Eastern bias, due to my own area of expertise), what is clear is that many of the developments that I outline here are trends that have been occurring simultaneously in, or that are of equal relevance to, the study of liturgy in other geographical areas and historical periods.[3]

For the first eight centuries, the study of Christian worship, its origins and its evolution, goes hand in hand with the study of the rise of Christianity as a religion. One of the most significant influences in the past two decades in this respect has been the field of Late Antiquity. By redefining the centuries between the classical Roman and Medieval worlds as a period not of decline but of transformation and by viewing them not through a (primarily) economic and political but a cultural and sociohistorical lens, this multidisciplinary field has given rise to an endlessly changing range of approaches and points of view.[4] What constitutes Late Antiquity is itself still under definition, with a variety of time ranges theorized.[5] For the study of liturgy, the most important point to

---

Alexopoulos, eds., *Inquiries into Eastern Christian Worship*, Eastern Christian Studies 12 (Leuven: Peeters, 2012).

[3] This is not surprising as what we are talking about here is a widespread change in historiography in recent decades, more generally characterized under the labels of postmodernism or postcolonialism.

[4] For reflection on the formation and development of the concept see the historiographical essays in both Philip Rousseau, ed., *A Companion to Late Antiquity* (Oxford: Blackwell, 2009), and Scott F. Johnson, ed., *The Oxford Handbook of Late Antiquity* (Oxford: Oxford University Press, 2012).

[5] So in his *World of Late Antiquity*, Peter Brown defined Late Antiquity as the period from 150–750 CE. In another iteration of this work, also published in 1971, the chronological termini were replaced by the names of significant individuals of roughly the same periods. See Peter Brown, *The World of Late Antiquity: AD 150–750* (New York: Harcourt Brace Jovanovich, 1971); Peter Brown,

note is that in its most generous interpretation the field essentially deals with the period between our earliest historical sources—the New Testament and associated writings—and, in the West, the early Medieval Period, in the East, middle Byzantium and early Islam.[6] The sheer breadth of the perspectives that this all-encompassing view of these critical centuries offers has had a profound impact on the study of the rise of Christianity, with a noticeable flow-on effect into the study of its worship practices.

The most important changes this reconceptualization of history has brought about are, in my view, the following. The first is a substantial alteration in how we view the parting of the ways between Christianity and Judaism, on the one hand, and the relationship between Christianity and so-called "pagan" religions, Greco-Roman philosophy, and magic on the other. The shift from a neat linear schema to one that is organic and much more chaotic is wonderfully illustrated by figures 1 and 9 published by Martin Goodman in *The Parting of the Ways*.[7] The broad implications of this change

---

The World of Late Antiquity from Marcus Aurelius to Muhammad (London: Thames and Hudson, 1971). A more restrictive view focuses on the Roman Empire, arguing that its later phase extends from the Diocletian tetrarchy to the beginning of the Arab conquest. See, e.g., Stephen Mitchell, *A History of the Later Roman Empire AD 284–641: The Transformation of the Ancient World* (Oxford: Blackwell Publishing, 2006). In response to ideological debates, the negotiation of the boundary between classical Antiquity, Late Antiquity, and the Middle Ages is ongoing, with the boundary at either end of Late Antiquity continuing to shift back and forth. An increasing interest in the rise of Islam and the transition into Islamic rule in the Mediterranean east is now influencing the terminus at the upper end. The Oxford Centre for Late Antiquity, for example, designates it as "the period between approximately 250 and 750 CE" (http://www.ocla.ox.ac.uk).

[6] The fields of study circumscribed by the Oxford Centre for Late Antiquity are particularly expansive: the later Roman Empire; the Sassanian world (Persia); Byzantium and the Christian East; Judaism and the Jewish world; Islam and the Islamic world; and the post-Roman West. Their web site (as cited in the previous note) is divided accordingly, with each field comprising its own researchers, graduate students, and events.

[7] Martin Goodman, "Modelling the 'Parting of the Ways,'" in *The Ways That Never Parted: Jews and Christian in Late Antiquity and the Early Middle Ages*, ed. Adam H. Becker and Annette Yoshiko Reed (Tübingen: Mohr Siebeck, 2003),

in perspective are profound: a move away from the language of Christianity to that of Christianities, for instance, and a move away from studying only those strands viewed as central (for example, the Eucharist, baptism, and these rites in orthodox/Nicene Christianity) to a growing appreciation of those on the periphery; a recognition, even, that what we thought was on the periphery may not, in fact, be so peripheral; and a constant reappraisal of when we thought certain benchmarks in the rise of Christianity—such as its emergence as a distinctly separate religion and the emergence of Nicene trinitarian Christianity as normative—took place.[8] A second important change is that, within a view of history that focuses on the cultural and the social, the life of the ordinary person, not just elites, becomes important. This has led to an interest in the laity, their personal and communal experience of the liturgy and even their influence on it, not just in the clergy who preside over or perform it.[9] An additional consequence is an increased emphasis on

---

121 and 129. In his introduction (119–20) Goodman points out the limitations of figure 9 and other two-dimensional illustrations, arguing that 3-D modeling would represent the complexity of the current perspective even more effectively.

[8] The various shifts in the way we view the emergence of Christianity as a distinct religion are amply illustrated by the essays published in Becker and Reed, *The Ways That Never Parted*; and in Simon C. Mimouni and Bernard Pouderon, eds., *La croisée des chemins revisitée. Quand l'Église et la Synagogue se sont-elles distinguées? Actes du colloque de Tours, 18–19 juin 2010*, Patrimoines, Judaïsme antique (Paris: Cerf, 2012). With regard to the emergence of Nicene Christianity as normative, the comments of James O'Donnell, *Bryn Mawr Classical Review* 2014.5.53, reviewing Jason D. BeDuhn, *Augustine's Manichaean Dilemma*, vols. 1–2 (2009, 2013) are illustrative: "BeDuhn emphasizes the creation of 'Nicene' and 'Catholic' Christianity in 379–381 CE and following, when Theodosius came to the throne. The emperor's church made the surprising choice of going back to the Nicene formulation that had been all but abandoned, even by Constantine, and using it to create an approved form of Christianity that passed under what was now a brand name of 'Catholic.'" (http://bmcr.brynmawr.edu/2014/2014-05-53.html). The fragility and the chaotic fate of Nicene Christianity in the fourth century is amply illustrated by Lewis Ayres, *Nicaea and Its Legacy: An Approach to Fourth-Century Trinitarian Theology* (Oxford: Oxford University Press, 2004).

[9] See, e.g., Ottorino Pasquato, *I laici in Giovanni Crisostomo. Tra Chiesa, famiglia e città*, Biblioteca di scienze religiose 144 (1998; 3rd ed., Rome: Libreria

viewing liturgical practices in their social, cultural, and geo- and church-political contexts. A third change has been a shift in how we approach our textual sources. Works that were once viewed as popular as opposed to serious literature, such as homilies, hymns, and saints' lives, are now studied in their own right, with their status substantially revalued. For liturgy, this has meant a growing acknowledgment of the central and dynamic role of the sermon in the Liturgy of the Word,[10] its association with pre- and post-baptismal instruction and ritual,[11] and its role in the context of the hagiographies that were read out during the liturgies enacted on the festivals of saints and martyrs. Surprising as it may seem, study of the origins and evolution of the homily and of preaching *per se* in the first eight hundred years has only been taken seriously since the 1990s.[12] A fourth change is a new appreciation of buildings built for the purposes of public worship (churches, synagogues, temples) as community hubs, that is, as complexes that have rooms for activities and liturgies (in the ancient sense) other than worship—for instance, for the storage of the church treasury, for the collection of linens and clothing for distribution to the poor, for communal meals.[13] That is, that the worship space of a church

---

Ateneo Salesiano, 2006); and Ramsay MacMullen, *The Second Church: Popular Christianity A.D. 200–400*, Writings from the Greco-Roman World Supplement Series (Atlanta, GA: Society of Biblical Literature, 2009).

[10] Although it should be noted that the division between the Liturgy of the Mass or Eucharistic Liturgy and the Liturgy of the Word reflects a distinctively modern Roman Catholic and Protestant point of view. Orthodox churches view the rites observed at a regular liturgical synaxis more holistically.

[11] See Wendy Mayer, "Catechetical Lectures and Homilies," in *The Oxford Handbook on Early Christian Biblical Interpretation*, ed. Paul M. Blowers and Peter W. Martens (Oxford: Oxford University Press, forthcoming).

[12] See Wendy Mayer, "Homiletics," in *The Oxford Handbook of Early Christian Studies*, ed. Susan Ashbrook Harvey and David Hunter (Oxford: Oxford University Press, 2008), 565–83.

[13] On synagogues as the locus for lodging, communal meals, and the storage of collections for poor relief, see David Instone-Brewer and Philip A. Harland, "Jewish Associations in Roman Palestine: First Century Evidence from the Mishnah," *Journal of Greco-Roman Christianity and Judaism* 5 (2008): 200–21; and Yael Wilfand Ben Shalom, "Poverty, Charity and the Image of the Poor in Rabbinic Texts from the Land of Israel" (PhD dissertation, Duke University, 2011),

or synagogue is only one part of a larger complex and that liturgy is embedded within and in relationship with those other activities. Perhaps even more self-evidently, like the relationship between preacher and audience, between the sermon and other parts of the liturgy, or between laity and clergy, this relationship, too, is not static but dynamic.[14] A fifth change is a move away from a Western bias that had been underwritten by historiographies concerned with the rise of Europe, with a resultant increasing interest in cultures and communities that worshipped in languages other than Greek or Latin.[15] Also relevant is an increased self-consciousness

---

352–61, who notes a discrepancy between the textual and archeological evidence. See further Gregg E. Gardner, *The Origins of Organized Charity in Rabbinic Judaism* (Cambridge: Cambridge University Press, 2015). For an example of the collection of linens and clothing for poor relief during Christian worship, see Wendy Mayer and Pauline Allen, *The Churches of Syrian Antioch (300–638 CE)*, Late Antique History and Religion 5 (Leuven: Peeters, 2012), 228–29; and see Justinian, *Novella* 128.15 (ed. Rudolfus Schoell and Guilelmus Kroll, *Corpus Iuris Civilis*, vol. 3 [Berlin, 1954]), where it is decreed that standard weights and measures for the purposes of measuring produce and other items paid in taxation be stored in a church in each city of the Eastern empire. Douglas Boin, "The City as a Stage, the City as Performer: Ostia's Forum Basilica and the Production of a Visible Christian Identity in the Fourth Century," in *Late Antique Cities and Religious Change*, ed. Philip Rousseau and Wendy Mayer (Washington, DC: Catholic University of America Press, forthcoming), argues persuasively for the social interconnectedness of religious buildings and their urban or peri-/sub-urban environment. The range of activities conducted in "religious" meeting spaces is also noted by Edward Adams, *The Earliest Christian Meeting Places: Almost Exclusively Houses?* (London and New York: Bloomsbury T & T Clark, 2013), esp. 121–24.

[14] That is, buildings are altered in response to changes in use or ritual over time. Concerning changes at the synagogue at Ostia, for instance, see Douglas R. Boin, *Ostia in Late Antiquity* (Cambridge: Cambridge University Press, 2013), 119–22 and 167–68. In the churches of Antioch, in a number of cases baptisteries were not original but added later. At the church in the lower city, Seleucia Pieria, the chancel was extended and doors added or sealed up as additional rooms were added to the complex, while in the case of the Church of St. Babylas, the use of external rooms changed, while interior and exterior tombs were added over time. See Mayer and Allen, *Churches of Syrian Antioch*, 32–40 and 59–61.

[15] We see this most clearly in the maturing of interest in the Syriac- and Coptic-speaking communities of Late Antiquity, and now also the growing

about historical methods and the biases of sources, resulting in a greater honesty about what is missing and what we can and cannot know on the basis of the evidence that we do have. Together, these changing perspectives go hand in hand with the impact of the development of new technologies for the study of material evidence (such as church buildings and the visual arts) on how we approach and view liturgy, a factor to which we shall turn toward the end of this chapter. As a curious aside and before we move on to explore these issues further with a range of illustrations from recent and current research, one final point is worthy of note. While Late Antique studies has had a profound influence on how we currently view liturgical practices and their evolution during these early centuries, not one of the recent handbooks on or companions to Late Antiquity devotes a chapter to the topic. The closest we come is a chapter on sacred space and visual art in *The Oxford Handbook of Late Antiquity*.[16] On the other hand, in *The Oxford Handbook of Early Christian Studies*, the now much-changed field of patristics (study of the church fathers) demonstrates this more socially and culturally contextualized view of liturgy, with seven chapters under the rubric "Ritual, Piety, and Practice,"[17] and with the inclusion of chapters on homiletics, martyr passions and hagiography, and poetry and hymnography under the rubric "Expressions of Christian Culture."[18]

Having set the background, what I shall do in the discussion that follows is to offer examples of recent work, both published

---

interest in Christianity within the Sassanid Empire and in Arabic- and Armenian-speaking communities.

[16] Ann Marie Yasin, "Sacred Space and Visual Art," in Johnson, *Oxford Handbook of Late Antiquity*, 935–69. Of seven chapters on "The Sacred" in Rousseau, *Companion to Late Antiquity*, none deals with Christian worship.

[17] See Susan Ashbrook Harvey and David Hunter, eds., *The Oxford Handbook of Early Christian Studies* (Oxford: Oxford University Press, 2008), where chapters 34 to 40 treat the topics of Christian initiation, eucharistic liturgy, prayer, asceticism, penance, martyrdom and the cult of the saints, and pilgrimage.

[18] Ibid., chapters 27 to 33. Hymnography is divided into three chapters (Christian Latin poetry, the Greek world, and Syriac).

and in progress, in order to raise questions about their implications for how we view liturgy in both past and present.[19] I have already mentioned a turn in research to the laity and their experience. A radical and challenging work that emerges from this perspective, within the setting of the blurry, chaotic religious worldview that is the new norm is Ramsay MacMullen's book *The Second Church*.[20] The fundamental question that he asks is this: in the period before 400 CE, how central to the common person's devotional life was clergy-led worship inside a church? The conclusion he arrives at is: scarcely at all. It was only a small part of their understanding of worship and religious life. He points to church attendance inside cities of only 1 to 8 percent of the Christian population.[21] By far, the majority of Christians were conducting their worship outside the city walls at the tombs of the martyrs and saints.[22] In pointing to the coexistence of two churches—the established church (dominant in our textual sources) and the Christianity of the many (visible in the archeological and epigraphic record), the two churches in tension with each other in matters of worship[23]—he raises important questions concerning whether in viewing the liturgy of the past

[19] In many cases the literature relevant to the topics under discussion is considerable. For the sake of conserving space, I offer only representative examples here. It is also important to acknowledge the anglophone bias in the examples cited. This reflects in large part the conferences I attended while preparing this paper, which proved a useful source for testing ideas. Although the trends described here are to some extent led by anglophone scholarship, there is much literature that could be cited that appears in many other languages.

[20] Cited at n9.

[21] MacMullen, *Second Church*, 101.

[22] Summed up at MacMullen, *Second Church*, 104–14.

[23] See, esp., MacMullen, *Second Church*, 95: "Various details . . . show bishops and the masses pulling in opposite directions. They had different ideas about the language of gesture and voice that one should use toward the divine, its style or propriety; different ideas about the reality of relations with the dear departed; and their own sense of what were the best answers for ordinary people faced with the needs of this secular life, not those of the life to come. . . . They didn't disagree with their bishop's teachings, but those teachings were not the whole of their religion."

our definition of liturgy, of religion, and of the actors involved has been and remains too restrictive and elite.[24]

Two current research projects highlight the importance of this challenge. In a paper delivered in 2013, Andrew McGowan, illustrating the gendered aspect of liturgy, drew out the evidence for the origins and evolution of the ritual of footwashing.[25] Quite apart from the details themselves, what was intriguing in this paper is where he located and how he described the transformation of this common, hospitable act performed by women into one that is liturgical. Throughout his paper, he talked about a "ritual act with practical benefit," something that became a "distinct sacramental performance," shifting in the fourth century "into a different kind of mode, sacramental, if not liturgical," and, in the end, as "piety performed in other places" (homes, prisons, cemeteries) as well as "worship." He also talked of how what was seen as worship in the second century is different from what was seen as worship in the fourth. In this language we see, I would suggest, the tension between a desire to engage with the full religious world of the

[24] MacMullen, *Second Church*, 95: "Our understanding of worship itself is . . . a problem for us still, an encumbrance to our reading of the past"; and (98) "to the extent that the modern model of religion derives from and reveals to us the Christianity of these great teachers and their classrooms everywhere, it must appear to be the possession of a very few. . . . History is a democrat. It is or it should be respectful of all human beings alike, not only those that dominate in the report through their position and their art." This raises interesting questions concerning the North American evangelical search to recover early liturgical tradition, as discussed in the chapter by Melanie Ross. Whether one's worship places emphasis on a sermon associated with the reading of Scripture and prayer or on ritual language and action perceived to originate in the first centuries of Christianity, it is now possible to conceive that both are worshipping equally in the tradition of the early church.

[25] Andrew McGowan, "Worship in Steps: Gender and the Construction of Liturgical Practice in Early Christianity," opening plenary address, *Early Christian Centuries I: Men and Women in Early Christianity*, Australian Catholic University, Melbourne, October 3–5, 2013. Some of this same material is dealt with in his book *Ancient Christian Worship: Early Church Practices in Social, Historical, and Theological Perspective* (Grand Rapids, MI: Baker Academic, 2014), where an attempt to define "worship" more broadly is undertaken in the introduction.

Christianity of the first four centuries, while still working from within a language and view of liturgy tied to the established church. We must ask whether that language would change and some of those distinctions disappear, if this ritual were viewed from the less easily defined perspective of MacMullen's "second church," taking into evenhanded account the Christianity of the many.

In a paper delivered only a short time later, Blake Leyerle, who has been working for some years on a book tentatively titled *Travelling Space: Theorizing Early Christian Pilgrimage*, offers among her examples one that raises some interesting questions about the boundary, if any, between common human behavior that takes place in a space associated with liturgy and gestures that are themselves liturgical.[26] The point that she makes regarding pilgrim graffiti scratched in stone or written in charcoal is that in general the leaving of graffiti by pilgrims was a performative gesture.[27] In some special cases, she remarks, this practice was even formalized by the custodians of the shrines who themselves inscribed scriptural verses and phrases at points throughout the buildings or caves to prescribe movement throughout the space and designate stations at which pilgrims could enact their devotion. These are performative acts that occur along a spectrum, so that what might not be labeled liturgical at one end shades into something distinctly liturgical at the other. The same could be said of impermanent gestures performed by pilgrims as part of the Christianity of the many—the leaving of perishable offerings,[28] the pouring and

[26] Blake Leyerle, "Pilgrim Graffiti," delivered at the Annual Meeting of the North American Patristics Society, Chicago, May 22–24, 2014.

[27] For examples, see the early fifth-century graffito "hail Mary" among other scratchings on a column base, Church of the Annunciation, Nazareth Custodia Terrae Sanctae, http://www.nazareth-en.custodia.org/default.asp?id=6249; and the Georgian descriptions discussed in Yana Tchekhanovets, "Early Georgian Pilgrimage to the Holy Land," *Liber Annuus* 61 (2011): 453–71 (esp. 457–65).

[28] So Severus of Antioch, *hom.* 27 (ed. Maurice Brière and René Graffin, Patrologia Orientalis 36, fasc. 4 [1974], 570–73), delivered June 18, 513, tells us that when Leontius's relics were processed the wagon was covered by the pious with items of clothing, bread, necklaces, and rings.

removal of oil from a casket,[29] the removal of dirt from the base of a stylite's pillar,[30] or performing a gesture associated with the history of the site, such as reclining on a bench at the site of the wedding of Cana.[31] Do we require words uttered at the same time as the gesture—whether spontaneous or formulaic—such as a prayer, to transform the action into something liturgical? Or, since the Piacenza pilgrim goes on to say that he filled one of two water jars at the site with wine, lifted it on his shoulder, offered it at the altar, and washed in the spring (or, possibly, font) for a blessing,[32] is it the intent of the performer that confers liturgical status? And, if an act is spontaneous, does it make it any less an act of worship?

Another point that this last example raises is the benefit of the dialogue between textual and material evidence for the historical period in question and between these two and contemporary evidence. At the 2013 Annual Meeting of the Society of Biblical Literature in Baltimore, at which Leyerle delivered an earlier version

[29] For examples of reliquaries and the various mechanisms for pouring oil into and collecting it from them, see the illustrations and discussion in Marie Christine Comte, *Les reliquaires du proche-orient et de Chypre à la période protobyzantine (IVe–VIIIe siècles): formes, emplacements, fonctions et cultes*, Bibliothèque de l'antiquité tardive 20 (Turnout: Brepols, 2012), 46–51 and 111–12.

[30] Pilgrim flasks, their numbers indicative of a flourishing industry and market, provided the means for pilgrims to have permanent contact with a saint. See, e.g., Gary Vikan, *Early Byzantine Pilgrimage Art*, rev. ed. (Washington, DC: Dumbarton Oaks, 2010); and Rangar H. Cline, "A Two-Sided Mold and the Entrepreneurial Spirit of Pilgrimage Souvenir Production in Late Antique Syria-Palestine," *Journal of Late Antiquity* 7, no. 1 (2014): 28–48. The full range of *eulogiai* (blessings) that pilgrims retrieved from sites included fruit, twigs, oil, soil, rocks, dew, and "manna." For the kinds of devotional practices associated with *eulogiai* after they were brought home, see Blake Leyerle, "Pilgrim *Eulogiae* and Domestic Rituals," *Archiv für Religionsgeschichte* 19 (2008): 223–38.

[31] *Antonini Placentini Itinerarium* 4 (ed. P. Geyer, Corpus Christianorum Series Latina 175 [Turnhout: Brepols, 1965], 130): *Deinde milia tria uenimus in Cana, ubi ad nuptias fuit Dominus, et accumsimus in ipso accubitu, ubi ego indignus nomina parentum meorum scripsi* ("Next we travelled three miles to Cana, where the Lord attended the wedding, and we reclined on the actual couch, where I, unworthy that I am, wrote the names of my parents." Translation mine.

[32] Ibid.: *ex quibus hydriis duae ibi sunt et impleui unam ex eas uino et in collo plenam leuani et obtuli ad altare et in ipsa fonte pro benedictione lauauimus.*

of her paper, Lee Jefferson reported on the state of excavations at Khirbet Qana in lower Galilee, where he and his colleagues have discovered a complex of four caves dating from the fifth century CE that had become filled with soil soon after the Crusader period. Situated in the vicinity of a Jewish village and part of a hillside complex that appears to contain a church and monastery, the subterranean pilgrimage site has rough graffiti scratched on its walls and in one chamber with plastered walls a sarcophagus lid on its side, displaying three crosses.[33] In his paper, Jefferson reported on the presence in the same chamber in close proximity to this putative altar of a number of stone water vessels. The association of the site with the miracle at the wedding at Cana is relatively compelling. This find broadens out our questions. If the presence of a church and monastery is subsequently confirmed, we see in the same context and side-by-side three settings for worship (monastic, established church, that of the Christianity of the many). At this period, this phenomenon was not uncommon across the Mediterranean world. What was the relationship between all three? How distinct were they? And what were the relative ratios of participation? How did the Jewish community and its rituals impact those of the Christians? Who had jurisdiction over the various parts of the complex? That is, who regulated and prescribed the various modes of worship that took place in each of the three settings? And, when the Christianity of the many is involved, is the established church, regardless of its view of acceptable behavior and its efforts to regulate it, even relevant? I pose this last question

[33] See the publicity articles with site description and photographs, "Lee Jefferson and Tom McCollough receive ACS funding to improve undergraduate research," May 2, 2014, http://www.centre.edu/lee-jefferson-and-tom -mccollough-receive-acs-funding-to-improve-undergraduate-research/; and "Religion professors receive $30,000 from International Catacomb Society," June 27, 2013, http://archive.centre.edu/news/2013/khirbet_qana.html. Tom McCollough and Lee Jefferson each delivered a fresh analysis of findings at the site at the Southeastern Commission for the Study of Religion (SECSOR) regional meeting, Nashville, TN, March 6–8, 2015, focused on the excavated synagogue and on the iconography of the pilgrimage crosses found on the Khirbet Qana site.

in light of the thought-provoking response by the art historian Gary Vikan to the panel in which Jefferson and Leyerle gave their papers. Describing his research into the devotion attached to Elvis Presley for his book, *From the Holy Land to Graceland*, Vikan noted how reverence at the holy site (Graceland) is policed not by security guards but the laity, who have their own rigid ideas of what is appropriate and inappropriate behavior.[34] He also pointed out how in the course of his researches across time and space, it became clear that one of the defining features of such ritual behavior is the sense of *communitas* experienced, even though individual pilgrims approach the same site or event or saint differently. Again, we see here how in taking the religion of the many into account, worship becomes something that is considerably more expansive than traditional definitions and approaches allow.

Another set of questions was raised early in 2014 when I was asked to respond to a panel on the theme "Sacred Objects, Mundane Origin" at the Annual Meeting of the American Society for Church History. A paper by Maria Dasios concerned an episode in a seventh-century hagiography, the Life of St. Theodore of Sykeon.[35] Theodore's condemnation of a silver chalice and paten purchased by a deacon for use in his monastery because of its secular origin (in this case silver allegedly reclaimed from a prostitute's chamber pot) highlighted for me something that I had been pondering in my own work on the churches of this same period in Syrian Antioch.[36] That is, whether acquisition was via purchase by the church in question or via donation, some liturgical vessels, particularly in earlier centuries, most likely started out as objects produced for the private household. Liturgical spoons, for instance, like patens, are of precisely the same type as those in domestic

[34] See Gary Vikan, *From the Holy Land to Graceland: Sacred People, Places and Things in Our Lives* (Chicago: University of Chicago Press, 2013).

[35] Maria Dasios, "Provenance Contaminates? Competing Forms of Capital in the Life of Theodore of Sykeon," delivered at the American Society of Church History Annual Meeting, January 2–5, 2014.

[36] See Mayer and Allen, *Churches of Syrian Antioch*, 223–24.

use.[37] Strainers could be used equally in either setting.[38] Is it context, then, that is, the simple act of transference from the private to the liturgical setting, that changes their status from secular to liturgical? Was any kind of ritual involved? On the other hand, many of the items in liturgical silver hoards have specifically Christian symbolism and votive inscriptions.[39] This suggests that they were commissioned intentionally by donors for a local church. Did these explicitly Christian symbols or inscriptions automatically confer on the vessels liturgical status? And what about the private devotional act engaged in commissioning and donating them? On the other hand, the anxiety that Dasios identifies in the *Life of Theodore* concerning the slippage of such objects from secular to sacred and back is also intriguing. To what extent is the lavish use of metals in liturgical objects (including the cladding on altars and on the columns of ciboria)[40] irrelevant to the liturgical status of objects, given that we find critiques of this same practice in private households in the discourse against wealth? I think here of couches, chairs, beds and not just chamber pots.[41] Given that even small churches held in their treasury a far greater quantity of liturgical vessels than they could possibly use or require for liturgical celebrations,[42] should we look instead to the monetary value of the metal from which

[37] For comparative examples of liturgical and domestic silver plates see Marlia Mundell Mango, *Silver From Early Byzantium: The Kaper Karaon and Related Treasures* (Baltimore: The Walters Art Gallery, 1986), figs 34.8, 95.1, 106.1 at 164, 269, 278. For spoons see ibid., entries 19–22 at 121–27.

[38] Ibid., figs 24.1–3, 26.2–4 at 131, 134.

[39] See ibid., entries 1–56 at 68–226.

[40] Mayer and Allen, *Churches of Syrian Antioch*, 221–23. An example of silver revetment from an altar (sixth century) is on display in the Byzantine Gallery of the Museum, Dumbarton Oaks, Washington, DC (BZ.1963.36.11).

[41] For a late fourth-century example of such invective, in which the use of silver chamber pots, chairs, and footstools is excoriated, see John Chrysostom, *In Col. hom.* 7 (Patrologia Graeca 62, 349–50).

[42] The silver hoard associated with the Church of St. Sergius, Kaper Karaon, a village in the limestone massif in the hinterland of Antioch, Syria, contains fifty-five items (crosses, patens, chalices, ewers, spoons, lampstands, fans, strainer) and a piece of silver revetment weighing a total of 82 lbs (37.2 kgs). See Marlia Mundell Mango, "The Monetary Value of Silver Revetments and Objects Belonging to Churches, A.D. 300–700," in *Ecclesiastical Silver Plate*

liturgical objects were made, viewing them simply as an expression of the wealth of donors and a transference into the liturgical sphere of the patronage ethos?[43] And what about the case of liturgical fans, which were used in the liturgy but had, at least initially, a purely pragmatic rather than symbolic ritual purpose?[44] (Here we are encouraged to think about the influence on worship of climate.) Again, is it the context in which they are used that makes them liturgical? In the end, is Dasios right, and does everything hinge on multiple, sometimes competing, discourses of perception?

To move to a not unrelated issue, just as MacMullen points out that the majority of our written sources for this period reflect the established church, so one of the consequences of the multidisciplinary approach brought to bear in the study of Late Antiquity is to view those texts and what they have to say about liturgical practice through a hermeneutic of suspicion. This engenders a

---

in Sixth-Century Byzantium, ed. Susan A. Boyd and Marlia Mundell Mango (Washington, DC: Dumbarton Oaks, 1992), 134.

[43] Discussion of the transformation of classical civic benefaction into euergetism directed in theory toward the poor but in reality often toward ecclesiastical institutions, particularly churches, is substantial. See, e.g., Peter Brown, *Through the Eye of a Needle: Wealth, the Fall of Rome and the Making of Christianity in the West, 350–550 AD* (Princeton, NJ: Princeton University Press, 2012); Sylvain Destephen, "L'évergétisme artistocratique au féminin dans l'Empire romain d'Orient," in *Les réseaux familiaux antiquité tardive et moyen âge in memoriam A. Laiou et É. Patlagean*, ed. Beatrice Caseau, Collège de France—CNRS, Centre de Recherche d'Histoire et Civilisation de Byzance, monographies 37 (Paris: ACHCByz, 2012), 183–203; and Ville Vuolanto, "Male and Female Euergetism in Late Antiquity: A Study on Italian and Adriatic Church Floor Mosaics," in Päivi Setälä and others, *Women, Wealth and Power in the Roman Empire*, Acta Instiui Romani Finlandiae 25 (Rome: Institutum Romanum Finlandiae, 2002), 245–302.

[44] As suggested by *Constitutiones apostolicae* 8.12.3 (Syria, c. 380; ed. Marcel Metzger, *Les constitutions apostoliques*, 3, Sources Chrétiennes 336 [Paris: Éditions du Cerf, 2008], 178): δύο δὲ διάκονοι ἐξ ἑκατέρων τῶν μερῶν τῶν θυσιαστηρίου κατεχέτωσαν ἐξ ὑμένων λεπτῶν ῥιπίδιον ἢ πτερὸν ταῶνος ἢ ὀθόνης, καὶ ἠρέμα ἀποσοβείτωσαν τὰ μικρὰ τῶν ἱπταμένων ζῴων, ὅπως ἂν μὴ ἐγχρίμπτωνται εἰς τὰ κύπελλα. ("Let two of the deacons, on each side of the altar, hold a fan, made up of thin membranes, or of peacock feathers, or of fine cloth, and let them discreetly drive away the small flying insects, so that they don't dart into the cups.")

deep distrust of what Christian literary texts across a wide range of genres have to say at face value—and here we include all of those traditionally used in the study of liturgy—on the basis that their underlying concern is distinguishing one particular version of Christianity from other religions or other forms of Christianity.[45] There is a reason why the shaping of Christian identity (in which performative ritual plays a part) is a topic that is currently exciting much attention.[46] In hindsight, this insight might seem self-evident, but there is rapidly increasing exposure of the profound extent to which the picture of distinctiveness promoted by these texts, particularly of discontinuity between Christian ritual and that of the social and cultural world within which it developed, has covertly shaped how we view liturgy. These issues are illustrated by a number of recent studies that revolve around amulets, the ritual use of scriptural incipits, exorcism, and baptism. Where terms like magic and superstition were once used pejoratively and seen as distinct from religion, they are now viewed as interconnected, the boundaries between them becoming to our view increasingly blurry. Once again, this area of research allows us greater access to the worship life of the second church, that is, insight into the cognitive and experiential world of the Christianity of the many.

In his article on Christian exorcism and spells, Theo de Bruyn seeks to assess the veracity of the claims of second- to third-century Christian apologists that by virtue of the simplicity of

---

[45] Two examples of the complete reappraisal of the function and meaning of texts brought about by this hermeneutic are: Aude Busine, "From Stones to Myth: Temple Destruction and Civic Identity in the Late Antique Roman East," *Journal of Late Antiquity* 6, no. 2 (2013): 325–46; and Douglas Boin, "Hellenistic 'Judaism' and the Social Origins of the 'Pagan-Christian' Debate," *Journal of Early Christian Studies* 22, no. 2 (2014): 167–96. In the first the author deconstructs narratives of temple destruction, which are shown to be later reconstructions of memory for contemporary purposes; in the second, the author deconstructs the dominant pagan-Christian dichotomy, showing that it is a construct of internal Christian identity formation.

[46] See the comments on this trend in Wendy Mayer and Geoffrey D. Dunn, "Introduction," in *Christians Shaping Identity from the Roman Empire to Byzantium: Studies Inspired by Pauline Allen*, ed. Geoffrey D. Dunn and Wendy Mayer, Supplements to Vigiliae Christianae (Leiden: Brill, 2015), 1–4.

their language (that is, appeals to the name of Jesus or short phrases from Scripture) their exorcisms are more effective.[47] By contrast, these authors argue, the incantations performed by other practitioners are elaborate and incomprehensible. In the process of reaching his conclusion—that the apologists are only partially correct and both the preservation of traditional elements and Christian innovation are widely variable—he makes the point that the rite of initiation has dominated the study of Christian exorcistic practice to the detriment of our understanding of ad hoc exorcism. He also points to amulets from the fifth to seventh centuries that contain in some cases extended liturgical invocations or petitionary prayer.[48] In one case, this involves an excerpt from the Lord's Prayer. This particular category of amulets and spells is one that de Bruyn has been working on for some time,[49] and it raises the issues of how ordinary Christians perceived the ritual power of formulaic phrases (for instance litanies, prayers, the chanting of psalm verses) within the established worship setting, and whether they perceived that power as intrinsic and transferrable to another context. That is, did words performed within the worship of the established church have the same or a different set of associations when performed within the context of the Christianity of the

[47] Theo de Bryn, "What Did Ancient Christians Say When They Cast Out Demons? Inferences from Spells and Amulets," in Dunn and Mayer, *Christians Shaping Identity*, 64–81.

[48] So the first six lines of *Supp. Mag.* I 23 (fifth century), discussed by Jitse Dijkstra, "The Interplay Between Image and Text: On Greek Amulets Containing Christian Elements from Late Antique Egypt," in *The Materiality of Magic*, ed. Dietrich Boschung and Jan Bremmer, Morphomata 20 (Paderborn: Wilhelm Fink, 2015), 271–92 at 278, include elements from the Creed.

[49] See Theo S. de Bruyn, "Ancient Applied Christology: Appeals to Christ in Greek Amulets in Late Antiquity," in *From Logos to Christos: Essays in Christology in Honour of Joanne McWilliam*, ed. Ellen M. Leonard and Kate Merriman, Editions SR / Éditions SR 34 (Waterloo: Wilfrid Laurier University Press, 2010), 3–18; and Theo S. de Bruyn and Jitse H. F. Dijkstra, "Greek Amulets and Formularies from Egypt Containing Christian Elements: A Checklist of Papyri, Parchments, Ostraka, and Tablets," *Bulletin of the American Society of Papyrologists* 48 (2011): 159–214.

many?[50] Nils Korsvoll answers these questions to some extent by applying cognitive ritual theory. This allows him to argue for a cognitive blending on the part of the user and ritual practitioner, which would not have been accepted by the "official" church.[51] Between them de Bruyn, Korsvoll, and Joseph Sanzo—whose doctoral research on the use of scriptural incipits in Egyptian amulets is now published[52]—elicit a number of additional factors of significance. All three point to the way in which these texts overturn an assumed relationship between ritual power and strict adherence to established ritual patterns. The ritual practitioners who create the spell show flexibility in what formulaic elements they use and how much or little of a text they inscribe in relation to the space available. This includes variability in the citation of scripture itself, with an appeal to the scholarship of others on the flexible scribal habit— that is, the flexibility exhibited by scribes of this period between word-for-word and free forms of transmission. What does this to have to say to the relative inflexibility that we assume from the fourth century onward in regard to the established church's liturgical practice? Jitse Dijkstra equally importantly, in his most recent publication on this material,[53] points out how scholars have habitually ignored the drawings, including crosses and orant (praying) figures, that occasionally accompany spells. In arguing that these "illustrations" are in fact integral to the spells as well as linked schematically and performatively to temple graffiti, he not only challenges us to draw together the performative aspect of spells

[50] Here recent work on inter-, meta-, and hyper-textuality also raises some of the same questions. See Daniel Stökl Ben Ezra, "Reading Ritual with Genette: Paratextual and Metatextual Aspects of the Bible in Ritual Performances," in *On the Fringe of Commentary: Metatextuality in Ancient Near Eastern and Ancient Mediterranean Cultures*, ed. Sydney H. Aufrère, Philip S. Alexander, and Zlatko Plese, Orientalia Lovaniensia Analecta 232 (Leuven: Peeters, 2015), 105–26.

[51] Nils H. Korsvoll, "Engaging with the Divine: A Cognitive Analysis of an Early Christian Apotropaic Papyrus" (MA dissertation, University of Oslo, August 2011).

[52] Joseph E. Sanzo, *Scriptural Incipits on Amulets from Late Antique Egypt: Text, Typology, and Theory*, Studien und Texte zu Antike und Christentum 84 (Tübingen: Mohr Siebeck, 2014).

[53] See n48.

and pilgrim behavior but also raises intriguing questions about the link in the Christianity of the many (and perhaps also the liturgy of the established church) between images, their performance, ritual action, and ritual words. Sanzo and Korsvoll also raise the importance of viewing such practices and practitioners within their local context, in this case, Egypt. Adducing the work of David Frankfurter and David Brakke, influential scholars of monasticism and Egypt in Late Antiquity, they point to the rise of the monk in this region as a local ritual specialist.[54] This parallels similar theorizing of the rise of the holy man or virtuoso ascetic as local Christian ritual specialist at this same period in Syria.[55] This, in turn, raises the question of liturgical authority and again introduces the monastic setting as another element that needs to be considered when we think of liturgy. Finally, the importance of Dayna Kalleres' work is that it ties all of this back into the ritual of the established church (in this case the prebaptismal rite of exorcism),[56] reminding us not only of the importance of the tension in this respect between the practices and perceptions of the established church and the Christianity of the many, and the fact that the two need to be viewed in concert, but also that in the view of human beings prior to the Reformation ritual words had power and were performative.

While all of this research has been going on and continues apace, research into the liturgical life of the established church during these centuries has also been reshaping the liturgical landscape. Here, we again see the influence of the sociocultural emphasis and

[54] Korsvoll, "Engaging with the Divine," 84–87; Sanzo, *Scriptural Incipits*, 171–75.

[55] Since Peter Brown's seminal article, "The Rise and Function of the Holy Man in Late Antiquity," *The Journal of Roman Studies* 61 (1971): 80–101, a substantial body of literature on the topic has been published. See in particular the special issue of *Journal of Early Christian Studies* 6, no. 3 (1998), with updated reflection by Brown. See, however, the recent challenge to Brown's reading of the rural monk as holy man by Jakob Ashkenazi, "Holy Man Versus Monk—Village and Monastery in the Late Antique Levant: Between Hagiography and Archaeology," *Journal of the Economic and Social History of the Orient* 57, no. 5 (2014): 745–65.

[56] Dayna S. Kalleres, *City of Demons: Violence, Ritual, and Christian Power in Late Antiquity* (Berkeley, CA: University of California Press, 2015).

multidisciplinary approaches brought to bear in the study of Late Antiquity. Earlier in this chapter, I mentioned the growing appreciation of preaching and the homily as an important liturgical act and element. The work on the preacher's audience pioneered by Mary Cunningham and Pauline Allen[57] that led to a volume on the medieval preacher's audience[58] is now reaching fruition in a third volume dedicated to Latin patristic preaching.[59] Study of the impact of liturgy on society and vice versa is exemplified in two recent works, one concerning seventh- to eighth-century Rome,[60] the other seventh-century Byzantium.[61] In the first, John Romano argues that in these critical centuries, public worship at Rome acted as a social glue, as a mechanism for inclusion and exclusion. In this respect, this important study reminds us that the worship of the established church was not only something that took place at a certain time and within a certain space but also was, in a much larger sense, socially performative. Here it ties in with other recent work that focuses explicitly on the demarcation and construction of space as part of religious boundary formation, appealing to theories from social and cultural geography.[62] That work in turn should be viewed side by side with studies that focus on architecture itself and its setting as active agents in the ritual process.[63] To

[57] Mary B. Cunningham and Pauline Allen, eds., *Preacher and Audience: Studies in Early Christian and Byzantine Homiletics*, A New History of the Sermon 1 (Leiden: Brill, 1998).

[58] Carolyn Muessig, ed., *Preacher, Sermon and Audience in the Middle Ages*, A New History of the Sermon 3 (Leiden: Brill, 2002).

[59] Johan Leemans, Gert Partoens, Anthony Dupont, and Shari Boodts, eds., *Preaching in the Latin Patristic Era: Sermons, Preachers, Audiences*, A New History of the Sermon (Leiden: Brill, forthcoming).

[60] John F. Romano, *Liturgy and Society in Early Medieval Rome* (Farnham: Ashgate, 2014).

[61] Phil Booth, *Crisis of Empire: Doctrine and Dissent at the End of Late Antiquity* (Berkeley, CA: University of California Press, 2013).

[62] Christine Shepardson, *Controlling Contested Spaces: Late Antique Antioch and the Spatial Politics of Religious Controversy* (Berkeley, CA: University of California Press, 2014).

[63] Bonna D. Westcoat and Robert G. Ousterhout, eds., *Architecture of the Sacred: Space, Ritual and Experience from Classical Greece to Byzantium* (Cambridge: Cambridge University Press, 2012), especially chaps. 7–12: Joan Branham,

return to the second book just mentioned, however, Phil Booth, like Romano, looks at a period in which a specific geographic region, this time the Eastern Roman Empire, underwent a profound transformation. Here he looks to the rise of the Eucharist as "the central aggregating icon of the Christian faith" amid what he describes as the "renegotiation of competing ascetical and liturgical narratives."[64] Again we see here liturgy and liturgical concerns permeating at least certain levels of society well beyond the interior space of the church building. In yet another recent book, which admittedly extends into a much later period, we see the nexus between liturgy and power brought out in relation to liturgical objects not yet mentioned in this chapter, clerical robes.[65]

The term "embodied" points to the study of two aspects of liturgy that are only just starting to emerge, the cognitive and experiential. Missing from dry texts and archeological remains is not only the full experience of what it was like to touch, feel, taste, smell, see, and hear the worship experience but also how ritual gestures and even the clothing one wears during worship affect the mind of the performer. In a provocative paper delivered at the 2014 meeting of the North American Patristics Society, Adam Serfass appealed to both Daniel Schwartz's recent study of the communal, cognitive, and ritual components of initiation and to enclothed cognition theory to tease out the reality of the baptismal robe and its subconscious impact.[66] Enclothed cognition theory, building on

---

"Mapping Sacrifice on Bodies and Spaces in Ancient Judaism and Early Christianity"; Jodi Magness, "The 'Foundation Deposit' from the Dura Europos Synagogue Reconsidered"; Ann Marie Yasin, "Sight Lines of Sanctity at Late Antique Martyria"; Robert G. Ousterhout, "The Sanctity of Place and the Sanctity of Buildings: Jerusalem vs. Constantinople"; Slobodan Ćurčić, "Divine Light: Constructing the Immaterial in Byzantine Art and Architecture"; and Vasileios Marinis, "Architecture as a Definer of Sanctity in the Monastery tou Libos in Constantinople."

[64] Booth, *Crisis of Empire*, 1.

[65] Warren Woodfin, *The Embodied Icon: Liturgical Vestments and Sacramental Power in Byzantium* (Oxford: Oxford University Press, 2012).

[66] Adam Serfass, "Enclothed Cognition and the Sanctifying Power of the Baptismal Robe in John Chrysostom's Catechetical Homilies," Annual Meeting of the North American Patristics Society, Chicago, May 22–24, 2014. See

theories of embodied cognition, describes the systematic influence that clothes have on the wearer's psychological processes.[67] In the course of a ritual program of prayer, good works, and daily exorcism, going barefoot, for instance, eliminates all footwear-related distinction of rank, but does it also make the brain of the catechizand more receptive? Similarly, how do the robes that priests wear affect the audience subconsciously, and do they make their wearer more ethical?[68] The same questions, applying embodied cognition, can be asked of the literal effect of bowing one's head and kneeling down during penitence or of the various positions engaged in prayer. Cognitive theories point to the fact that in all of these cases, and most probably across the full range of ritual clothing, gestures, and utterances in liturgy, the physical experience will have been as significant as the symbolic meaning, the two going hand in hand.[69] A few other examples of recent scholarship that try to bring us closer to the experience of worship in the early Christian past are Carol Harrison's emphasis on listening as part of Christian practice—particularly in relation to sermons and prayer—on the basis that nearly everything written down in the ancient world and well into Late Antiquity was performed aloud.[70] Giselle de Nie turns to a quite different set of theoretical models from psychiatry, psychoneuroimmunology, and anthropology in her attempt to recover the affective experience of miracles in the Latin-speaking West, in particular the transforming power of images, both verbal and visual.[71]

Daniel L. Schwartz, *Paideia and Cult: Christian Initiation in Theodore of Mopsuestia*, Hellenic Studies 57 (Washington, DC: Center for Hellenic Studies, 2013).

[67] See Hajo Adam and Adam D. Galinsky, "Enclothed Cognition," *Journal of Experimental Social Psychology* 48 (2012): 918–25.

[68] These questions were posed by Serfass, "Enclothed Cognition."

[69] This understanding underlies Derek Krueger's groundbreaking *Liturgical Subjects: Christian Ritual, Biblical Narrative, and the Formation of the Self in Byzantium*, Divinations: Rereading Late Ancient Religion (Philadelphia, PA: University of Pennsylvania Press, 2014).

[70] Carol Harrison, *The Art of Listening in the Early Church* (Oxford: Oxford University Press, 2013).

[71] Giselle de Nie, *Poetics of Wonder: Testimonies of the New Christian Miracles in the Late Antique Latin World*, Studies in the Early Middle Ages 31 (Turnhout: Brepols, 2011).

Her work has potential for trying to understand at a level deeper than sight the visual aspects of worship. This is quite different from the approach of Robin Jensen, for instance, who in her recent publications on baptism pulls together a wide range of evidence in order to help us understand the conscious mind of the participant when exposed in ritual to the visual.[72] Her work is in some ways a milestone in the study of early Christian art in the way in which it contextualizes this art.

An impact on how we both study and understand past worship which I have not mentioned thus far, and that requires reflection as we draw to a close, is that of recently developed, in particular computer-assisted, technologies. 3D computer imaging, employing software developed within the discipline of architecture, offers an obvious advantage in allowing us to reconstruct the space in which worship took place, particularly when the evidence is partial and fragmentary. This has considerable potential in terms of providing us with a more embodied sense of the lived experience of worship in these distant centuries than our imagination can supply. At present, 3D reconstruction of liturgical space, on the other hand, is constrained by the view of liturgy applied by the modeler, and it should be pointed out that the available models are at present highly variable in terms of their utility. So, for instance, the project Byzantium 1200 for the most part provides only exterior-view reconstructions of church buildings in middle Byzantine Constantinople, without 360-degree view capability.[73] A rare exception is two interior views of the baptistery of Hagia Sophia.[74] Of perhaps

[72] Robin M. Jensen, *Baptismal Imagery in Early Christianity: Ritual, Visual and Theological Dimensions* (Grand Rapids, MI: Baker Academic, 2012); and Robin M. Jensen, *Living Water: Images, Symbols and Settings of Early Christian Baptism*, Supplements to Vigiliae Christianae 105 (Leiden: Brill, 2011).

[73] See "Hagia Eirene," http://www.byzantium1200.com/eirene.html; "Holy Apostles," http://www.byzantium1200.com/apostles.html; and "Saints Sergios and Bacchos," http://www.byzantium1200.com/sergio.html. The results, it must also be pointed out, are also dependent on the reading of the sources, both textual and material, used.

[74] "Hagia Sophia," http://www.byzantium1200.com/hagia.html. Both employ the same perspective.

greater use are the static reconstructions of fora and statues, public space through which liturgical processions passed.[75] On the other hand, associated YouTube videos of landmarks within the city, with their mobile perspective, now supplement and enhance the static views of the city's buildings.[76] Similarly, the reconstruction of the interior of the church in the lower city at Seleucia Pieria, the port of Syrian Antioch, produced as part of the multivenue ancient Antioch exhibit coordinated and curated by Christine Kondoleon in 2000, is indicative of an older view of liturgical space, as it ignores the plethora of rooms, including baptistery, that formed part of the complex.[77] In its infancy is application of these same technologies and visualscape theory to line-of-sight research. The articles to which I refer here do not deal with Christian architecture per se but offer an example of future possibilities.[78] Ethan Gruber and John Dobbins, for instance, produced a 3D model of a villa with dining floor mosaics and water features from late antique Antioch

[75] For example, "Forum Constantine," http://www.byzantium1200.com /forum-c.html.

[76] See, e.g., "Column of Leo," https://www.youtube.com/watch?v= othETzXU0IA; and "Porta Aurea—Golden Gate (Sunrise Version)," https:// www.youtube.com/watch?v=q0fflXZvaNk. In the latter the interests of the creator (military, rather than social-historical) are evident.

[77] Compare figs. 1 and 2 (3D reconstruction) in W. Eugene Kleinbauer, "The Church Building at Seleucia Pieria," and fig. 1 (3D reconstruction with decorations in situ) in Susan Boyd, "The Relief Decoration of the Church Building at Seleucia Pieria," with fig. 1 (2D site plan) in Christine Kondoleon, "The Mosaic Pavement of the Church Building at Seleucia Pieria," in *Antioch: The Lost Ancient City*, ed. Christine Kondoleon (Princeton, NJ: Princeton University Press and Worcester Art Museum, 2000), 217–19, 221.

[78] Eleftheria Paliou, "Reconsidering the Concept of Visualscape: Recent Advances in Three-Dimensional Visibility Analysis," in *Computational Approaches to Archaeological Spaces*, ed. Andrew Bevan and Mark Lane, UCL Institute of Archaeology Publications 60 (Walnut Creek, CA: Left Coast Press, 2013), 243–64; Graeme Earl and others, "Formal and Informal Analysis of Rendered Space: The Basilica Portuens," in ibid., 265–82; and Ethan Gruber and John Dobbins, "Illuminating Architecture: The House of the Drinking Contest at Antioch," in *CAA2010: Fusion of Cultures, Proceedings of the 38th Annual Conference on Computer Applications and Quantitative Methods in Archaeology, Granada, Spain, April 2010*, ed. F. Contreras, M. Farjas, and F. J. Melero (Oxford: Archaeopress, 2013), 71–76.

to which they applied algorithms for the movement of sunlight. This allowed them to show that at certain hours of the day sunlight hit certain mosaic panes in the floor, which correlated with the hours for dinner parties and dining. One can see the potential for studying the play of light on visual art and furnishings within churches in terms of the worshiper's experience. One study that has been conducted along these lines is that of Ioannis Liritzis and Helen Vassiliou, who examined twelve Greek Byzantine churches dating from the fifth to eighteenth century.[79] While their results were not consistent, they were able to show that the alignment of most ensured that sunrise hit the church around the equinoxes, and in some cases near the date of the summer solstice or on the feast day of a particular saint. Again, this adds another dimension to our understanding of the worship experience. So, too, does the new capacity to enjoy virtual tours of early Christian spaces. The web site offering the capacity to tour from one's desk the Catacombs of Priscilla in Rome is the fruit of recent collaboration between the Pontificia Commissione Archaeologia Sacra and Google Maps.[80] What it offers is a limited but valuable opportunity to explore, at the very least, the visual experience of moving through the catacombs and to do this repeatedly, getting a better feel for what it must have been like to worship in the chambers of that underground venue.[81]

---

[79] Ioannis Liritzis and Helen Vassiliou, "Does Sunrise Day Correlate with Eastern Orientation of Byzantine Churches on Significant Solar Dates and Saint's Days? A Preliminary Study," *Byzantinische Zeitschrift* 99 (2006): 523–34.

[80] "Catacombe di Priscilla," https://plus.google.com/+Catacombedi PriscillaRoma/about. To access the tour, move down the web page to the image labelled "See inside" and click on the arrow. Navigation into and through various galleries and corridors is achieved via clicking on sections of the image (or arrows that appear); the scene can be rotated by up to 360° using the compass to the bottom right of the image. Images on the walls of the catacomb can be enlarged (retaining resolution) using current trackpad gestures.

[81] Missing is the damp feel of the underground galleries and these are lit by powerful modern lighting that illuminates and casts shadows on the wall decorations in a manner quite different from that of the torches or lamps that would have been used by worshippers of the first Christian centuries. Absent,

What has been offered in this chapter is a whirlwind tour of a multitude of changes in historiography, art and architecture, archaeology, and related disciplines that are rapidly changing how we view liturgy in the first eight centuries that followed the emergence of Christianity. So whirlwind has it been, in fact, that we have not even entered into the topic of gender studies[82] or the nascent influence of disability studies,[83] both of which deserve consideration in their own right. What remains is to take a step back to regain our breath and to reflect in these closing paragraphs on some significant ways in which our understanding of the landscape of liturgy in those centuries has already changed or is in the process of changing in response to the developments discussed. First, the social and cultural turn in late antique studies encourages us to view worship as embedded in society. Similarly, it encourages us to view developments that occur as not linear or static but local or regional and untidy. More important, it challenges us to acknowledge that what we call "the liturgy" refers to the worship life of the established church and is only one of a number of equally valid worship options. The other settings, in our current reimagining of liturgy's past, are the Christianity of the many—this includes the cult of the martyrs, saints and angels, pilgrimage, and ritual practices relating to the demonic and the divine—and one that we have barely touched on here, the ascetic and monastic setting. That is, what we have in the past viewed as rites that are original, central, and normative—the liturgies of the Word and the Eucharist, or baptism—developed in parallel and in interaction

---

too, is any sense of smell or experience of how sound moves through the restricted and less restricted spaces.

[82] See Teresa Berger's essay in this volume and her book, *Gender Differences and the Making of Liturgical History: Lifting a Veil on Liturgy's Past* (Farnham: Ashgate, 2011).

[83] Although the application of disability studies to biblical studies is a growing trend, its relevance to how we view liturgy in this period is only just starting to be explored. It has considerable relevance for liturgical rites of the established church that require mobility, such as baptism by immersion and processions, and the worship of the Christianity of the many, such as pilgrimage and incubation at healing shrines, to name but a few.

with a range of other forms of worship. In fact, for the first four centuries and, in some regions, possibly even later, the established church was a minority, and the bulk of worship took place outside of that context. And so, too, we should expand our scope beyond the confines of the church building. Here we are reminded of Goodman's modeling of the development of Christianity.[84] If we were to swap out the labels for ones specific to worship, our current view of the development of liturgy would be markedly similar. The blurring of boundaries between the secular and sacred, between Christianities, and between these latter and Judaisms and other religious options as a result of this changed point of view now leaves us floundering somewhat as we struggle to come up with models and definitions that are holistic and inclusive. On the other hand, what we look for when we now think of liturgy in this period has, as a result of these conceptual changes, expanded considerably. We now look for not only what is prescribed in worship but also the spontaneous—on the part of all of its performers. That we now look at all of its performers, not just those in the established church or who preside, is in fact another change that has taken place. We also look at flexibility in ritual expressed in a wide variety of ways and at an expanded range of ritual gestures, acts, and utterances. We now look to recover the sensory, cognitive and experiential in addition to the more traditional approaches to the visual that drive the study of Christian architecture and art—and by cognitive, I mean that we now engage in attempting to recover the performer's subconscious and automatic as well as conscious attitude or response. It is in this area of study, one suspects, in

---

[84] See the figures cited in n7, which model the old, traditional linear view of Christianity's development against a variety of newer multidimensional chaotic and interactive models. Fig. 9 (Goodman, "Modelling," 129) includes within this picture: Platonism, magic, Second Temple Judaisms, post-70 Judaisms, Christianities, Ebionites, judaizing Christians, "proto-orthodox" Christianity, "heresies," "gnostics, etc.," Marcionites, Jewish Christians, judaizing gnostics, Talmidei Hakhamim, "Sadducees," and "Essenes," in repeated contact with "varieties of paganism," all laid over a background labelled "culture of Graeco-Roman world."

addition perhaps to the field of disability studies, that we will see some of the most interesting developments.

If I were to attempt to sum up the change in mindset that has in recent decades occurred in scholarship concerning the first eight centuries of Christianity, it would be the importance now placed on multidisciplinarity, multiple kinds of evidence, and on context.[85] If I were to sum up the influence of this change in mindset on how we now view Christian worship in the past, it would be encapsulated in the phrase "think outside the box." If the twentieth century was focused on looking inside the box at the worship of the established church, the twenty-first century is in the process of ripping open the box's sides, flattening it out, and watching the contents spill out and mingle with everything outside it. Concerning the different imagined past that results, liturgical historians at the end of this century will no doubt have their own interesting things to say.

[85] Maxwell Johnson's chapter in this volume introduces a cautionary note. If contextualization is important for the ancient evidence, it is also important for its contemporary interpreter. As we engage in our task as liturgical historians, we are challenged continually to ask ourselves why we are asking the questions that we ask or reading the evidence in a particular way.

Contributors

Teresa Berger is professor of liturgical studies at the Yale Institute of Sacred Music and Yale Divinity School, where she also holds the appointment as Thomas E. Golden Jr. Professor of Catholic Theology. Her publications include *Gender Differences and the Making of Liturgical History* (2011) and a volume of essays based on the 2011 Yale ISM Liturgy conference, *Liturgy in Migration: From the Upper Room to Cyberspace* (2012).

Harald Buchinger is professor of liturgical studies at the University of Regensburg, Germany, where he also served as dean of the faculty of Catholic theology from 2013 to 2015. His publications include the two-volume dissertation *Pascha bei Origenes* (2005). In 2012–2013, he was a Senior Research Fellow and Visiting Professor at the Yale Institute of Sacred Music.

Emmanuel Fritsch, CSSp, is an independent scholar who has been engaged in the study of the liturgical tradition of the Ethiopian Orthodox Tewahedo Church since 1985. He serves the Ethiopian Catholic Church as secretary of the Bishops' Liturgy Committee and is a fellow of the French Centre of Ethiopian Studies in Addis Ababa. His publications include "Pastophoria and Altars: Interaction in Ethiopian Liturgy and Church Architecture" (2007, with M. Gervers), "The Anaphoras of the Ge'ez Churches: A Challenging Orthodoxy" (2013), and a number of entries in the *Encyclopedia Aethiopica*.

Bruce Gordon is the Titus Street Professor of Ecclesiastical History at Yale Divinity School. He also teaches in the Department of History at Yale and is currently Director of Graduate Studies for the university's European and Russian Studies graduate program. He is the author of *Calvin* (2009) and the forthcoming *John Calvin's Institutes of the Christian Religion* (2016). He is completing a project on the Protestant Latin Bibles of the sixteenth century.

Maxwell E. Johnson is professor of liturgical studies in the Department of Theology, University of Notre Dame, and a pastor in the Evangelical Lutheran Church in America. Recent publications include *Praying and Believing in Early Christianity: The Interplay between Christian Worship and Doctrine* (2013) and *The Church in Act: Lutheran Liturgical Theology in Ecumenical Conversation* (2015).

Wendy Mayer is research fellow in the Centre for Early Christian Studies at Australian Catholic University and also research associate in the College of Humanities, University of South Africa. Her publications include, in addition to numerous articles on aspects of early Christian preaching, *The Churches of Syrian Antioch (300–638 CE)* (2012) and the collection of essays *Christians Shaping Identity from the Roman Empire to Byzantium* (2015).

Melanie Ross is assistant professor of liturgical studies at the Yale Institute of Sacred Music and Yale Divinity School. In 2010, she coedited, with Simon Jones, *The Serious Business of Worship: Essays in Honour of Bryan D. Spinks.* Her first authored book, *Evangelical versus Liturgical? Defying a Dichotomy*, appeared in 2014.

Miri Rubin is professor of medieval and early modern history at the School of History, Queen Mary University of London, UK. She studies the religious cultures of medieval Europe through a broad range of sources, materials, and methods. Her publications include *Corpus Christi: The Eucharist in Late Medieval Culture* (1991); *Gentile Tales* (1999); and *Mother of God: A History of the Virgin Mary* (2009). She has recently translated the *Vita et passio Willelmi Norwicensis*, published by Penguin Classics (2014).

Bryan D. Spinks is Bishop F. Percy Goddard Professor of Liturgical Studies and Pastoral Theology at the Yale Institute of Sacred Music and Yale Divinity School. His most recent publications include *The Worship Mall: Contemporary Responses to Contemporary Culture* (2010) and *Do This in Remembrance of Me: The Eucharist from* *the Early Church to the Present Day* (2013). He is the current president of the Society of Oriental Liturgy.

Karen B. Westerfield Tucker is professor of worship at Boston University, a position she has held since 2004. Among her many publications are *American Methodist Worship* (2001) and (edited with Geoffrey Wainwright) *The Oxford History of Christian Worship* (2006); the latter publication will soon appear online in a revised and expanded version. A past president of the international and ecumenical Societas Liturgica, she is also the former editor-in-chief of the society's journal, *Studia Liturgica*.

Index

Brakmann, Heinzgerd, 42, 45
Bray, Gerald, 231
bread and wine
    and A. Campbell, 240
    and Zwingli, 185, 192, 194, 198,
        199, 200
    See also Eucharist
Breen, Timothy H., 7
    Imagining the Past, 3–5
Brenz, Johannes, 192
Brick, Michael, 206
    *A Brief Discourse of the Troubles
        Begun at Frankfort*, 207–9, 219, 223
Brigittine nuns, 29
Bristol Cathedral, 30–31
Browe, Peter, 125–26
Brown, Andrew, 34
Brown, Peter, *World of Late Antiquity*,
    276n5
Brown, Phoebe, 261
Bruges, 34
Bullinger, Heinrich, 187, 192, 201
Burgess, Clive, 31
Busine, Aude, "From Stones to Myth,"
    290n45
Butler, Judith, *Gender Trouble*, 134
Bynum, Caroline, 27
Byzantine area, iconostasis in, 69
Byzantine Rite, 14, 116
Byzantium, 277, 294
Byzantium 1200 project, 297

Calvin, John, 192, 208, 220, 221, 231,
    234, 236
    "The Form of Prayers and
        Ecclesiastical Chants," 100
Calvinism, 246
Cambrai, 26–27
Cameron, David, 205n1
Campbell, Alexander, 234, 235–41, 242,
    245, 248
    The Christian System, 240–41
    "A Restoration of the Ancient
        Order of Things," 239
Campbell, Thomas, 236, 240, 248
    Declaration and Address, 237
Camp Hymns, 254
Camp Hymns in Alphabetical Order, 264
Campolo, Tony, 231

camp revivals, 259
Cannadine, David, 6, 18
Cannon, Jon and Beth Williamson, *The
    Medieval Art, Architecture and History
    of Bristol Cathedral*, 30–31
Canons of Hippolytus, 117
Canterbury, 12
Carolingians, 16, 24
    and Gregorian chant, 147, 149–50,
        152, 153, 154
Carr, E. H., *What Is History?*, 5
Cartwright, Thomas, 216
Castanhoso, Miguel de, 71, 72, 91
Castelli, Elizabeth, 180, 191
castrati, 137
castration, history of, 125–26
catacombs, 299
catechumenate, 167, 169, 173
    and *Apostolic Tradition*, 100,
        109–10, 115, 116
    in early third century, 97
    and *Ordo Romanus 11*, 161–64
    See also baptism; initiation
Catholicism, 233
    and Nevin, 244, 245, 247
    post-Tridentine, 145
    See also Roman Catholic Church
Cecil, William, 210
Celestine I, Pope, 151
Certayne Psalmes, 222
Certeau, Michel de, 249
Cerulli, Enrico, 83
Chambers, Richard, 208
Champion, Matthew, 20
chantries, 31
Charlemagne, 24
Chartres Cathedral, 17
"Chicago Call: An Appeal to
    Evangelicals," 231–34, 248
Christianity
    and *Apostolic Tradition*, 95–120
    and Christianities, 278, 301
    democratization of, 235–36
    early, 95–120, 181, 198, 244
    and Judaism, 277, 286
    of the many, 282, 284, 286, 287,
        290, 293, 300
    and Nevin, 244
    orthodox/Nicene, 278

Hartker, St. Gall, Stiftsbibliothek 390 codex, 150
Hatch, Nathan, 237
Hebrews, 181
Heilsgeschichte, 101
Helen, St., 78
Hen, Yitzhak, 24, 25
Henry, John N., 255
Henry III, Emperor, letter of *intitulatio* of, 34
hermeneutics, of suspicion, 113
Hermesdorff, Michael, 145
Higginson, Thomas Wentworth, "Negro Spirituals," 256–57
Hilaria, 41
Hildegard of Bingen, 28, 130
Hippolytus, 10–11, 93, 94, 95
histoire croisée, 21–22
historicism, 145
historiography, 5
    comparative, 113, 123
    critical analysis of, 127
    evolutionary approach to, 123–24
    gender-attentive, 122–29
history/historical analysis, 281
    and biases of sources, 281
    and Breen, 3, 4–5
    causation vs. meaning and understanding in, 5, 6
    changes in study of, 276–81
    cliometric, 22
    cultural, 5
    cultural and social, 278–79
    implications of for worship, 234, 240–41, 245–47
    and Lavater, 201–3
    local, 127
    material object of, 128
    and Mercersburg theologians, 247
    and Nevin, 242, 244–45
    objectivity in, 5
    of ordinary people vs. elites, 278
    postmodern approaches to, 113
    precedents in, 101
    and present views, needs, and concerns, 6–7
    and Reformers, 181
    subjectivity in, 5, 6
    theology of, 101

twentieth century innovation in, 127–28
    viewpoint and predilections in, 112
    Western bias in, 280
    wrong side of, 205–6, 228
    and Zwingli, 179–80, 182, 183–86, 190, 191, 204
    See also past
Hodge, Charles, 247
Hogue, David, 4
Holifield, Brooks, 243, 244
Holt, David, 258n22
Holyday, Adam, 210
Holy Land, 84
    See also Jerusalem
holy man, 293n55
Holy Roman Empire, 144
Holy Spirit, 98, 99, 104
    as Mother, 111
    and Nevin, 244
    and Zwingli, 190, 193, 194, 200, 204
homilies, 15, 75, 190, 279, 281, 294
    See also preaching; sermons
Hooker, Richard, 227
Hopkins, John, 222, 223, 224, 225, 226
Horsey, Sir Edward, 210
Hosius, Bishop, 59
hospitals, American Civil War, 261
Host, 28, 177–78
Hostetler, Joseph, 241
hours, books of, 32
hours, liturgy of, 115
Howard, Deborah and Laura Moretti, *Sound and Space in Renaissance Venice*, 31
"How Firm a Foundation" (hymn), 256, 258
Hugh of St. Victor, 233
Hutchinson, William, 218
    The History and Antiquities, 211, 212
Hutton, Matthew, 217
Huycke, William, 208, 220
hymnals, Civil War
    configuration of, 252
    context of, 252–61
    and doctrine, 251–52
    organization of, 264–65
    production and distribution of, 253–55

and Lavater, 183, 201–3
and Nevin, 244
and Zwingli and Zurich church,
176–204
and Zwingli's dream, 187–91
See also Eucharist; Jesus Christ
Lucernarium, 100, 110
Luther, Martin, 101, 187, 234
and A. Campbell, 239
and Lavater, 202–3
and Zwingli, 183, 189, 191–92
Lutheran Book of Worship (1978), 105, 107
Lutheran Church, 105–8
Lutherans, 201, 271–72

Macarius II, of Alexandria, Pope, 64
MacDuff, J. R., *Soldier's Textbook*, 262
MacMullen, Ramsay, 289
The Second Church, 282–83, 284
magic, 277, 290
Magnificat, 29
Mainz, 17–18
Makāna Śellāsē, church of, 72, 79
Malka Ṣēdēq, Archbishop, 77
Malone, Carolyn Marino, 15
Mamluk period, 69
manuscripts, 34–35, 41
Maqāryos, Abbā, 57
Maqdas, 76–77
Marcombe, David, 215, 217
Marḥa Krestos, 70, 82
Marini, Stephen, 265
"Hymnody as History," 268
Marinis, Vasileios, 17
Mark, St., eucharistic prayer of, 91–92
Marot, Clémont, 223
Marshall, Paul V., 107–8
Martyr, Peter, 214, 215
Martyrdom of Polycarp, 110
martyrium, 89, 90
martyrological texts, 180
martyrs, cult of, 300
Marxist history, 127
Mary, 30, 31, 32–33
Māryām Nāzrēt, church of, 60–65, 91, 92
Māryām Qorqor
murals of, 89
Mary I, Queen, 207, 213, 216, 220, 222

masculinities, 133–34
Massaja, Guglielmo, 40
mästäbqʷaʼat, 46
Mastabqʷeʼat (*"Supplications"*), 44
material culture, 5
material environment, 30
Maurists, 23
Maxwell, Jack, 246
Mayer, Josephine, 126, 127, 130
McCarthy, Daniel P., *Appreciating the
Collect*, 9n20
McGowan, Andrew
Ancient Christian Worship, 132
"Worship in Steps," 283
McKinnon, James, 156, 167–68
Mecham, June, 29
medievalism, romantic interest in, 145
medieval period, 277
medieval preachers, 294
medieval reform movements, 180
medieval sources, 185
Meens, Rob, 25
memory
and Protestant Reformers, 179
and Reformers, 180
and Zwingli, 190, 191, 193, 194,
197, 200–201
Mercersburg Movement, 234, 242–47
Merovingian society, 24
Merviel, 28
messālēnnat, 78
meta-narratives, 132
Methodist Episcopal Church, South,
254–55, 266–67
Methodists, 235, 253, 259, 267
Mikāʼēl, Metropolitan, 57–65
Miracles of Mary, 41
missionaries, 253
Mitchell, Nathan, 246
Mocquereau, André, 147
monasticism, 44, 81, 286, 293, 300
Montaillou, 28
Morgan, Nigel, 11
Morgan, Robert, 8, 9, 11
Mosman, Chesley, 270–71
Muḥammad ibn Ibrāhīm al Ġāzī, *ǧihad*
of, 41
Mulford Farmstead, 3
Muller, Richard, 13

317